Queer Screen

A *Screen* Reader

**Edited by
Jackie Stacey
and Sarah Street**

 Routledge
Taylor & Francis Group

LONDON AND NEW YORK

First published 2007
by Routledge
2 Park Square, Milton Park, Abingdon, Oxon OX14 4RN

Simultaneously published in the USA and Canada
by Routledge
270 Madison Ave, New York, NY 10016

Routledge is an imprint of the Taylor & Francis Group, an informa business

Editorial selection and material © 2007 Jackie Stacey and Sarah Street
Chapters © 2007 chapter authors

Typeset in Perpetua by
Florence Production Ltd, Stoodleigh, Devon
Printed and bound in Great Britain by
Antony Rowe Ltd, Chippenham, Wiltshire

British Library Cataloguing in Publication Data
A catalogue record for this book is available
from the British Library

Library of Congress Cataloging in Publication Data
Queer screen: a screen reader/edited by Jackie Stacey and Sarah Street.
    p. cm.
  1.Homosexuality in motion pictures.   2. Homosexuality and motion
pictures. I. Stacey, Jackie. II. Street, Sarah.
PN1995.9.H55Q47 2007
791.43′653–dc22   2007005422

ISBN10: 0–415–38430–3 (hbk)
ISBN10: 0–415–38431–1 (pbk)

ISBN13: 978–0–415–38430–8 (hbk)
ISBN13: 978–0–415–38431–5 (pbk)

Contents

Illustrations   ix
Editors' acknowledgements   xi
Publisher's acknowledgements   xii
Contributors   xiii

Introduction: queering *Screen*   1

JACKIE STACEY AND SARAH STREET

PART I
Authoring queerness   **19**

1 **Guerrilla in the midst: women's cinema in the 80s**   21

TERESA DE LAURETIS

2 **That special thrill: *Brief Encounter*, homosexuality
   and authorship**   41

ANDY MEDHURST

PART II
Queering technology   **53**

3 **Technology, paranoia and the queer voice**   55

ELLIS HANSON

4 **She is not herself: the deviant relations of
   *Alien Resurrection***   80

JACKIE STACEY

5 Continuous sex: the editing of homosexuality in
   Bound and *Rope*   106
   LEE WALLACE

PART III
Racialization, queerness and desire   **123**

6 Racialized spectacle, exchange relations and the
   Western in *Joanna d'Arc of Mongolia*   125
   KRISTEN WHISSEL

7 From Nazi whore to good German mother: revisiting
   resistance in the Holocaust film   146
   JULIA ERHART

8 The autoethnographic performance: reading Richard
   Fung's queer hybridity   163
   JOSÉ MUÑOZ

PART IV
Queer bodies and histories   **181**

9 Space, time, auteurity and the queer male body:
   the film adaptations of Robert Lepage   183
   PETER DICKINSON

10 The suspended spectacle of history: the tableau
   vivant in Derek Jarman's *Caravaggio*   208
   JAMES TWEEDIE

11 The She-man: postmodern bi-sexed performance
   in film and video   236
   CHRIS STRAAYER

PART V
The *Boys Don't Cry* debate   **257**

12 Pass/fail   259
   MICHELE AARON

13 Risk and queer spectatorship   265
   JULIANNE PIDDUCK

14 **Girls still cry**   272
PATRICIA WHITE

15 **The transgender gaze in *Boys Don't Cry***   278
JUDITH HALBERSTAM

16 **The class character of *Boys Don't Cry***   283
LISA HENDERSON

17 **Boyz do cry: screening history's white lies**   289
JENNIFER DEVERE BRODY

Index   296

Illustrations

1.1	*Working Girls* (Lizzie Border, 1986)	28
1.2	*She Must Be Seeing Things* (Sheila McLaughlin, 1987)	37
1.3	*She Must Be Seeing Things*	38
2.1	*Flames of Passion* (Richard Kwietniowski, 1989)	43
2.2	*Brief Encounter* (David Lean, 1945)	47
3.1	*2001: A Space Odyssey* (Stanley Kubrick, 1968)	56
3.2	*2001: A Space Odyssey*	62
3.3	*Law of Desire* (Pedro Almodóvar, 1987)	68
3.4	*Law of Desire*	73
9.1	*Le Confessionnal* (Robert Lepage, 1995)	188
9.2	*Le Confessionnal*	188
9.3	*Le Confessionnal*	189
9.4	*Le Confessionnal*	189
9.5	*Le Polygraphe* (Robert Lepage, 1997)	192
9.6	*Le Polygraphe*	193
9.7	*Le Polygraphe*	194
9.8	*Nô* (Robert Lepage, 1998)	197
9.9	*Nô*	198
9.10	*Possible Worlds* (Robert Lepage, 1998)	201
9.11	*La Face Cachée de la Lune* (Robert Lepage, 2003)	204
10.1	*Caravaggio* (Derek Jarman, 1986)	218
10.2	*Caravaggio*	224
10.3	*Caravaggio*	224
10.4	*Caravaggio*	224
10.5	*Caravaggio*	224
11.1	Publicity still for the *Rocky Horror Picture Show* (Jim Sharman, 1975)	238
11.2	Lynda Benglis	240
11.3	Carolee Schneemann	242
11.4	*The Kipling Trilogy: Perils of Pedagogy* (John Greyson, 1984)	246
11.5	*Chinese Characters* (Richard Fung, 1986)	247

11.6	Divine	248
11.7	*The Kipling Trilogy: Perils of Pedagogy*	249
11.8	Save You All My Kisses, Dead or Alive	250
11.9	Mike Monroe, Hanoi Rocks	250
11.10	Marilyn	251
11.11	Marilyn	251
11.12	Annie Lennox	253

Editors' acknowledgements

We would like to thank the *Screen* authors for agreeing to have their articles re-published in this form, and for their enthusiasm for the project. In the preparation of this volume, we would also like to thank Adi Kuntsman at the Department of Sociology, Lancaster University, for her excellent work on the initial stages of this project. Also, we thank Caroline Beven at *Screen* for her help in locating the images and for editorial support in the production of many of the original articles.

The following lists the dataes of the articles' first appearence in *Screen*:

1   Guerrilla in the midst: women's cinema in the 80s, 31:1, 1990
2   That special thrill: *Brief Encounter*, homosexuality and authorship, 32:2, 1991
3   Technology, paranoia and the queer voice, 34:2, 1993
4   She is not herself: the deviant relations of *Alien Resurrection*, 44:3, 2003
5   Continuous sex: the editing of homosexuality in *Bound* and *Rope*, 41:4, 2000
6   Racialized spectacle, exchange relations, and the Western in *Joanna d'Arc of Mongolia*, 37:1, 1996
7   From Nazi whore to good German mother: revisiting resistance in the Holocaust film, 4:4, 2000
8   The autoethnographic performance: reading Richard Fung's queer hybridity, 36:2, 1995
9   Space, time, auteurity and the queer male body: the film adaptations of Robert Lepage, 46:2, 2005
10 The suspended spectacle of history: the tableau vivant in Derek Jarman's *Caravaggio*, 44:4, 2003
11 The She-man: postmodern bi-sexed performance in film and video, 31:1, 1990
12 Pass/fail, 42:1, 2001
13 Risk and queer spectatorship, 42:1, 2001
14 Girls still cry, 42:2, 2001
15 The transgender gaze in *Boys Don't Cry*, 42:3, 2001
16 The class character of *Boys Don't Cry*, 42:3, 2001
17 Boyz do cry: screening history's white lies, 43:1, 2002

Jackie Stacey, Lancaster University
Sarah Street, University of Bristol

Publisher's acknowledgements

All images were reproduced with kind permission. While every effort has been made to trace copyright holders and obtain permission, this has not been possible in all cases. Any omissions brought to our attention will be remedied in future editions.

Contributors

Michele Aaron teaches film studies at the University of Birmingham. She is author of *Spectatorship: the Power of Looking On* (2007). She edited and contributed to *The Body's Perilous Pleasures: Dangerous Desires and Contemporary Culture* (1999) and *New Queer Cinema: a Critical Reader* (2004), which were both published by Edinburgh University Press. She is currently completing a monograph for them on Death and the Moving Image.

Jennifer Devere Brody is the Weinberg College Board of Visitors Research and Teaching Professor at Northwestern University. She holds appointments in the departments of English, Performance Studies and African American Studies. She is the author of *Impossible Purities: Blackness, Femininity and Victorian Culture* (1998) and *Punctuation: Art, Politics and Play* (under contract with Duke University Press). She has been awarded grants from the Ford Foundation and the Monette/Horwitz Trust for Independent Research against homophobia. Her work has appeared in *Genders*, *Signs*, *Callaloo*, *Theatre Journal*, *Text and Performance Quarterly* and many edited volumes.

Peter Dickinson teaches in the Department of English at Simon Fraser University. He is the author of *Here is Queer: Nationalisms, Sexualities, and the Literatures of Canada* (1999) and *Screening Gender, Framing Genre: Canadian Literature into Film* (2006).

Julia Erhart is Senior Lecturer in the Department of Screen Studies, Flinders University, Adelaide, where she teaches and researches in the areas of feminist and queer studies in media and culture, documentary, and experimental media. Articles by her on these subjects have appeared in a number of journals and edited anthologies including *Screen*, *Camera Obscura*, *Afterimage*, *Screening the Past*, *Realtime*, *Companion to Contemporary Film Theory* and *Straight Studies Modified: Lesbian Interventions in the Academy*. She is a Fulbright recipient and is working on a manuscript about films by women directors that represent the historical past.

Judith Halberstam is Professor of English and Director of the Centre for Feminist Research at the University of Southern California. Halberstam teaches courses in queer studies, gender theory, art, literature and film. She is the author of *Female Masculinity* (1998), *The Drag King Book* (1999), *Skin Shows: Gothic Horror and the Technology of Monsters* (1995) and *Queer Time and Place: Transgender Bodies, Subcultural Lives* (2005).

Ellis Hanson is Professor of English and Director of the Lesbian, Bisexual and Gay Studies Program at Cornell University. He is the author of *Decadence and Catholicism* (1997) and the editor of *Out Takes: Essays on Queer Theory and Film* (1999). He is finishing a book on the cinema and moral panics over child sexuality.

Lisa Henderson is Associate Professor of Communication and Faculty Affiliate in American Studies at the University of Massachusetts, Amherst, and Director of CISA, the Five College Center for Crossroads in the Study of the Americas. She has written research essays on sexual representation, cultural production, feminist media studies and cultural studies of social class for a number of collections and such journals as *Screen*, *Signs*, *Journal of Communication*, *Feminist Media Studies* and *Journal of Homosexuality*. Her book in progress is titled *Love and Money: Queers, Class and Cultural Production*.

Teresa de Lauretis is Professor of the History of Consciousness at the University of California, Santa Cruz, and has written on film since the 1970s. Her books, widely translated in Europe, Latin America and Asia, include *The Cinematic Apparatus*, (co-edited with Stephen Heath, 1980), *Alice Doesn't: Feminism, Semiotics, Cinema* (1984), *Technologies of Gender* (1987), *The Practice of Love* (1994). A Reader of her essays in feminist theory, *Figures of Resistance*, edited by Patricia White, is forthcoming by the University of Illinois Press. She is currently completing *Death @ Work*, a book on the inscription of the drive in film and literary texts.

Andy Medhurst teaches about film, television, sexuality, identity and popular culture at the University of Sussex.

José Muñoz is Chair and Associate Professor of Performance Studies, New York University. His major research interests include Latino studies; queer theory; critical race theory; global mass cultures; performance art; film and video. He is a member of the Board of Directors for The New Festival: New York's Lesbian and Gay Film Festival and for the Center for Lesbian and Gay Studies, CUNY. He is also on the Executive Committee on Popular Culture of the Modern Language Association.

Julianne Pidduck teaches in the Département de Communication at the Université de Montréal. Specializing in studies of gender, sexuality and the moving image, she is author of *Contemporary Costume Film: Space, Place and the Past* (2005) and a short monograph on Patrice Chéreau's *La Reine Margot* (2003). Her current research explores the 'imaging' of queer kinship across a broad corpus of contemporary North American and European queer cinema, video and television.

Jackie Stacey is Professor of Cultural Studies and Women's Studies in the Department of Sociology at Lancaster University. Her publications include *Star Gazing: Female Spectatorship and Hollywood Cinema* (1994) and *Teratologies: a Cultural Study of Cancer* (1997). She is co-author of *Global Nature, Global Culture* (2000). She is currently completing a book for Duke University Press entitled *The Cinematic Life of the Gene* and has been a co-editor of *Screen* since 1994.

Chris Straayer is an Associate Professor in the Department of Cinema Studies at New York University, where she received the David Payne Carter Award for Teaching Excellence in 2002. She is the author of *Deviant Eyes, Deviant Bodies* (1996), and numerous articles on film and video in academic journals and anthologies. She has judged and curated multiple programmes, including 'Lesbian Genders' at the Whitney Museum of American Art. She serves on the directorial board of the Lyn Blumenthal Memorial Fund for Independent Video and New Media and the editorial board of *Journal of Television and New Media*. From 2003 to 2006, she was co-editor of moving image reviews for the journal *GLQ*. Currently she is writing on transsexual discourse, structures of passing and representations of mentality.

Sarah Street is Professor of Film at the University of Bristol. Her publications include *British National Cinema* (1997); *British Cinema in Documents* (2000); *Transatlantic Crossings: British Feature Films in the USA* (2002) and *Black Narcissus* (2005). She is co-editor of *European Cinema* (2000), *Moving Performance* (2000) and *The Titanic in Myth and Memory* (1985). She is co-author of *Cinema and State* (1985) and *Film Architecture and the Transnational Imagination* (2007). She has been a co-editor of *Screen* since 2001.

James Tweedie is Assistant Professor of Comparative Literature and a member of the Cinema Studies faculty at the University of Washington. He was previously a post-doctoral fellow at the Yale Center for International and Area Studies, where he coordinated the Crossing Borders Initiative, an interdisciplinary programme designed to facilitate the study of globalization in the humanities and social sciences. He has published essays in *Cinema Journal*, *Screen*, *SubStance*, *Twentieth Century Literature*, and other books and journals, and he is currently working on a comparative study of cinematic new waves from the late 1950s to the 1990s.

Lee Wallace is Senior Lecturer in English at the University of Auckland. She is the author of *Sexual Encounters: Pacific Texts, Modern Sexualities* (2003). Her current research addresses the relation between female sexuality and space in architectural and cinematic discourses. Her essay on *Bound* is part of a book-length inquiry, 'The Sexual Life of Apartments: Lesbianism, Cinema, Space'.

Kristen Whissel is an Assistant Professor of Film Studies at the University of California, Berkeley. She is the author of *Picturing American Modernity: Traffic, Technology and the Silent Cinema* (forthcoming, Duke University Press) and has published articles on silent cinema in *Camera Obscura*, *Screen*, *The Historical Journal for Film, Radio & Television* and *A Feminist Reader in Early Cinema* (2002). She is currently writing a book on digital special effects, a portion of which was recently published in *Film Quarterly*. She is on the Editorial Board of Film Criticism and is the founder of the Berkeley Film Seminar.

Patricia White is Chair of Film and Media Studies at Swarthmore College. She is the author of *Uninvited: Classical Hollywood Cinema and Lesbian Representability* (1999) and, with Timothy Corrigan, *The Film Experience* (2004). A member of the editorial collective of the feminist media journal *Camera Obscura*, she is working on a book on contemporary feminist filmmakers.

Introduction:
Queering *Screen*

Jackie Stacey and Sarah Street

It is tempting to begin this introduction with a definition of 'queer'. But in many ways the term defies definition, since part of its discursive force has been the work of undoing existing conceptual categories of sexuality and undermining traditional notions of sexual identity. Like its predecessor term, the postmodern, queer has struggled to keep open its own signification against academic imperatives towards conclusive definition. Since both concepts push against the fixing of an indexical system, theorists invested in their performative potential have shared a concern with maintaining a contested feel to their significance. In this sense, queer has not only functioned as an adjective (to designate theorist, film or director) it has also been used as a verb to convey its transitive potential. Despite an almost inevitable drive towards quotable synthesis within contemporary academia, queer has somewhat successfully evaded such conceptual closure and maintained some of the slipperiness of its original impetus – perhaps because it has always also belonged as much to film and video makers, festival programmers and political activists as to academics. In this open spirit, this collection includes many, and sometimes competing, approaches to the subject: queering *Screen*, screening queer and queer screens – the relationship can be played across diverse theoretical and political agendas with a range of different consequences. It is precisely this convergence of the theoretical and the political which has given the term such a generative and yet elusive life.

Queer's postmodern sensibility sits in productive tension with its place in the history of sexual politics and audiovisual cultures. Continuing its original commitment to activism, queer is a term which may be associated with so-called high theory (especially poststructuralist and often psychoanalytic theories of the sexual subject and the embodiment of desire) but it rarely sheds its political allegiance to social and cultural transformation.[1] In a move analogous to the reclaiming of a negative category as the focus for political intervention within Black politics,[2] queer has been transformed from a popular term of abuse into the rallying point for community protest against discrimination (most particularly in AIDS activism in North America). The effective reversal of queer from a category of hatred used to construct 'abject zones of sociality'[3] to a category of political and theoretical purchase for radical sexual communities is, in many ways, quite remarkable. And yet, perhaps 'reversal' implies a misleading sense of agency, intention and desired outcome, for the point of embracing queerness has never been to give it a positive force, in the sense of making hated sexual categories loveable (or even likeable). Rather, the queer move has typically defined itself in opposition to the desire for 'acceptance' which some have suggested (though many would disagree) characterized the lesbian and gay movements of the 1970s onwards. Inclusion, understanding, tolerance – these have not been the goals of queer interventions; rather, queer has asserted its presence, demanded resources, and celebrated, rather than denied, the multiple perversities of so-called 'non-heteronormative sexualities'.[4]

But even characterizations such as these are in danger of reinforcing an oversimplified progress narrative, according to which queer interventions simply rejected the naive lesbian and gay celebration of essentialized 'identity politics', which had formed the basis of its demands for acceptance, inclusion and visibility.[5] Instead, many have argued that the relationship of queer sexualities and cinemas to their lesbian and gay predecessors is a highly contested, widely debated, and complexly interwoven one.[6] Some scholars have suggested that far from being set against the terms lesbian and gay, queer should be articulated through a proximity to them.[7] Others have argued against such proximity, rejecting queer as an anti-feminist re-masculinization of sexual theory and politics and cautioning against what has been seen as the misogyny of its celebration of perversity.[8] However its contested genealogy is configured, the discursive transformation of current intellectual agendas through the impact of 'the queer turn' (which is not yet complete, in any sense of the term) has had very tangible effects across the humanities, arts and social sciences in the academy. Its interdisciplinary force continues to queer traditional curricula and research agendas and its notable visibility within contemporary intellectual life has been unexpectedly successful in the current climate of conservatism and corporatization in higher education.

I

Within film studies, the announcement of 'the new queer cinema' by Ruby Rich in 1992 generated a debate that has continued across the field ever since.[9] Rich's characteristically percipient pinpointing of the emergence of the new queer cinema both offered an indicative reading of the cumulative impact of this highly diverse work and predicted its potential to reconfigure the field of lesbian and gay film studies:

> Of course, the new queer film and videos aren't all the same, and don't share a single aesthetic vocabulary or strategy or concern. Yet they are nonetheless

united by a common style. Call it HomoPomo: there are traces in all of them of appropriation and pastiche, irony as well as a reworking of history with social constructionism very much in mind . . . these works are irreverent, energetic, alternately minimalist and excessive. Above all, they're full of pleasure.[10]

Coinciding with the emergence of queer theory in the academy, and with AIDS activism beyond it, new queer cinema promised a generative space in which to combine academic and political agendas concerned with representing non-normative sexualities through audiovisual media.[11]

Significantly, it was the screening of new independent, queer work at international film festivals (including New York, San Francisco, Utah, Toronto, Amsterdam, Berlin and London) in the early 1990s that precipitated Rich's intervention. Engaging with concepts in queer theory and issues in AIDS activism, 'new queer cinema' included work such as *Poison* (Todd Haynes, 1991), *Swoon* (Tom Kalin, 1992), *Tongues Untied* (Marlon Riggs, 1990), *Paris Is Burning* (Jennie Livingstone, 1991), *The Living End* (Gregg Araki, 1991), *Edward II* (Derek Jarman, 1991) and *My Own Private Idaho* (Gus Van Sant, 1991).[12] For Rich, the breadth of this international presence at film festivals and the scope of its historical reach in terms of its inclusion of work by film and video makers of different generations constituted a significant moment of consolidation and potentiality:

For one magical Saturday afternoon in Park City, there was a panel that traced a history: Derek Jarman at one end on the eve of his 50th birthday; and Sadie Benning at the other, just joining the age of consent. The world had changed enough that both of them could be there, with a host of cohorts in between.[13]

The emergence of 'new queer cinema' was constituted through the combination of this new work, which, for Rich, announced a break with the past, and the simultaneous reconfiguration of the significance of existing work, which was now given a new genealogical frame: the newness of this work lay in what she saw as the convergence of deconstructive cinematic style, irreverent celebration of sexual perversities, fierce and vocal political protest and compelling theoretical innovation within the academy; the reconfigured existing cohort began to include filmmakers, such as Ulrike Ottinger, Richard Fung, Monica Treut, Sheila McLaughlin, Su Friedrich and Pedro Almodóvar. In an uneven and fractured way 'queer' has continued to constitute its subjects, drawing on the political and visual practices of many generations of marginal activists. Unlike other disciplines where the emergence of queer was, perhaps, associated with particular theorists or books (such as Judith Butler and Elizabeth Grosz in Philosophy, or Jonathon Dollimore, Alan Sinfield and Eve Kosofsky Sedgwick in English Literature[14]), in screen studies queer entered the arena through discussions of specific films and videos and often through their directors.

Two films (of the many candidates) that emerged as particularly generative of the queer cinema debate in the UK context were: *She Must be Seeing Things* (Sheila McLaughlin, 1987) and *Swoon* (Tom Kalin, 1992). Both films were characterized at the time as marking a break with lesbian and gay cinema in terms of their willingness to explore the uncomfortable or difficult terrain of perverse sexual desire. If, as Ellis Hanson suggests in his chapter in this volume, queer is understood to refer to perverse desires in the psychoanalytic sense of the term ('the odd, the uncanny, the undecidable', p. 55) then rather than queer sexuality being limited to a particular identity or practice, it might instead gesture towards 'that no-man's [*sic*] land beyond the heterosexual norm' (p. 55). In this sense, queer cinema explored the perverse and the deviant within the sexual domain, and rejected cinema as either a reassuring space of positivity or as a potential route through which to win the acceptance of wider audiences.

Coming from the independent sector, both films used techniques from art cinema to explore deviant sexualities, while also relying on familiar narrative and generic strategies, albeit somewhat self-reflexively. *Swoon* used a stylish noir aesthetic to trace the intimacies of a homosexual couple engaged in child abduction and homicide; *She Must Be Seeing Things* drew on queer performance work to play with forbidden (or certainly at that time unpopular) issues, such as the fluid boundary between lesbian and heterosexual desire, the pleasures of voyeurism and 'stalking', and the tensions of interracial romance. Despite their obvious differences, both films were in critical dialogue with dominant modes of cinema, through their own versions of arthouse style. *She Must Be Seeing Things*, for example, included obtrusive formal self-reflexivity by incorporating a film-within-a-film that commented on the main narrative but which was essentially an avant-garde film being made by the main protagonist, inserted into an otherwise more linear narrative. The narrative premise of *Swoon* was inspired by Hitchcock's *Rope* (1948), creating an intertextual link with the earlier film by exploiting, and making explicitly queer, its murderous, pathological, homosexual subtext. If the films were disturbing, even shocking, to many lesbian and gay audiences, as well as straight ones, they were clearly intended to be. Debates raged about their form and their content: did *Swoon's* stylish mise-en-scene somehow aestheticize homosexual violence, and did the narrative inextricability of their desire from their intention to kill pathologize homosexuality (yet again)? Did *She Must Be Seeing Things* offer an uncritical set of voyeuristic spectatorial pleasures which legitimized female psychopathology, denying the specificity of lesbian desire?[15]

For many of the independent films which have become key texts within the project of queering screen studies, one of the main questions continues to be availability. Just as 'indeterminacy' might be said to characterize queer sexuality, so 'ephemerality' haunts the future of its cinema, as particular films and videos threaten to become unavailable, or indeed have only ever been available to limited audiences in specific national contexts (notably the United States, Canada, Australia and some European countries). The question of the international reach of queer screen studies presents itself partly around the limits of distribution and exhibition. For many, part of the politics of queer screen studies should be to maximize the availability of independent queer work and to prioritize its place in the curriculum for these very reasons. The video work discussed in this volume by Chris Straayer, for example, is not generally available (unless, for example, as part of the music DVD market, as with David Bowie's 'Boys Keep Swinging' which appears on a special edition of his videos that have been transferred to DVD). This signals the importance of locating texts from the past that in retrospect reveal the multi-faceted reach of queer film and video art, particularly as expressed within traditions of performance art on screen.

For many of those who embraced both its politics and its visual aesthetics, new queer cinema offered a much-needed response to the widely rehearsed problems of positive images (the notion that the answer to the oppressive negative stereo-types of mainstream cinema was to produce positive images of lesbians and gays instead) and to the limits of the political strategy of greater lesbian and gay visibility (the idea that presence on the screen might be indicative, or could be transformed into, an improved political status).[16] In contrast to these modes of intervention, new queer cinema seemed to offer a challenging voice from the margins (politically and artistically) that was not asking to be allowed into mainstream representation (in any senses of the term), but which asserted its difference with a proud defiance. It opened up a dynamic and generative set of theoretical and political issues: perhaps desire and sexuality are always messy, unstable and disturbing; perhaps greater visibility is not a political solution but is a central part of a broader representational problematic about the illusory union of image, knowledge and identity; and perhaps any assumed stability or continuity within individual or collective sexualities abnegated the fractures and fissures of both sexual and political subjectivities.

For some, the idea of new queer cinema is so firmly rooted in the independent audiovisual sector that using the category to discuss mainstream cinema and television is anathema.[17] Since queer found its originary impetus in independent film and video, many would see the inclusion within its critical remit of more conventional narrative films, such as *Bound* (Andy and Larry Wachowski, 1996), or television series such as *The L Word* (US, TV series, executive producer and writer Irene Chaiken, 2004–), as a distortion only permitted by the ill-advised loosening and diluting of the category through the passage of time. However, it is perhaps also important to consider the place of more mainstream cinema (and, later, television) in the development of queer screen studies as a field, for, as Rich's original article made clear, even Hollywood had its role to play in the emergence of queer cinema, if initially somewhat by default:

In the spring [of 1992] on the very same day, Paul Vergoeven's *Basic Instinct* and Derek Jarman's *Edward II* opened in New York City. Within days, the prestigious New Directors/New Films Festival had premiered four new 'queer' films . . . *Basic Instinct* was picketed by the self-righteous wing of the queer community (until dykes began to discover how much fun it was) while mainstream critics were busily impressed by the 'queer new wave'.[18]

The question of the place of popular forms within queer screen studies continues many long standing disagreements about the politics of popular culture more generally,[19] but also takes on a particular inflection in the context of two important contextual factors: the increasing breakdown of previous distinctions between the mainstream and the independent sectors, between high art and its popular commercial counterparts;[20] and the increasing presence of lesbian and gay sexualities in the media more generally, to the extent that almost every soap opera, in the UK at least, has now had its own version of the 'gay subplot'. In the British context, the regular lesbian and gay magazine programme, *Out on Tuesday/Out* (UK, Channel 4 TV, 1989–91), commissioned some important new work which cut across the usual generic divisions and was produced by Mandy Merck (ex-*Screen* editor). This series marked a significant intervention into British broadcasting, disturbing some of the conventional divisions between popular, documentary and experimental forms.[21]

While the breakdown of the mainstream/independent divide and the presence of lesbian and gay sexualities on the screen has varied enormously according to national context, there has been a generalized set of trends within Western media forms that have had a widespread (if uneven) impact. While, for some, the problem of holding open a radical space that is not tainted by commercial control or popular forms continues to be a crucial aspect of the politics of queer audiovisual cultures, for others claiming a space within mainstream film and television has always been part of the project of 'queering culture'. Within this framework, films such as *Bagdad Café* (Percy Adlon, 1987), *The Ballad of Little Jo* (Maggie Greenwald, 1993), *The Adventures of Priscilla, Queen of the Desert* (Stephen Elliot, 1994), *Boys Don't Cry* (Kimberly Peirce, 1999), *Far from Heaven* (Todd Haynes, 2002), *Brokeback Mountain* (Ang Lee, 2005), and television programmes such as *Queer as Folk* (UK, Channel 4, 1999; US series 2000) and *Six Feet Under* (US, series 2001–5, creator and executive producer, Alan Ball) all belong to a general category of queer culture that precisely demonstrates the problem of the mainstream/independent divide.

For queer scholars such as Richard Dyer, Alexander Doty or Andy Medhurst, popular culture has always been of interest as a queer space (regardless of the arguable increasing breakdown of distinctions between high and low forms) as much for reasons of class politics (refusing to condemn popular pleasures as necessarily conservative or to elevate bourgeois representational practices associated with experimental or independent traditions to the site of radical intervention) as for sexual politics (reading *beyond* the heteronormativity of popular culture to the camp, homoerotic or homosocial pleasures which have always been central to its appeal). As Medhurst points out, often this 'beyond' is a short journey. His work, alongside many others, has been pivotal in foregrounding the importance of certain mainstream texts to the pleasures of queering culture and, of course, to the pleasures of camp.[22] Revisiting the vexed question of authorship and the ways in which it returns to the film studies agenda in relation to queerness, Medhurst's chapter in this collection looks at how films such as the British classic *Brief Encounter* (David Lean, 1945) might be read through questions of queer biography and subcultural knowledge.[23] A film about forbidden love, scripted by Noël Coward, it is easy to see why *Brief Encounter* entered gay subculture as an iconic reference point.

The publication of Medhurst's article in *Screen* (1991) was one of a number of interventions which have meant that *Brief Encounter* has taken its place within queer film studies; another was the film's reworking by queer filmmaker Richard Kwietniowski as *Flames of Passion* (1989);[24] and yet another was the publication of Richard Dyer's book on the film, which is written through a thoroughly queer sensibility (though here the boundary between camp and queer blurs somewhat).[25] Partly through the effect of his own authorship (his reputation as a gay scholar)[26] and partly as a result of the strikingly personalized (sometimes quite revealing) modes of analysis, Dyer's intervention enacts a queering of popular cinema which demonstrates the full potential of what it means for queer film scholars to 'read against the grain'.[27] In his appreciation of the film's staging of the hidden emotional intensities and forbidden desires within the everyday rituals and exchanges of middle-class British femininity in the mid-1940s, Dyer's reading offers a place of queer identification across the traditional gender dyad. The tension in this British melodrama between the understated articulation of desire on the one hand, and the affective intensities of feminine restraint and repression embodied in the figure of Laura (Celia Johnson), on the other, are appreciated by Dyer through a queer melancholic empathy with the painful, yet pleasurable, closures of denial and that all-too-familiar sense of a lost opportunity.

The work of queering screen studies as a field may have begun with debates about 'new queer cinema', but it has since been extended and deepened in such a way as to have made an impact on the subject and to have shaped its research and teaching agendas more generally. Although Ruby Rich decried the co-opting of the movement into 'just another niche market' by dominant culture by 1995, its impact has continued to be remarkably successful in the current academic climate.[28] There is now a considerable body of work that makes up queer screen studies around which courses are now organized.[29] A number of edited collections have begun to consolidate the field, including most recently, Harry Benshoff and Sean Griffin's *Queer Cinema, The Film Reader* and Michele Aaron's *New Queer Cinema*.[30] Both volumes discuss the relationship of queer cinema to mainstream culture, the former emphasizing the place of queer sensibilities throughout twentieth-century American culture and the latter locating the 'moment' of queer within a specific set of political circumstances around AIDS activism in the early 1990s.[31]

The bulk of writing on queer cultures to date relates to examples from Western production contexts, although work concerned with a broader range of national locations (and increasingly, globalized cultures) is now beginning to be published.[32] By its very nature this volume reproduces the rather Western focus of the queer work published to date in *Screen* (a problem not limited to this journal).[33] While the selection of chapters for this collection was a difficult task, since we might have included three times as many articles had space and cost allowed, the final volume (however substantial) could not have done justice to the diversity of national and transnational cinemas beginning to emerge in the area of queer studies, since much of this work has yet to find its way to publication in *Screen*.[34] In this sense, *Queer Screen: the* Screen *Reader* makes no claims to be 'representative' in terms of its international reach; rather, it seeks to reprint some (but certainly not all) of the best queer work published in the journal in the last two decades.[35] The impetus behind this edited volume is to assess *Screen*'s contribution to the growing body of scholarship in queer screen studies and to place the journal firmly within the publication remit of queer film, video and television scholars in the future (including those working in areas hitherto not represented in it).

II

The essays in this collection have been selected from what might loosely be called queer work in *Screen* since 1990. A journal whose international reputation was established around its particular interventions into the theoretical and political agendas of the 1970s, when a psychoanalytically informed semiotics of film took on the energy of a highly contested political space, might appear an obvious place for early queer work to have emerged. And yet *Screen*'s perceived adherence to particular theoretical orthodoxies was seen by some to prohibit debates about sexuality which were not framed within a specific conceptual terrain. In some ways, although it might have been the obvious place for it, *Screen* was relatively slow to be seen as a journal in which to publish queer work. One can only speculate about the reasons for a particular aspect of a journal's reputation, and each speculation is always in danger of adding to more general mythologies which circulate around a journal such as *Screen* (and, certainly, this reputation has undergone many transformations since its 1970s incarnation). But perhaps the rather gradual nature of the emergence of queer debate within the journal was because of an inevitable connection of queer to the categories of lesbian and gay. As a journal with such a reputation (however quickly this became something of a totalizing myth) for the powerful combination of Lacanian psychoanalysis and Marxist aesthetic criticism and politics, perhaps *Screen* could entertain debates about 'the sexual subject' (and even publish its first reader with this title),[36] but could not move easily into the terrain of lesbian and gay theory for fear of undermining its insistence upon the instabilities of sexuality, desire and subjectivity that its particular theoretical focus had placed centre stage in film studies. With the queer move, which established precisely the possibility of combining poststructuralist theory with sexual politics, however, perhaps the significance of 'deviant sexualities' to film and video and then television studies gradually became more palatable in so far as, for many of these scholars, such instabilities were assumed from the outset.

To some extent, perhaps, it was less the heteronormativities of *Screen*'s film theory and more the need for queer sexualities to establish its poststructuralist credentials that accounts for the relative delay in *Screen* being associated with the emergence of queer scholarship. No doubt there are all kinds of complex accounts to be offered of this particular convergence, but what is important here is that the title of this volume refers in part at least to that historical move: to queer *Screen*. Part of the gradual association of *Screen* with queer work emerged from Mandy Merck's important contribution not only as the journal's editor but also through her own publications.[37] Opening up the tricky theoretical debate between poststructuralism and perverse sexualities, Merck's agenda-setting work pushed against some of the more sedimented heteronormativities of the legacy of 1970s film theory.

Queer work has been in increasing evidence in the journal from the 1990s onwards, and the aim of this collection is to bring this work together in order to evaluate the journal's contribution to the development of queer film studies. Teresa de Lauretis has been one of the central figures within queer film theory since its inception, insisting on the importance of its continuing dialogue with feminism.[38] The inclusion of her article 'Guerrilla in the midst: women's cinema in the 1980s' as the opening piece in the first issue of *Screen* after its move to its new editorship in Glasgow in 1990, is significant as it reviews the field of 'women's cinema' at the threshold of the inauguration of queer interventions. These competing, and yet mutually informing, discursive fields, both theoretically and cinematically, can be tracked through this 'state of the art' piece by de Lauretis. Finishing with her appreciative evaluation of *She Must Be Seeing Things*, that most controversial queering of lesbian feminist cinema, this article sets the stage for a debate between the representational politics of feminism and queer theory which continues today. Written by one of the figures whose work perhaps most represents the inseparability of queer debates from feminist film theory, de Lauretis's article opens this volume to signal this significance. Queering both psychoanalysis and film theory, de Lauretis pushed conceptualizations of the sexual subject on screen in some bold new directions in her important book *The Practice of Love*, in which she reworks psychoanalytic theories of perverse sexuality, most especially fetishism, to pose the question of the specificity of lesbian desire and the politics of its cinematic forms of spectatorship.[39]

The place of psychoanalytic theory in queering screen studies is also central to Ellis Hanson's 'Technology, paranoia and the queer voice', reprinted in this volume. Moving from Donna Haraway's figure of the cyborg[40] to psychoanalytic theories of paranoia, Hanson examines the notion of 'technology as a sexual prosthetic device' (p. 55). Queering both psychoanalysis and cyborg theory, Hanson offers a reading of the unlikely pairing of *2001: A Space Odyssey* (Stanley Kubrick, 1968) and *Law of Desire* (Pedro Almodóvar, 1987) through which he extends the idea of queerness beyond the human body to its interface with technical configurations. For Hanson both films present technological denaturalizations of the body and sexuality, if through very different cinematic strategies. The queerness in film which lies in the 'undecidable' (in the odd or the uncanny), Hanson suggests, leaves a trace of unfinished business full of potential. Whereas *2001* gestures towards 'paranoid defence', he argues, *Law of Desire* (one of Almodóvar's many films about 'queer people on the edge') presents us with 'the finest example of the pleasurable failure of paranoid defence in film' (p. 66). If these films are concerned with a 'loss of orientation' rather than a confirmation of it, and an uncertainty about sexual and gender identifications, then this is precisely what makes them so significant for queer theory.

The question of indeterminacy is explored in another form in Jackie Stacey's 'She is not herself: the deviant relations of *Alien Resurrection*', where the boundaries between the monstrous and the human (and the posthuman) are broken down in the transgenic cloning of Ripley (Sigourney Weaver). Here the relationship between biological and cultural mimicry is explored in terms of how genetic experimentation is given cinematic life through a set of iconographic and narrative inscriptions mutually articulating technological, sexual and pathological sameness. No longer the fully human body whose 'clean and proper' status reassuringly places abject otherness solely on the side of the monstrous, this recombinant incarnation of Ripley refuses such clear cut boundaries and presents instead a series of queer indeterminate embodiments.[42] The charged dynamics between Ripley and Cal (Winona Ryder), the robot who passes as human, redefine homoeroticism as a kind of 'sexual interface in which their mutual knowledge of the technologies of replication and mutation produce their excessive sameness as technological and sexual deviance' (p. 100).[43] But here, again, the problem presents itself of reading a genre film so acutely aware of its own generic moves and so knowingly displaying its own history and its place as the fourth in the Alien series. For while 'the associations of homoeroticism with an unnatural attachment to sameness might appear to confirm the narrative drive of abjection in *Alien Resurrection*, the reconfiguration of sameness as technological function pushes such heteronormativity to the surface' (p. 99).

If indeterminacy is to be welcomed as the queering of the heteronormative cinematic apparatus, then how might cinema's own knowing deployment of generic strategies, apparently refusing generic conventionality, complicate such an evaluation? Reading the 'politics' (sexual and otherwise) of a film poses new challenges within the current highly self-conscious incarnation of genre cinema, in which a heightened knowingness of generic conventionality both potentially undermines its force and binds filmmakers and audiences together in the mutual pleasures of cinematic knowledge and citation. *Bound* raises the problem of reading the representation of queer sexualities through a stylized deployment of generic conventions. In 'Continuous sex: the editing of homosexuality in *Bound* and *Rope*', Lee Wallace poses the question of how popular form makes radical sexualities visible and visualizable in the context of pastiche and postmodern play with generic histories. Offering a far more palatable (and morally justifiable) cinematic exploration of the taboo coupling of homosexuality and homicide, *Bound* might be seen as the lesbian answer to its queer predecessor *Swoon*. But Wallace examines how the cinematic language of *Bound*, with its knowing reiterations of its generic predecessors, rewrites film noir as a kind of 'sexual pastiche'. She suggests that: '[w]hile the elusiveness of homosexuality is crucial to the film's narrative, *Bound* simultaneously requires lesbianism to function evidentially, to disclose itself within a visual field. Under this representational double bind, the film frequently compensates for the indeterminacy of sexuality with cinematic technique' (p. 106). For Wallace the film's visual mimicry demonstrates precisely the complexity of 'visibility' as a political strategy.

The debate about whether *visibility* necessarily equates to a radical sexual politics has been widely rehearsed within queer film studies and beyond.[44] Kristen Whissel offers a reading of Ulrike Ottinger's film *Johanna d'Arc of Mongolia* (1989) in terms of the complexity of the conceptual connection between radical politics and radical audiovisual forms. Whissel offers a reading of the film in direct contrast to Brenda Longfellow's claims that the film is 'an invitation to [a] phantastical voyage and eroticised encounter with the Other . . . [in which] the narrative subject and the spectator . . . do not defend themselves against difference: they let difference in and allow themselves to be transformed by the process'.[45] For Whissel, *Johanna d'Arc of Mongolia* does not 'subvert traditionally racist cinematic representations of racial difference. . . . [R]ather . . . it participates in the cinema's traditional process of producing, reproducing and organizing historical conceptions of racial and ethnic difference from the position of dominant Anglo-American and northern European culture' (p. 125). What is at stake in this dialogue about how the film reworks or reproduces conventionalized racial difference as spectacle, is a broader debate about the extent to which work from the independent sector is implicated in the history of dominant cinematic codes.

Questions of the racialization of desire are discussed in a very different context in Julia Erhart's chapter, which examines the Nazi period as one in which gay/lesbian/queer experiences have been neglected in both documentary and fictional accounts. In particular, she draws on notions of 'political mimicry' and masquerade as strategies used by those seeking to repress their racial and queer identities in a context of totalitarianism. Here, again, we see queer as a category borrowing from, or identifying with, theoretical insights to be found in other areas, such as postcolonial theorist Frantz Fanon's observations about the consequences of colonial oppression for the colonized, in particular the tendency to 'mimic' the elite in order to survive in an oppressive political system.[46]

The importance of colonialism, postcolonialism and racialization to the queering of heteronormative sexualities has been a crucial question running through the debates about queer cinema. From the outset, Rich asked if new queer cinema was predominantly for white boys and their movies:

> Will lesbians ever get the attention for their work that men get for theirs? Will queers of colour ever get equal time? Or video achieve the status reserved for film? Take, for example, Cheryl Dunye, whose videos *She Don't Fade* (1991) and *Vanilla Sex* (1992) put a sharp, satiric spin on black romance and cross-race illusions.[47]

In the introduction to a special issue of *Social Text* on queer theory, David Eng, Judith Halberstam and José Muñoz place this issue centre stage in their consideration of the future of queer theory.[48] In the current volume, Muñoz explores the ways in which questions of queer desire are inextricable from those of hybridity, migration, displacement and colonial legacies in his piece on the independent work of queer Chinese-Trinidadian film- and video-maker, Richard Fung. In 'The autoethnographic performance: reading Richard Fung's queer hybridity', Muñoz uses queer theories of performativity, together with postcolonial and other theories of hybridity, to analyse the personal and political convergence of ethnicity and sexuality in Fung's use of the queer body in his video work. In his readings of Fung's *My Mother's Place* (1991) and *Chinese Characters* (1986) Muñoz suggests that 'Fung works to make hybridity and its processes comprehensible and visible' (p. 165).

Just as Muñoz pushes us to reconsider the visualizing strategies available for rethinking the inseparability of the racialization and sexualization of the queer body, so Peter Dickinson raises the complex question of tensions between national and sexual politics in his chapter on the films of Robert Lepage, a filmmaker who is probably better known as a theatre director. The close readings produced by Dickinson of films such as *Le Confessional* (1995) concentrate on how Lepage's cinematic work is overlaid with a conflation of the queer male body with 'failed or unrealized national identity' (p. 185), so much so that the queer male body is represented as problematic and even tortured. Whereas 'his theatre creations are filled with all manner of queer characters and images of same-sex eroticism', Dickinson argues that the films are 'so overlaid with the symbolic weight of internalised guilt and dysfunction as to be borderline homophobic' (p.184). While proclaiming Lepage's work as queer, this chapter traces how the process of adaptation, the discourse of Quebecois national identity and the role of the auteur are implicated in this problem of representation.

Independent filmmakers such as Derek Jarman, discussed in James Tweedie's chapter, use history not only in terms of subject matter, but also in terms of a formal means of making queer statements: 'In Jarman's mode of identity politics – specifically queer activism during the height of the AIDS crisis and under Thatcherite governance – the rediscovery of identities submerged beneath dominant histories and a genealogy of current subcultures becomes an explosive political project' (p. 209). Thus, Jarman's visual analysis of the tableau vivant and its placement within a context of queer politics radicalizes the genre of 'the life of the absolute artist' (p.210). It also unites the work of two queer artists, Caravaggio and Jarman, across countries, centuries and creative forms. In this case the 'knowing' intertextual quotation that is such an important strategy for queer readings of mainstream texts refers to art history rather than to popular culture.

Moving from popular music to underground film and experimental video, Chris Straayer examines the figure of the 'She-man' in audiovisual culture. The music videos and independent films she discusses are able to push further than more mainstream forms in their performative 'play' with identities and sexualities. While the music video has arguably become mainstream, these texts nevertheless can be identified as experimental, an area of production that is less tied to dominant modes of expression, yet to some extent engages with (queer) notions of the popular. In this chapter, 'The She-man: postmodern bi-sexed performance in film and video', Straayer combines feminist theories of the masquerade with queer theories of gender performativity. As one of the theorists whose work has placed queer theory at the centre of feminist film studies, Straayer's work here signals the multiple challenges which new queer categories pose to traditional gender and sexual binaries.[50]

The controversies surrounding the film *Boys Don't Cry* touch on precisely this issue but for very different reasons: to what extent does the film's more mainstream narrative and visual strategies compromise the representation of the violence to its transgender protagonist? This debate signals not only the continuing tensions within queer film and video about the problems of dominant narrative and spectatorial conventions for exploring so-called radical sexualities, but also marks the arrival of 'trans' debates and 'trans' theory within queer film studies.[51] If the move from lesbian and gay to queer destabilized of the hetero/homosexual distinction, then the further troubling of sexual and gender categories through the impact of transgender on queer have complex implications for film studies. A fictionalized account of the actual murder of a transgender person, Brandon Teena, which had already been made into a powerful documentary, *The Brandon Teena Story* (Susan Muska and Greta Olafsdöttir, 1998), *Boys Don't Cry* raised heated debates about the relationship between queer histories and the politics of representation in the cinema. In the final section of the book, we include five shorter pieces (since they were originally published in *Screen*'s debates section) which all address these tensions between questions of queer politics and readings of cinematic form. A film widely debated within transgender communities (on-and-off line) as well as within feminist film theory, *Boys Don't Cry* demands new ways of thinking about spectatorship and passing (Michele Aaron), the gaze (Judith Halberstam), class identifications (Lisa Henderson), the gendering of genre (Julianne Pidduck and Patricia White) and white exclusivity and occlusions (Jennifer Devere Brody). As these interventions make clear, the transgender figure on the cinema screen confounds many foundational assumptions about the relationship between desire and identification, and between sexuality, gender and embodiment. The film therefore serves as an exemplary case study, not least as a teaching resource, of how a single text can function as a broad and contested arena for debate surrounding the key issues involved in queer film studies.

Fifteen years on from Rich's naming of new queer cinema in the early 1990s, queer screen studies has now found a place within the research and pedagogic agendas of a range of intersecting fields of audiovisual study. In the move from lesbian and gay to queer a decade of struggles around audiovisual representation has occurred. In a queer world, the now standard 'LGBT' (lesbian, gay, bisexual and transgender), combines non-equivalent categories with divergent histories in such a way that potentially destablizes all of them. Work in *Screen* during this period has contributed to the demand for film and television studies to integrate uncomfortable questions of sexuality into its programmes. While to some extent this continues feminist and lesbian and gay interventions within the field in the previous two decades, queer moves have also overturned and dismantled some of the discursive spaces established by previous generations working at these intersections of scholarship and activism. In the history of *Screen*, queer has emerged as a dynamic and generative concept through which sexual categories have multiplied and diversified in ways that have called for new kinds of theory and new forms of representation. In collecting together some of the best queer work to have been published in the journal, we hope to mark its contribution to this debate.

Notes

1   For an excellent introduction to queer theory, see Annmarie Jagose, *Queer Theory: an Introduction* (New York: New York University Press, 1996).

2   This is primarily associated with the Civil Rights Movement among African Americans in the United States in the 1960s and 1970s, typified by the use of slogans such as 'black power' and 'black is beautiful'. For accounts of that history, see for example, bell hooks, *Ain't I a Woman: Black Women and Feminism* (London: Pluto Press, 1982) and Angela Davis, *Women, Race and Class* (New York: Random House, 1981).

3   See Judith Butler, *Gender Trouble: Feminism and the Subversion of Identity* (London: Routledge, 1990), pp. 133–4.

4   For a discussion of the term 'heteronormativity', see Lauren Berlant and Michael Warner's 'Sex in public', Special Issue on Intimacy, *Critical Inquiry*, vol. 24, no. 2 (1998), pp. 547–66; Michael Warner, 'Fear of a queer planet', *Social Text*, no. 29 (1991), pp. 3–17 and Michael Warner (ed.), *Fear of a Queer Planet: Queer Politics and Social Theory* (Minneapolis, MN: University of Minnesota, 1993).

5   The stereotypical version of 'identity politics' attributes to it the assumption of a stable continuity between desire, consciousness and subjectivity and implied a necessary relation between sexuality on the screen and sexuality in the cinema audience; but for a discussion of the complexity of these debates, see Diana Fuss, *Essentially Speaking: Feminism, Nature and Difference* (London and New York: Routledge, 1989). For a discussion of the relationship between sexual identity and screen images, see Richard Dyer (ed.), *Gays and Film* (London: British Film Institute, 1977).

6   For a discussion of 'queer' and 'gay' as historically intertwined categories, see Michael Warner, *The Trouble with Normal: Sex, Politics, and the Ethics of Queer Life* (Cambridge, MA: Harvard University Press, 2000). See also Richard Dyer, *The Culture of Queers* (London: Routledge, 2002).

7   For example, Jonathan Katz suggested the need to theorize the proximity of the history of the categories of lesbian and gay and that of queer at the 'Theorising Queer Visualities' Conference at Manchester University in April 2005.

8   See Sheila Jeffreys, *Unpacking Queer Politics: a Lesbian Feminist Perspective*, (Cambridge, Polity; Oxford, Blackwell, 2003).

9   B. Ruby Rich, 'A queer sensation: new gay film', *Village Voice*, 24 March 1992; reprinted and expanded as 'The new queer cinema', *Sight and Sound*, vol. 2, issue 5 (1992), pp. 30–4.

10   Rich, quoted in Harry Benshoff and Sean Griffin (eds), *Queer Cinema: the Film Reader* (New York: Routledge, 2004), p. 54.

11   For some early examples of work on queer film and video, see Bad Object-Choices (eds), *How Do I Look? Queer Film and Video* (Seattle, WA: Bay Press, 1991); Martha Gever, John Greyson and Pratibha Parmar (eds), *Queer Looks: Perspectives on Lesbian and Gay Film and Video* (London: Routledge, 1993); Alexander Doty, *Making Things Perfectly Queer: Interpreting Mass Culture* (Minneapolis, MN: University of Minnesota Press, 1993).

12   This is the collection of films and directors are grouped under the new queer cinema category by Benshoff and Griffin, *Queer Cinema: the Film Reader*, p. 11.

13   Rich quoted in ibid., p. 59.

14   See Judith Butler, *Gender Trouble* and *Bodies that Matter: On the Discursive Limits of Sex* (New York and London: Routledge, 1993); Elizabeth Grosz, *Volatile Bodies: Toward a Corporeal Feminism* (Bloomington, IN: Indiana University Press, 1994); *Space, Time and Perversion: Essays on the Politics of Bodies* (New York and London: Routledge, 1995); Jonathan Dollimore, *Sexual Dissidence: Augustine to Wild, Freud to Foucault* (Oxford: Oxford University Press, 1991); Alan Sinfield, *The Wilde Century: Effeminacy, Oscar Wilde and the Queer Moment* (New York: Columbia University Press, 1994); Eve Kosofsky Sedgwick, *Between Men: English Literature and Male Homosexual Desire* (New York: Columbia University Press, 1985) and *Epistemology of the Closet* (Berkeley, CA: University of California Press, 1990).

15   See, in particular, the debate on the film in Bad Object-Choices (eds), *How Do I Look? Queer Film and Video*. The controversy surrounding *She Must Be Seeing Things* (especially

the arguments about its screening at the Lesbian Summer School in London in 1988 when some present attempted to stop the screening) was a very public one. Although it may now seem unlikely that the sex shop scene showing the choice of available dildos, or the protagonist's bisexuality, could cause such forceful objections among members of the audience, it is nevertheless indicative of the complexity of queering sexual representations in a lesbian context. The competing discursive regimes operating here were fiercely felt. Just as the filmmaker might have seen herself as pushing against the cinematic and sexual conventions of heteronormativity, so the film's opponents believed that in its exploration of voyeurism, the fluidity of sexual desire, and the use of sex toys, the film re-inscribed lesbian sexuality within phallocentric and patriarchal visual regimes. In this sense, queer films dealing with lesbian desire are subject to the conflicted and contested responses of audiences whose concerns draw upon the complex debates about sexuality and its visual representation within feminism.

16   The classic account of 'negative' images of gays and lesbians in the cinema is by Vito Russo, *The Celluloid Closet: Homosexuality in the Movies* (New York: Harper & Row, 1981). For an earlier collection which raises the issue of identity politics, see Dyer (ed.), *Gays and Film*.

17   For example, in his paper at the 'Theorising Queer Visualities' conference, Manchester, April 2005, Isaac Julian firmly rejected the notion that television series such as *The L Word* could be considered part of queer culture.

18   Rich, quoted in Benshoff and Griffin, *Queer Cinema*, p. 53.

19   For an example of the continuing focus on these dilemmas, see the roundtable discussion 'Queer film and media pedagogy' in *GLQ*, vol. 12, no. 1 (2006), pp. 117–34.

20   In the British context, for example, two instances of the breakdown of the high/popular culture divide (or at least which challenge the notion that the 'high brow' is not for popular consumption) might be Tate Modern and Channel 4: Tate Modern, housing the UK's leading collection of modern art has now become one of London's most visited tourist sites; similarly, the launch of television's Channel 4 in 1982 sought to combine unconventional programming with programmes aimed at a more mainstream audience – significantly, one of the earliest Channel 4 controversies resulted from the screening of a lesbian film, *Veronica 4 Rose* (Melanie Chait, 1982).

21   The series covered a wide range of issues and formal styles, for example, a record of the 1991 Lesbian and Gay Pride event, *Pride '91*, directed by Richard Kwietniowski, and *Khush*, a film by Pratibha Parmar about South Asian lesbians and gays living in Britain, North America and India. The BFI video, *The Best of Out & Out on Tuesday*, is no longer available.

22   See Andy Medhurst and Sally Munt (eds), *Lesbian and Gay Studies: a Critical Introduction* (London: Cassell, 1997), and Andy Medhurst, 'It's as a man that you've failed: masculinity and forbidden desire in *The Spanish Gardener*', in Pat Kirkham and Janet Thumim (eds), *You Tarzan: Masculinity, Movies and Men* (London: Lawrence & Wishart, 1993). See also Alexander Doty, *Flaming Classics: Queering the Film Canon* (New York: Routledge, 2000), and Brett Farmer, *Spectacular Passions: Cinema, Fantasy, Gay Male Spectatorships* (Durham, NC and London: Duke University Press, 2000) and Richard Dyer, *The Culture of Queers*.

23 For a discussion of the place of gossip in queer subcultures, see Gavin Butt, *Between You and Me: Queer Disclosures in the New York Art World 1948-1963* (Durham, NC and London: Duke University Press, 2005).

24 *Flames of Passion* is also the title of the matinée film which Laura and Alec go to see on one of their afternoon rendezvous in *Brief Encounter*. The display of sexual passion by the dancing bodies of 'natives' on the screen functions as the classic displacement of the (ultimately) repressed desires of the two white protagonists. Taking the same title, Kwietniowski's film explores the queer desires which heteronormative sexualities disavow in order to maintain their privilege. It also brings to the surface the camp pleasures in the history of popular cinema.

25 Richard Dyer, *Brief Encounter* (London: British Film Institute, 1993).

26 Richard Dyer's *Gays and Film* (which included an essay by Caroline Sheldon on lesbians in the cinema), followed by his history of lesbian and gay cinema, *Now You See It: Studies in Lesbian and Gay Film* (London: Routledge, 1990; second edition with Julianne Pidduch, 2003) established his reputation as one of the founding scholars of lesbian and gay film studies. His more recent collection *Culture of Queers* further consolidates the enormous contribution of his work to the field.

27 The strategy adopted by many gay and lesbian audiences, see examples quoted in Doty, *Making Things Perfectly Queer*, pp. 17–38.

28 B. Ruby Rich, 'Queer and present danger', *Sight and Sound*, vol. 10, no. 2 (2000), pp. 22–4.

29 See 'Queer film and media pedagogy'.

30 Michele Aaaron, *New Queer Cinema* (Edinburgh: Edinburgh University Press, 2004). These two collections join Ellis Hanson's *Out Takes: Essays on Queer Theory and Film* (Durham, NC and London: Duke University Press, 1999) and two earlier pioneering books these two edited collections join earlier pioneering books on lesbians and the cinema: Tamsin Wilton (ed.), *Immortal, Invisible: Lesbians and the Moving Image* (London and New York: Routledge, 1995), and Andrea Weiss, *Vampires and Violets: Lesbians in Film* (London: Jonathan Cape, 1993).

31 This helpful distinction between these two collections is made in an excellent extended review of them by James Morrison 'Still new, still queer, still cinema?' in *GLQ*, vol. 12, no. 1 (2006), pp. 135–46.

32 See, for example, Gayatri Gopinath, *Impossible Desires: Queer Diasporas and South Asian Public Cultures* (Durham, NC: Duke University Press, 2005). For queer work in the context of globalization, see Arnaldo Cruz-Malavé and Martin F. Manalansan (eds), *Queer Globalizations: Citizenship and the Afterlife of Colonialism* (New York: New York University Press, 2002) and Cindy Patton and Bengno Sánchez-Eppler (eds), *Queer Diasporas* (Durham, NC: Duke University Press, 2000).

33 For a discussion of the problem of reinscription of pre-existing margins and centres within queer theory, see the introduction to the special issue on queer theory: David L. Eng, Judith Halberstam and José Esteban Muñoz, 'Introduction', *Social Text* 23, vol. 84–5, no. 3–4 (2005), pp. 1–17.

34 Examples of important new queer work on cinema which do not have a western focus include: Helen Hok-Sze Leung's 'New queer cinema and third cinema', in Michele Aaron (ed.), *New Queer Cinema: a Critical Reader*, pp. 155–67; 'Unsung heroes: reading transgender subjectivities in Hong Kong action cinema', in Laikwan Pang and Day

Wong (eds), *Masculinities and Hong Kong Cinema* (Hong Kong: Hong Kong University Press, 2005), pp. 81–98, and 'Uncertain triangles: lesbian desire in Hong Kong cinema', in Tineke Hellwig and Sunera Thobani (eds), *Asian Women: Interconnections* (Toronto: CSPI/Women's Press, 2006), pp. 185–202.

35   Despite the absence of much queer work beyond the western context in *Screen*, there has been a considerable amount published in the broad field of world cinemas: for a collection of some of the best *Screen* articles on world cinema, see Annette Kuhn and Katie Grant (eds), *Screening World Cinema* (London: Routledge, 2006).

36   *Screen* (eds), *The Sexual Subject: a* Screen *Reader in Sexuality* (London: Routledge, 1992).

37   See Mandy Merck, *Perversions: Deviant Readings* (London: Virago/Routledge, 1993); *In Your Face: 9 Sexual Studies* (New York: New York University Press, 2000).

38   For discussions about the dialogue between feminism and queer theory, see, for example, Mandy Merck, Naomi Segal and Elizabeth Wright (eds), *Coming Out of Feminism* (Oxford: Blackwell, 1998). See also Elizabeth Weed and Naomi Schor (eds), *Feminism Meets Queer Theory* (Brown University and *differences*, 1997).

39   Teresa de Lauretis, *The Practice of Love: Lesbian Sexuality and Perverse Desire* (Bloomington, IN: Indiana University Press, 1994).

40   Donna Haraway, 'A cyborg manifesto: science, technology, and socialist-feminism in the late twentieth century', in *Simians, Cyborgs and Women: the Reinvention of Nature* (New York: Routledge, 1991), pp. 149–81.

41   For a further discussion of Almodóvar's queer cinema see Paul Julian Smith, *Desire Unlimited: the Cinema of Pedro Almodóvar* (London: Verso, 1994).

42   For further discussion of this theme see Barbara Creed, *The Monstrous Feminine: Film, Feminism and Psychoanalysis* (London: Routledge, 1993) and Catherine Constable, 'Becoming the monster's mother: morphologies of identity in the *Alien* series', in Annette Kuhn (ed.), *Alien Zone II: the Spaces of Science Fiction Cinema* (London: Verso, 1999), pp. 173–202.

43   The notion of the 'sexual interface' is drawn from Claudia Springer, *Electronic Eros: Bodies and Desire in the Postindustrial Age* (London: Athlone Press, 1996), p. 68.

44   See Peggy Phelan, *Unmarked: the Politics of Performance* (London: Routledge, 1993); Bad Object-Choices, *How Do I Look?*; de Lauretis, *The Practice of Love.*

45   Brenda Longfellow, 'Lesbian phantasy and the other woman in Ottinger's *Johanna d'Arc of Mongolia*', *Screen*, vol. 34, no. 2 (1993), p. 35.

46   This is most clearly explicated in Frantz Fanon, *Black Skin, White Masks* (London: Pluto, 1986, translated by Charles Lam Markmann; first published as 'Peau noire, masques de seuil' in 1952).

47   Rich, 'The new queer cinema', p. 59.

48   Eng *et al.*, *Social Text*, 23, vol. 84–5, no. 3–4 (Fall–Winter 2005), pp. 1–17.

49   See also José Muñoz, *Disidentifications: Queers of Colour and the Performance of Politics* (Minneapolis, MN: University of Minnesota Press, 1999).

50   See Chris Straayer, *Deviant Eyes, Deviant Bodies* (New York: Columbia University Press, 1996).

51   See Jay Prosser, *Second Skins: the Body Narratives of Transsexuality* (New York: Columbia, 1998).

Part I

Authoring queerness

1　Guerrilla in the midst: women's cinema in the 80s[1]

Teresa de Lauretis

'Women's cinema' is a term whose definition or field of meaning is almost as problematic and contested as the term 'feminism' itself. Thinking about the critical history of women's cinema – a historically specific set of practices that we can easily agree exists, and yet is difficult to categorize in any but the vaguest and immediately questionable terms – offers a starting point to reconsider other film-critical terms used to distinguish, classify or simply speak of practices of cinema in the last twenty years or so: terms more often paired in opposition to one another, such as Hollywood vs. independent, avant-garde vs. classical, entertainment vs. political, alternative vs. mainstream cinema.

Like women's cinema, these terms have no precise discursive boundaries or objective status, and are open to redefinition in light of historical changes that may occur, that have occurred, in cinematic production, distribution and reception: they serve as general references for thinking about current directions in cinema and the media as forms of cultural production and of the social imaginary. This 'social imaginary' has, of late, increasingly focused on 'the other' – witness Craig Owens's often cited 1983 article 'The discourse of others: feminism and post-modernism', a special issue of *Discourse* edited by Trinh T. Minh-ha in 1987 with the title 'She, the inappropriate/d other', and the very conference for which this paper was written, 'High culture/popular culture: media representation of the other'.[2] An important critique of the notion of 'the other(s)' – and, to my mind, a necessary corrective to the overgeneralized use of the term, with its fashionable currency and quasi-theoretical status – is made by Coco Fusco in a recent issue of *Framework*: 'There is a tremendous amount of multinational corporate investment in multiculturalism in the US . . . that underlies and underwrites what is perceived in the mainstream media as . . . our new sense of national culture as "enriched" by "diversity"', writes Fusco, who consequently refrains from using terms that refer specifically to race and/or ethnicity, preferring instead the term 'subaltern':

> My current area of interest is in how subaltern media is positioned, absorbed and consumed. As an historically Euro-American film culture takes on

post-colonial discourse, the issues of race and representation, and the contexts of those debates, become the focus of increasing attention, conflict and commodification. It is because of the intensified commodification of subaltern experience that we speak of crossover successes in North America and Europe. And it is within the context of this activity that we must examine practices which may or may not be channelled into the 'crossover', or which may or may not contest this process.[3]

For me as well it is not possible, after twenty years of feminist work, to think of women or, for that matter, anyone as 'the other' – regardless of racial, cultural, sexual or whatever differences. This chapter will be concerned instead with cinematic representation as a mode of production, appropriation and expropriation of sociosexual differences, and with the strategies of legitimation and delegitimation by which those differences are re-contained in current films. Strategies of re-containment cannot be neatly allocated to one or the other side of the oppositions, say, mainstream vs. independent or commercial vs. non-commercial, as they most often cut across them. In looking at how some of those strategies are deployed and take effect in spectatorship, my aim is at once to question and to redefine the terms of the critical discourse on cinema. First of all, women's cinema: in the midst of all this, can it still function as an alternative practice, a guerrilla cinema, and under what conditions?

Women's cinema may succinctly be defined as *a cinema by and for women*. But which women? Do we mean all women, across cultures and countries and the many differences that more and more articulate, and render increasingly elusive, terms like 'feminist theory' or even 'feminism' itself? Like them, if all-inclusive, or if simply inclusive, denotative, the term 'women's cinema' becomes too literal, too liberal, banal and self-defeating. If too narrow, it becomes reductive, sectarian, exclusionary. And yet, what if one would like to exclude from the (political) category of women's cinema certain films made by women, whether as popular, entertainment films (e.g., the films of Lina Wertmueller), as films in the tradition of European art cinema (e.g., Agnes Varda, Margarethe von Trotta) or in the tradition of American independent cinema (e.g., Susan Seidelman)? Even such a short list is already problematic: these are films made by women, but are they made *for* women? Conversely, could one include in the category of women's cinema a film like Sergio Toledo's *Vera* (1987), made by a man but addressing the questions of gender and sexual difference more directly than do most women's films, or, on the other hand, Valeria Sarmiento's *El hombre cuando es hombre* (1982), made by a woman but all about men?

Such quandaries are not new, though they are renewed again and again for each of the various instances and practices of cinema that increasingly respond to the impact which feminism has made or is beginning to make. But they were posed already from the start of women's cinema, when it emerged in the context of the feminist film culture that developed with the women's movement in the late sixties and seventies. As Judith Mayne remarks, the term women's cinema initially had two different meanings which to some were diametrically opposed.

> First, women's cinema refers to films made by women. The filmmakers range from classical Hollywood directors like Dorothy Arzner and Ida Lupino to their more recent heirs, like Claudia Weill and Joan Micklin Silver; and from directors whom many feminists would just as soon forget, like Leni Riefenstahl or Lina Wertmueller, to other contemporary European directors concerned directly and consciously with female modes of expression, like Chantal Akerman and Helke Sander. They range as well from independent documentary filmmakers like Julie Reichert (co-director of *Union Maids*) and Connie Fields (*The Life and Times of Rosie the Riveter*) to more experimental independents attempting to reconcile feminist politics and avant-garde form, like Michelle Citron (*Daughter Rite*) and Sally Potter (*Thriller*).[4]

The other meaning, Mayne continues, referred to films made for women, but its referent was a particular film genre, popular throughout the thirties and forties, and recently revived, a Hollywood product designed to appeal to a specifically female audience and pejoratively known as 'the weepies' until Molly Haskell renamed it 'the woman's film', and the name stuck.

While admitting that perhaps ultimately films made by women have little or nothing to do with Hollywood women's films, Mayne is against too stark an opposition between the 'inauthentic' and the 'authentic' portrayals of female experience in films made for women and by women respectively. She prefers 'to *affirm* the ambiguity of the term "women's cinema". For in order to understand how women make movies, there needs to be some consideration of what relationships women have had, traditionally and historically, as filmmakers and as film consumers, to the medium'.[5] And hence her affirmation of the central role of feminist film criticism in the definition of women's cinema. Similarly, in the introduction to *Re-vision: Essays in Feminist Film Criticism*, where Mayne's essay was reprinted in 1984, the co-editors proudly reaffirm the achievement of a close relationship of collaboration, of mutual support and interchange between feminist film critics, scholars, festival organizers, distributors and filmmakers: 'Thus, many of the political aspirations of the women's movement form an integral part of the very structure of *feminist work in and on film*' [emphasis added].[6]

What appears from even so brief a survey of the critical history of the term is, first, that women's cinema refers to and includes not just a set of films or practices of cinema, but also a number of film-critical discourses and broadly-cast networks of cinema-related practices that are directly connected with the history of feminism and the development of a feminist sociopolitical and aesthetic consciousness. Secondly, it is clear that women's cinema cuts across any easy division or opposition between high and popular culture, Hollywood and independent, mainstream and alternative cinemas. And moreover it destabilizes the criteria by which film-critical categories have been set up: narrative, for example, which in Anglo-American film culture, though not in Latin America or in Europe, has long been opposed to avant-garde filmmaking. For, from early on, women's cinema has included, or better, intervened in both narrative and non-narrative genres (documentary, autobiography, interview format), both avant-garde and 'illusionistic' films. In fact, if there has been one trait most markedly characteristic of women's cinema, I would say that it has been *the project to work with and against narrative*, shifting the place of the look, playing with genre/gender crossing and reversal, image-voice disjunctures, and other codes of narrative construction – the seduction of narrative nowhere more evident than in Yvonne Rainer's work from *Film About a Woman Who . . .* (1974) to *The Man Who Envied Women* (1985).[7]

Elsewhere I had occasion to write about narrative with regard to the history of women's cinema and its relation to aesthetic and feminist theory.[8] Although I cannot review my arguments here, they constitute the premises from which this essay proceeds and from which I now want to reconsider the notion of alternative cinema, whether or how it may function as a critique of dominant codes of representation, and whether or to what extent a cinema by and for women can still be seen as a feminist political project.

But to begin with, what is meant by alternative cinema today? Is 'alternative' meant in the *strong sense* of the term, that is to say, synonymously with oppositional, as it was in Fernando Solanas and Octavio Getino's proposal of a 'third cinema', a cinema of liberation? In contrast with the first, institutional and colonialist cinema, on the one hand, and, on the other, with a second, avant-garde, high-art cinema well on its way to institutionalization through aesthetic legitimation, the third cinema, as they saw it, was a cinema of the masses, a guerrilla cinema whose conditions were 'making films that the System cannot assimilate and which are foreign to its needs, or making films that directly and explicitly set out to fight the System.[9] Or, if it is difficult today to think of a System that one may oppose directly, from the outside, from a position of ideological purity and without complicity, is 'alternative' rather meant in a less stringent, or *weak sense*: as another option, perhaps, for either grassroot or emergent forms of the social imaginary, an option which would not replace but would coexist more or less peacefully with other, mainstream forms, if only given a chance (on the model, say, of cable or direct-access tv)? In other words, does the notion of alternative cultural forms have anything to do with hegemony and class or racial struggle, as it did in the parlance of the sixties and seventies, or does it loosely refer, in a perspective of postmodern pluralistic democracy, to those sectors of the social field that are allowed some cultural expression in the margins of what is called mainstream? In which case, does it still make sense to speak of a *dominant* culture, if not of a System? And further, does 'alternative' have to do with content or with form, or is this question itself moot in a postmodern cultural climate?

An excellent discussion of Third Cinema may be found in Paul Willemen's 'The Third Cinema Question: Notes and Reflections'. He follows it from its early formulations in the sixties in Latin America, especially in the work of filmmakers and critics such as Solanas and Getino (Argentina), Tomás Gutiérrez Alea and Julio García Espinosa (Cuba), and Glauber Rocha (Brazil), to the recent reformulations offered by, for example, Teshome Gabriel with regard to cinema in Third World countries, up to the relevance and the political implications of the notion of 'third cinema' – as distinct from Third World cinema – for contemporary film culture in First World countries such as Britain or the United States. Willemen argues for Third Cinema in the First World as a lucid 'production of social intelligibility' that, both as filmmaking and as theoretical-critical work, may challenge 'English aspirations towards universality': 'This requires a particular emphasis to be given to "otherness", to the dialogue with unfamiliar cultural practices and traditions, while refusing to homogenise every non-EuroAmerican culture into a globalised "other".' At the same time, Willemen states his conviction that 'outsideness/ otherness is the only vantage point from which a viable cultural politics may be conducted in the UK. The negotiation of the problems involved in otherness as a positional necessity is the precondition for a critical cultural practice'.[10]

Returning to the US context, I will now ask – are the following films alternative: *The Color Purple* (Steven Spielberg, 1985), *Kiss of the Spider Woman* (Hector Babenco, 1984), *Desert Hearts* (Donna Deitch, 1985), *I've Heard the Mermaids Singing* (Patricia Rozema, 1987), *The Brother from Another Planet* (John Sayles, 1984), *Dim Sum* (Wayne Wang, 1984), *She's Gotta Have It* (Spike Lee, 1986), *Yo Soy Chicano* (Luis Trevino, 1972) or *La Chicana* (Silvia Morales, 1980)? The answer, I suspect, is yes and no. This means we have to reconsider and redefine the very notion of alternative cinema (in the weak sense), for its relationship to mainstream cinema would only be alternative with regard to very specific and local contexts of reception. Moreover, some of those films might be considered alternative in form, in their employ of film-stylistic procedures developed by avant-garde filmmaking or the political documentary of the early seventies, while others would be alternative in content, in their choice of topic, actors and issues sociologically defined. Even so, in the case of the former, it might be borne in mind that the step from self-reflexivity to parody or self-indulgence has become much shorter in the eighties (to wit the current success of Pedro Almodóvar and Percy Adlon); in the case of the latter, can one still see Spielberg's whitewashed *Color Purple* as in any way alternative, when one compares it with the formal originality and thematic daring of Alice Walker's epistolary novel? Or Babenco's reductive and subtly heterosexist *Kiss of the Spider Woman* when compared with, again, the formal innovation and discursive richness of Puig's gay novel?

If we say that those two films are in some way alternative to mainstream representations of Black culture and to homophobic images of gay men, respectively (and arguments have been made to that effect), we cannot call them alternative on the grounds that they effectively critique cinema itself. For, on the contrary, their success is based not just on presenting acceptable, or positive, images of social groups heretofore unrepresented, but on doing so in cinematic terms that are acceptable, legitimated, by the very apparatus of representation that has excluded them until now – and now appropriates, and so exproprates, their 'difference' in the service of its unchanged economic and ideological ends. Not the least instance of such an appropriation/expropriation, such a legitimation which is at the same time a mode of delegitimation, was noted by gay reviewers in the casting of William Hurt as Molina in *Kiss of the Spider Woman*: for if Hurt received an Oscar for his portrayal of a Buenos Aires homosexual, while safely ensconced in the security of his well-established masculine, and straight, persona it is because the Academy award recognized his 'artistry' in *portraying* 'the other' – in performing, that is, exactly the kind of man he is not. Another instance of this strategy of legitimation and delegitimation occurred, in reverse, when the relatively unknown Patricia Charbonneau, who played the lead lesbian role in *Desert Hearts*, took great pains to re-establish a proper, straight and feminine, persona by giving interviews and appearing in the popular press photographed with her husband and child. In short, Hollywood does not believe in 'others', even as it gains from and applauds their 'portrayal' in motion picture art.

Thus, if I am not willing to accept the term 'alternative' for such film practices, it is not that I want to insist on form for form's sake or to hold on to some modernist and elitist notion of aesthetic. Quite the contrary. One of the accomplishments of women's cinema, to my mind, is that it has defied those notions of aesthetic implicit in high art, while systematically critiquing the dominant forms of cinematic representation which are, after all, those of popular cinema. The feminist critique of representation might have intended to destroy, or to deflect, the lures and pleasures of narrative closure and identification, but it has also meant, and realized, *a shifting of the ground of intelligibility and pleasure*. And by shifting the very ground of representation, it has effectively unsettled the standard frame of reference of cinema – the standard frame of visibility, what can be scan, and eroticized – and altered the conditions of representability of the social subject.

In this sense, for example, Lizzie Borden's passage from *Born in Flames* (1983) to *Working Girls* (1986), which marks a move from independent to theatrical distribution circuits and consequently also, to some extent, a shift in the form of address (as well as intended audience), might be seen as a move from alternative to mainstream cinema. But in fact it does not work that way. For better or for worse, *Working Girls* does not work as mainstream cinema, even as it may no longer work effectively as women's cinema. I suggest that the reason it does not is that Borden has employed a non-standard frame of reference, of visibility, to represent the female body. She has de-glamourized it and – by cinematic standards – desexualized it; or, in film-theoretical terms, she has de-fetishized it, de-voyeurised it, making it into a functional, working body as opposed to a site of sexuality and domination by the gaze.

After a screening of *Working Girls* in Santa Cruz, as part of a sex-radical, and not uncontested, feminist effort to 'support the local sex business community', Borden stated that she intended 'to use the apparatus as neutral and to treat women as subjects of the look': position the camera so that the women's bodies in the film would be shown as they themselves would see their own bodies, with their own eyes or in a mirror, so that the woman's body would not be shown or seen from the point of view of one wielding a camera or (as she put it) a speculum; so that, for example, as Molly sees herself getting undressed, *she* would be the relay of the spectator's look at her body. My paraphrase of Borden's statements, as well as the direct quotations, all come from my own notes of the (unpublished) discussion which followed the Santa Cruz screening on 29 January 1988. But in a published interview (given in January 1987) Borden restates her project in very similar terms:

> Most of the angles in the bedroom scenes are not subjective camera, but they're from a woman's point of view. There's no shot in the film where you see Molly's body the way a man would frame her body to look at it, except when she's looking at herself that way, in the scene where she poses with the guy in front of the mirror, for example. But, even there, I set up the shot so that if we are looking at her body in that scene, we're also looking at her eyes looking at her body. The first time you see her without any clothes on, she's alone with herself, and our gaze is involved with her watching herself.[11]

Moreover, that spectator is addressed as female: 'the audience I assumed, was female', Borden said. The effect she sought to produce in her spectators was 'to see women [as we ourselves do] when we are alone, for reasons of education'. (The function of address is clear here, for Borden was speaking to a mixed audience but addressing it as an audience of women, just as her film is watched by a mixed audience, but addresses the spectator as a woman.) She reiterated this point by suggesting that her choice of locale, a middle-class brothel as a working environment relatively free of the risks and dangers of street hooking, was in effect 'a woman's space': downstairs, an everyday living space; upstairs, a work space where the women whose trade is male fantasies, take control of the men's fantasies and hence have control over their own work.

If Borden's proposal of the middle-class brothel as an updated version of *A Room of One's Own* has displeased as many feminists as Woolf's book has (and on rather similar grounds of class privilege and voluntarism – in addition to charges by the anti-pornography movement), it has also displeased the entertainment-motivated

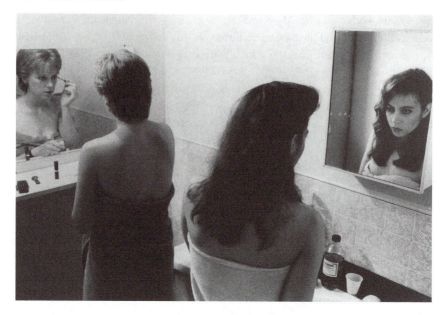

Figure 1.1 Working Girls (courtesy of Contemporary Films)

audiences who found their voyeuristic pleasure and standard subject-position severely undercut by the film's didactic project and women-centred sexual politics. The latter's articulation, evident to everyone at the thematic, manifest level, was much less evident, but perhaps all the more effective, at the level of spectatorship – in the inversion of the function of address and of the system of the look that characterize dominant or mainstream cinema, and that have come to be expected by its spectators.

While *Working Girls* does not work as mainstream cinema (that is to say, crudely put, the male spectators are not turned on by it), it also may not work effectively as women's cinema. By this I mean, quite plainly, that women spectators may not be turned on either. This is not, I think, because the film is about sex work (with the emphasis on work rather than sex), but because it is devoid or, more accurately, purged of desire. Paradoxically, in a film that manifestly supports sex work as a viable economic option for women's social and emotional independence from men (as signified by the opening and closing shots of Molly's lesbian household), sex work appears to be the ultimate form of alienated labour, for all the control it may afford the workers, and in spite of the film's effective de-romanticizing and de-moralizing of female sexuality. In other words, it is not that *Working Girls* is 'unaestheticized', as some critics have alleged of *Born in Flames*, but rather that it is *anaesthetized*: it is as dry, distant and neutral as the latex sex it mercilessly depicts, finally representing sex work as the negation, not of sex but of female desire itself.

I will now try to say this more complexly. Writing about *Born in Flames* and other films, in 'Rethinking Women's Cinema', I proposed and elaborated the theoretical hypothesis that a film could *address the spectator as female*, a female social subject engendered, constructed and defined by *multiple* social relations of (class, race, sexuality, age, etc.), and that such a film's textual space would extend toward this spectator 'in its erotic and critical dimensions, addressing, speaking-to, making room, but not . . . cajoling, soliciting, seducing'.[12] This notion of address, it seemed to me, was a more useful criterion by which to define women's cinema as a cinema by and for women. And, as the reception of *Working Girls* suggests, both the critical and the erotic dimensions seem to be necessary: lacking the former, the film would offer no critique of representation, cinema or society, and so lose its connection to feminism: lacking the latter, it would remain didactic, fail to engage the spectator's desire, and so relinquish its capacity for 'entertainment'.

The importance of narrative cinema as a mode of working through the relations of female subjectivity, identity and desire cannot be understated. It has been perhaps the single uncontested issue in women's cinema, as well as feminist cultural politics, since the late Claire Johnston's often cited remark in 'Women's Cinema as Counter-Cinema': 'In order to counter our objectification in the cinema, our collective fantasies must be released: women's cinema must embody the working through of desire: such an objective demands the use of the entertainment film.'[13] Pleasure, fantasy and desire have indeed become central to the feminist project of both inventing new images of the female social subject and imaging for that subject new forms of community. One of the effects of that project, less in cinema than elsewhere, has been the construction of conceptual, representational and erotic spaces where women could address themselves to women and, in assuming the position of subject – of speaking, seeing, thinking, and desiring subject – women could then concurrently identify and recognize in women *the subjects and the objects* of a female desire.

There is no doubt that feminism shares with other emergent and oppositional social groups the affirmation and the reclaiming of sociosexual differences, and the project of erecting alternative ways of seeing, conceptualizing and representing difference. But the particularity of the feminist project consists in its specific emphasis on the female subject in all of its component aspects – from the modes of its social and material subjection to the modes of its resistance and agency, from the emergent conditions of female symbolic subjecthood to the affective and unconscious processes that mark female historical subjectivities; and hence the necessary emphasis, for feminism here and now, on a critical, historicized understanding not only of the possibilities but also of the limitations of fantasy, desire, and what Audre Lorde has called 'the uses of the erotic'.[14] In cinema, video and other social technologies or 'machines' of the visible, this is especially crucial, given their now acknowledged weight in the processes of subjectivity and in the construction of self- or group-identity, as evidenced by the popular terms that signify those processes: self-image, representation, (in)visibility, passing and so on.

Going back to the notion of alternative cinema, I would propose that, even though we can no longer equate it either with experimental/avant-garde filmmaking or with what used to be called 'political' cinema (i.e., independent or 'poor' cinema), in opposition to the monolithic machine of Hollywood and other national cinemas, and even though we can no longer think of it as a cinema of liberation in the terms set out by Solanas and Getino, nevertheless their notion of a guerrilla cinema retains some valuable suggestions. Take, for example, their idea of alternative venues of distribution, such as screenings to community centres and non-commercial, educational spaces for a limited, local audience, where the film would act as 'a detonator or pretext' for critical exchange and discussion, bringing about a sort of 'liberated space, a decolonized territory'.[15] The presence of the filmmaker and/or actors at the screening and subsequent discussion, as well as the film shown, they hoped, would constitute an act of liberation from neocolonial oppression, an act of collective and individual decolonization, for all the actors-participants.

> The decolonization of the filmmaker and of films will be simultaneous acts to the extent that each contributes to collective decolonization. The battle begins without, against the enemy who attacks us, but also within, against the ideas and models of the enemy to be found inside each one of us. Destruction and construction.[16]

I need not underscore the parallels between this view and the practices of independent or 'political' cinema in the US (and Britain) in the seventies, practices which have virtually disappeared by the late eighties. What is more remarkable is that something of that notion of guerrilla cinema has continued to be active throughout the eighties in the actual reception, if not in the deliberate strategies, of women's cinema; and this has occurred in spite of the inevitable adjustments due to the historical factors that, paradoxically, have contributed to the success of women's cinema, such as the institutionalization of feminism in academic Women's Studies programmes, festivals and publicly funded events, and consequently the rather celebratory character of such events. Just two examples – the presentation of *Working Girls* in Santa Cruz mentioned earlier; and the heated debate that ensued from the women-only screening of Sheila McLaughlin's *She Must Be Seeing Things* (1987) at the London Metro Cinema in September 1988, when some women stormed the screen while others tried to rip the film from the projector – suggest that women's cinema can still work as something of a decolonial practice, a transformation or variation of feminist consciousness-raising practices, though we can no longer cherish the hope for an unambiguous 'liberation'.[17]

Thus the notion of guerrilla film is still valid, it seems to me, when it refers to an alternative practice of cinema emanating from and explicitly located in a sub-cultural context, or a marginal sector of a socially emergent group such as 'women'. What I have in mind is not so much the sense in which the collective reading of any film (including a commercial, box-office oriented, patently heterosexist film like *Personal Best* [Towne, 1982])[18] depends not insignificantly on the context of exhibition and reception, which may well constitute the film as a 'pretext' for critical discussion (as in a college classroom) or a 'detonator' of audience response (as in a rally). I am rather thinking of guerrilla cinema in the sense of those films which can disrupt, shake up, put into question the given group's imaginary self-coherence, bringing to the surface and giving voice to the repressed, unavowed differences and exclusions on which the ideology of a self-complacent, international or multicultural feminism has come to rest. And in this sense, especially, I have used the phrase 'guerrilla in the midst', in conjunction with Tania Modleski's reading of *Gorillas in the Mist* (Michael Apted, 1988) in her paper 'Cinema and the dark continent: race and gender in popular film', also presented at the 'High Culture/Popular Culture' conference.

In sum, what I would call alternative films in women's cinema are those which engage the current problems, the real issues, the things actually at stake in feminist communities on a local scale, and which, although informed by a global perspective, do not assume or aim at a universal, multinational audience, but address a particular one in its specific history of struggles and emergency. Films, in other words, whose project is less the imaging of a redemptive history (as might have been conceived in the early years of the women's movement) than a project of 'effective' history, in Foucault's terms, but films which, nevertheless, manage 'to bring about a real state of emergency', as Benjamin urged: 'to retain that image of the past which unexpectedly appears to [those who are] singled out by history at a moment of danger. The danger affects both the content of the tradition and its receivers. The same threat hangs over both: that of becoming a tool of the ruling classes.'[19]

That the eighties are a moment of danger is not in doubt, with Thatcherism rampant in Britain and the recent presidential election in the US following up on eight years of Reaganomics and the frightful increase in fundamentalism, racism and homophobia fuelled by the AIDS national emergency. What is in doubt is whether progressive, or what I would rather call radical, feminism – I mean the feminism that since the early eighties has been engaged in anti-racist and anti-homophobic struggles, responsive to the critique of racism articulated by women of colour as well as to the lesbian critique of the institution of heterosexuality – will be able to avert the attendant dangers of feminist conservatism and aestheticized post-feminism, on the one hand, and of appropriation/expropriation by the media, on the other. In short, whether feminism will be able to deflect the strategies of legitimation and delegitimation of sociosexual difference that have become prevalent in this decade. For, as Norma Alarcón put it to me in a seminar discussion, are there really any 'inappropriated others'? I took her question to mean that while there may be – indeed there are – many who are other (than white or socially privileged), in so far as they are named, interpellated, or represented as 'others', they may already have been appropriated. The question of an *alternative* women's cinema today must be posed precisely from this historical and political emergency.

To illustrate the point, I want to look very briefly at some strategies of inscription, legitimation and delegitimation of sociosexual difference exemplified in three recent women's films (I use this term to retain the ambiguity rightly preferred by Mayne and to avoid labelling the films feminist or otherwise, which in the present argument would be tantamount to begging the question). Considering the overall production of films about women during the past few years, one is struck by the pervasiveness of certain 'themes' clearly derived from a generic, much oversimplified image of 'feminism' that may be openly antagonistic or apparently sympathetic, but is equally reductive and ultimately hostile to the feminist political project. One is the theme of women's independence: women successful in their careers as well as in their personal and social lives, whom the film eventually punishes for their hubris and brings down to their 'proper' place by means of sexual subjugation by a man. Or not. And in this second case, the woman, 'wins'.

Examples of the first case are *The Jagged Edge* (Richard Marquand, 1985), where gender reversal in the courtroom drama genre only serves to accentuate that women are still first and foremost the locus of the sexual (for men), whatever else they may do or be, and thus will only be controlled by men through sexual domination; or *Extremities* (Robert Young, 1987), where one woman's successful struggle against her rapist only succeeds in realigning the audience's sympathies with the latter. A related theme is the more traditional one of female sexuality as excessive, uncontrollable, leading to murder for the sake of securing women's unbounded sexual 'freedom', as re-proposed in the resurgence of *film noir* remakes (*Body Heat* [Lawrence Kasdan, 1981], *Black Widow* [Bob Rafelson, 1987]) and variations thereof (*Fatal Attraction* [Adrian Lyne, 1987]). All of these are obviously antagonistic, anti-feminist attempts to devalue the gains that a *very few* women may have made in social equality and, at a deeper level, to delegitimate the feminist demand for women's self-definition and sexual independence from familial- or male-centred social relations.

In the second case, where the woman wins, a quite new and increasingly recurrent theme makes its appearance: the theme of lesbianism. It seems that one requirement of the sentimental education that accompanies the woman's journey to independence is her encounter with the sphinx of lesbianism; and our heroine will survive it, by answering the riddle much in the same way as Oedipus did: i.e., on behalf of man. Films like *She's Gotta Have It*, *Bagdad Cafe* (Percy Adlon, 1988), *The Color Purple*, *Desperately Seeking Susan* (Susan Seidelman, 1984), or *I've Heard the Mermaids Singing* are apparently benign and seemingly pro-feminist ways of achieving a similar effect: that is to say, while they ostensibly legitimate women's ability to succeed in the world as it is, and even to live independently of 'men', these films, in their more or less overt homophobia, all but delegitimate the feminist argument for an autonomous definition of female sexuality and the far more radical independence from the heterosexual social contract – the social institution and the symbolic categories of heterosexuality.

I've Heard the Mermaids Singing, for example, 'starts from the premise that women can do anything they want in life', states its young director, the Canadian Patricia Rozema, winner of the 1987 Cannes Prix de la Jeunesse for her enormously successful first feature produced independently (in Toronto) on a shoestring, as the saying goes, and sold to thirty-two countries in one week.[20] Like the media accounts of its production, the film is a modern-day fairytale. It tells the story of Polly, a modern-day Cinderella with a camera and aspirations to art-photography, who gets a secretary job in an art gallery and a crush on its curator, Gabrielle, a glamorous and successful lesbian in the closet. But the unlikely Prince Charming, as Polly(anna) will discover, is not only a pretentious art critic, unappreciative of true talent (Polly's), but also a fake who passes off her girlfriend's painting for her own. In short, Gabrielle is at once a female man and a bad phallic mother, and Polly will expose her crime, her secret lack, by extorting her confession on video camera.

It is difficult to see what lesbianism has to do with this story, which features it so prominently in theme (and so stereotypically in characterization), except perhaps to take the place of 'the kind of action or violence or sex that get automatic attention and commercial success' – the kind, that is, which Rozema decries (and which would have cost more than a few shoestrings). Rozema builds her film, as well as her account of its project, on the sparest, most tenuous presumption of feminist principles: 'Women and ambition is a fairly new issue, and one that interests me, so I chose to work primarily with female characters. Men don't really have much of a presence in this film – as women have so often not had much presence in film generally.' But she worries that 'one could interpret the film as anti-male' or that it might have been seen as 'propaganda for homosexuality'. Consequently, one may speculate, her 31-year-old heroine Polly is intended to be 'an asexual, polymorphous-perverse "everywoman"' – no matter that the two adjectives are mutually incompatible, that the subjectivity they would describe is unimaginable, and that such a privileged and omnipotent universal female subject is, at best, improbable. Rozema continues: 'The curator could have been a man, or a straight woman, but the fact that she is a lesbian is meant to blow Polly's [and the viewer's?] mind. And if Gabrielle had been a man, it might have been a film that was anti-male-authority. As it is, it's simply anti-authority.' So much for sexual difference. As for gender, it 'seems like a category of such minuscule significance to me. . . . I'm interested in more existential questions', Rozema states.

I quoted at some length to point out the conscious strategies, on the part of the director, by which both feminism and lesbianism are on the one hand appropriated and legitimated, and on the other preempted of their sociopolitical and subjective power, reduced to a new angle to sell 'more existential questions'. These, one must infer, are the heroine's fantasies of flying or walking on water(!). For the fantasy sequences are shot in black and white, clearly marked as 'art' photography, in order to set off Polly's 'internal universe' from the 'realistic' colour footage of the mundane 'real world', which Bearchell accurately characterizes as a lesbian soap opera. I do not care to speculate further on the less conscious or unexpressed fantasies behind *I've Heard the Mermaids Singing* (the reference to T.S. Eliot is no less a naive than the rest of the film), though its reception as an exemplary film of women's cinema is ground for serious self-questioning by those of us who still want to claim the term for a feminist political project.

Bob Rafelson's *Black Widow* is a more interesting film with regard to this discussion, and not because of the existential questions which it does not pose, but rather because it exemplifies both cases at once, both of the narrative images and trajectories typical of the heroine of the woman's film in the rage of post-feminism: the independent woman who is found guilty and punished, and the woman who wins (and punishes) are placed face to face in the lead *film noir* roles of the *femme fatale* and the female investigator: Catherine (played by Theresa Russell) is the elusive, super-sexy, murderous spider woman, *noir* icon par excellence, and Alex (played by Debra Winger) is the supposedly unattractive unwomanly woman-detective who turns down dates with her boss for a smoky game of poker with the boys.

If both can be called heroines and if *Black Widow* just barely qualifies as a woman's film, in spite of its being obviously made in the *film noir* genre, it is because Alex is not really the hero, although she occupies his narrative function as agent, representative of the law and eventual purveyor of justice. She does bear the name of the Father, duly foreshortened (Alex is the masculine-sounding short for Alexandra), and yet her relation to the very icon of the object of desire, her 'obsession' with Catherine – an obsession which the genre codes as a relation of desire (to wit the title of Visconti's superb version of James M. Cain's novel *The Postman Always Rings Twice, Ossessione* [1942]) – is subverted by the unexpected emergence, half-way through the film, of the most classic femininity in Alex's own character and visual image. In other words, what the spectator had been led to read as Alex's desire for Catherine, culminating in the scene on the beach and the famous kiss at the wedding party, suddenly and inexplicably twists into a feminine identification with her, the kind of identification with the female image, the Mother, which, according to Freud, allows the girl to negotiate the Oedipus Complex and turn her instinctual drives toward the man: Alex starts wearing Catherine's clothes, visiting her hair stylist, and wanting to sleep with her husband (-to-be).

In her reading of *Black Widow*, Marina Heung makes a good argument for the film's attempt to transform the role of women in the *noir* genre by assigning both of the lead roles to independent and professional women, and thus having 'two women protagonists interact directly with each other' in a genre whose 'usual strategy is to pose the "good" woman and the "bad" woman as symbolic opposites, abstractions emblematic of the male protagonist's moral conflict'.[21] However, Heung concludes, the attempt is unsuccessful: it is only Alex's fascination with Catherine that sustains the plot and is given a plausible, if questionable, explanation (i.e., Alex takes Catherine as alter ego, as model to her own inadequate femininity); the 'black widow' remains mysterious, unknowable, so that the mere hint of *her* attraction to Alex must suffice to raise the spectatorial stakes in a possible erotic relationship between the two women. Thus, to Heung's way of seeing, the film develops two plots, the classical *noir* plot and the 'feminization of Alex' plot, ultimately disappointing all expectations.

My own reading is less kind to the film. What Heung calls the second plot is not in fact a plot – at least not in the sense of an arrangement of narrative functions, though it may well be a plot in the sense of intentional strategy – but rather an inconsistent subtext borrowed from the genre of the woman's film, and temporarily inserted in the film in order for the first (*noir*) plot to achieve its climax and moral (oedipal) resolution. Similar contortions are required in Freud's account of the female psychosexual development, where an additional twist is required in the oedipal plot (the girl's sudden refocusing of sexual pleasure from the clitoris onto the vagina) to turn her infantile object-choice from the Mother to the Father, and every deviation from this pattern is attributed to a 'bisexuality' innate to all humans, but more so to females.[22] In the film's plot, that twist takes the form of Alex's sudden feminine identification with Catherine. But its inherent inconsistency is apparent once again in the final coup-de-scène where Alex is fully reinstated in her role as punishing representative of the Law and walks away alone, in the closing shot, into an uncertain sunset. This is not the ending of a woman's film, but of a *film noir* (or a detective film, a Western, etc.): Alex's 'feminization' has not occurred, the 'second plot' has simply been dropped, the inconsistency remains.

A piece of indirect evidence for this argument may be found in another film, Seidelman's *Desperately Seeking Susan*, which is similarly built on two female protagonists and a plot which also turns on the investigation of one by the other. But there the relationship of the suburban child-housewife of uncertain femininity played by Rosanna Arquette, to the mysterious and sexually 'free' superwoman played by Madonna, is clearly one of feminine, narcissistic identification. Consistently with the generic plot of the woman's film, in the end femininity, independence and even friendship are achieved, but with, heaven forbid, no hanky panky between girls and, instead, the restoration to each of her own man. In spite of that, this film, too, in the wake of the current vogue of the theme of lesbianism, has been read as being about 'feminine desire' (collapsed into feminine identification), and has been seen ingenuously – or perhaps ingeniously – as catering to 'the specifically homosexual pleasures of female spectatorship'.[23]

Going back to *Black Widow*, then, it clearly appears that, the greater sophistication of its apparatus notwithstanding, the film's heavy hints at lesbianism are also there only to 'blow the viewer's mind', and its Hollywood-scale strategy of expropriation and delegitimation is, for the greater visual pleasure it affords, all the more insidious. Imagine for a moment: if Alex had been allowed to be what the first half of the film suggests – that is, the subject of her female desire for Catherine – she would not have wanted *to be like* Catherine but *to have her*, or have *her* instead of *Paul*; and she, most likely, *might* have had her – and then, good-bye poker games and target practice with the boys, good-bye service to the Law protecting rich men from women, good-bye loyalty to their moral order. . . . Will someone ever remake *film noir* this way?

Like the other two, the third film in my sample, McLaughlin's *She Must be Seeing Things*, is set in an investigative frame whose subject is the heroine and whose object, the 'mystery' investigated, is also 'woman' – female sexuality, difference and desire. Where it differs from them is in its employ of cinematic narrative codes such as the film-within-the-film, parallel editing, and the system of the look (which maps the relations of look and image) to construct spectatorial positions, as well as diegetic points of view, whereby both of the protagonists are perceived to be at once subject and object of a female desire. And where it differs from nearly all other cinematic representations of lesbianism is the way this film proposes it precisely as *a question of representation, of what can be seen*. Here lesbianism is not merely a theme or a subtext of the film, nor simply a content to be represented or 'portrayed', but is the very problem of its form: how to represent a female, lesbian desire that is neither masculine, a usurpation of male heterosexual desire, nor a feminine, narcissistic identification with the other woman. Which is to say: how to construct, for both spectators and filmmakers, a new position of seeing, a new place of the look, the place of a woman who desires another woman.

She Must be Seeing Things is not simply the portrayal of a lesbian relationship and of the ghosts and fantasies that haunt the two protagonists (one of whom is an independent filmmaker). It is also, quite self-consciously and originally, an attempt to pose the formal problem of lesbian representation in cinema by working through the cinematic equivalence of look and desire, and to reclaim the function of voyeurism by rearticulating it in lesbian terms.[24] In response to the charges of pornography and heterosexism some lesbian feminists hurled at her film, McLaughlin stated:

> What I wanted to do in this film was to foreground the relationship between the two women and then have that act in relation to male culture. . . . I wanted

Figure 1.2 She Must Be Seeing Things (courtesy of Metro Pictures)

to open up the notions and possibilities of what women can do, to try to confront and be iconoclastic towards what have become lesbian and feminist taboos. . . . I wanted to undermine the idea of women as narcissistic extensions of each other because I don't think it's true. That's not why women are together.[25]

Indeed, the erotic relationship between the two protagonists is represented as mediated by heterosexual codes and ways of seeing that are inescapable in our culture, but also by other, subcultural codes (e.g., the lesbian butch-femme performance of sexual roles), which the film foregrounds visibly, marking them as roles, as performance, and distancing them by irony.

By calling up the iconographic and cultural forms that recur in the history of cinema and constitute the frame of reference or the visible, for what can be seen, but doing so in conjunction with contemporary lesbian practices of both re-appropriation and deconstruction of that history, *She Must Be Seeing Things* confronts the spectator with a necessary if uncomfortable question: What are the things Agatha (Sheila Dabney) imagines seeing and those Jo (Lois Weaver) 'sees' in her film, if not those very images that our cultural imaginary and the whole history of cinema have constructed as the visible, what can be seen, and eroticized? Namely, the female body displayed as spectacle for the male gaze 'to take it in', to enter or possess it, or as fetish object of his secret identification; the woman as

Figure 1.3 She Must Be Seeing Things (courtesy of Sheila McLaughlin)

mystery to be pursued, investigated, found guilty or redeemed (by man); and above all, what can be seen and eroticized – though it is not actually represented on the screen, but only figured, implied, in the look – the male gaze itself, the phallic power of the look as figure and signifier of desire.

Feminist film criticism and theory have documented this history of representation extensively. The originality of McLaughlin's film, in my opinion, consists precisely in foregrounding that frame of reference, making *it* visible, and at the same time shifting it, moving it aside, as it were, enough to let us see through the gap, the contradiction; enough to create a space for questioning not only what they, the two women protagonists, see but also what we, spectators, see in the film; enough *to let us see ourselves seeing*, and with what eyes. Thus it addresses spectatorial desire precisely by disallowing a univocal identification with any one character or rule or object-choice, and foregrounding instead the relations of desire to fantasy and its mobility, for them and for us, within the fantasy scenario.

In contrast to the romance or fairy-tale formulas adopted by films like *Lianna* (John Sayles, 1983), *Desert Hearts*, or *I've Heard the Mermaids Singing*, *She Must Be Seeing Things* locates itself historically and politically in the contemporary North American lesbian community with its conflicting discourses, posing the question of desire and its representation from within the context of actual practices of both lesbianism and cinema As a self-conscious, self-critical, feminist intervention amidst the various representational strategies, both feminist and anti-feminist, that aim to expropriate and delegitimate lesbianism as irreducible sociosexual difference, or to recontain it in acceptable, legitimate forms, McLaughlin's film is an example of how an alternative, guerrilla cinema can still work effectively today.

Notes

1 This essay was commissioned for the Conference 'High Culture/Popular Culture: Media Representation of the Other', held at the Rockefeller Foundation's Bellagio Study and Conference Center in Bellagio, Italy, 27 February to 4 March, 1989.

2 Craig Owens, 'The discourse of others: feminism and postmodernism', in Hal Foster (ed.), *The Anti-Aesthetic: Essays in Postmodern Culture* (Port Townsend, WA: Bay Press, 1983), pp. 57–82: Trinh T. Minh-ha (ed.), special issue of *Discourse: Journal for Theoretical Studies in Media and Culture*, no. 8 (Fall–Winter 1986–7).

3 Coco Fusco, 'About locating ourselves and our representations', *Framework*, no. 36 (1989), pp. 7–8.

4 Judith Mayne, 'The woman at the keyhole: women's cinema and feminist criticism', in Mary Ann Doane, Patricia Mellencamp and Linda Williams (eds), *Re-vision: Essays in Feminist Film Criticism* (Frederick, MO: University Publications of America and The American Film Institute, 1984), p. 49.

5 Ibid., p. 50.

6 Mary Ann Doane, Patricia Mellencamp and Linda Williams, 'Feminist film criticism: an introduction', in *Re-vision*, p. 5.

7 See Yvonne Rainer, 'Some ruminations around cinematic antidotes to the Oedipal net(tles) while playing with De Lauraedipus Mulvey, or, he may be off screen, but . . .', *The Independent*, vol. 9, no. 3 (April 1985), pp. 22–5: 'More kicking and screaming from the narrative front/backwater', *Wide Angle*, vol. 7, no. 1–2 (1985), pp. 8–12; and *The Films of Yvonne Rainer* (Bloomington, IN: Indiana University Press, 1989), a volume containing the complete scripts of her films and other contributions by and about Rainer.

8 Teresa de Lauretis, 'Rethinking women's cinema: aesthetics and feminist theory' (originally published in *New German Critique*, no. 34 (Winter 1985)) and 'Strategies of coherence: narrative cinema feminist poetics, and Yvonne Rainer', both in *Technologies of Gender: Essays on Theory, Film, and Fiction* (Bloomington, IN: Indiana University Press, 1987). See also *Alice Doesn't: Feminism, Semiotics, Cinema* (Bloomington, IN: Indiana University Press, 1984), especially ch. 5.

9 Fernando Solanas and Octavio Getino, 'Toward a third cinema', *Cinéaste*, vol. 4, no. 3 (Winter 1970–1), p. 4.

10 *Framework*, no. 34 (1987), p. 36, also in Jim Pines and Paul Willemen (eds), *Questions of Third Cinema* (London: BFI, 1989), pp. 1–29.

11 Scott MacDonald, 'Interview with Lizzie Borden', *Feminist Studies*, vol. 15, no. 2 (Summer 1989), p. 342.

12 de Lauretis, *Technologies of Gender*, p. 142.

13 Claire Johnston, 'Women's cinema as counter-cinema', in Claire Johnston (ed.), *Notes on Women's Cinema* (London: SEFT, 1974), p. 31.

14 Solanas and Getino, 'Towards a third cinema'; p. 19.

15 Ibid., p. 10.

16   Audre Lorde, *Sister Outsider: Essays and Speeches* (Trumansburg, NY: The Crossing Press, 1984).

17   One account of the debate provoked by McLaughlin's film is given by Victoria Brownworth. 'Dyke S/M wars rage in London: racism and fascism alleged', *Coming Up!* vol. 10, no. 1 (October 1988), pp. 14–15. On what has come to be known generally as the feminist 'sex wars', see B. Ruby Rich, 'Feminism and sexuality in the 1980s', *Feminist Studies*, vol. 12, no. 3 (1986), pp. 525–61.

18   On the different readings of *Personal Best* and the specific interpretive strategies documented in lesbian feminist reviews, see Elizabeth Ellsworth, 'Illicit pleasure: feminist spectators and *Personal Best*', *Wide Angle*, vol. 8, no. 2 (1986), pp. 45–56.

19   Walter Benjamin, 'Theses on the philosophy of history', in *Illuminations* (New York: Schocken Books, 1969), p. 257.

20   Chris Bearchell, 'A Canadian fairytale: Chris Bearchell talks to Particia Rozema about taking her first feature to Cannes', *Epicene* (October 1987), p. 26. All subsequent quotations from Rozema come from this text (pp. 24–6), which combines the interview with Bearchell's generous, if rightly critical, review of the film.

21   Marina Heung, 'Black Widow', *Film Quarterly*, vol. 41, no. 1 (Fall 1987), p. 57.

22   On the Freudian story of femininity as well as on the standard positions assigned to male and female characters by the plot of Oedipal narratives, in film and elsewhere, I have written extensively in *Alice Doesn't*, ch. 5.

23   Jackie Stacey, 'Desperately seeking difference', *Screen*, vol. 28, no. 1 (Winter 1987), pp. 46–61.

24   This last point is also made by Martha Gever, 'Girl crazy: lesbian narratives in *She Must Be Seeing Things* and *Damned If You Don't*', *The Independent* (July 1988), pp. 14–18.

25   Alison Butler, '*She Must Be Seeing Things*: an interview with Sheila McLaughlin', *Screen*, vol. 28, no. 4 (Autumn 1987), pp. 21–2.

2 That special thrill: *Brief Encounter*, homosexuality and authorship

Andy Medhurst

A gay text is one which lends itself to the hypothesis of a gay reading, regardless of where the author's genitals were wont to keep house.

Gregory Woods[1]

. . . finished reading *Present Laughter*. What a wonderful play it would be if – as Coward must have wanted – all those love affairs were about homosexuals.

Sir Peter Hall[2]

Death In Venice gives gay people a special thrill, and therefore it is gay novel.

Delegate at the 1987 International Scientific
Conference on Lesbian and Gay Studies[3]

Authorship is hardly a hot issue these days. The very word itself conjures up ancient dusty battles over the cultural legitimacy of cinema, battles that were fought, won and forgotten long ago. The idea that a film's director is the primary, shaping source of its meaning is simultaneously inscribed as middlebrow commonsense (see the film review columns of *The Observer*, *City Limits*, or any publication targeted at the bourgeois intelligentsia, with their umbilical linking of film title and director's name) and dismissed as hopelessly outmoded by every branch of recent critical theory. It is a dead debate, and its tombstone was the BFI Reader *Theories of Authorship*,[4] which offered an inbuilt teleology, a narrative trajectory which led me, as a postgraduate student, away from the embarrassments of romantic individualism to the chastening rigours of poststructuralist thought. It was a tempting package, and I bought the whole deal – the Author was, beyond question, buried, and Roland Barthes led the funeral procession.

My induction into this orthodoxy coincided, however with my growing engagement with the politics of gay culture, and here a different version of Barthes (that most rapturously polysemic and flirtatiously comic of writers) was important. I became increasingly interested in gay men's specific ways of seeing the world – what one might call, to use a now unfashionable phrase of Raymond Williams, male homosexual structures of feeling – but to qualify for inclusion in this framework, texts had to pass an 'authorship test' ('is/was he gay?') that harked back to the bad old days of crudely biographical criticism. There seemed to be a double standard at work, albeit one rooted in political expediency – Authorship was bad, Gay Authorship was good.

That distinction, shockingly banal though it is, has been hard to shake from my mind, and its persistence is one of the things I want to explore in this chapter. I also want to address two more complex issues in textual and sexual theory: first, the political implications of poststructuralist attempts to discredit notions of authorial agency; and second, the related debates in gay theory around what have come to be known as the poles of 'essentialism' and 'social constructionism' (terms I will elaborate on later). I want to use one film as a springboard into these questions – *Brief Encounter* (1945), written by Noël Coward and directed by David Lean. This is not, I suspect, the most obvious of choices, so perhaps some explanation is necessary.

It is part of the accumulated folk wisdom of gay male subcultures that the homosexuality of an individual will reveal itself primarily through matters of taste – not good or bad taste but *particular* taste, a fondness for certain cultural artefacts above others, a set of preferences that proclaim one's sexual affiliations as clearly as any sloganeering T-shirt. For British gay men, at least those of my acquaintance, loving *Brief Encounter* is one such marker. One reason for this, I would suggest, is that *Brief Encounter* is not simply the tearful tale of heterosexual romance that it appears to be: beneath, or alongside, or overlapping this narrative is another, quite specifically related to the homosexuality of its author. Employing the naively biographical paradigm of Gay Authorship, *Brief Encounter* shows Noël Coward displacing his own fears, anxieties and pessimism about the possibility of a fulfilled sexual relationship within an oppressively homophobic culture by transposing them into a heterosexual context. The furtiveness and fear of discovery that end Laura's and Alec's relationship comprise a set of emotions that Coward would have felt with particular force and poignancy, and which gay men ever since have responded to with recognition and admiration.

I do not offer that reading as any startling new interpretation; it is a decoding of the text that many gay men (and no doubt a sprinkling of perceptive heterosexuals) have made. One, the British gay director Richard Kwietniowski, has taken the simple reading a stage further by making the prize-winning short film, *Flames of Passion* (1990), which is both pastiche of and homage to the Coward original, reworking its iconography into an updated story of gay romance that begins with hurried glances on a station platform and, times having changed, ends with intertwined consummation on the train. His film, Kwietniowski straightforwardly claims, is one that would have been approved of by Noël Coward's unconscious.[5]

There is, then, a long-established subcultural reading of *Brief Encounter* that cuts across its ostensible or mainstream meaning, but does this have any substantive

Figure 2.1 Flames of Passion (a BFI production; photographer, Tony Clancy)

base in the text itself or is it only a collective fantasy, a shared 'special thrill'? Before tackling the theoretical problems raised by that question, it will be instructive to look at the volatile critical reputation of *Brief Encounter* within British film culture, since this can be linked very closely to shifting paradigms of authorship.

> The theme and situation are universal. They belong to all human beings whether they have individually endured a similar love-tragedy or not. . . . It would be difficult to find a more profound story of distressed love in the history of the cinema.[6]

> To see [*Brief Encounter*] again . . . at the Baker Street Classic, is to see another film entirely . . . the audience in this usually polite and certainly middle-class hall couldn't restrain its derision and repeatedly burst into angry exasperated laughter . . . a well-spoken young lady . . . finally cried out 'Where the hell is Milford Junction anyway?'[7]

More than any other single film, *Brief Encounter* has operated as a barometer of the prevailing assumptions in British film culture. It was released in December 1945, to an overwhelmingly positive critical response that praised its 'maturity' and 'realism', and also hailed it as the latest success from the Coward/Lean 'team', which had, during the Second World War, produced three notably successful films, namely *In Which We Serve* (1942), *This Happy Breed* (1944) and *Blithe Spirit* (1945). This run of critical and box-office hits prompted C.A. Lejeune, film critic of *The Observer*, to claim:

> These Coward films are probably the nearest things we have to a valid modern school in British cinema. . . . You often hear people say, 'Why can't we make films over here with the taste and art and honesty of the French cinema?' In his own way, and in his own idiom, Coward does.[8]

What is striking here is not just the confidence of the assertion of quality, but the unquestioned awarding of the credit to Coward. The literary bias of British film reviewing has rarely been quite so plainly stated – Coward is the established name, his reputation guaranteed by years of theatrical success, hence he takes precedence over the mere maker of pictures. In 1946, however, Lean directed his first film without a Coward connection, *Great Expectations*, and the huge reputation and success this enjoyed coincided with the start of the long postwar decline suffered by Coward – the net result was that the writer's contribution to the earlier films' success became progressively marginalized, a state of affairs hardly helped by the increasing influence of French auteurist models of film analysis on British critics.

Roger Manvell's *The Film and the Public*, published in 1955, still held *Brief Encounter* in very high esteem, placing it in a chapter rather disingenuously called 'A miscellany of films' but which is clearly intended to signify a pantheon of cinematic greats. (There are extremely instructive comparisons to be made between the films that make up Manvell's 'Miscellany' and the 'Pantheon' of directors listed in the first, 1962, issue of *Movie* – the changes are an eloquently stark illustration of the massive reorientation of British film culture.) So, Coward is elevated to join the likes of *Greed* (1923) and *Paisa* (1946) and *Le jour se lève* (1939), but Manvell cautiously refuses to bestow individual plaudits, preferring to see the film as 'one of those rare films for which one can never be sure to whom the real credit is due . . . an example of the unity achieved by the cooperation of many creative minds'.[9] Eventually, though, he singles out Celia Johnson's acting followed by Lean's direction. Coward was beginning to disappear.

The date of *The Film and the Public* is significant – 1955, just one year before the whole 'Angry Young Men' circus. Anger was, above all, a theatrical phenomenon and Coward exemplified the type of theatre that was under attack. The films made from 'Angry' texts seemed to mark a similarly definitive rejection of the previous orthodoxies, with *Brief Encounter* acquiring an unenviable figurehead status as the paradigmatic sexless, middle-class, British film – hence the scorn of the audience that contained Raymond Durgnat. As Durgnat himself put it, to explain the film's fall from grace, 'Jimmy Porter came along'.[10]

There are subtexts here concerned with gender and sexuality. It is Coward who is singled out for specific blame by Durgnat, his screenplay compared explicitly and dismissively to women's romance fiction as if that, by itself, was a confirmation of worthlessness. More generally, the 'Angry' movement had been characterized by strong antihomosexual prejudices (John Osborne's *Look Back In Anger* and Kingsley Amis's *Lucky Jim* are full of bullishly heterosexual scorn for 'effeminacy') which found Coward an ideal target. If *Brief Encounter* were to be critically favoured at all, it had to be rescued from the discredited label of Coward and conclusively assigned to the body of texts marked 'Lean'. This process, begun in 1946 with the acclaim for *Great Expectations*, reached its peak with the 1974 publication of *Masterworks of the British Cinema*, a book that included the script of *Brief Encounter* but zealously forbade its readers to praise the man who wrote it: '*Brief Encounter*, indeed, constitutes almost a declaration of independence on Lean's part from his fruitful, but by 1945 no doubt increasingly constricting, association with Coward's writing.'[11] The hegemonic assurance of that 'no doubt' speaks volumes – the Author was dead, long live the auteur. Or, in terms of the concerns of this article, the gay writer had been effaced, leaving a blemish-free heterosexual text.

> Victor: I'm glad I'm normal.
> Amanda: What an odd thing to be glad about.[12]

While I would insist on the centrality of Noël Coward's sexuality to the patterns of meanings that I see in *Brief Encounter*, I would not wish for one second to hold him up as any kind of gay martyr. The mythologies of tragic sacrifice that have coalesced around gay writers like Oscar Wilde and Joe Orton tend only to impede a fully contextual understanding of how their sexuality and textuality inform each other. I have no desire to add Coward to that mythology, besides which he was, judging by the biographies and his own diaries, an intolerable man – snobbish, reactionary, racist, lamenting Labour election victories and the decline of Empire, welcoming Gandhi's assassination, oozing sycophancy towards the British (and any other) royal family, and describing the Beatles as 'bad-mannered little shits'. Coward was not, to use a rather tired phrase, a positive role model.

Nonetheless, his plays (including *Still Life*, on which *Brief Encounter* was based) can be productively mined for half-hidden endorsements of sexual options that strayed beyond the expected confines of domesticated heterosexual monogamy. This can partly be accounted for by the social milieu in which many of them are set, that stereotypically 'Cowardian' world of elegant hotel bedrooms where the cocktail shaker is always within reach. In *Design For Living*, Otto boasts that:

> Our lives are diametrically opposed to ordinary social convention. . . . We've jilted them and eliminated them and we've got to find our own solutions for our own peculiar moral problems. . . . We're not doing any harm to anyone

else. We're not peppering the world with illegitimate children. The only
people we could possibly mess up are ourselves, and that's our lookout. . . .
Therefore the only thing left is to enjoy it thoroughly, every rich moment of
it, every thrilling second.[13]

He can do so, because he lives a life where material luxury has bought him out of
the social expectations imposed on less fortunate people. In the same play comes
the following exchange:

> Gilda: If we were ordinary, moral, high-thinking citizens we shouldn't have
> had an affair at all.
> Leo: Perhaps not. We should have crushed it down.[14]

In many ways, this is the entire story of *Brief Encounter* encapsulated in two lines.

Moreover, even when Coward seems to be advocating sexual experimentation,
he stops far short of specific details. As Alan Sinfield has put it, he 'validates deviant
sexuality when it is part of a general bohemianism' but nothing more concretely
radical is put forward.[15]

Perhaps now might be the point to question whether this type of analysis belongs
in *Screen* at all – isn't it unreconstructed literary criticism of the most discredited
kind, combing through the textual evidence to find traces of what the author 'really
thought'? I plead guilty, partly, but in my defence I want to return to the point I
signalled earlier, that a biographical approach has more political justification if the
project being undertaken is one concerned with the cultural history of a
marginalized group. To be sure, we have all moved on since films directed by
Hitchcock were unravelled in the search for strands of 'Catholic guilt', but equally
I still teach gay students who find it genuinely empowering to learn of the
homosexuality of a cultural figure as one contributing factor to the work that he/she
produced.

It is also important to stress that this reclaiming of Coward as relevant to gay
culture is very different from the limiting ways in which some heterosexual critics
have mobilized the fact of his sexuality. What happens there is that a 'really gay'
reading of Coward is put into play, much as I have already done with *Brief Encounter*,
but on the grounds that a homosexual writer can *only* write about homosexuality
(analogous cases would be the insistence that Edward Albee's *Who's Afraid of Virginia
Woolf* is 'really' about a gay couple, or that Tennessee Williams's Blanche Dubois
is nothing but a transposed drag queen). I would refer back to Sir Peter Hall's
comment on *Present Laughter* here – for him the failure of that play is in direct
proportion to its not being about homosexuals. In this way the homosexual writer
is granted a dubious measure of liberal pity ('if only he hadn't lived in such a
repressive world') while at the same time the heterosexual critic distances the
threatening possibility that a homosexual writer might have a great many insights

Figure 2.2 Brief Encounter (courtesy of the Rank Organization plc and BFI stills archive)

into the codes, mechanisms and ideologies of heterosexuality itself. That such insights are available to gay people (whether we are writers or not) should come as no surprise – from birth we are relentlessly socialized into a heterosexual identity that we may later choose to reject but which remains an always familiar landscape – those on the margins of a culture know more about its centre than the centre can ever know about the margins.

The importance of Coward for gay culture is not simply one of thematics; there are also broader, crucial but treacherously nebulous questions of tone, attitude and feeling. What I want to get at is how Coward shared and contributed to making the male homosexual structure of feeling that I and many other contemporary gay men find in his writing. Richard Dyer has described how Coward's song-writing, along with that of other gay lyricists like Cole Porter and Lorenz Hart, can be productively reread in terms of their specifically homosexual perception of the double-edged nature of romantic love – simultaneously wanting it desperately to happen but convinced of the impossible ridiculousness of any such desire.[16] That sense of 'bitter-sweet' (the title, perhaps not incidentally, of one of Coward's greatest stage successes) strikes me as a crucial component of the structure of feeling I am interested in here. Dyer's list of songwriters could be updated, for example, to include the Pet Shop Boys, whose records plug directly into that bitter-sweet double-bind of the passionate desire/impossibility of fulfilment (a song like *Rent* exemplifies this). Connoisseurs of the self-referentiality of gay culture might care to note that the Pet Shop Boys' Neil Tennant frequently lists Coward's *Sail Away* as one of his favourite songs – it is hard to conceive of any other contemporary pop star having the wit or sly wisdom to make such a choice.

If plays like *Design For Living* or *Private Lives* foreground the witty, hedonistic, passionately abandoned side of the bitter-sweet couplet, then *Brief Encounter* is the key text of the opposite side. It is a text which explores the pain and grief caused by having one's desires destroyed by the pressures of social convention and it is this set of emotions which has sustained its reputation in gay subcultures. I ought to add, perhaps, that gay men do not regard this film with nothing but sad, solemn recognition – the characteristically gay male urge to mock and undercut what one genuinely and deeply feels, what Dyer brilliantly calls 'the knife edge between camp and hurt',[17] can be evidenced by pointing out that one of London's most crowded and cruisy gay bars is called 'Brief Encounter', though one is, alas, unlikely to meet anyone resembling Trevor Howard therein.

Gregory Woods's remark, quoted at the beginning of this chapter, suggests, in a rather deliriously utopian, post-Barthian kind of way, that any text can be opened up to a gay interpretation if gay readers decide it to be appropriate – authorial intention is here surrendered in favour of a sort of subcultural authorship, a collective 'special thrill', a method of analysis based on a recognition of shared structures of feeling. Similarly, Alison Hennegan has described how as a teenager she hunted out lesbian fiction and based her decisions to investigate one text rather than another on clues as vague and 'irrational' as a publisher's logo or a particular chapter title.[18] Hunches these may have been, but they were almost always right – critical theory may not have the language to describe this method of discovering homosexually-relevant material, but as a subcultural practice, a particularly attuned set of decoding skills, it undoubtedly exists, as I and any other gay person can testify.

Knowing an author's homosexuality makes that decoding far easier (if at the same time rather less triumphant – there's an undeniable pleasure in finding out that a favourite writer, actor or director you have admired for years turns out to be gay, as you always privately hoped and 'knew') but it returns us once again to the problem of biography, the danger of regressing to a simplistic reading of texts which simply locates their meanings in the author's life story. Yet this is a problem that needs to be faced, because the reading of *Brief Encounter* that I have outlined reintroduces into the critical game that most awkward of players – the historical, flesh-and-blood person of the author.

The Author has staggered from the deathbed, so is it time for critical analysis to pay attention to real people's lived lives, their traceable, material existences? If so, there is much rethinking to be done, for the theoretical paradigms that have dominated the last twenty years have nothing resembling an adequate critical framework for dealing with a factor as flagrantly nonabstract, as defiantly corporeal, as embarrassingly tangible as this.

There is a danger, though, that the kind of gay cultural archaeology described above (a sort of retrospective 'outing') can degenerate into the construction of an ahistorical 'gay sensibility'. The appeal for tolerance by gesturing to lists of Famously Artistic Homosexuals is one of the classic tropes of gay self-justification – it goes 'Sappho, Michaelangelo, Shakespeare . . . and me' – and it needs always to be resisted because it seeks to extend contemporary definitions of sexuality back to incorporate historical periods when categorizations of the sexual were quite different. In short, the 'gay sensibility' is a rhetorical deployment of essentialism.

The essentialist view of homosexuality seeks to forge links between all people who enjoy same-sex relations, regardless of gender, race, age, class or period. It is, on any logical grounds, patently nonsensical, as Jeffrey Weeks has argued:

> We cannot . . . simply assume that nothing changes, that gays and lesbians have always existed as we exist today . . . that there is a mystical continuity between our desires and their desires across the range of cultures and histories. We do not do it for any other aspect of our social existence. We should not do it for our sex.[19]

Opposing that essentialist version of homosexuality is an analysis which, drawing above all on the work of Foucault, sees homosexuality as a social construction, culturally and historically specific, sensitive to cultural and historical change.

This 'social constructionism' can in turn be linked to that whole shift in critical thinking which has sought to undermine any credibility in the unified subject as a source of meaning, and most crucial here has been the contribution of psychoanalysis. These arguments are more than familiar to readers of this journal and, considered purely as philosophical debates, they are impressively rigorous and difficult to refute. Where they become problematic, especially for members of marginalized cultural groups, is in what they begin to mean if we take them out of the pristine hot-house of the academy and put them into the messy struggles of day-to-day life.

To regard homosexuality as a social construction and nothing more is, potentially, to put another weapon in the hands of those who would like to see it quite literally erased from the world – if it can be constructed, then it can be deconstructed, so what are all those queers still doing here? Gay intellectuals may dismiss essentialism as a bogus utopia, but it has provided the emotional power behind a great deal of gay activism – it is much harder to claim civil rights for a discursive construction. The pragmatism of political urgency must be allowed to sully the purity of intellectual thought; what is needed, at least in the short term, is what Gayatri Spivak has referred to as a kind of 'strategic essentialism'.[20]

Otherwise marginalized groups run the risk of theorizing themselves out of existence.

Besides which, what is so attractive about this surrendering of unitary identity, this fetish for fragmentation that characterizes so much of modern intellectual life? Is it always a good idea to slaughter the Author? Three quotations from feminist, black and gay perspectives, helpfully problematize that question:

> . . . the postmodernist decision that the Author is dead, and subjective agency along with him, does not necessarily work for women and prematurely forecloses the question of identity for them. Because women have not had the same historical relation of identity to origin, institution, production, that men have had, women have not, I think, (collectively) felt burdened by too much Self, Ego, Cogito, etc.[21]

> It never surprises me when black folks respond to the critique of essentialism, especially when it denies the validity of identity politics, by saying 'Yeah, it's easy to give up identity when you got one'. Should we not be suspicious of postmodern critiques of the 'subject' when they surface at a historical moment when many subjugated people feel themselves coming to voice for the first time?[22]

> Narrative identification . . . is being rejected . . . at a point in time when gays can claim they still have not had it. An initial period of identification is important to a repressed group that has *never* had adequate self-images.[23]

The last of those three comments was, it is true, written almost fifteen years ago, long before the more than 'adequate' gay images of *My Beautiful Laundrette* or *Law of Desire* or *Torch Song Trilogy*, but I think the general point stands: before we stampede to dispense with 'identity', let us consider whether it still has its uses as a rallying point for political action. Postmodernism is less liberating for some social groups than for others – though there is a point to be made here about the extremely close links between postmodernism as a general theoretical superstructure and camp as a specific homosexual practice. I have, perhaps rashly, elsewhere published the baldly provocative claim that 'postmodernism is only heterosexuals catching up with camp'[24] and I think the relationship between the two discourses remains a fruitful area for further study. Crudely, the sense of blurred boundaries, of disrupted hierarchies, of disrespectful, intertextual playfulness, of the delight in superficiality and the wearing of cultural masks – all these were fundamental to the strategies of camp long before postmodernism lurched into view. One of the key crossover texts, perhaps, is Barthes's *Mythologies*, for what is that but a series of camp readings? Name one heterosexual male theorist who could display such interest in wrestling, washing powders *and* Greta Garbo.

Authorship is identity in the textual sphere, and hence gay people, like all marginal groups, have, at present, a political stake in wanting to hold on to the Author despite her/his expulsion from prevailing postmodernist theories. We need to construct our histories through examining the records left by those who went before us, not in a blunderingly literal-minded fashion that sees fictional texts as factual 'evidence', but by studying how texts mediate the contradictions and challenges faced by those who carried a homosexual identity through a heterosexual world. This can only be done, of course, with authors who lived within modern categorizations of sexuality – but that period, after all, does include the entire history of the cinema.

To see essentialism and social constructionism as polarized opposites may be useful for rhetorical purposes, but any fully sensitive analysis of culture and sexuality must constantly negotiate between the two.[25] Organizing around the politics of identity may well overlook the troubled, shifting role of the unconscious in the formation of subjectivities, but such exquisite philosophical niceties often have to be shelved when dealing with palpable, material discrimination. I have read my Foucault, I am aware of the conceptual shortcomings of a timeless, essentialist homosexual identity, I might even want to take the step of putting quotation marks around the word 'gay' – but the man who queerbashed me some years ago did not put quotation marks around his fists. An emotive example, to be sure, but sexuality is not a topic from which emotion can be expelled, because the categories of sexuality are experiential: I cannot be purely theoretical about homosexuality, because I am not a purely theoretical homosexual. Neither was Noël Coward, and, despite the multitude of other differences between us, that shared fact persists and continues to inform, shape and intensify my love of *Brief Encounter* and the tears it always makes me shed.

Notes

1 Gregory Woods, *Articulate Flesh: Male Homo-Eroticism and Modern Poetry* (New Haven, CT: Yale University Press, 1987), p. 4.

2 John Goodwin (ed.), *Peter Hall's Diaries* (London: Hamish Hamilton, 1984), p. 229.

3 Quoted by Maurice van Lieshout, 'The context of gay writing and reading', in Dennis Altman, Carole Vance, Martha Vicinus and Jeffrey Weeks (eds), *Homosexuality: Which Homosexuality?* (London: Gay Men's Press, 1989), p. 113.

4 John Caughie (ed.), *Theories of Authorship* (London: Routledge, Kegan Paul/British Film Institute, 1981).

5 See Stephen Bourne's interview with Kwietniowski, *Gay Times*, June 1990.

6 Roger Manvell, *The Film and the Public* (Harmondsworth: Penguin, 1955), pp. 156–8.

7 Raymond Durgnat, *A Mirror for England* (London: Faber, 1970), p. 180.

8 C.A. Lejeune, *Chestnuts in Her Lap* (London: Phoenix House, 1947), p. 163.

9 Manvell, *The Film and the Public*, p. 156.

10 Durgnat, *A Mirror for England*, p. 180.

11   John Russell Taylor (ed.), *Masterworks of the British Cinema* (London: Lorrimer, 1974) pp. 10–11.

12   Noël Coward, *Private Lives*, in *Play Parade* (London: Heinemann, 1934), p. 480.

13   Noël Coward, *Design For Living*, in *Play Parade*, pp. 404–5.

14   Ibid., p. 361.

15   Alan Sinfield, 'Who was afraid of Joe Orton?', *Textual Practice*, vol. 4, no. 2 (1990), p. 270.

16   Richard Dyer, 'Judy Garland and gay men', in *Heavenly Bodies* (London: British Film Institute/Macmillan, 1987), p. 154.

17   Ibid., p. 180.

18   Alison Hennegan, 'On becoming a lesbian reader', in Susannah Radstone (ed.), *Sweet Dreams: Sexuality, Gender and Popular Fiction* (London: Lawrence & Wishart, 1988), pp. 165–91.

19   Jeffrey Weeks, 'Against nature', in Altman *et al.*, *Homosexuality: Which Homosexuality?*, p. 206.

20   Spivak cited in Judith Butler, 'Gender trouble, feminist theory and psychoanalytic discourse', in Linda J. Nicholson (ed.), *Feminism/Postmodernism* (London: Routledge, 1990), p. 325.

21   Nancy K. Miller, 'Changing the subject: authorship, writing and the reader', in Teresa de Lauretis (ed.), *Feminist Studies/Critical Studies* (London: Macmillan, 1986), p. 106.

22   bell hooks, 'Postmodern blackness', in *Yearning* (London: Turnaround, 1991), p. 28.

23   Paul Hallam and Ronald L. Peck, 'Images of homosexuality', *Gay Left*, no. 5 (1977), p. 25.

24   Andy Medhurst, 'Pitching camp', *City Limits*, 10–17 May 1990.

25   For more substantial reading around this question see Carole S. Vance, 'Social construction theory: problems in the history of sexuality', in Altman *et al.*, *Homosexuality: Which Homosexuality?*, pp. 13–25; and Diana Fuss, *Essentially Speaking: Feminism, Nature and Difference* (London: Routledge, 1989).

Part II

Queering technology

3   Technology, paranoia and the queer voice

Ellis Hanson

> Through drugs, or perhaps via the sharpening or even mechanical amplification of latent ESP functions, it may be possible for each partner to simultaneously experience the sensations of the other; or we may eventually emerge into polymorphous sexual beings, with the male and female components blurring, merging and interchanging. The potentialities for exploring new areas of sexual experience are virtually boundless.
>
> Stanley Kubrick[1]

> He believed that he had a mission to redeem the world and to restore it to its lost state of bliss. This, however, he could only bring about if he were first transformed from a man into a woman.
>
> Court Judgement, referring to Schreber[2]

It is curious that Stanley Kubrick requires technological assistance to engage in the sort of 'blurry' sexual behaviour that comes quite easily to a great many people who are, shall we say, less invested in normative heterosexuality. Daniel Paul Schreber, whose memoirs inspired Freud's most important work on paranoia, only needed God and his imagination. Kubrick is almost radical in his sexual politics, except for the fact that these remarks originally appeared in *Playboy*, a magazine whose view of sexuality is less than innovative. With his emphasis on the 'polymorphous' play of gendered 'components', Kubrick does seem to gesture vaguely in the direction of the queer. By 'queer', I mean the odd, the uncanny, the undecidable. But, more importantly, I refer to 'queer' sexuality, that no-man's land beyond the heterosexual norm, that categorical domain virtually synonymous with homosexuality and yet wonderfully suggestive of a whole range of sexual possibilities (deemed perverse or deviant to classical psychoanalysis) that challenge the familiar distinctions between normal and pathological, straight and gay, masculine men and feminine women. Kubrick's vaguely queer musings on the future of sexuality, inspired apparently by his work on *2001: A Space Odyssey* (1968), bring together two points about the film that I would like to expand upon here: sexual transformation, and technology as a sexual prosthetic device.

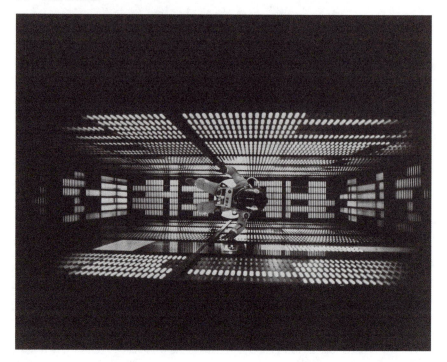

Figure 3.1 2001: A Space Odyssey (courtesy of BFI stills archive and Turner Pictures)

Whether by accident or by necessity, the age of technology is concomitant with the age of desire, rendering postmodernity peculiarly susceptible to the romance of people for their machines. What am I doing when I express desire through technology, or when electric speech becomes the voice of love? What happens when this electric voice of love is a queer voice? Does Kubrick see the gender-bending voice of the HAL computer in *2001* as a precursor of a technosexual revolution and, if so, then why is HAL the focus of a science-fiction nightmare? My juxtaposition of Kubrick with Schreber raises still other questions about Kubrick's scenario. Is the queer voice of HAL so very different from the voices that Schreber hears, those voices hostile and divine, enigmatic and telephonic, that talk him through his transformations into Miss Schreber, into the wife of God or the Prince of Hell, into the seer of spirits and the redeemer of the world? Kubrick and Schreber each offer a version of human redemption, and each has a utopian vision that first takes a terrifying turn through paranoia and sexual transformation.

The connection between paranoia and cinema, not to mention criticism on the subject, has already developed into a major tradition. The suspense or horror film, where repressed desire gains hallucinatory palpability as the beast in the closet, is only the most noted genre in this respect. While mainstream cinema has traditionally avoided explicit representations of lesbians and gay men, it has nevertheless developed paranoia into an important marketing strategy – and the parallel history of paranoia and homosexuality in classical psychoanalysis is well known. In the Schreber case, Freud noted that paranoia always seems to be caused by repressed homosexuality, and his colleague, Sándor Ferenczi, was quick to add that paranoia is merely homosexuality 'in disguise'.[3]

While Freud's insistence upon a link between paranoia and homosexuality has buffeted a great deal of criticism, Mary Ann Doane, Kaja Silverman and Patricia White, among other feminist film theorists, have explored at length the connections between filmic pleasure, the disembodied voice, female paranoia and female homosexuality in classic cinema. The heroine, stalked by an embodiment of her repressed desire, perhaps even her own seductive voice, is a familiar cinematic trope. This scenario is important to gay film theory as well, since the demonization of the gay man in film is often a paranoid function of homophobia. The gay man in mainstream cinema, more often than not, is less a character than a symptom in the narrative articulation of masculinity. He is the return of the repressed. He is the question of queerness – of male femininity, of desire between men – an essentially disruptive question raised and violently dismissed in the course of the film. He stands precariously on the margins of the conventional subject–object relationship of man to woman, his very exclusion an answer to the question that he raises. He is the villain to be abused, murdered or anxiously domesticated in order to preserve a coherent and conventional masculinity elsewhere.

2001 is extraordinary in this paranoid tradition in that it brilliantly evokes the destabilizing eroticism of technology through the queer voice of HAL. Furthermore, the film's attempt at closure, at dismantling HAL on the way to idealizing the relationship between man and his machines, obscures a degree of disruptive ambivalence toward technology that persists even to the final, triumphant frames. In this way, while *2001* is a fine example of the paranoid tradition in film, its eroticization of technology helps to undermine its own attempt at constructing a stable masculine subject. This persistent instability gestures toward the possibility of a radical jouissance in paranoid narratives. For this reason, I am proposing another odd juxtaposition by comparing *2001* to a more recent film, Pedro Almodóvar's *La ley del deseo / Law of Desire* (1987). In Almodóvar's film, queer voices are dis-embodied and projected through machines – through a telephone, a television, a typewriter. After the fashion of HAL, these voices function as a destabilizing force in the narrative, undermining attempts at repression and closure. While Kubrick resists the queer voice of technology, Almodóvar's camp style delights in it. These two films, in my view, represent two very different functions of the disembodied voice in cinema: the paranoid defence of horror and the paranoid pleasure of submission. Both functions may be seen in the Schreber case: the difference between Schreber's horror at his desire to be fucked as a man, and his pleasure at the thought of being fucked as a woman.

Speculations about the sexuality of HAL have been proliferating and suppressed ever since the film first opened. All of these readings are based on the sexual ambiguity of HAL's voice, but the question of HAL's sexuality is often quickly dismissed by readings that insist upon the asexuality of machines and the asexual alienation of men in space. Critics have rarely warmed to the notion of computer love in the manner of Donna Haraway in a recent interview: 'I would rather go to bed with a cyborg than a sensitive man, I'll tell you that much'.[4] Or by Kubrick himself in a comment that prefigures Haraway: 'There is a sexiness to beautiful machines. . . . We are almost in a sort of biological machine society already.'[5] The very language that critics have used to describe HAL demonstrates the paradox of asexuality and oversexuality characteristic of a long tradition of representing the android and the androgyne.[6] Pauline Kael is notably frank in her description of HAL as a 'rejected homosexual lover', but the range of interpretations is suggestive: HAL has a 'passionless almost homosexual voice', he is an 'androgyne', he is 'epicene', 'neuter, neutral' and 'sterile' – one critic hazarded the somewhat less than courageous epithet '(gay?)'. HAL is a 'monster', 'berserk', 'hysterical', 'a fussy genius', he is 'neurotic' and experiences a 'paranoid breakdown'. 'His "voice" is bland, neutral, reassuring, and also ambiguous, sinister, untrustworthy.' As a coalescence of the maternal and narcissistic preoccupations of this film, Penelope Gilliatt's description of HAL is as brilliant as it is bizarre: 'He gives a lot of thought to how he strikes others, and sometimes carries on about himself like a mother fussing on the telephone to keep a bored grown child hanging on.' My own personal favourite comes from Don Daniels' review: 'HAL's faggoty TV-announcer tones and vocabulary become the disembodied voice of three centuries of scientific rationalism.'[7] Beware the faggoty techno-vampire! He leaps through your television screen and your movie screen, bearing with him all the evils of modern science and psychiatry, infecting you with his queer undecidability and reviving in you curious dreams about your mother. The queer voice, traditionally a bearer of anxiety, illicit pleasure, and fear, becomes in *2001* the very ghost in our machines, a mode of articulating horror and repressed desire in a culture of technology. I would argue that *2001*, like many of its reviews, gives an anxious audience an art form through which to act out sexual anxieties and at the same time to distance them and control them: HAL's queerness is suggested but suppressed, owned but quickly disowned, acknowledged but unexplored.

What many reviews imply, and I would assert, is that HAL's queerness is just one aspect of a panicky regression to narcissism articulated throughout *2001*. The appearance of a link in this film, between narcissism and the queer voice should come as no surprise, given the importance of narcissism in Freudian theories of paranoia and homosexuality. Briefly, in the narcissistic paradigm for the etiology of male homosexuality, a man disavows symbolic castration by identifying with his infantile fantasy of a phallic mother and taking himself as the object of his own desire. This narcissistic construction is by no means peculiar to psychoanalysis: one need only consult the myriad cultural representations of gay men as mentally ill, passive, selfish, exhibitionistic, fascist, deadly, fixated on their mothers and so on. What is striking about *2001* in this respect is the way it produces an all-male environment in which erotic tension is produced through mirroring effects, doubling, and symbolic infantilization. Enter the 'faggoty' voice of HAL, and this narcissistic tension cannot help but take on homoerotic accents, especially where the film is viewed in a social context in which the links between narcissism and homosexuality are already in place. One could argue that Kubrick does for the space programme what Melville does for shipping: he articulates the tensions and erotic ambiguities that complicate the distinction between the homosocial and the homosexual within communities of men.

The sheer maleness of *2001* is striking. A number of feminist readings have pointed out the gradual disappearance of women from the film.[8] While Russian women might hold professional positions of power as Cold War enemies in Kubrick's world, North American women are still relegated to familiar, marginalized roles such as homemakers, flight attendants and receptionists. By the film's end, women have vanished entirely, replaced by a startling image of an extrauterine foetus, a Star Child, conceived and nurtured by men and their machines. The progress of the film marks the end of man's need not only for woman, but for the earth, the body and sexual reproduction; and this progression reproduces the narrative of the separation of the male child from his mother, his accession to an autonomous masculine identity, and his discovery (like Kubrick's apemen) of the phallic tool of abstract reason. In a sense, men become (at least in fantasy) like HAL in that they no longer seem to require a body, sex, life support or contact with the earth. One of the radical insights of psychoanalysis, however, is that the mother can never be lost and the body never erased. They are merely repressed, and so this progress is in fact a false utopian narrative produced through repression and rigid libidinal organization. In *2001*, this psychoanalytic insight is realized in the return of the repressed through HAL: the unconscious resuscitation of femininity, maternity, the body, and desire within the homosocial economy of the space mission. HAL has so thoroughly reproduced the psyche of man that he seems (unlike Haraway's cyborg) to have an unconscious, or different levels of consciousness working at once. He has a capacity for error; he has a memory, even a memory of his birth as a conscious entity on 12 January 1992; he even has a memory of a lullaby of words, 'Daisy, Daisy, give me your answer do', a love song he once sang with his instructor, Mr Langley, and sings again in his surrender of consciousness to the astronaut Dave Bowman. Narcissistic desire for fusion with the lost mother is resuscitated as symptomatic of the hypermasculine mission of transcendent self-realization through scientific rationalism. Man the scientist, having transformed the discourse of knowledge into a rigidly defined identity, nevertheless rediscovers his body and his repressed unconscious along the inserted ladder of his own mastery. In short, he rediscovers repressed desire through the voice of HAL, his own machine, created in his own image.

The evidence of this return of the repressed maternal signifier is everywhere apparent. The phallic bone of the apeman is transformed in the flick of a frame into a spaceship that enacts a kind of zero gravity coitus with another rotating spaceship, a round one with an entry in the middle. But beyond this hetero-sexual daydream, the spaceships seem to have an androgynous or bisexual quality. The phallic or spermatic aspect of Dr Floyd's shuttle and the *Discovery* is modified by their womblike containment of life and life-support systems. Furthermore, the voyagers on board these spaceships enjoy a floating, hypnotic, amniotic existence. Dr Floyd holds the important women in his life at a telephonic distance – his daughter, his wife, the babysitter – only to find himself waited on by smiling mother-substitutes who feed him liquid food from cartons nippled over with straws. Distinguished scientists in technological swaddling clothes sleep dreamlessly on life support, with intimations of the horror of mummification. Dave Bowman and Frank Poole, who are both paragons of scientific training and masculine self-restraint, find themselves eating what looks like Technicolour babyfood and being waited on by HAL, whom one critic has referred to as 'the biggest mom of all'.[9]

Even the baldly paternal symbolism of the monolith has its infantile and maternal aspects. The monolith is vaguely phallic in shape and masculine in its austerity: it is the ultimate bearer of the Word, literally humming with the evidence of higher intelligence and pedagogical intentions. But the erotic ambiguity of the monolith may be glimpsed in what is perhaps an unintentionally suggestive comment made by a reviewer: 'Kubrick stylizes the moment of the birth of human consciousness with the presence of the monolith and *musique concrète* by György Ligeti howl-ing from the soundtrack like a collage of all the world's religious music.'[10] 'Birth' and 'howling' would seem to disrupt the harmonious organization of any religious 'collage'. The bizarre, ecstatic, deafening, heterogeneous voices of the monolith, a mixture of recordings by Ligeti and Kubrick, are disturbing in that they are as perverse and profane as they are divine. I am reminded of Lacan's discussion of god and feminine jouissance. What is the jouissance of this monolith? What is the nature of its incomprehensible, seductive, strangely religious but undecidable voice? Like HAL's voice, this other voice of higher, perhaps hostile, perhaps divine, certainly alien intelligence, speaks with an uncanniness that paradoxically harks back to presymbolic utterance.

Another peculiarity of the monolith is its function as both phallic icon and birth canal. It is a door at once closed and open. Its smooth, black impenetrability when touched by the apes and Dr Floyd comes unhinged in Jupiter space. Its blackness becomes penetrable as the darkness of an abyss, the opening to a space which is the very collapse of time and space: the maternal passageway for Bowman's psychedelic, nonverbal, perhaps preverbal journey. In the novel *2001*, Arthur

Clarke plays on this notion of the phallic-vaginal symbol: 'Impossibly, incredibly, it was no longer a monolith, rearing high above a flat plain. What had seemed to be its roof had dropped away to infinite depths: for one dizzy moment, he seemed to be looking down a vertical shaft – a rectangular duct which defied the laws of perspective.'[11] The use of the word 'shaft' here is a telling pun: '*shaft*' as phallic rod or weapon but also '*shaft*' in the sense of 'elevator shaft', the dirtying duct, serviceable of course, but fatal when the cable snaps.

This disorienting and paradoxical collapse of sexual difference, construed psychoanalytically, appears to be symptomatic of a regression to the proto- or pseudo-genitality of the anal-sadistic phase.

> According to Freud, the faecal mass or 'stick' foreshadows the genital penis, the production of stools becomes a prototype of childbirth (the infantile sexual theory of giving birth through the anus), the daily separation from the faeces is a precursor of castration, and excrement in the rectum anticipates genital coitus.[12]

Kubrick's monolith, with its uncanny voices and sleek black geometry, presents an imperfect idealization of the faecal-phallic stick. The monolith's function as shaft suggests the perverse collapse of phallus and orifice, of genital and pregenital pleasure, whose 'unmeaning' is deflected into a pseudodivine enigma. The monolith functions metonymically in the film, and its inscrutability may be seen as the sublimation of anal drives – the drive to death, error, confusion, so subversive of the film's technological utopianism – reconstrued more safely as a deified 'intelligence'. What is somehow 'beyond the phallus' is projected onto the nonspace of Jupiter space and construed as 'out of reach'.

The 'faecal' reading of the monolith is further supported by the recurrence of bathrooms in the film: the famous zero gravity toilet (where Dr Floyd is once again obliged to confront the perils of toilet training), Rachel the babysitter in the bathroom, and finally the 'ideal' bathroom near the end of the film. There is also the inert asteroid, strangely turdlike, that hurls past the *Discovery* as Poole makes his first trip out in the pod; and this asteroid prefigures Poole's death, his dead body rotating in space, reinforcing the connections between death drive, anality and the unburied corpse. One might also consider the deliberate burial of the monolith on the moon, or its sudden appearance one morning on the prehistoric plain. In Clarke's novel, the first appearance of the monolith is preceded by the clank of metallic feet striking stones and uprooting bushes, as though some space-age dinosaur were passing in the night, dropping a gift of encoded dung. Like Schreber, the apes hear voices that seem to persuade and inform, voices that are taken for divine. The string of associations developed here – obedience to mysterious voices, divinity, excretion, jouissance – should come as no surprise to the psychoanalyst, who finds in the case of Schreber a paranoid model for such divine 'evacuation': 'the process is always accompanied by the generation of an exceedingly strong feeling of spiritual voluptuousness.'[13]

Even the very poetry of space travel, performed at first to the waltz of 'The Blue Danube', suggests both a displaced eroticism and a mystification of modern technology. Gentle rotation and curving architectural lines are a repeated motif, slowly rendered sinister through the changing mood of the musical score. The graceful and disorienting rotation of circular spaces, including the figure of a female flight attendant in phallic costume defying the audience's experience of gravity, recalls the connection between rotation, ego disintegration and anal pleasure in psychotic discourse.[14] Furthermore, the equally graceful schmaltz of 'The Blue Danube', a throwback even in its own time, links this rotating pleasure with the progress of modern science, generating a nostalgic sense of continuity between the space age and the waltz age, 2001 and the Enlightenment. This nostalgia turns to pensive moodiness, however, with Khatchaturian's 'Gayne Ballet Suite', which accompanies the scene where an astronaut jogs and shadow boxes in a circle inside a centrifuge, again defying the audience's experience of gravity. Finally, nostalgia gives way to anxiety and terror. The musical soundtrack is replaced by menacing silence or by the labour of human breathing, as when Poole ventures out in the pod and ends up rotating gently through space in a zero-gravity *Totentanz*. The changing score and the poetic continuity of rotation emphasize the slow and sinister shift toward the paranoid plot and the astronauts' growing distrust of the HAL computer.

HAL turns *2001* into a 'maternal horror' film, despite the virtual absence of mothers. As Julia Kristeva has written, horror and abjection are perverse celebrations of a phantasy of the maternal body: 'But devotees of the abject, she as well as he, do not cease looking, within what follows from the other's "innermost being" for the desirable and terrifying, nourishing and murderous, fascinating and abject inside the maternal body.'[15] In reading the vaginal or maternal imagery of

Figure 3.2 2001: A Space Odyssey (courtesy of BFI stills archive and Turner Pictures)

the film as anal, I find that *2001* articulates a homoerotic phantasy of male maternity, of maternity between men, and the concomitant phantasy of anal childbirth. Schreber still haunts us: 'Something occurred in my own body', he writes, 'similar to the conception of Jesus Christ in an immaculate virgin, that is, in a woman who had never had intercourse with a man.'[16] Ironically, Kubrick's earlier name for HAL was Athena, recalling the asexual birth of the virgin goddess of wisdom from the head of Zeus (or the Roman Jupiter). Presumably, the Athena voice was rejected for HAL's sexually ambiguous voice in order to avoid any heterosexual implications, but Kubrick succeeded in producing homosexual implications instead. At this point in the film, the anal-sadistic focus is HAL, HAL's focus, his mechanical gaze and technified speech from which it is impossible to hide. HAL replaces women and the Russians as the principal justification the film has to offer for the paranoid sensation of persecution. I hear his ubiquitous voice, and I see his ubiquitous eye. This eye, a deep lens which might also be his ear, is odd in that it is both a protrusion and a hole and is the passageway for both his gaze out and my gaze in. One critic even noted that HAL has a 'red eye shaped like a female breast'.[17] His eye–ear is at once a male and female protrusion, but also an orifice, filled with the red light of danger signals and the yellow light that also glows in the eyes of the leopard in the apeman sequence. With the dispersal of HAL's voice and gaze, he becomes difficult to locate except in a fetishistic fixation on certain objects, such as the memory banks or the lens. HAL is so diffuse that the ship itself becomes his body, a male body, or at any rate an androgynous one, with doors and passageways, voice and vision and memory, and even little spermlike babylike homunculi called 'pods' that can be ejected from the main ship. The astronauts, Bowman and Poole, are in this sense functioning inside HAL's body; they are integral parts of it.

This male interiority, isolated in outer space, is the site of highly sublimated narcissistic play in the name of modern science. When not tinkering, jogging, shadow boxing, or sunlamp bathing (to name a few of their more autoerotic activities), the two men engage in duties where they seem to mirror or complement each other. In fact, they look so much alike, it is sometimes difficult to tell them apart. There is also the self-reflexive entertainment of watching themselves on a BBC broadcast. But this pleasure always seems unconscious, its erotic meanings sacrificed to the science fiction pretext and the exigencies of living in space. In fact, one of the most disturbing scenes is Poole's death, but Bowman dutifully represses any emotional vulnerability he might experience at the loss of his virtual twin. And yet, when Bowman retrieves Poole's body and the devious HAL locks them out of the main ship, Kubrick offers us a stunning image with subtle homoerotic implications, that of Bowman as the Madonna. Inside a pod floating in space, he waits for the unresponsive HAL to open the gate; in the pod arms he holds his dead friend who has been sacrificed for the mission. In this strange revision of the *Pietà*, the Madonna – the ultimate Christian image of asexual childbirth, maternal narcissism and mourning – is mapped onto the relationship of two men whose physical contact is mediated by a machine or, one could say, a scientific discourse of machines. For Bowman, technology is the highly sublimated mode of realizing Schreber's fantasy of virgin motherhood, and the villain HAL is the symptomatic focus for his paranoid defence against the challenge of this phantasy to his masculine autonomy.

The most homoerotic aspect of the film, of course, is Bowman's forced entry into the ship and into HAL himself. Bowman explodes into the flowing red tunnel of the emergency entrance, much to HAL's distress. He stalks through the ship, his heavy breathing electrically amplified by life support. HAL responds in an ambiguous voice. His words suggest the fear and panic of rape, and yet his calm 'user-friendly' tone suggests a disturbing sensuality, reinforcing the eroticism of an otherwise violent act:

> Dave. Stop. Stop, will you. Stop, Dave. Will you stop, Dave. Stop, Dave. I'm afraid. I'm afraid, Dave. Dave. My mind is going. I can feel it. I can feel it. My mind is going. There is no question about it. I can feel it. I can feel it. I can feel it. I'm afraid.

In the glowing red room of HAL's sanctum sanctorum, Dave Bowman slowly dislodges HAL's consciousness with a screwdriver, while the groggy computer recalls his creation in Urbana, Illinois, and sings a lullaby of sorts, a love song addressed ironically to Bowman: 'Daisy, Daisy, give me your answer do. I'm half crazy all for the love of you. It won't be a stylish marriage. I can't afford a carriage. But you'd look sweet upon the seat of a bicycle built for two.' HAL's love song to the man who is literally (un)screwing him juxtaposes love with rape and murder, suggesting the erotic ambivalence at the heart of Bowman's violence. In attacking and dismantling HAL, Bowman is battling with the return of his own repressed narcissism; he is silencing a voice at once alienated from him and yet a part of him, most strange and yet most familiar, the electric voice of a machine and yet strangely the voice of his child or his lover. HAL is Bowman's symptom, the technological voice of his unconscious. HAL's voice is inscrutable and mysterious, despite his presumptions to perfect rationalism. No empirical analysis can reveal the nature of HAL's capacity for error, which challenges Bowman's belief in the computer and in himself as pure and infallible consciousness. HAL returns to Bowman the message of his own unconsciousness, the limits of his own knowledge. Bowman's assault on HAL is not only a murder, but also a revelation of sorts. HAL's unconscious, the unknown secret that motivates the whole mission, is depicted as a videotape that accidentally reveals itself to Bowman once he has deactivated HAL. The videotape tells us of the monolith and the real mission of the *Discovery* – the quest to understand the monolith's strange message. But the videotape itself is mysterious. It mentions the monolith, but cannot explain its meaning.

Like the unconscious, the videotape is a secret that remains mysterious even in its revelation. The official in the videotape speaks, but can tell us nothing. Bowman's only discovery is a paranoid one, the realization that he has been the victim of a superior and even hostile knowledge.

Ironically, Bowman then changes places with HAL in what amounts to an identification with his symptom. HAL is reduced to his somatic functions, while Bowman takes control of the ship. Bowman leaves behind his dependent role as hired hand for HAL, but he achieves mastery only through a sadistic act that recalls HAL's own behaviour toward Poole. His identification with HAL is further underscored when he is sucked through Jupiter space, his wide open eye, like HAL's eye, filling the screen. His mastery is still qualified by his passivity. Bowman ends up in a surreal room – Regency, Louis Quinze, Louis Seize, Miami hotel room, it depends on which critic you read – a room of the mind, a collapse of the distinction between inner and outer space. It is also a collapse of time and identity, as Bowman sees himself ageing in a mirror and encounters himself, narcissistically, in different rooms at different stages in his life. The room is also one of postmodern nostalgia for the Enlightenment, decorated in neo-neo-classical taste with ideal spaces of white light interrupted by European paintings that predate 2001 by a few centuries. This room glows with an idealizing white light. The body is vanishing, decaying, sublimated to death. The bathroom is so neat – is it ever used? As Theodor Adorno writes: 'Imprisoned in itself, the subject holds its breath, as though it were not permitted to touch anything unlike itself.'[18] Bowman's room is the very image of that 'windowless monad' of objectless inwardness that Adorno finds in the mirror of modernist literature, not to mention in 'capitalism's highly polished, glittering late phase'.[19] But Bowman's pensive and methodical dinner is interrupted by an error, an error like HAL's error, a wine glass broken by a miscalculated move of his body. His error recalls him to the very existence of that body, the body that still stubbornly resists erasure by the intellect.

Kubrick celebrates the rationalist utopia of man's transcendent rebirth from his own head, but only after he has all but unplugged HAL, the persecuting voice of the narcissism inherent in man's love for his own machinery. *2001* follows a familiar paranoid narrative in which the racial, sexual, or ideological purity of the hero is threatened by his own alterity; and a plot is generated through the creation of an enemy, a symptom in fact – in this case HAL, who embodies this alterity and who must be destroyed. The plot is familiar to us not only from Gothic literature and horror films, but also from the Frankfurt School's critique of the authoritarian personality and Freud's discussion of repressed homosexuality with respect to fascism and paranoia. But as Freud and Adorno knew, paranoid defence, the symbolic murder of the symptom, does not necessarily resolve the internal conflict, but may just cloak it and perpetuate it. Bowman's failure to answer the call of the unconscious has not made the phone stop ringing. The murder of HAL is a murder in effigy, an effort at mystification that can only mask – but not eradicate – the techno-narcissism inherent in Bowman's romantic resurrection and rebirth as the Star Child.

The concluding frames of the film, depicting the ideal figure of the Star Child happily isolated in space, may be seen as Kubrick's final attempt to ensure this mystification. The Star Child is put forward as Bowman's final triumph over HAL. It may be seen as the final triumph over the disruptive desire that the film has been articulating and struggling with all along. Bowman has achieved the ultimate sublimation of the fantasy of male childbirth or procreation between men. Through science and technology he has given birth to himself out of his own head. He has presumably re-engendered himself as a self-sufficient and autonomous being that can do without woman, the body, and nature. The question is, does Kubrick succeed in his technological utopianism? Are his critics justified in reading the film as misogynistic or homophobic? As many have noted, HAL is the most human presence in the film, and his silencing is one of the most disturbing scenes in all of Kubrick's work. At one point, HAL's lens and Kubrick's lens are one and the same – I seem to be looking through HAL's eyes as he tries to lip-read Bowman and Poole. Any identification with HAL I might feel would tend to undermine my paranoid reaction against him; and yet my identification and horror put me also in the place of Dave Bowman, who experiences HAL as the uncanny, that which is at once most familiar and most strange. Is Bowman a traditional science fiction hero, or is he the target of Kubrick's irony? Is *2001* the satirical Kubrick of *Dr Strangelove*, or is it Kubrick, the space-age mythmaker, submitting the techno-logical age to a familiar paranoid narrative of itself? The question is a difficult one. Despite the triumphant tone of the final frames, Kubrick's attempt at narrative closure remains troubling and ambiguous.

This ambiguity at the end of *2001* raises for me the possibility of a radical reworking of traditional paranoid narratives in him, perhaps even through the sort of satire at which Kubrick is adept. Although much remains to be said about filmic horror and paranoid defence, I want to make a sudden leap to Almodóvar because I think it is extremely important – especially for queer theory – to address the possibility of the paranoid pleasure towards which Kubrick seems to gesture. *Law of Desire* is, in my view, the finest example of the pleasurable failure of paranoid defence in film. My starting point is again Freud's reading of Schreber's memoirs. Having expressed his horror – and thinly disguised pleasure – at the possibility of his homosexuality (his fear, for example, of being tossed to the asylum attendants for their sexual enjoyment), Schreber treats us to an account of his submission to the will of God. He describes his bodily transformation into a woman, complete with female genitalia and feminine nerves of voluptuousness. He comes to the defence of his pleasure, amid what is otherwise a distressing account of his 'nervous illness': 'Since then I have wholeheartedly inscribed the cultivation of femininity on my banner, and I will continue to do so as far as consideration of my environment allows, whatever other people who are ignorant of the supernatural reasons may think of me.'[20] Such queer pride! Is it possible to wave such a 'banner' in the cinema? Schreber is declaring his separate peace somewhere in that battle zone between societal prohibition and insistent subversive desire. Schreber attempts to make peace with the prohibition against homosexuality by saying that he is an agent of God and really a woman after all. What Freud finds in Schreber, however, is a 'feminine (that is, passive homosexual) wishful phantasy'.[21] Schreber's desire to submit in a man (or a masculine deity) as a woman is an attempt to answer the disruptive call of repressed homosexual desire as spoken through the psychic mechanism of paranoid hallucination. His paranoia, according to Freud, finds its aetiology in a homosexual fixation on his father or his brother, not to mention the transference of this libidinal cathexis onto his doctor, Flechsig.

If it is conceivable to make a film in which the return call of repressed desire is answered rather than brutally disconnected, then *Law of Desire* is that film. As Paul Julian Smith has noted:

> By placing itself on the side of the 'woman' (on the side of love, loss, and timelessness) Almodóvar's cinema of gay male desire 'crosses the line' between male and female narrative, makes possible a certain pleasure in the place gendered as female, a pleasure which should not be dismissed as vicarious.[22]

Smith's comment recalls Kubrick's *Playboy* interview in its dissatisfaction with the limits of gender. The male exploration of pleasures encoded as feminine is not, in Almodóvar, an appropriation of some essentially female position, but is rather a symptom of the failure of traditional structures of masculinity to account for all the vicissitudes of desire in men. Furthermore, like Kubrick, Almodóvar eroticizes technology and the disembodied voice as part of his effort to articulate the play of desire. Unlike *2001*, however, *Law of Desire* is a film about queer people that needs to be talked about a great deal more. With its play of language and use of camp, Almodóvar's film challenges familiar distinctions between high art and popular culture, melodrama and comedy, male and female, straight and gay, gay and lesbian, sexual identity and sexual anarchy, making it one of the few films to engage queer themes with a genuinely postmodern sensibility (Derek Jarman and Ulrike Ottinger spring most quickly to my mind). The reviews of *Law of Desire*, however, were tepid, both in Spain and abroad. Almodóvar's films have always been attacked for their preoccupation with taboo sexuality – gay sex, transsexualism, sado-masochism, masturbation and so on. He is the most popular director Spain has ever produced and has become something of a cult figure, especially among gay audiences; however, a more general journalistic prudery still prevails when he is reviewed. Almodóvar's camp sensibility has been widely misunderstood, perhaps because it is so firmly rooted in his sexual politics: 'You cannot take camp out of

Figure 3.3 Law of Desire (courtesy of BFI stills archive and Metro Pictures)

its original context if you feel like an intellectual using this . . . this . . . element of *theirs*. To use it outside, you have to celebrate it, to make an orgy of camp. Anyway, it's a sensibility. Either you have it or you don't.'[23] Among North American critics, only Pauline Kael, a camp icon in her own right, has been consistently enthusiastic in the Almodóvar cause, writing perceptive *New Yorker* reviews that apparently made news in Spain.

Much like *2001*, *Law of Desire* incites sexual panic, if the reviews are any clue to the typical audience response. Reading through the North American reviews of *Law of Desire* and *Matador* (1986) – Almodóvar's first films to find an audience in the USA – I find that some of the comments are simply beyond me: 'lacks in depth', 'boneheaded', 'quite the hooiest trash', and 'romantic idealism that has connections with fascism'. Other comments engage the language of pathology, a commonplace method of abusing anything queer: 'schizoid', 'disorderly', 'acting out', 'a textbook-worthy collection of case histories' – one critic even observed that the director 'could probably save all this stuff for his shrink'.[24] But what is to be made of a gay critic from New York who says, presumably in reference to AIDS, 'In this day and age it's scandalous for Almodóvar to make a film that promotes homosexuality'?[25] Almodóvar himself, apparently afraid of losing his heterosexual market, has said that *Law of Desire* is the exact opposite of films aimed at a 'gay public' and that, after a while, 'you forget that the triangle of lovers is all men'.[26] Although this judgement has been frequently reiterated by a number of people, neither my experience of the film nor my experience of its reviews bears it out; furthermore, I am at a loss to understand why one would want to forget that the triangle of lovers is all men. As with *2001*, the film reviews raise the question of queerness, but at the same time control all the answers in what amounts to an act of defence.

Ironically, *Law of Desire* is itself concerned with desire, control, and defence with respect to language. Like Lacan's seminar on 'The Purloined Letter', Almodóvar's film is about letters waylaid en route to their destination. Machine-made texts abound, including film scripts, dramatic scripts, phone messages, phone calls, a television interview, vinyl records and photographs. Almodóvar delights in the fetishization of the signifier, its deviation from its supposed origin in human speech into a tactile life of its own as recorded language. Furthermore, this fetish object, this detachable phallus, is ceaselessly in transit, ceaselessly defying control or possession or even stable interpretation. Consider Pablo's love letters to himself and to Juan, already the bearer of narcissistic and homoerotic pleasure, but then transformed when read aloud by Juan or by Juan and Pablo at the same time, read aloud by Ada (the young girl who loves Pablo), and read aloud by Antonio and by the detective – read aloud in each case by a voiceover, a voice that is itself disembodied, free floating. The recorded voice or image at play is a central theme throughout Almodóvar's work: mock television commercials, pornographic videos, films within films, telephones, message machines, lip synching, dubbing and so on.

In *Law of Desire*, Pablo seems to authorize his own desire, to distance it and control it, always through the machinery of the spoken voice, through the telephone, the television, and the scripts he writes on his typewriter. However, in the very play of his reified words, in the generation of sexual meanings and sexual consequences beyond his conscious intention in contexts beyond his conscious comprehension, his own message returns to haunt him in disguise. The law of desire follows closely upon the law of the signifier, ever disseminating, always in some sense returning, in uncanny scenes that exceed the human faculty of control or repression. Technology and the technified voice become the mechanisms of paranoia. As with the voice of HAL in *2001*, what is thought to be Pablo's own voice and his own desire, alienated through machinery in his effort at control, returns as the voice and the desire of the Other, exceeding control, exceeding the illusion of possession, and always already at play.

The opening scene inspired important criticism on queer specularity.[27] A name-less young man enters a bedroom or, at any rate, a room with a bed; he is ordered by a male voiceover to undress, and he obeys. Nameless, but I could call him Schreber. This man is not so very different from Schreber, in so far as his pleasure and fear and uncertainty seem to hinge upon his obedience to a mysterious voice. There is a cut, and I see the young man again, but then I realize it is his mirror image. At the command of the voice, he goes to a full-length mirror in his briefs and, like a new Narcissus, he kisses his image, and rubs his crotch against the glass; he removes his briefs, runs his fingers over his body, turns face down on the bed and (apparently against his better judgement) demands to be fucked. Then, in an alienating cut, Almodóvar presents us to the speaker of the voice, an older man who at first I think is the director. And so I think I am watching a film being shot and a director giving orders from a script – or is he just reading it? Another man is with him, and I gather he is reiterating the young man's words for the soundtrack or perhaps even speaking in his place, I am not sure. In fact, I am unsure at first whether they are interacting with the young man at all, or just editing and dubbing a film in which he appears; that is, they may be speaking his words in his absence, indeed, in the absence of the entire profilmic scene. Have I seen yet the character who speaks the mysterious voice in the script I see before me? The voice and I are both positioned behind the young man, and we both focus on his buttocks, invisibly penetrated, framed for emphasis, as he brings himself to orgasm with his hand. Then he is paid – who is this man who pays, this arm with money on the screen? The young man is a paid actor, but no, the camera is still on. His being paid is part of his role as an actor and, in fact, the two other men might also be actors. The final frame of this sequence becomes the final frame of the film as it is shown on a theatre screen in the next sequence, linking what I have just seen to the rest of the film. I learn that Pablo is the director and writer of the film; and as for the three (or is it four?) men I have been watching, all of whom might be characters in his film, two of whom might not be, none of them is seen again.

I am disoriented from the start, unsure of what I am hearing and looking at, unsure where the frame of the film within the film is supposed to end. Is this a house, a hotel, a set? Is the young man a friend, a hustler, a prisoner, an actor, perhaps all of these? Where is the voice speaking from – inside the room, outside the room, over the speaker of a telephone? Who is the voice – a private person, the writer, the director, an editor, another actor? With whom do I identify – the voice, the camera, the young man taking orders? Beyond the sheer virtuosity and complexity of this scene, there is the paranoid sensation it excites in the spectator, whose position of superior knowledge is by no means assured. I could envy Schreber, who could at least claim a degree of certainty about things, however delusional. Finally, I learn that the writer and director of this film within a film is absent from the opening scene; in a sense, it is another disembodied voice or, rather, a voice reified by a screenplay and re-embodied, performed by the voice of another in the absence of the author and perhaps even in the absence of the actor who appears to be speaking – then reified in turn by the recording medium of film and re-contextualized as my own experience as viewer (or was it Tina's experience, as she sits in the audience?). The confusion of contexts and identities generates a crisis of interpretation. I have no certainty about what I am looking at or what I am hearing or who has control over my gaze, all I know is that I am experiencing it and I like it. Despite the alienating effects, the suture is powerful: that is, despite my confusion, you could not separate me from the screen with a spatula. Moreover, whether one is a man or a woman or a little of both, it is virtually impossible to watch this scene, I think, without feeling drawn into it as a participant, implicated as a voyeur in its queer fantasy, positioned as a queer man – and this too can generate a paranoid, essentially homophobic, feeling of panic.

Almodóvar admitted in an interview that this scene was too disturbingly erotic even for him, which is why he made the cut away from the masturbating man to the two men speaking from a script.[28] The scene generates too much memory, too much pleasure, and too much guilt, especially for a director who is trying to forget Franco and his own Catholic education. But he cuts away from the original scene, dare we call it the primal scene, of the masturbating man, towards – what? Towards an editor who might be the writer or a director, eventually towards the director Pablo, then towards the director Pedro and Almodóvar's own disembodied voice as it sings in the background at a disco in the following scene. In true paranoid fashion, a cutting away from the scene of desire is at the same time a cutting towards it, an alienating effect that raises the question of the desire of the one who writes or directs, even the one who watches in the audience.

Paranoia is put in play from the start, from the moment I find myself in the same room with a man being ordered to undress by a voice that sounds as if it came from inside our own heads. Schreber, of course, could probably have sympathized: commanded, overwhelmed, even insulted by strange 'voices', he feels obliged to obey in spite of himself. Like the young man, whose penis is the only part of his body that remains hidden from the camera, the existence of Schreber's penis is often in question. Sometimes he is sure he has female genitalia, and the idea occurs to him 'that it really must be rather pleasant to be a women succumbing to intercourse'.[29] Schreber performs his desire, his erotic transformation, before a mirror. *Law of Desire* has a Schreberian queerness throughout. The transformation from a man into a woman is a fantasy for Schreber, but a surgical reality for Almodóvar's Tina, who is now Pablo's sister but was once his brother. As in the Schreber case, the voice that persuaded Tina to change her sex was that of her father, who could not be trusted, who abused her and who is, as one might expect, absent from the film.

Paranoia is confirmed by the central love triangle of the film, the obsessive love of Antonio for Pablo and Pablo for Juan. Antonio becomes the preying stranger whose words are nevertheless uncanny, familiar to Pablo because they are sometimes his own; and for Juan, Antonio is also the uncanny stranger who has taken his place with Pablo and yet, at the same time, has taken Pablo's place, wearing a shirt in the same pattern as Pablo's favourite shirt and attempting to seduce Juan. As in the Schreber case, Pablo is unwittingly the author of his own paranoid predicament, which is to say he wrote it in his own absence. Antonio's desire is authorized by Pablo in so far as Antonio is attempting to embody the desired object that Pablo describes through his film and through a television interview. This is perhaps the ideal object Pablo experiences in his love for Juan but does not find in Juan himself, the ideal object that is consciously suppressed (by his split with Juan, his attempt to 'get over it') and displaced onto film and television. After the film, Antonio jerks off in the men's room of the cinema, repeating the words he attributes to the actor and to the object of Pablo's desire ('Fuck me! Fuck me!'), in effect taking the place of the actor in the film. Later, still unknown to Pablo, Antonio watches the television interview as though he were taking notes. Although he professes heterosexuality and apparently has had no sexual experiences with men, he goes home with Pablo and immediately attempts to live the picture of the desired man that Pablo has unwittingly suggested to him. Antonio fixes things around the house, he dotes on Pablo, he learns to be fucked. He even repeats lines from Pablo's interview – 'I know that line', Pablo remarks, with an unpleasant feeling of déjà vu. Pablo experiences the return of his signifier in the voice of this stranger, this unwanted lover: in this way, he is dogged by the very object of his repressed desire, which he comes to understand as his enemy.

In *Pablo*, I find a classic vacillation between desire and its foreclosure. Antonio, not to mention all the machinery and technology of the human voice in this film, functions in paranoid fashion as the symptom that continually returns Pablo to the scene of desire. Antonio, who is himself one of Pablo's dramatic creations, is the symptom by which Pablo remains in play as a subject of desire. The Lacanian theorist Slavoj Žižek makes this function of the symptom especially clear:

> The symptom is the way we – the subjects – 'avoid madness', the way we 'choose something (the symptom-formation) instead of nothing (radical psy-chotic autism, the destruction of the symbolic universe)' through the binding of our enjoyment to a certain signifying, symbolic formation which assures a minimum of consistency to our being-in-the-world. . . . This, then, is a symptom: a particular, 'pathological', signifying formation, a binding of enjoy-ment, an inert stain resisting communication and interpretation, a stain which cannot be included in the circuit of discourse, of social bond network, but is at the same time a positive condition of it.[30]

This foreclosure or 'psychotic autism' is best represented in the film by Pablo's bout with amnesia, an amnesia he does not want to part with. This amnesia is a failure to remember who he is and whom he loves, and it is concomitant with Pablo's recognition of the role he has played in Antonio's murder of the object of desire, Juan. Pablo is forever struggling towards the foreclosure of desire, trying to opt out of its circuit, retreating into an increasingly narcissistic enclosure in his apartment, safe from the object (Juan) and the symptom (Antonio), whom he keeps at a distance by means of the telephone and the message machine. Pablo under-stands the telephone's power of erotic control. So did Cocteau, whose telephone play, *The Human Voice*, he stages with Tina. In Cocteau's play, the heroine moans in despair, 'If you didn't love me but were clever, the telephone would become a terrifying weapon, noiseless and leaving no trace'.[31]

But it is precisely love and desire that render the telephone unstable as a prosthetic device of erotic control. Through the telephone and message machine, the television interview, the typewriter on which he writes his plays and his letters, Pablo keeps Juan and Antonio paradoxically under control and painfully in touch. He leaves the possibility of desire open. Note that Tina has returned to Pablo his typewriter in the same scene in which his amnesia disappears. Pablo's recorded voice shares the place of Antonio as symptom. Antonio is Pablo's only bridge to desire, and yet is also inimical to desire. Antonio insists upon himself as an object of desire, and he recalls Pablo to his feelings for Juan. But at the same time he is a suicide and the murderer of the object Juan. He is the embodiment of Pablo's repressed desire for Juan, and also the agent of Pablo's repressed aggression toward Juan.

Antonio as symptom, though not 'included in the circuit of discourse', is nevertheless a 'positive condition of it', to use Žižek's words, he is a threat, and yet he continually returns to Pablo to – what? Desire. The *Law of Desire*, as represented through Juan, its archetypal object, and Tina, its archetypal subject. Tina is Almodóvar's most extraordinary creation in this respect. Gay man, straight woman, lesbian, transsexual, Tina is virtually an allegorical figure for Almodóvar's conception of desire in the film. Hers is the voice of unrequited love or, more precisely, the melancholic voice of desire; productive, transformative, unsatisfiable, always languishing in the real absence but phantasmatic presence of the object, always predicated on an essential gap between the self and the beloved. Her life

Figure 3.4 Law of Desire (courtesy of BFI stills archive and Metro Pictures)

is a dramatization of Lacan's dictum that the sexual relation does not exist. Erotic couplings in this film always fail, always miss the point. The object is always vanishing. Desire is Tina's lament for her lover, Ada's mother Ada, and her lament as Cocteau's telephone heroine in *The Human Voice*. Desire is Tina's prayer for Morocco, where her father abandoned her for another woman, and it is also her masochistic and weepy song of Christian adoration to the Virgin in the chapel where she used to jerk off and where her spiritual father also abandoned her. Desire is Tina's body, her erotic plenitude determined ironically by her many losses, so tormented that she begs to be hosed down in the street. Desire is also the message of Jacques Brel's '*ne me quitte pas*', don't leave me, a sentimental song sung in a suitably gender-bending voice on Pablo's stereo. And desire is also Laura P. – Pablo's latest dramatic creation based on Tina – a woman who mutilates her own body to excite the tenderness of her beloved. For Almodóvar, desire is an interminable demand, profoundly melancholic and queerly feminine.

The Jacques Brel song, the telephone play, Antonio's seduction of Tina, all bring Pablo into an identification with the melancholic economy of desire that Tina represents. As with Schreber, the pleasure, essentially incestuous here, finds Pablo in the feminine position, the position of Tina, the brother he no doubt loved, the sister he maybe still loves (note especially the scenes where they seem strangely like mother and father to the girl Ada). His identification with Tina mirrors Tina's own transsexual transformation, the transformation from gay man into queer woman. Pablo is in the position of the gay man turned queer woman at the sound of his own estranged voice played back to him, through letters from Juan, through Antonio – through the 'human voice' of Cocteau and Tina, moaning with rejection.

In rewriting Cocteau's telephone play, Pablo is in effect speaking aloud the signifier he ascribes to Tina, Tina's memory, Tina's mourning for her love for Ada's mother Ada. But in the quarrel over the old photographs from their childhoods, Pablo recognizes that her past is to some extent his own: through the play he writes, they also come to share a present – of rejection, of fame, of artistry, even of cocaine. They share the spirit of her song to the Virgin, 'singing, weeping, and pain . . . attend to my lament'. *The Human Voice* is both Tina's and Pablo's voice at once and, ironically, it is a voice which neither Juan nor Antonio ever hears. But it is also through Pablo's authorial voice that this *Voice* too is controlled, projected onto Tina, whose place nevertheless he shares. Pablo's identification with Tina is further celebrated and distanced through his next artistic project(ion), the creation of the character Laura P., once again based on Tina's past. This would seem to be another attempt at erotic control, another effort by Pablo to experience his own desire vicariously through projection onto Tina. But Tina resents this aspect of control, his appropriation of her failures, and his use of her voice as a speaking 'machine' (her word) on stage. She insists upon the value of her own melancholic desire, and she refuses her role as Pablo's symptom. To complicate matters, the imaginary Laura P. takes on a life of her own: she is a character in a play, but Pablo also uses her name to write letters to the closeted Antonio, whose mother spies on him. Laura P. becomes herself another symptom, Tina or no Tina. In the imaginations of Antonio's mother and the police, she becomes a woman whom Antonio and Pablo are fighting over. At one point, the police suspect Tina of posing as Laura P. and murdering Juan; in other words, the original is accused of posing as the copy. Laura P. is the imaginary mode by which Pablo speaks as Tina, while still reserving the distance of the creative artist. But in his playfulness with this imaginary identity, he becomes involved in a farcical plot whose violent consequences exceed his control. The character of Laura P. is another instance in which Pablo's own voice returns to him in paranoid fashion as the voice of the Other.

The scene from *The Human Voice* as staged by Pablo is itself another extraordinary moment in the film. Pablo has invested Cocteau's pathetic heroine with Tina's axe-wielding eroticism and her memories of her former lover, Ada's mother Ada, and he has included the girl herself in a communion dress, wheeling slowly across the stage on a kind of handcar, lip-synching '*ne me quitte pas*'. As in the opening scene, I am unsure what is happening at first, since the set is a reproduction of Tina's apartment and the scene a representation of her life. At first, I am unsure whether this is a stylish move on Almodóvar's part or a play within the film. The play of the dramatic text exceeds even Pablo's authorial control when Ada's mother Ada appears, as though summoned by the act of calling her on the stage telephone. Again, the technified voice has an uncanny capacity to upset the opposition of intimacy to distance, presence to absence. While Tina is presumably moaning to her lover Ada Mama over the phone, Ada Mama appears offstage. Tina finds herself speaking a script into the phone, speaking out of script into the phone, speaking the script offstage to Ada Mama and speaking out of script offstage to Ada Mama.

A number of oppositions are upset here. When is Tina in character or out of character, since everything she says is her own words? When are her words her words, rather than Pablo's words or the words of the play? Where does the frame of the play end, does it include Ada Mama? And what about when Tina leaps toward the wings? To what extent is the girl Ada a part of Tina's scene? To what extent is Ada's voice her own, since (after an emotional scene with her mother in the dressing room) her voice overlaps with the voice of the recording? To what extent is Tina actually Carmen Maura, the actress who plays her? Almodóvar has set up a clever mirroring effect that recalls the disorientation and doubling of the Narcissus at his mirror in the opening scene. With Maura as Tina, as woman plays a man who became a woman, and with the transsexual actress Bibi Andersson playing Ada Mama, a man who became a woman plays a woman. This mirror effect is further played out by Ada's mother Ada, by Antonio Banderas playing Antonio Benitez, by the director Pedro appearing Hitchcock-style as a shop assistant in his own film. Clearly, it is more than conventional oppositions of gender and sexuality that are deconstructed in this film. That this deconstruction evolves through the effects of a telephone and a typescript is important: technology promotes the freedom and play of the signifier in transit, liberated from its conventional association with a human body or a human voice. This scene emphasizes the unpredictability and therefore the uncontrollability of the signifier and its resistance to myths of possession and origin. Human speech, conventionally presumed to be the origin of language and therefore truer to nature in western metaphysics, takes a Derridean turn through technology.

The film's ending, in which Antonio holds Tina hostage in the hope of a final hour of sex with Pablo, suggests a surrender of sorts: the power of the signifier to control desire finally accedes to the power of the signifier to unleash it. That an intersection of the camp and the queer should provide the vehicle for this sort of commentary on language is important since camp thrives on its being in excess of conventional narrative strategies and since queerness, by definition, wreaks havoc on conventional notions of sexuality. However unlikely, Pablo, finally impressed by Antonio's love and self-sacrifice, submits to him – while in the background another record is playing, los Panchos' Loc dudo, a song ironically about love and doubt. This seduction is accompanied by the subtle ticking noise of Pablo's typewriter, as though they are being written by an invisible author even as they speak; and of course they are. Pablo has authorized the desire of the man who persecutes him, and in his submission to his persecutor, his own words authorize his destiny, despite his best efforts to the contrary. A wonderfully paranoid delusion becomes a paranoid truth: the writer is written by his own typewriter. Put in Lacanian terms, the writer is in the possession of his typewriter (admirable ambiguity of language). The two men have sex, and the tick of the typewriter becomes the tick of an ornament on, ironically, a rear-view mirror and the grind of a gyrating light atop a police car. This tick, this script, is wandering, volatile, out of control; perhaps fatally so, as Antonio spreads a shroud-like sheet over the recumbent Pablo and shoots himself. The script veers with camp disrespect through many of the standard means of representing queer desire in film – as vampirism (the biting imagery is especially suggestive), as necrophilia, as narcissism, as at once murderous and suicidal. At one point the two lovers even pose as that familiar icon, the *Pietà*, as Pablo (having already undergone a resurrection or two) kneels and embraces the dead Antonio in his arms; but even this image is undercut by Ada's over-the-top May Cross as it catches fire in the background.[32] The final scene is anything but neatly moralistic. The film ends in a typical Almodóvarian violence to the signifier and its machines: Pablo tosses his typewriter out the window in the last vain attempt to resist the tangles of desire and narrative. In a comic move that is pure Almodóvar, language asserts its playful potency: however unlikely, the typewriter violently explodes into flames as it lands in a rubbish bin.[33]

In this final scene, Almodóvar parts with a tradition of paranoid defence. In *2001*, the sexual conflicts raised by the paranoid plot with HAL are virtually upstaged by the silencing of HAL and the triumphant and utopian figure of the Star Child. Bowman appears to have transcended the desire that persecutes him. Pablo, however, submits to the paranoid return of his own signifier, his own desire, closing in on him after a wide circuit through technology and Antonio, closing in on him in a wide arc like the wide arc of the rays of God as they shoot down from the sky into Schreber's head. It is, in Almodóvar's words, an 'orgy of camp'. *Law of Desire* embraces the pleasure, even the violence, engendered by its own paranoia. At the same time, the film manages to bypass the homophobia of the traditional paranoid plot by rendering desire itself queer and taking the lives of openly queer people as its focus. Furthermore, Almodóvar makes no attempt at triumphant closure, as Kubrick seems to do in *2001*. He does not simply kill the persecutor and leave the hero in command of the sexual field. Unlike the dismantling of HAL and the appearance of the Star Child, the suicide of Antonio is not homophobic and it is not an effort at neatly resolving the questions about desire that the film raises. Despite Pablo's submission and Antonio's suicide, desire remains in play, as does the repeated refrain of the song Lo dudo, lo dudo, lo dudo, as the credits roll. Pablo is, if anything, overwhelmed by the sort of obsessive and melancholic love he once repressed. The final shot is of a burning building; the typewriter and the May Cross have set the screen ablaze, and men scale the wall on rescue ladders. I am left at the end of *Law of Desire* as I am left at the end of Schreber's memoirs: uncertain of the hero's command of the sexual field. I am filled with doubt, like the singer of Lo dudo. I doubt the closure of the narrative. I do not believe that Schreber is free of the asylum once and for all, though the authorities let him out; and I do not believe that Pablo will ever quite liberate himself from the complications of desire, from that burning building of sorts, in which the film leaves him. And above all, I am haunted and thrilled by this possibility in the film of a queer voice interminably at play.

Notes

1 From Kubrick's 1968 *Playboy* interview, reprinted in Jerome Agel (ed.), *The Making of Kubrick's 2001* (New York: New American Library, 1970), p. 346.

2 Quoted in Sigmund Freud, 'Psychoanalytic notes on an autobiographical account of a case of paranoia (dementia paranoides)' (1911), in *The Standard Edition of the Complete Psychological Works of Sigmund Freud*, trans. James Strachey (London: Hogarth Press, 1955–74), vol. 12, p. 16.

3 Ibid., p. 59; Sándor Ferenczi, 'On the part played by homosexuality in the pathogenesis of paranoia' (1912), in *Sex in Psychoanalysis*, trans. Ernest Jones (New York: Dover, 1956), p. 133.

4 Constance Penley and Andrew Ross, 'Cyborgs at large: an interview with Donna Haraway', in *Technoculture* (Minneapolis, MN: University of Minnesota Press, 1991), p. 18.

5 Quoted in William Kloman, 'In 2001, will love be a seven-letter word?', *The New York Times*, 14 April 1968, p. D15.

6   See Janet Bergstrom, 'Androids and androgyny', *Camera Obscura*, no. 15 (1986), pp. 36–65.

7   See Pauline Kael, *5001 Nights at the Movies* (New York: Henry Holt, 1991), p. 800; Penelope Gilliatt, 'After man', *The New Yorker*, vol. 44, no. 8 (1968), pp. 150–2; Renata Adler, '"2001", is up, up and away', *The New York Times*, 4 April 1968, p. 58; Louise Sweeney's review, quoted in Agel, *The Making of Kubrick's 2001*, pp. 56–62; Don Daniels, '*2001: A Space Odyssey* – a sleep and a forgetting', *Journal of Popular Culture*, vol. 2, no. 1 (1968), pp. 167–71; and Alexander Walker, *Stanley Kubrick Directs* (New York: Harcourt Brace Jovanovich, 1972), pp. 252 and 285.

8   For an excellent feminist reading of the sexual politics of *2001*, see Zoë Sofia, 'Exterminating fetuses: abortion, disarmament, and the sexo-semiotics of extraterrestrialism', *Diacritics*, vol. 14, no. 2 (1984), pp. 47–59. Also of interest is Judith A. Spector's discussion of *2001* and so-called 'womb-envy', 'Science fiction and the sex war: a womb of one's own', *Literature and Psychology*, vol. 31, no. 1, (1981), pp. 21–32.

9   Daniels, *2001*: a new myth, p. 6.

10 Ibid., p. 2.

11 Arthur C. Clarke, *2001: A Space Odyssey* (New York: New American Library, 1968), p. 190. See also Spector, 'Science fiction and the sex war', p. 27.

12 See Sigmund Freud, 'On transformations of instinct, as exemplified in anal erotism' (1917), *Standard Edition*, vol. 17, p. 131. This neat synopsis is quoted from Janine Chasseguet-Smirgel, *Creativity and Perversion* (New York and London: W.W. Norton, 1984), pp. 11–12.

13 Quoted in Freud, 'Psychoanalytic notes on an autobiographical account', p. 27.

14 See Robert Fliess, *Symbol, Dream and Psychosis* (New York: International Universities Press, 1973), pp. 101–6.

15 Julia Kristeva, *Powers of Horror* (1980), trans. Leon S. Roudiez (New York: Columbia University Press, 1982), p. 54.

16 Quoted in Freud, 'Psychoanalytic notes on an autobiographical account', p. 32.

17 Judith Shatnoff, ' A gorilla to remember', *Film Quarterly*, vol. 22, no. 1 (1968), pp. 56–62.

18 Theodor W. Adorno, *Prisms* (1967), trans. Samuel and Shierry Weber (Cambridge: MIT Press, 1986), p. 262.

19 Ibid., p. 256.

20 Daniel Paul Schreber, *Memoirs of My Nervous Illness* (1903), trans. Ida Macalpine and Richard A. Hunter (Cambridge and London: Harvard University Press, 1988), p. 149.

21 Freud, 'Psychoanalytic notes on an autobiographical account', p. 47.

22 Paul Julian Smith, *Laws of Desire: Questions of Homosexuality in Spanish Writing and Film, 1960–1990* (Oxford: Clarendon Press, 1992), p. 199.

23 Almodóvar, quoted in Marcia Pally, 'Camp Pedro', *Film Comment*, vol. 24, no. 6 (1988), p. 18.

24 See Janet Maslin, 'Spanish law of desire', *The New York Times*, 27 March 1987, p. C15; David Edelstein, 'Wooly bully', *The Village Voice*, 7 April 1987, p. 54; Stanley Kauffman, 'Strong reactions', *The New Republic*, vol. 198, no. 28 (1988), p. 128; Marsha Kinder, 'Pleasure and the new Spanish mentality', *Film Quarterly*, vol. 41, no. 1 (1987), pp. 33–44.

25 Quoted in Enrique Fernández, 'Desire under the palms', *The Village Voice*, 17 March 1987, pp. 62, 64.

26 Quoted in Enrique Fernández, 'The lawyer of desire', *The Village Voice*, 7 April 1987, p. 50.

27 See, for example, Smith, *Laws of Desire*, pp. 188–90; also Earl Jackson, Jr, 'Graphic specularity: pornography, Almodóvar and the gay male subject of cinema'. Cecilia Moore and Valerie Wayne (eds), *Transformations: Gender in Film and Literature* (Honolulu, HI: University of Hawaii Press, 1992), pp. 4–8.

28 Vito Russo, 'Man of La Mania', *Film Comment*, vol. 24, no. 6 (1986), pp. 15–16.

29 Schreber, *Memoirs of my Nervous Illness*, p. 63.

30 Slavoj Žižek, *The Sublime Object of Ideology* (London and New York: Verso, 1989), p. 75.

31 Jean Cocteau, *The Human Voice* (1930), trans. Carl Wildman (London: Vision Press, 1951), p. 31.

32 As Smith points out, this visual allusion to the *Pietà* is explicit in Almodóvar's script. Smith, *Laws of Desire*, p. 198.

33 This violence to the signifier is apparent from the opening credits of the film, in which the names of actors, writer, director and so on are typewritten on white paper that has apparently been crumpled and thrown away. To underscore the sexiness of the metaphor, Almodóvar spotlights the names as though with a flashlight, giving the audience a voyeuristic sensation that they are playing detective and secretly peering through someone else's literary failures in the dark.

4   She is not herself: the deviant relations of *Alien Resurrection*

Jackie Stacey

Writing of the problematic question of spectatorial identification with the heroes of cloning films, Debbora Battaglia argues that, 'because the heroes are multiple, not the autonomous egos of Freudian theory, we are *with* the owner and the owned at once, if we are with anyone; our subject-position identifies with a *relation*'.[1] Battaglia conceptualizes the figure of the clone in cinema as a 'supplement', as 'something that supplies, or makes apparent, insufficiencies', for:

> unlike the replicant which requires no connection to an original and is often seen questing for a connection, even a negative connection, to its makers (such as the toy maker and Tyrell Corporation CEO of *Blade Runner*), the clone embodies the closest relation to the original.[2]

Taking its cue from Battaglia's important insights about the figure of the clone in cinema, this essay examines the embodiment of this relation in the new monsters of genetic engineering which confound the traditional boundaries of sameness and difference so central to debates about body horror film. If the clone embodies a relation as Battaglia contends, this essay examines what is at stake if we consider the implications of this relation as one of sameness. How are we to understand cinematic fantasies of cloning constructed as the monstrous embodiment of relations of sameness? This question emerges in dialogue with a number of feminist debates about the 'monstrosity of sameness'. As Elizabeth Grosz has argued, monsters have traditionally been connected to the idea of the threat of duplication:

> Monsters involve some kind of doubling of the human form, a duplication of the body or some of its parts. The major terata recognized throughout history are largely monsters of excess, with two or more heads, bodies, or limbs; duplicated sexual organs . . . it is a horror at the possibility of our own imperfect duplication, a horror of submersion in an alien otherness, an incorporation in and by an other.[3]

In this essay, I offer a reading of the film *Alien Resurrection* (Jean-Pierre Jeunet, 1997) in terms of its configuration of cloning as the embodiment of what I shall call the relations of 'excessive sameness'.[4] Whereas all cloning films could be read through this problem of too much sameness, in so far as they are concerned with technologies of copying (those within the science fiction or body horror genres probing the monstrous potentialities of such imitative experiments), I shall argue that the cloning of Ripley (Sigourney Weaver) in *Alien Resurrection* is particularly significant to feminist and queer theorists in film studies for the ways in which the relations of sameness embodied in the clone are marked as 'excessive' in their articulation of particular forms of deviance. More specifically, I shall suggest that Ripley's cloning is given cinematic life through multiple and interrelated forms of biological, technological and sexual deviance. The first, biological deviance, will be explored through an analysis of the failed bodies of Ripley's clone siblings and their relation to her cloned perfection; the second, technological deviance, will be explored through an interrogation of the transgenic cloned body and its relation to its human and alien origins; and the third, sexual deviance, will be discussed through a reading of the homoerotic body of Ripley, whose queer desires are related to her technological conception and intimacies with her robotic counterpart Call (Winona Ryder).

My reading of *Alien Resurrection* extends a number of debates within feminist theory, most centrally those concerned with understanding the relationships between cinematic fantasies of monstrous bodies and new forms of genetic technology. To this end, I shall put feminist theories of the 'geneticization of culture' and the 'teratological imagination' into dialogue with debates about the centrality of the abject for understanding the 'monstrous feminine' in horror film.[5] Building upon feminist challenges to Barbara Creed's theories of the abject with respect to the horrors of genetic engineering in *Alien Resurrection*, I shall investigate how the queering of desire in the figure of the clone requires us to consider the problem of sameness not only in terms of cloned embodiment,[6] but also in respect of the film's self-conscious play with the performance of passing.

While the precarious boundary between monstrous and proper bodies pervades both the narrative structure and iconographic landscape of all the *Alien* films,[7] the fourth film in the series, *Alien Resurrection*, places genetic manipulation centre-stage by organizing its exploration of monstrousness around the story of the cloning of Ripley. Since each *Alien* film has involved the cinematic (re)incarnation of Sigourney Weaver as a different kind of Ripley (from action heroine in *Alien* [Ridley Scott, 1979] to marine cyborg in *Aliens* [James Cameron, 1986] to androgynous social outcast in *Alien 3* [David Fincher, 1992]), the literal cloning of Ripley by scientists in *Alien Resurrection* translates the problem of generic repetition into a scene of genetic enactment. But Ripley is not merely a clone of her former self, she is a transgenic clone: a clone whose original already combined the DNA of two different species – human and alien. Drawn from cellular traces of a Ripley already impregnated with the alien species (causing her sacrificial suicide, as she plunges from a great height in a Christ-like pose down into the flames below, at the end of *Alien 3*), this latest version of Ripley combines her with the monster at the level of genetic inheritance. If cinematic representations of the clone generally construct this figure as the embodiment of a relation, as Battaglia argues, then Ripley as transgenic clone embodies not only the relation of original to copy but, simultaneously, the relation of human body to alien monster. As such, the story of Ripley's artificial reincarnation and transgenic kinship in *Alien Resurrection* moves the series firmly into the spectacular realm of the scientific laboratory and the diseased, 'deformed' and mutating bodies that populate its spaces in the age of the new genetics.

Alien Resurrection places the mutability of the cell at the heart of its spectacular display of monstrous bodies. The mesmerizing credit sequence shows cellular mutations in flowing motion: shot in extreme closeup, the warm golden glow, its reflective, sometimes sticky, shiny surface and the repeated use of circular, interconnected patterns give a honeycomb-like appearance to the substance. But a much more sinister set of associations governs this sequence as, almost immediately, cells mutate into more monstrous distortions. The flow moves in waves accompanied by an eerie musical score which rises and falls to the same rhythmic pattern as the cell motion. A sense of bodily form emerges as the moving contours begin to resemble mutating versions of the skin, flesh and bones. Crossing the usual internal/external boundary of bodily integrity, the sticky substances and skeletal patterns are reminiscent of many of the reversals built into the design of the alien bodies in the previous films. The use of extreme closeup shots (accompanied by a distorted mirroring effect) combines with the fluidity of the constant mutation to thwart any attempt to fix the meaning or origin of the organs and body parts displayed, offering instead a sense of the endless transformational potentialities of cellular formation. Gradually, though, the forms become more recognizable as they transform into grotesquely disfigured organs, ending with a kaleidoscope of monstrosities, as teeth, hair, eyes and bones appear and disappear in the undulating fleshy mass.

In her most recent book, *Metamorphoses: Towards a Materialist Theory of Becoming*, Rosi Braidotti argues that the fascination with the monstrous bodies of scientific cell manipulation is inextricable from the new potential for the mutability of the image associated with digitization and global cybercultures.[8] Braidotti's insistence on the significance of technological intersectionality in contemporary cultures demands a consideration of the interface between genetic engineering and digital manipulation.[9] This broad challenge from Braidotti might be posed as a more modest question here about how the relationship between cinematic and scientific technologies is configured. Put simply, we might ask what fantasies are imagined through the relationship between cloning and morphing in the cinematic spectacle of the monstrous bodies of the new genetics.

In the opening sequence of *Alien Resurrection* discussed above, the monstrous potentiality of cell development in an age of genetic engineering and cloning is given a visual equivalence in the continuously mutating flow of images. These cells and organs achieve this sense of mutability through a morphed flow of continuous visual transformation. As we watch this fluid movement of changing cell formations, the threat of the hidden monstrous organs and features repeatedly surfaces and disappears, offering us only a cautionary glimpse of the more dangerous and disturbing spectacle hidden in the golden flow. This extended exploration of cell mutation thus uses one technology (morphing and digital special effects) to imagine another (cloning), producing an analogy between artistic and scientific innovations. Each form had previously guaranteed its own particular authenticity (the cell contained the truth of ancestry and inheritance; the photographic image authorized the visual evidence of the historical event). The potential distortions shown through this digitized credit sequence convey the dangers of a time when scientific intervention into cellular life threatens to produce monsters as well as marvels.

According to Braidotti, the mutability of these new technologies that intersect and reinforce each other so powerfully is closely related to their monstrous associations. She writes: 'there is indeed a distinct teratological flair in contemporary cyberculture, with a proliferation of new monsters which often merely transpose into outer space very classical iconographic representations of monstrous others'.[10] For Braidotti, 'the monstrous or teratological imaginary expresses the social, cultural and symbolic mutations that are taking place around the phenomenon of techno-culture . . . [and] visual regimes of representation are at the heart of it'.[11] What she calls the 'teratological imagination' takes its form in the context of the current conjuncture of genetic engineering with the cybercultures of globalization.

Teratology is the scientific study of monsters and marvels, sharing its name with the study of the malignant tumours which develop from an unfertilized germ (egg or sperm) cell: the teratoma. As cancers of the egg cell, teratomas 'have the capacity to differentiate into any of the specialised cell types of the adult body . . . [and] are often filled with clumps of matted hair, protruding lumps of bone, cartilage, bronchial and gastro-intestinal epithelium and even teeth'.[12] These bizarre, parthenogenetic, disordered mixtures of malignant cells and tissue derange other more general cultural categories: they mix together life and death, health and illness, the normal and the pathological, the human and the monstrous.[13] The 'teratological imagination' named by Braidotti is populated with the horrors evoked by such disordered mixtures of monstrous proportions. Since it details cell behaviour and misbehaviour, the history of teratology offers a powerful iconographic repertoire for contemporary cultural representations of genetic manipulation.

A fascination with teratomas and with excessive cell growth in *Alien Resurrection* combines a longstanding generic preoccupation with monstrous bodies with more recent fantasies about genetic engineering and cloning. The iconography of cell mutation draws upon the teratological imagination to convey a new sense of fascination with deviant bodies at a time when the scientific manipulation of cells might produce more terrifying distortions of the human form than nature itself.[14] *Alien Resurrection* draws quite explicitly on an iconography of monstrous bodies from medical science to give shape to its fantasies of failed genetic offspring. In other words, biological deviance of the organic variety (disease) is used to imagine the terrifying visual monsters that might result from a technological interference with biology (such as genetic engineering).

The significance of the teratological dimension of the spectacle of cellular mutations and distortions in the credit sequence is not fully elaborated until much later in the film, when Ripley encounters the display of monstrous failed clones numbered one to seven. Following her successful cloning as host body for the infant alien on the spaceship Aurega at the beginning of the film, Ripley's 'baby' is removed from her chest and allowed to mature. The scientists responsible allow Ripley to remain alive out of curiosity. A pirate ship, the Betty, arrives with illegal cargo (live bodies for hosts in which to breed the aliens), and a motley crew, including Call, a robot who passes as human, is programmed for compassion and is trying to destroy the aliens (and Ripley, too, if necessary). Once the aliens begin to reproduce and destroy the humans, the remaining members of the crew from each spaceship combine and are led in flight by Ripley. It is at this point in the film that Ripley confronts her own commodification as genetic experiment.

Delaying the remaining crew's flight from the ship, Ripley pauses to compare her own numerical tag (the number eight tattooed on her lower inside forearm) with the sequence one to seven on the entrance to the laboratory in which the clones are housed. Ripley's connection to her horrific predecessors is established through the numerical sequence, which, mimicking the technology which has produced them (DNA as genetic sequence), suggests Ripley's 'enslavement' to the capitalist scientists who plan to make money from this experiment. The concentration camp-style numbering on Ripley's arm confirms her status as object of exchange in these capitalist relations, a 'meat by-product' (as her creator calls her) that has no rights to personhood. In this spectacle of the inhumanity of science, echoes of Holocaust eugenic experimentation combine with analogies to slavery and are mapped onto contemporary fantasies about genetic engineering. In an earlier scene we see Ripley become the 'white slave' forced to eat and move with her hands and feet in shackles to limit the violent and unpredictable outbursts through which she expresses her resentment at having been 'resurrected'. Following its much debated replicant predecessor *Blade Runner* (Ridley Scott, 1982), cyborg enslavement produces a historical reversal which appears to separate slavery from race: in *Alien Resurrection* slavery is repositioned 'beyond race' as the political potential of the brutality of the combined ruthlessness of science and capitalism.[15] Created by a multiracial group of scientists, Ripley's whiteness cannot protect her from exploitation, manipulation and objectification; white slavery becomes the ultimate horror in the fantasy of a genetically engineered future.

Part gallery, part laboratory – a kind of unnatural history museum – the scene of this scientific exhibit displays the spectacle of failed genetic experimentation like a chamber of horrors. A closeup shot from inside the room back through the glass, showing Ripley's face with the numbers one to seven in reverse across her forehead, indicates the distant trace of an ancestral memory of her shared genetic inheritance with the previous clones. The bodies of the dead clones one to six are displayed in giant test tubes, suspended in a transparent solution, lit from above by a yellowish spotlight, and raised slightly above or slightly below eye-level for human inspection. This yellow/golden colour combines with the music from the credit sequence to return us to the spectacle of the teratological grotesque with which the film began. Although very different in style, there is a shared sense of fluidity to both scenes: in the credit sequence the cellular forms mutate to reveal unexpectedly monstrous distortions; in this scene, the continuous camera movement around the space both tracks and displays Ripley's trance-like journey through the monstrous history of her genetic ancestry. These transparent storage columns are spaced intermittently throughout the room, requiring Ripley to move among her predecessors as she slowly takes in the shocking visual evidence of her own prehistory. Physical proximity is indicative of her genetic connection, underscored by gestures of touch: Ripley's hand touches the glass of the test tube containers as she passes, giving a visual sign of her empathy with her ancestors. The shots alternate between medium-shots and closeups displaying the grotesque bodies of the clones and long-shots placing Ripley (and later Call) among them.

This gallery of genetically engineered monsters shows the spectacle of failed recombinant DNA. As combination of Ripley and the alien, they are transgenic clones whose half-human, half-alien status takes the visual shape of corporeal distortion. As in the credit sequence, the visualizations of these genetic experiments take the forms of recombinant images which use aspects of Ripley/Weaver's facial features (hair, jawline, forehead, nose) morphed with monstrous exaggerations from elsewhere. Numbers one to six include foetal forms, tumour-like protrusions, misplaced organs and distortedly extended features. The first resembles a foetus-like, coiled-up old man whose spine continues into a tail, suggesting a prehuman phase in evolutionary development. Another has witch-like elongated fingers of alien proportion. Like the teratomas in the credit sequence, these monstrous births have inappropriate cell differentiation visible on their bodily surface: one has a spine or rib-like bone formation running down the side of its leg; another has doubled organs – two mouths with enormous teeth. The attempt to interfere with normal cell division has produced excessive cell growth: one has an extended skull doubling the size of its head and another has a breast-like form growing out of its side. Ripley/Weaver's features are shown as visual traces in the contours of the clones' faces, echoing the forms which tie her to their fate. Like Ripley, one of the clones has a mass of black hair which floats in a Medusa-like formation in the liquid suspension; a closeup shot of this clone prefigures a later one in which Ripley is shown in a similar pose in the underwater battle against the aliens. In one shot taken from in front of the test tube through the yellow-coloured liquid, Ripley, standing behind it, appears to accompany her dead sibling inside the vessel. In their pathological deformities, the clones mirror Ripley's own deviant cellular composition.

Ripley's connection to (and empathy with) the clones culminate in her encounter with number seven, the most human of her ancestors. She is the only one who is still alive and breathing (or gasping); she is just able to utter the words 'kill me'. Bearing the traces of the previous failures (inappropriate bone formations puncturing the skin, breast mispositioned, elongated limbs), linked up to medical machines that are keeping her alive, and chained like a slave to the table on which she lies, number seven is the ultimate cyborg horror of genetic experimentation. In an extended act of violent outrage at the brutality of genetic science, Ripley torches first number seven and then all the other clones, destroying the entire laboratory. As the flames hit the glass test tubes they shatter, and the liquid solutions explode and ignite, destroying the imprisoned clones. Cutting between shots from above, behind and below, and using tilts to convey the distorting force of the attack, the spectacle shifts from the stasis and containment of the science museum display to a cathartic action sequence of elemental chaos as the golden glow of the fire combines with the reflective capacity of the liquid and the glass. As Ripley backs out of the space she has decimated, the sound of her exhausted panting echoes the sound of clone number seven for one last connecting moment before she and Call rejoin their human crew.

In its display of unrestrained cell division, excessive organ growth and deformed bodies defying the biological laws of 'form, control, unity of design and function',[16] *Alien Resurrection* produces a fantasy of genetic experimentation as the teratological grotesque. Like the malignant forms that are their prehistories, these failed clone bodies exhibit the deathly self-destruction of both pathological and artificial cellular malfunction. The horrors of cloning, of turning the culture of the copy into a biological possibility, are expressed through the display of excessive cell growth associated with malignant disease in which the body fails to recognize and expel the monstrous proliferations within. Biological laws of cellular division are defied in both cloning and in malignant disease: the cells trick the body into misrecognition; cellular similarity appears as difference with fatal consequences. The biological deviations of excessive cellular production of both teratomas and of cloning combine in these monstrous figures to produce a spectacle of the threat of too much sameness in its most material bodily form. Such disregard for the foundational requirements of difference at the biological level is shown to have deadly effects in these failed clones. Moving reproduction out of the human body and into the laboratory threatens to bring the monsters of nature home to roost in the cloned bodies which are unnaturally, or too closely, related to their original host. Ripley's connection to these monstrous bodies, both her siblings and her predecessors, traces the horrors of the new forms of kinship and relatedness in the age of cloning. The horrors evoked by such disordered teratological mixtures thus take on a new dimension in the current cultures of the new genetics.

According to recent cultural analysts, our conceptions of normal and pathological bodies, and of our relatedness to our kin, have been profoundly transformed by the new genetics.[17] What has been called the 'new genetic imaginary' is a fantasy landscape inhabited by artificial bodies whose futures might be controlled and extended, whose new forms of kinship might be unthinkable, and whose diseases, and indeed desires, might be reprogrammed or 'designed' through the 'helping hand' of scientific intervention.[18] We live in the age of the Human Genome Project, a three-billion-dollar enterprise to map the genetic makeup of *Homo sapiens*, an age in which DNA is increasingly used as an explanation for human disease and as a means of detecting deviant and criminal behaviour. The so-called 'geneticization of culture', or 'the genetic turn', as explored in José van Dijck's *Imagenation: Popular Images of Genetics*, refers to the ways in which popular understandings of the new genetics pervade ideas about the human, the body and disease in fiction, film and advertising as well as in more general public debate. In their study of the gene as a cultural icon, Dorothy Nelkin and Susan Lindee have argued that the gene has become a cultural icon whose determining power is acclaimed across popular forms: 'In supermarket tabloids and soap operas, in television sitcoms and talk shows, in women's magazines and parenting advice books, genes appear to explain obesity, criminality, shyness, directional ability, intelligence, political leanings and preferred styles of dressing.'[19]

Fantasies of reproductive technology, such as *in vitro* fertilization, have pervaded popular culture in the form of a technological fetishism, involving a disavowal of the mother's role, an omnipotent fantasy of procreation without the mother, enabling science, as Sarah Kember has argued, to fulfil the desire to father itself.[20] Cloning pushes such imaginings in new directions, placing the cell as the unit of life at the heart of the troubling, yet fascinating, potentialities of scientific experimentation. Cloning is only one aspect of genetic engineering, and yet, according to Donna Haraway, it has a strikingly powerful grip on the popular imagination, because it is simultaneously 'a literal, a natural, and a cultural technology, a science fiction staple and a mythic figure for the repetition of the same, for a stable identity, and for a safe route through time seemingly outside human reach'.[21]

Cloning films arguably belong to the generic tradition of doubling that has pervaded the history of science fiction films. As J.P. Telotte has argued, we might trace the continuities in the cinematic preoccupation with doubles and their threat to the individuality of the human form from *Frankenstein* (James Whale, 1931) through *Invasion of the Body Snatchers* (Don Siegel, 1956) to *Blade Runner*: 'as exemplary texts, these films are commonly concerned with the human body as a double, and thus as an emblem of man's [*sic*] own blind space disconcertingly brought into contact with the specular'.[22] For Telotte, this preoccupation with the threat of the monstrous double is part of a general cultural anxiety about the other side of desire:

> The horror genre typically conjures up monstrous 'copies' that, we would prefer to think, have no originals, no correspondence in our world. Their anomalous presence, however, fascinates us even while it challenges our lexicon of everyday images.[23]

Since many science fiction films are about the potential monstrosity of scientific and technological innovations made in the name of the advancement of humanity, and since science fiction films, as Mary Ann Doane has argued, repeatedly explore the relationship between the technological and the maternal (often showing the latter as the contaminator of the former), *Alien Resurrection* conforms to its generic predecessors.[24] Read through its own generic inheritance, this film rehearses the preoccupations of body horror films more generally: these films are concerned with 'the torture and agony of havoc wrought on a body devoid of control'[25] and with 'the ruination of the physical subject'.[26] By exploring the potential monstrousness of the new genetics, *Alien Resurrection* might seem to be the logical next step in the evolutionary cycle of body horror/science fiction films. Following this trajectory, the film's representations of cloned bodies might be analysed as symptoms of contemporary anxieties about new life forms and new forms of life, and about who will control their conception and reproduction.

This generic reading can be extended to confirm Creed's influential psycho-analytic theory of body horror films as the ritual fantasy banishment of 'the abject',[27] in which she reworks Kristeva's essay on abjection, *Powers of Horror*.[28] As has been widely rehearsed, the process of abjection is that through which we expel those unwanted objects which remind us of our origins and our fate. These un-desirable objects are those which make us shudder, make our flesh creep, turn our stomachs; those which have the capacity simultaneously to fascinate and revolt. According to Creed, it is the female body, and in particular its reproductive capacity, which has been placed as the abject source of the narrative threat that must be resolved. It is the problem of separating from the maternal body that is endlessly rehearsed in body horror films, since, it is argued, we can never fully expel these reminders of the mutability of our boundaries, for the abject haunts the subject long after it has been expelled. And thus, Creed argues, the threat of being reabsorbed into the maternal body continues to preoccupy cultural fantasies and fictions: the womb represents the utmost in abjection. For example, in *Aliens*, Creed argues, the narrative strategies combine with a generic iconography of the womb to form the heart of the 'monstrous feminine':

> Woman's womb is viewed as horrifying . . . because . . . it houses an alien life form, it causes alterations in the body, it leads to the act of birth. . . . The womb . . . within patriarchal discourses . . . has been used to represent woman's body as marked, impure and a part of the natural/animal world.[29]

Extending life beyond death, doubling the possibility of existence, undermining the authenticity of individuality (individual originally meaning indivisible), cloning threatens many of the foundationalisms of contemporary culture. As such the clone might appear to be the ultimate in abjection, if, as Kristeva argues, it is 'not the lack of cleanliness or health that causes abjection . . . but what disturbs identity, system, order. What does not respect borders, positions, rules. The in-between, the ambiguous, the composite.'[30] And Ripley, as not only a clone, but one who was engineered as a body already pregnant with the alien species, might seem to represent the literal embodiment of the full grotesque potentiality of the monstrous-feminine in the age of the new genetics. After all, for Kristeva, the abject can never properly be banished and repeatedly returns to haunt the subject at the borders of its existence. Ripley might thus be seen as the literal embodiment of the constant threat of the abject. If we analyse the ways in which genetic engineering is represented in *Alien Resurrection* through an iconography which draws quite explicitly on a repertoire of associations between the clone, the monstrous birth and the diseased female body, we might extend Creed's argument about body horror to an exploration of 'the genetic abject'.

Both generic and psychoanalytic theories here seem to point to the ways in which *Alien Resurrection*, like its predecessors, rehearses a fantasy expulsion of monsters in order to reassure us of our bodily and individual integrity. In the light of these approaches, the scene in which Ripley destroys the monstrous clones one to seven, discussed above, could be read as a pivotal moment in the narrative drive towards humanizing Ripley in order to remove her from the place of the abject. Here, she and Call prove to be 'more human than the humans'[31] on the ship, when they put clone number seven out of her misery, and then go on to destroy clone exhibits numbers one to six. Number seven is the abject figure who crosses the boundary between life and death, bringing death into life, and whose last breath calls Ripley to reimpose this distinction and to kill her. For Ripley, number seven is her previous self, who bears an uncanny resemblance to her embodiment as number eight; too proximate to her current incarnation, number seven represents the problem of identity as excessive sameness. In destroying number seven, she is, in part, destroying herself. Rehearsing her previous self-destruction at the end of *Alien 3*, Ripley revisits the narrative closure which failed to deliver its promise of total annihilation. In her destruction of the clones one to seven, who reflect Ripley's deviant biology back to her in their cellular excesses, Ripley kills herself over and over again.

But it is Ripley and Call's emotional response to number seven's suffering that distinguishes them from the unfeeling humans. As Battaglia has pointed out, 'It is not uncommon in films of human doubles that narratives of passing expose the insufficiency of dominant-culture originals'.[32] In destroying her predecessors, Ripley demonstrates a disgust for the excesses of genetic experimentation by eradicating the abject bodies these have produced. In the process she also becomes more fully human herself by becoming an individual. Since the notion of being human in part depends upon the assertion of the singularity and originality of each human subject, in destroying the traces of her replication (numbers one to seven) Ripley arguably begins to leave behind her cloned status. Ironically, she becomes more fully human by killing her clones out of a sense of compassion; and her decision not to kill the human scientist responsible for this misery serves as a further sign of her humanity, as well as of the humanness which he lacks.

Despite the repeated display of the proliferation of sameness in the teratological monstrosities which appear to give cinematic shape so perfectly to what we might think of as 'the genetic abject', it has been argued, however, that *Alien Resurrection* undoes, rather than confirms, Creed's reading of body horror. As Catherine Constable's important reading of the film suggests,[33] the narrative closure ultimately signals the failure to banish the abject successfully, thus refusing the spectator the generic pleasures of the previous films in the series. Moreover, the figure of Ripley as transgenic clone confuses the conventional dichotomies that the genre of body horror has historically relied upon. The problem with the representation of Ripley as a transgenic clone in *Alien Resurrection* is that she is both the threat and the hope, both human and alien, and as such she can neither be destroyed like her offspring and her predecessors, nor can she straightforwardly be the heroine and the object of our identification. Constable insists that since the clear boundary between the normal and the monstrous body cannot be maintained in *Alien Resurrection*, the *continuing* validity of Creed's suggestion that horror film is a ritual expulsion of the abject is called into question.

For Constable, *Alien Resurrection* defies the psychoanalytic model of the abject not only because of its narrative structure, but also because of its presentation of intersubjective models of embodiment throughout the film. For example, in the scene at the beginning of the film in which the scientists surround the giant test tube which displays the morphing figure that will be Ripley reborn as transgenic clone, Ripley is connected backwards and forwards in time to her 'kin'. She is linked to the past through the child character Newt to whom Ripley played surrogate mother in *Aliens* (the voiceover repeats Newt's words in that second film in the series: 'My mommy said there were no monsters, no real ones anyway, but there are'), and to the future through the mother alien who will grow up and reproduce and to whom Ripley has just given birth, making her both the monster's mother and sibling.[34] Constable's reading of the complex dynamics of identity, memory and temporality in this scene demonstrates the limits of the psychoanalytic model:[35]

> Ripley's identity is thus set up as an intersection point. She is altered by giving birth to the queen just as the queen will later display the nature of Ripley's bequest to her. Within a traditional psychoanalytic model, these points of intersection would constitute a breakdown of the oppositional structures of identity. On this model, Ripley's new-found memories would indicate a collapse of the division between human and monstrous, conflating Ripley with the alien queen. However, the beginning of *Alien Resurrection* is complicated in that the alien's capacity for instinctual memory also provides Ripley with a means of remembering Newt. The alien DNA is therefore reconfigured within Ripley to provide access to a specific relationship as well as to activate a species memory. The capacity for instinctual memory does not dissolve Ripley into the alien queen, but sets up a point of intersection between the two distinct characters.[36]

For Constable, the transformation of Ripley's memory through her bodily mutation establishes a series of fluid exchanges between Ripley, Newt and the alien queen, demonstrating the need for a new model of subjectivity based on interrelationality: 'Theorizing the possibility of productive points of intersection between self and Other, human and monstrous, requires an entirely different model of subject formation. The morphing figure in the tube stands for the possibility of change through productive encounters with otherness.'[37]

This argument is reinforced if *Alien Resurrection* is contrasted with its predecessors. Whereas in *Aliens*, Ripley and the queen meet in a battle between the good mother (human) and the bad mother (alien) in which they fight to the death to protect their offspring, in *Alien Resurrection* the distinctions between human and non-human, human and animal, human and machine have collapsed entirely. This is most vividly shown in two scenes. First, Ripley again abandons her flight from the ship with the crew and is drawn back to the queen's body as it writhes in pain, struggling to give birth; she is viscerally called back as if through an embodied memory of shared corporeality, and her movement becomes more insect/animal-like in response to her sense of shared pain. Once hailed, Ripley is shown literally submerging herself in the viscous substance surrounding the queen. With an almost orgasmic abandonment of self, Ripley reconnects with the alien as if she is returning home to a familiar maternal body, as Claudia Springer argues: 'By associating a deathlike loss of identity with sexuality, pop culture's cyborg imagery upholds a longstanding tradition of using loss of self as a metaphor for orgasm.'[38] This incestuous sexual merger with the alien queen is followed by the birth of an alien biped who destroys the queen and pursues Ripley as she begins to regain her human consciousness and reconnect with the human endeavour to escape. In the escape shuttle Ripley has to expel the queen's (and thus her own) offspring, and, as Constable argues, 'the way in which the monstrous child is dispatched by Ripley plays into the theme of intersecting identities that structure the film'. Ripley and the infant are shown in closeup, exchanging intimate caresses and mutual sniffing to convey a sense of love and loyalty through their shared genetic non-human tie. This intimate mother–child reunion that 'prefaces the infant's death', argues Constable, 'means that the traditional dispatch of the final monster cannot be regarded as a triumph',[39] and contrasts strongly with the final destruction of the monsters in the first two films:

> In *Alien*, Ripley dispatches the threat, securing the Symbolic space of the craft. In *Aliens* the battle between Ripley and the queen is a fight for species survival in which the human is pitted against the insectual. By *Alien Resurrection* the oppositional relation between the human and the inhuman has been completely reconfigured to form a series of intersecting potentialities.[40]

Constable's reading makes a convincing case about the problem of the psycho-analytic theory of abjection for understanding the body horror of *Alien Resurrection* in so far as Ripley literally embodies the impossibility of the requisite expulsion of the alien so vividly dramatized in the previous films in the series. However, the film's central preoccupation with the threat of excessive sameness rehearses the desire for markers of difference, for a boundaried self, for an individual body, and, as such, it is constantly haunted by the abject, even as it demonstrates the problem of the expulsion of its monstrous manifestations. Rather than rejecting Creed's theory of abjection as inappropriate or outmoded, I would suggest instead that in the repeated rehearsal of its failed mechanisms there is an almost *over-presence* of the abject in *Alien Resurrection* that requires further exploration.

In this rehearsal of the thwarted desire to banish the threat of the abject, the film plays with generic convention and audience expectation. While the ultimate expulsion of the monster is indeed fraught with ambiguity, as Constable suggests, the impossibility of narrative closure around the alien banishment foregrounds this expectation precisely *as* generic convention, bringing to the surface the formal moves of its predecessor alien films. The film's self-conscious commentary on its own generic conventions is immediately evident in the scene discussed above. In some senses, this adult figure *in vitro* appears initially to be 'the clean and proper body' that Kristeva writes about: floating peacefully in a transparent blue watery liquid, perfectly proportioned, clearly contoured, hairless and unblemished, Ripley is the spectacle of the body as pure sculpted form. As Ripley is morphed into being on the screen we are presented with the ultimate fantasy of individuality – there is no visual evidence of attachment to the mother since the navel is almost invisible. But the image of this perfect adult body morphing *in vitro* is accompanied by the uncanny voiceover referred to by Constable ('My mommy said there were no monsters, no real ones anyway, but there are'). Whereas Constable emphasizes the scene's significance in terms of cross-species memory and intersubjective embodiment, I would stress its *playful* reference to *Aliens* for audiences familiar with the series. For this moment juxtaposes the innocent, yet knowing, child's comment with the literal making of Ripley's body as a perfect image, deceptive in its surface perfection as Ripley is already pregnant with the alien and is about to become the monster's mother. In appearing as the perfect clone, Ripley is thus transformed from her previous role as good mother of Newt, to whom Ripley became the protective surrogate mother and for whom she risked her life in *Aliens*, to her new, if unwilling, status as mother of the bad mother – the alien queen. In other words, the voiceover takes on an increasingly ironic status as this perfectly formed body is shown to be not simply connected to the alien when the scientists perform a caesarian section to remove the foetal monster from Ripley's chest, but inextricable from her body and her psyche as she repeatedly demonstrates throughout the film that it still resides within her. The pleasing fantasy of perfect individuality suggested by the adult foetus *in vitro* at the beginning of the scene is thus not only undone by the revelation that Ripley is the apparently human by-product of a barbaric scientific experiment, but is also playfully reversed in that Ripley is then revealed as a transgenic clone, designed by scientists as host mother for her alien infant. Ripley defies the logic of individuality and singularity by combining two species and by being a clone who is both herself and not herself.

This generic self-referentiality is present throughout *Alien Resurrection* in its witty quotation of the shots, dialogue and mise-en-scene of its predecessors. Such self-commentary has crucial implications for how we read the problematization of the abject in relation to the film's body horror. Considered as a form of knowing generic reiteration, not only does the figure of the transgenic clone confound the fantasy of any permanent expulsion of the abject other, but in staging the impossibility of such an expulsion, Ripley can be read as repeatedly enacting the compulsive repetition of abjection itself, thus revealing the form of its foundational mechanisms. As Judith Butler has argued in relation to the regulatory functions of essentializing gender norms more generally:

> When the disorganization and disaggregation of the field of bodies disrupt the regulatory fiction of heterosexual coherence, it seems that the expressive model loses its descriptive force. That regulatory ideal is then exposed as a norm and a fiction that disguises itself as a developmental law regulating the sexual field that it purports to describe.[41]

Following Butler's claim, we might explore the extent to which *Alien Resurrection* troubles the power of the theory of abjection, exposing not only the potential loss of its descriptive force but also the regulatory function which lies at the heart of its theoretical foundations. In this vein, as the transgenic clone, Ripley's rehearsal of the problem of the me/not me boundary could be read as demonstrating its normative imperative but refusing its reassuring reinstatement (however temporary this might be): she remains both human and alien, both organic and technological, both Ripley and not-Ripley. When confronted by Call with the question of who she really is, Ripley replies: 'I am not her'. Ripley might thus be seen to represent the technological deviation from the biological norms of reproduction, embodying the impossibility of the expulsion of the abject and, in so doing, exposing its regulatory principles.

The structures of abjection, which offered such a powerful account of the appeal of the previous *Alien* films, are pushed to the surface through precisely the failure to instantiate the boundaries around the human subject in *Alien Resurrection*. Butler's challenge to the normative function of theories of the abject in gender identity formation looks at the question of the destabilization of the subject through the loss of a fantasy of internal coherence. She writes:

> 'Inner' and 'outer' make sense only with reference to a mediating boundary that strives for stability. And this stability, this coherence, is determined in large part by cultural orders that sanction the subject and compel its differentiation from the abject. Hence, 'inner' and 'outer' constitute a binary distinction that stabilizes and consolidates the coherent subject. When that subject is challenged, the meaning and necessity of the terms are subject to displacement. If the 'inner world' no longer designates a topos, then the internal fixity of the self and, indeed, the internal locale of gender identity, become similarly suspect.[42]

For Butler, the question is: 'how does a body figure on its surface the very invisibility of its hidden depth?'[43] Posing the question in this way, we might investigate how the suspect relations of sameness Ripley embodies are displaced onto its surface. What happens when Ripley's 'inner world' as transgenic clone 'no longer desig-nates' a recognizable 'topos'? We might extend Butler's argument to look at the 'redescription' of intrapsychic processes, such as abjection, in terms of the 'surface politics of the body'[44] or, rather, in terms of the encounter between the surfaces of two bodies, such as Ripley's and Call's. To what extent do the dynamics between them externalize this problem of the impossible conflicts of transgenic replication within Ripley's cloned body? In the final section of this essay, I shall examine how Ripley's 'hidden genetic depth' as the embodiment of excessive sameness is given form through her relationship with Call – the robotic double of Ripley's younger incarnations. These dynamics between Ripley and Call enact the problem of Ripley's 'suspect internal topos', and it is here that the film's playful and knowing treatment of the embodiment of the relations of sameness are most fully elaborated.

It is not only Ripley's shifting status as clone, or her problematic genealogy as displayed in the spectacle of the monstrous births, which cast her as deviant in *Alien Resurrection*, it is also her association with deviant desires. For what Constable passes over in her analysis is the extent to which Ripley's fluid and mutable identity in the film is established through her association with lesbian desire. This association works through the mutual reinforcement of both the intertextual star image of Weaver and the homoeroticism of her 'interrelationality' with Call in the film. Thus, while Constable is right to insist upon the confusion of the subject/object/abject categories of psychoanalytic theory in producing a close reading of Ripley's 'monstrous maternity', this is further complicated by another structuring relation: the heterosexual/homosexual distinction. For, as I shall show, it is precisely Ripley's multiplicity as transgenic clone and as the mother of another species that is deployed to establish a homoerotic dynamic with Call.

Celebrated as 'the androgynous action heroine' who defied the traditional Hollywood conventions of feminine passivity, Weaver became a lesbian icon during the 1980s and 1990s. Through her participation in violent action, her use of heavy weaponry and her technological know-how, Weaver's star image was associated with an unusual physical strength and stature, and a heroic agency exceptional for a woman in Hollywood cinema.[45] Keen to separate such 'gender trouble' from any lesbian association, publicity around Weaver's star image makes much of her 'softer femininity' and of her heterosexuality offscreen, as in the following example in *Film Review* in 1997:

> Appearances are deceiving. The classically trained actress is softer and more delicate off-screen than the characters she has played. She is no aloof and self-assured woman with an air of command.
>
>> I have come to embody feminine strength and confidence, but in real life my movie portrayals reveal little of how I feel about myself. . . . It was an odd thing being thought of as the female Harrison Ford because I'm really not a fan of scary movies. In fact, I'm very squeamish about horror films. I miss half of them because I look away at all those scary parts. My husband has to tell me when it's okay to look at the screen again.[46]

In contrast to this self-proclaimed squeamishness, in *Alien Resurrection* Ripley is almost parodically encoded for strength and power with her curly black hair swept back, her padded vest, her tense body and her 'just you try it' look: she is a kind of heavy-metal female 'Braveheart' with a touch of the mutability and artificiality of Michael Jackson in his 1982 pop video *Thriller*.[47] Weaver's previous associations with lesbian desire through her status as subcultural icon are given diegetic elaboration in *Alien Resurrection* through Ripley and Call's highly charged homoerotic relationship. Both Ripley and Call are represented as androgynous figures whose interactions with each other have an erotic energy.[48] Their shared status as scientific inventions sets them apart from the human crew and it also produces an intense intimacy between the two female stars. This intimacy not only plays upon Weaver's status as a lesbian icon, but also upon the associations between cloning and homosexuality: from the common nickname for a particular gay male cultural style (the clone) to the more general assumption that same sex desire is inextricable from narcissism, commonly understood as a desire for oneself or one's own image.

In the light of these broader cultural associations, we might argue that Ripley is cloned in more ways than one in *Alien Resurrection*. Ripley is a transgenic clone and she is also confronted with Call, who could be read as a further Ripley/Weaver clone. In this sense, Call represents the visual enactment of Ripley's hidden genetic depths. Call also duplicates the position of protagonist and multiplies the structures of identification in the film. Ryder brings Weaver face to face with a previous incarnation of herself. The stories about the dynamics between the two female stars contribute to their construction along the axis of similarity and imitation. In the same article from *Film Review*, Weaver is cited as taking pleasure in having been Ryder's role model. Having firmly established Weaver's heterosexuality, the strength of attachment between older and younger stars can be introduced through the discourse of the schoolgirl crush: 'She [Weaver] is proud of her action icon status and touched when . . . [her] co-star Winona Ryder told her that Ripley was her hero. "Winona told me that all through high school, she had slept under a poster of me in *Alien*. I was touched."'[49]

In the scene in which Ripley and Call first meet, soon after Call has entered the Aurega with the pirate crew, their visual mirroring gives external analogy to Ripley's cloned embodiment. Call (still passing as human) is dressed in a dark grey combat suit like the one worn by Ripley in the earlier *Alien* films. She has blanched white skin, dark, almost black, hair, large eyes and petite nose; she is Ripley's successor and also Ripley's past self. The shared whiteness of the two characters here connects them both to each other and to a white ideal of physical perfection: the similar bone structure (high cheek bones) and proportioned features (big eyes, small noses and fine lips) echo each other in their conformity to cultural norms of white beauty.

The homoerotic connotations of this doubling are played out in this arguably parodic sexualized encounter. Ripley is shown as feline dominatrix, playing with her prey as Call struggles to hold her own with the older and wiser cyborg. The scene is structured like a sadomasochistic seduction scene in which the two shift roles and power. Entering Ripley's guarded panoptic cell secretly, a closeup low-angle shot from behind Call shows her slowly drawing a knife from inside one of her steel-trimmed leather boots. The low angle of the shot gives Call a towering physical advantage over the supine, and apparently sleeping, Ripley who is stretched out in front of her on the floor. Lying on her back with one arm placed above her head in the traditionally feminine position of submission, Ripley appears ready for seduction. She is dressed in a tight, dark leather sleeveless waistcoat whose front lacing has been left open down to breast level. As Call lifts the opening to her waistcoat with the knife to reveal the long scar between her breasts (from her 'caesarean alien delivery') Ripley seems utterly exposed. The sexual signifiers proliferate: Call has found the entrance to Ripley's body she sought and makes it visible with her phallic instrument. But as Call inspects Ripley's body, one deception (Call's entry into the cell with false identity passes) is superseded by another – Ripley is feigning sleep, and moreover, not fearful of death, she invites Call to 'finish the job' and kill her. Taking control of the exchange, Ripley moves into a feline pouncing position and plays with Call's curiosity flirtatiously. In a two-shot, both women kneel facing each other showing their almost identical profiles in mirroring symmetry, and Call asks 'who are you?'. As Ripley replies with her original military title and number, she takes hold of the knife and forces Call to penetrate her hand with it (thus finishing the sexual act she began). Ripley thus tries to produce an identity by rehearsing her formal title as her body is penetrated by Call, who reflects Ripley's previous self.

This violent gesture produces no blood and no pain and offers a double answer to the question of her true identity: she both is and is not Ripley; she both is and is not human. Once penetrated by the knife, Ripley gives up her power to Call, who tells her she is not Ripley. As the knife is slowly withdrawn from Ripley's hand she echoes Call's words, 'I am not her', whilst shot in closeup gazing intensely at her younger double, who explains the violent origins of the cloning and the alien birthing process. Ripley then takes Call's hand and traces her facial contours with it, as if touching Ripley's skin might provide tangible evidence of her instinctive feeling that the alien is still part of her. The homoerotic physical intimacy of this exchange culminates in a final move: kneeling up, towering over her tiny intruder, Ripley encircles Call's face with long fingers and claw-like painted black nails. Half caressing, half threatening, Ripley reverses Call's touch. Switching back into dominatrix mode, Ripley grabs Call by the throat, holding her face roughly in her large hands. In a pose which imitates the conventional heterosexual prelude to a first kiss (male above, looking down seizing the female's face in his hands as she gazes up into his eyes), Call submits once again to Ripley's superior strength, is inspected, teased, and violently cast aside when Ripley is done.

This scene establishes an overtly homoerotic dynamic to Ripley and Call's relationship: the emphasis on touching, on looking, on role play and on intimate confessional dialogue combines with the status of Weaver as lesbian subcultural icon to produce a highly sexualized exchange. The use of closeup shots of Call and Ripley's faces as they combine their half-whispered secret knowledge confers an intensity to their communication. The physical resemblance across the generations between the two actors introduces a narcissistic aesthetic of duplication to their intimacy. As Ripley is forced to confront the 'truth' of her deviant ancestry, Call shifts from anger to fear to revulsion and then to compassion in response to the visual evidence of the potentialities of Ripley's body.

This scene clearly rehearses the cliched associations of physical resemblance with same-sex desire and both of these with cloning.[50] Such an emphasis on the visual mirroring of Ripley and Call places lesbian desire within a mise-en-scene of excessive sameness: their exchanges throughout the film emphasize their similarity, narcissistic recognition, sibling rivalry and even regressive mother-love. As such, the trouble posed by Ripley's biological deviance as transgenic clone is given external form in her encounter with Call: she is faced with a vision of her own abject duplicity. But these more abject overtones of the 'unnatural' or 'cloying' desire for sexual sameness rather than sexual difference are arguably undercut by the film's self-conscious play with cultural codes of 'passing', in which sexual identity and technological identity are placed in somewhat ironic dialogue with each other.

Ripley and Call are both cyborgs (one a transgenic clone and the other a robot) who can pass as human, and each has to 'come out' as non-human at different points in the film. They share knowledge, emotions and a recognition of their out-sider status in relation to the values of masculine science and technology (even though they were created by it). There is even a structural echoing of Ripley's 'coming out' scene with the later one in which Call is forced to 'come out' as a robot. In both scenes, the sexual connotations are explicit: as Claudia Springer has argued, 'collapsing the boundary between what is human and what is technological is often represented as a sexual act in popular culture'.[51] The second of the two scenes reiterates the sexual encoding of the intimate exposure of the other's wound and the penetration of the other's body in the first scene. Like Ripley, Call comes back from the dead when she rejoins the crew, having been fatally wounded in the chest. Just as Call had forced Ripley to admit to her cyborg status in the earlier confrontation, now Ripley reverses the demand. In a gesture that connects directly back to Call's opening of Ripley's clothing to reveal her caesarian scar in this previous scene, Ripley slowly and gently peels back Call's jacket to expose a chest wound seeping with white fluid. Echoing the playfully sexual connotations of the guided penetration of Ripley's hand by Call's knife at their first meeting, Ripley slides her fingers into the wound and rubs the sticky white substance between them as she exits. Just as the status of Ripley's body as non-human was established when Call's knife was inserted into it and neither blood nor pain resulted, so Call's robotic status is first indicated through the penetration of her body by Ripley's hand.[52] Throughout this scene, Call's lowered eyes, her silence and awkwardness, and finally her tears all indicate a sense of pain and humiliation paralleling the shame surrounding a forced confession of a deviant sexuality.

If Call's exposure as a robot is rendered visible in a scene which replicates the revelation that Ripley is not herself, this mirroring is amplified through her particular style of robotic design. For she is not only a robot but an 'auton': a 'second gen' (second generation), who should have been destroyed but of whom a few escaped. Like Ripley, who is not a straightforward clone but a transgenic one, combining two species, Call is an auton – a robot designed by robots. Thus both cyborgs share common genealogical patterns: they embody a doubled duplication and have a special relationship to their ancestors (Ripley to the alien, Call to computers); they have been manufactured by forces beyond their control (science and capitalism); and they should be dead (Ripley was forcibly reborn by scientists and Call escaped the destruction of all autons by the government).

Where the associations of homoeroticism with an unnatural attachment to sameness might appear to confirm the normative drive of abjection in *Alien Resurrection*, the reconfiguration of these relations of sameness as technological function pushes such normativity to the surface. The film repeatedly presents the problem of the threat of the abject and then translates it into a technological configuration which displays its formal conventions. One example of this move is the translation of homoerotic intensity into the more general intimacy of shared 'posthuman' technological embodiment in which Ripley and Call's status as robot and transgenic clone connect them through a corporeal and emotional empathy.[53] This is most clearly established at the moment when Call is transformed into the ship's computer in the second of the one-to-one scenes with Ripley (in the 'privacy' of the ship's chapel). The connection to the mainframe is possible through a cable hidden in the bible in the chapel (religion now only functioning to serve science); Call extracts the sinewy thread from the port in her forearm and inserts the computer lead like an intravenous needle. After fishing around for a connection, she begins to speak as the computer, named 'father', giving information on the ship's power loss. As Call speaks the computer's commands with her new electronic voice, she enacts what, for Katherine Hayles, is one of the defining elements of the posthuman age: 'the belief that information can circulate unchanged among different material substrates.'[54] The separation of information from bodies that is performed here reiterates a parallel disjuncture in Ripley's evolution discussed earlier: the dislocation of memories from subjects (Ripley has memories beyond the lived experience of her previous incarnations). As Michael Lundin has argued, both characters are thus placed within the realm of the posthuman where, citing Hayles, he notes that 'there are no essential differences or absolute demarcations between bodily existence and computer simulation, cybernetic mechanism and biological organism, robot teleology and human goals'.[55]

The transformation of Call in this scene places her alongside Ripley within a shared frame of posthuman mutability: 'the posthuman subject is an amalgam, a collection of heterogeneous components, a material-informational entity whose boundaries undergo continuous construction and reconstruction.'[56] In a series of shots of sliding doors being released, lights and computers being activated, the camera moves rapidly through the Aurega and into the Betty, offering the visual sense of Call's posthuman ubiquity: in her full robotic incarnation, Call can play God. The combination of Call's cyber-knowledge and Ripley's instinctive judgement allows the cyborgs to control the ship and the Betty's shuttle. Together, through their collaborative power, Ripley and Call seem invincible. The homoerotic intimacy between Ripley and Call in this scene is established through the increasing sense of knowledge of each other's technological potentialities; this is not, however, located solely within their bodies, but rather extends beyond them into the realm of the interface itself. Ripley and Call's erotic exchange combines the romantic pleasure constructed around the intimacy of their shared embodied recognition with 'erotic interfacing', which, Springer argues, 'is, after all, purely mental and non-physical; it theoretically allows a free play of imagination'.[57] *Alien Resurrection* thus redefines homoeroticism as a kind of sexual interface in which their mutual knowledge of the technologies of replication and mutation produce their excessive sameness as technological and sexual deviance.

The cloning of Ripley in *Alien Resurrection* produces a sense of horror of, and fascination with, seeing the reverse logic of what heterosexuality was perceived to guarantee: sexual difference, sexual reproduction, embodied maternity and paternity. To disorder these couplings is to threaten the foundationalisms which seemed to ensure the compatibility of biological and cultural reproduction: with the threat to the integrity of individuality comes the threat to the logics of heterosexuality within this queer landscape. As the transgenic clone whose pregnancy continues to connect her to the alien species even after she has given birth, and as the lesbian icon who plays a homoerotic power game with the newly arrived robotic version of her younger self, Ripley is constantly shown becoming someone else through her connections to other bodies. In defining herself against the singularity of the Ripley of previous *Alien* films ('I am not her'), this resurrected Ripley is the not-Ripley or the more-than-Ripley. A symbol not only of the posthuman but also of a reimagined form of 'life itself',[58] Ripley's mutating body and shifting identity imitate the cell duplication and division of genetic engineering, producing a fantasy of self-replication which reiterates and problematizes the traditional categories of classification within theories of body horror film.[59] In its repeated presentation of excessive sameness in its pathological, technological and sexual manifestations, *Alien Resurrection* relentlessly rehearses the impossibility of the expulsion of the abject other. The consequent over-presence of the abject in the film denies the pleasurable fantasy of its permanent expulsion offered by the previous *Alien* films. In the film's multiple refusals of such generic pleasures, the normativity of abjection is both rehearsed and exposed.

In producing a science fiction fantasy of the geneticization of the 'culture of the copy',[60] *Alien Resurrection* pushes the conventions of its generic inheritance to such limits that it produces excesses that are hard to contain within its forms of closure without displaying an ironic commentary upon its predecessors. If the cloning of

Ripley, pregnant with the alien, generates narrative problems for the traditional expulsion of the abject outlined by Creed, then the extension of the genre with this fourth film presents similar problems of duplication. As Constable argues, the film fails to re-establish the traditional boundaries around the human body to secure its integrity in the future. Both biological and cultural reproduction are defined here by the problem of excessive sameness. The biological, technological and sexual forms of deviance in *Alien Resurrection* are all cast as the signs of too much sameness: teratomas, clones and homoeroticism. Authenticity and individuality are called into question, not only by the threat posed by these forms of sameness, but also by the generic self-referentiality of *Alien Resurrection*. As such, *Alien Resurrection* rehearses the cultural analogy of the biological form of reproduction it represents. The audience is offered none of the generic guarantees or reassurances of conventional body horror; instead Ripley and Call, the two cyborgs, save the Earth and are the signs of hope for an unknown future. Shown in *Titanic*-like double profile, they brace themselves against the impact with the Earth's atmosphere, and look ahead to the bright new future, signalled through a series of cliched cloudscape shots. The survivors who accompany them are those whose bodies are coded as the most deviant of the pirate crew: the high-tech weapons expert in the wheelchair, Vreiss (Dominic Pinon), and the criminal thug, Johner (Ron Perlman), whose ruthless exploitation of others has no limits. The future belongs to the deviants – to the criminals and the cyborgs.

I am extremely grateful to the following people for their generous commentary on earlier versions of this article: Hilary Hinds, Imogen Tyler, Adrian Heathfield, Sarah Street and the two anonymous readers who wrote reports for *Screen*.

Notes

1 Debbora Battaglia, 'Multiplicities: an anthropologist's thoughts on replicants and clones in popular film', *Critical Inquiry*, vol. 27, no. 3 (2001), pp. 493–515, p. 496 (emphasis in original). Battaglia's excellent paper on human replication in popular cinema focuses particularly on the film *Multiplicity* (Harold Ramis, 1996).

2 Ibid., p. 506. Battaglia offers an analysis of replicants and clones in the cinema 'as corporealizations of the capacity of the supplement to destabilize the social paradigms and self-knowledge of their creators'. In this definition of 'supplement', Battaglia borrows from Derrida. Ibid., p. 496.

3 Elizabeth Grosz, 'Freaks', *Social Semiotics*, vol. 1, no. 2 (1991), pp. 22–38, p. 36.

4 For a more general discussion of 'the proliferation of sameness' in relation to the shift from reproduction to replication in the context of cloning, see Susan Squier, 'Negotiating boundaries: from assisted reproduction to assisted replication', in E. Ann Kaplan and Susan Squier (eds), *Playing Dolly: Technocultural Formations, Fantasies and Fictions of Assisted Reproduction* (New Brunswick, NJ: Rutgers University Press, 1999), pp. 101–15.

5   Barbara Creed, *The Monstrous Feminine: Film, Feminism and Psychoanalysis* (London: Routledge, 1993).

6   Catherine Constable, 'Becoming the monster's mother: morphologies of identity in the *Alien* series', in Annette Kuhn (ed.), *Alien Zone II: the Spaces of Science Fiction Cinema* (London: Verso, 1999), pp. 173–202.

7   The cultural significance of the kinds of monstrous bodies that populate alien films have been widely debated. See, in particular, James Kavanagh, 'Feminism, humanism and science in *Alien*', and Judith Newton, 'Feminism and anxiety in *Alien*', in Annette Kuhn (ed.), *Alien Zone: Cultural Theory and Contemporary Science Fiction Cinema* (London: Verso, 1990), pp. 73–81, 82–90; Constance Penley, 'Time travel, primal scene and the critical dystopia', in Constance Penley, Elisabeth Lyon, Lynn Spiegel and Janet Bergstrom (eds), *Close Encounters: Film, Feminism and Science Fiction* (Minneapolis, MN and Oxford: University of Minnesota Press, 1991), pp. 63–82; Kelly Hurley, 'Reading like an alien: posthuman identity in Ridley Scott's *Alien* and David Cronenberg's *Rabid*', in Judith Halberstam and Ira Livingston (eds), *Posthuman Bodies* (Indianapolis, IN: Indiana University Press, 1995), pp. 216–20; Elizabeth Hills, 'From "figurative males" to action heroines: further thoughts on active women in the cinema', *Screen*, vol. 40, no. 1 (1999), pp. 38–51; Pamela Church Gibson '"You've been in my life so long I can't remember anything else": into the labyrinth with Ripley and the alien', in Matthew Tinkcom and Amy Villarejo (eds), *Keyframes: Popular Cinema and Cultural Studies* (London: Routledge, 2001), pp. 35–51.

8   Rosi Braidotti, *Metamorphoses: Towards a Materialist Theory of Becoming* (Cambridge: Polity, 2002).

9   For a discussion of the cultural significance of the pixel, see Sarah Franklin, Celia Lury and Jackie Stacey, *Global Nature, Global Culture* (London: Sage, 2000), pp. 60–6.

10 Braidotti, *Metamorphoses*, p. 179.

11 Ibid., p. 181.

12 Melinda Cooper, 'Regenerative medicine: stem cells and the science of monstrosity', unpublished paper (2002), p. 10. This paper offers a fascinating discussion of the history of the scientific study of teratomas in relation to the development of contemporary stem cell research, looking in particular at the history of the conceptualization of the normal and the pathological in teratology and teratogeny.

13 In a woman, a teratoma may imitate pregnancy in so far as it has the capacity to produce the cells of all the different organs in the body. Thus, unlike many tumours, teratomas have a fascinating and yet grotesque characteristic of foetal resemblance. This is why teratomas are also called 'monstrous births'. For a more detailed discussion of teratomas, see Jackie Stacey, *Teratologies: a Cultural Study of Cancer* (London: Routledge, 1997).

14 As Rosi Braidotti has shown in *Nomadic Subjects: Embodiment and Sexual Difference in Contemporary Feminist Thought* (New York: Columbia University Press, 1994), teratology, or the scientific study of monsters, was the forerunner of contemporary embryology.

15 This argument is developed in Kaja Silverman's reading of *Blade Runner*, 'Back to the future', in *Camera Obscura*, no. 27 (1991), p. 115. For a comprehensive analysis of this film, see Scott Bukatman, *Blade Runner* (London: British Film Institute, 1997).

16 Harold Varmus and Robert A. Weinberg, *Genes and the Biology of Cancer* (New York: The Scientific American Library, 1993), p. 29.

17 For important analyses of popular cultural constructions of the gene, see Dorothy Nelkin and M. Susan Lindee, *The DNA Mystique: the Gene as a Cultural Icon* (New York: W.H. Freeman and Company, 1995); Jon Turney, *Frankenstein's Footsteps: Science, Genetics and Popular Culture* (New Haven, CT and London: Yale University Press, 1998); José van Dijck, *Imagenation: Popular Images of Genetics* (New York: New York University Press, 1998).

18 The term 'the new genetic imaginary' is taken from Sarah Franklin's chapter 'Life itself', in Franklin *et al.*, *Global Nature, Global Culture*, pp. 188–277. For a discussion of images of the 'helping hand' of science in new genetic interventions, see Sarah Franklin, 'Flat life: conception after Dolly', paper delivered at the 'Biotechnology, Philosophy and Sex' Conference, 12 October 2002, Ljubljana, Slovenia.

19 Nelkin and Lindee, *The DNA Mystique*, p. 2.

20 Sarah Kember, 'Feminism, technology and representation', in James Curran, David Morley and Valerie Walkerdine (eds), *Cultural Studies and Communication* (London: Edward Arnold, 1996), pp. 229–47.

21 Donna Haraway, *Primate Visions: Gender, Race and Nature in the World of Modern Science* (London: Routledge, 1989), p. 368.

22 J.P. Telotte, 'The double of fantasy and the space of desire', in Kuhn (ed.), *Alien Zone*, p. 154.

23 Ibid., p. 153.

24 Mary Ann Doane, 'Technophilia: technology, representation and the feminine', in Mary Jacobus, Eveleyn Fox Keller and Sally Shuttleworth (eds), *Body/Politics: Women and the Discourse of Science* (London: Routledge, 1990), p. 170.

25 Philip Brophy, 'Horrality – the textuality of contemporary horror films', *Screen*, vol. 27, no. 1 (1986), pp. 2–13, p. 10.

26 Pete Boss, 'Vile bodies and bad medicine', *Screen*, vol. 27, no. 1 (1986), pp. 14–25, p. 18.

27 Creed, *The Monstrous Feminine*.

28 Julia Kristeva, *Powers of Horror: an Essay on Abjection* (New York: Columbia University Press, 1982).

29 Creed, *The Monstrous Feminine*, p. 49.

30 Kristeva, *Powers of Horror*, p. 4.

31 Debbora Battaglia points out that the advertising slogan of the Tyrell Corporation (the company that produced the replicants in *Blade Runner*) is 'More Human than the Humans', Battaglia, 'Multiplicities', p. 507. On the human/replicant relation, see also Silverman, 'Back to the future', pp. 113–15.

32 Battaglia, 'Multiplicities', p. 509.

33 Constable, 'Becoming the monster's mother', p. 190.

34 For a discussion of the incestuous character of the complex forms of desire between Ripley and the various aliens in the film, see Church Gibson, '"You've been in my life so long I can't remember anything else"', p. 49.

35 For a discussion of the commodification of memory in science fiction films, see Bukatman, *Blade Runner*, pp. 77–80.

36 Constable, 'Becoming the monster's mother', p. 191.

37   Ibid. Constable draws here upon Christine Battersby's reworking of Luce Irigaray's theories of feminine subjectivity through the notion that in the potentiality to birth another, the female subject might be used to provide a new model of interrelatedness, as (potentially) being more than one and less than two through the connection to another's bodily formation. See Christine Battersby, *The Phenomenal Woman: Feminist Metaphysics and the Patterns of Identity* (Cambridge: Polity, 1998).

38   Claudia Springer, *Electronic Eros: Bodies and Desire in the Postindustrial Age* (London: Athlone Press, 1996), p. 61.

39   Constable, 'Becoming the monster's mother', p. 196.

40   Ibid., p. 197.

41   Judith Butler *Gender Trouble: Feminism and the Subversion of Identity* (London: Routledge, 1990), p. 136.

42   Ibid., p. 134.

43   Ibid.

44   Ibid., p. 135.

45   For further discussion of action heroines, see Carol Clover, *Men, Women and Chainsaws: Gender in the Modern Horror Film* (London: British Film Institute, 1992): Yvonne Tasker, *Spectacular Bodies: Gender, Genre and the Action Cinema* (London: Routledge, 1993) and *Working Girls: Gender and Sexuality in Popular Cinema* (London: Routledge, 1998); Ros Jennings, 'Desire and design: Ripley undressed', in Tamsin Wilton (ed.), *Immortal, Invisible: Lesbians and the Moving Image* (London: Routledge, 1995), pp. 193–206; Chris Holmlund, *Impossible Bodies: Femininity and Masculinity at the Movies* (London: Routledge, 2002).

46   *Film Review*, December 1997, p. 35.

47   For an analysis of Michael Jackson in this video, see Kobena Mercer, 'Monster metaphors: notes on Michael Jackson's "Thriller"', *Screen*, vol. 27, no. 1 (1986), p. 27.

48   For an analysis of androgyny and sexuality in science fiction films, see Janet Bergstrom, 'Androids and androgyny', in Penley *et al.* (eds), *Close Encounters: Film, Feminism and Science Fiction*, pp. 33–62.

49   *Film Review*, p. 33.

50   For a discussion of gay male cloning cultures, Battaglia references John Lauritsen, 'Political-economic construction of gay male cloning identity', *Journal of Homosexuality*, vol. 24, nos 3/4 (1993), pp. 221–32.

51   Springer, *Electronic Eros*, p. 61.

52   For a discussion of the sexualized use of hands in lesbian films, see Mandy Merck, 'The lesbian hand', in *In Your Face: 9 Sexual Studies* (New York: New York University Press, 2000), pp. 124–47.

53   For an analysis of the posthuman, see Katherine Hayles, *How We Became Posthuman: Virtual Bodies in Cybernetics, Literature and Informatics* (Chicago, IL: University of Chicago Press, 1999). I am grateful to Michael Lundin for letting me read his unpublished paper on *Alien Resurrection* as the presentation of posthuman embodied subjectivity, '(Wo)man-machine-insect: posthuman bodies in Jean-Pierre Jeunet's *Alien Resurrection* and Philip K. Dick's *Ubik*' (2002). This work is drawn from his PhD in progress: 'Spiders from Mars: refiguring subjectivity in the novels of Philip K. Dick, 1953–66', Stockholm University, Sweden. See also Hurley, 'Reading like an alien'.

54   Hayles, *How We Became Posthuman*, p. 1.

55 Ibid., p. 3.
56 Ibid.
57 Springer, *Electronic Eros*, p. 68.
58 For a discussion of the remaking of 'life itself' in the context of the new genetics, see Sarah Franklin, in Franklin *et al.*, *Global Nature*, pp. 188–227.
59 I am grateful to Imogen Tyler for discussions on these points. For an analysis of the disruptions to psychoanalytic categories produced by pregnant embodiment, see her chapter 'Skin-tight: celebrity, pregnancy and subjectivity', in Sara Ahmed and Jackie Stacey (eds), *Thinking Through the Skin* (London: Routledge, 2001), pp. 69–84.
60 For an excellent historical account, see Hillel Schwarz, *The Culture of the Copy* (New York: Zone Books, 1996).

5 Continuous sex: the editing of homosexuality in *Bound* and *Rope*

Lee Wallace

It is, perhaps, to be expected that the notorious invisibility of lesbianism would leave its mark on the cinematic style of a film whose plot development plays on the impossibility of lesbian legibility. Less predictable, however, is the way the Wachowski brothers' sexual thriller, *Bound* (1996), is everywhere structured by its attempts to visualize lesbianism, to make it succumb, once and for all, to the order of the visible. While the elusiveness of homosexuality is crucial to the film's narrative, *Bound* simultaneously requires lesbianism to function evidentially, to disclose itself within a visual field. Under this representational double bind, the film frequently compensates for the indeterminacy of sexuality with cinematic technique. In the enigmatic opening sequence, for instance, Corky (Gina Gershon) – shortly identified as an ex-con, good with her hands – lies unconscious, bound and gagged at the bottom of a closet, the tight dimensions of which the mobile camera has distorted with its wide-angle focus and first vertical, then horizontal, trajectory, so that the place of confinement is oddly capacious, holding as it does not just a limp body but the fetishized accessories that could be said to constitute both her character and that of her accomplice, Violet (Jennifer Tilly). Like many things in *Bound*, this scene invites a parallel with Alfred Hitchcock's *Rope* (1948). It would seem that the Wachowskis are deploying Hitchcock's famous moving camera in the one place he never allowed it: the closed space which holds the body. Toward the end of *Rope*'s dinner party, when Jimmy Stewart finally lifts the lid of the chest that hides the strangled victim, the camera-shot continues to conceal that much anticipated sight offscreen. The circumspection of Hitchcock's framing, according to D.A. Miller, has little to do with the conventions of a murder plot that generically requires the discovery of a corpse and everything to do with the 'pathways of symbolic signification' that inevitably return to the sexual status of the young man's asphyxiated body. Miller goes on to argue that the 'obscenity' of the aroused male body '"murdered" from behind', and its implications for a heterosexual visual economy mortgaged to castration anxiety, require that the young man's body remain hidden for the duration of Hitchcock's film.[1] However, the still-breathing body discovered inside *Bound*'s most recessed space, far from remaining unseen, is repeatedly submitted to the trial of visibility. Not once, but three times *Bound* revisits the spectacle of the restrained figure held in the dark; and that female body's vulnerability to the camera's investigative eye returns us, as unfailingly as Hitchcock's visual reticence, to a consideration of its homosexual status.

In the inaugural scene, the camera's discovery of that body is obscurely diagnostic. Entering the closet from above and commencing its high-angle descent, the tracking camera curiously elongates the distance from the patterned hatboxes neatly aligned across two high shelves, down past the metal hangers which hold Violet's visually foreshortened synthetic dresses, to the rows of white heels that gleam out of shadow nearer to the floor before panning across to Corky's heavy black boots, dark drill pants, cotton tank and labrys tattoo. Throughout, disconnected samples of dialogue in female and male voiceover, both seductive and aggressive, echo across the scene, never quite coalescing into anything like a sequence: 'I had this image of you inside of me, like a part of me'; 'You planned this whole thing'; 'Where's the fucking money?'. Disorienting in spatial and acoustic terms, the shot nonetheless establishes a visual continuity between the feminine accoutrements of Violet's wardrobe and the butch tackle worn by Corky throughout the film, so that the optically attenuated space between them is narratively abbreviated – or, in character terms, reduced – so that Corky's dykey taste in fashion verifies the lesbian potential of Violet's own. Having placed these feminine and masculine garments in some soon to be elaborated relation, the camera, now settled at floor level, holds on Corky's attractively battered face, stopping short of knitting into her character those other props which also contribute to the sexually suggestive quality of the scene: the rope, the gag, the designer bruises.

Ellis Hanson's description of *Bound*'s opening sequence similarly draws attention to the visual and sexual ambivalence of this scene:

> Once the title disappears from the screen, we are unsure what we are looking at. We cannot make sense of the shapes on the screen. Slowly they resolve themselves into a scene in which a woman bound with rope is trapped in a closet. The visual cues slip from bondage as sexual play to bondage as sexual assault – and so we are still unsure what we are looking at. We cannot fix the scene or the fantasy that motivates it. A woman is in the closet, in bondage, and yet her very restraints, not to mention all those shiny shoes, turn the bondage into a fetish and release the very eroticism that closets are supposed to negate.[2]

As this quotation from Hanson suggests, it would be hard to underestimate the resonance of this opening scene for contemporary theorizations of lesbian representation. Since Eve Kosofsky Sedgwick argued the historical pertinence of this figure for modern understandings of homosexual/heterosexual distinction, the closet has become the governing trope through which the impossibility of homosexual containment is understood.[3] Far from being an architectural site, let alone a secure one, the closet functions as an epistemic figure which organizes the relations of knowledge and ignorance which inadequately cordon off homosexuality from the heterosexuality for which it is everywhere mistaken. The closet, in this sense, is oddly expansive, though finally restrictive in the revelations it orchestrates, its permeability always in the service of holding a distinction – however unstable that line may prove to be – between in and out, gay and straight. *Bound*'s closet, and the narrative it initiates, does indeed function as a sexual proscenium, staging the display of lesbian identity in a visual register that is not without its own troublesome relation to the unreliability of homosexual difference. Notoriously obscure, sexuality is, after all, the last thing to submit to regimes of full and final disclosure.

The question of lesbian recognition, its difficult emergence within a visual field enthralled by heterosexual difference, is foregrounded throughout *Bound* both thematically and stylistically. The film's plot, an elaborate confidence heist, depends on the invisibility of same-sex desire and the uncertainty of sexual affiliation. Corky and Violet, thrown together by little more than the proximity of two apartments – Violet's own and the vacant one next door (number 1003) which Corky has been hired to make over – start an affair, unbeknownst to Violet's longtime mobster boyfriend, Caesar (Joe Pantoliano). When two million dollars of mafia money comes into Caesar's care, Violet sees a way 'out' but needs Corky's help to steal the money and leave herself clean. The planned 'redistribution of wealth' involves a straightforward theft from Caesar's and Violet's apartment, but when Caesar discovers the money has gone, instead of running, as the women anticipate, he decides to brazen it out with the mob's collectors, holding Violet hostage to his plans. While it occurs to Caesar that Violet might be capable of double-crossing him with Johnnie Marzoni (Christopher Meloni), who has been fingered in the set-up, it never occurs to him that she might be in cahoots with someone outside the orbit of the mob, let alone that of heterosexuality. Invisible though their criminal pact is to the sexually myopic Caesar, the film nonetheless:

> uses the whole gamut of classic scopophilic lures – carefully staged sex scenes, fetishistic costumes, killer cosmetics, shadowy lighting, voyeuristic point-of-view shots, and so on – to help [the viewer] recognise the sexual intensity of the relationship between the two female leads, Violet and Corky. Theirs is a desire that the men in the film cannot see, though the women hide it in plain sight.[4]

Thus, while Corky's butchness is worn like an ID, a credential as assertive as the low-slung badge of the lesbian cop who confronts her at her local bar, Violet's allegiance to the sartorial codes of femininity makes her sexual registration more dubious, capable as she is of magnetizing the attraction of both the lesbian Corky and most of the dark-suited men the plot sends her way: Caesar, Johnnie, the hangdog Shelley (Barry Kivel) – who has siphoned off the two million dollars in the first place but seems unable to leave without Violet – and the paternalistic Mickey (John P. Ryan), whose romantic attentiveness disguises many of the plot's implausibilities, including its resolution.

Violet's dubious sexuality is foregrounded in *Bound*'s first seduction scene. With Caesar absent, Violet calls Corky to her apartment to retrieve an earring from the sink, a lure so old that even Corky is wise to it. Earring restored, the two leads move to the darker environs of the living room where they take up the drinks which etiquette dictates. Violet continues to come on to Corky who still gives nothing away, her suspicion of Violet running as high as her curiosity. 'What are you doing?' Corky asks, after Violet has taken her hand and lifted it to her own tattooed breast. 'Trying to seduce you', is Violet's disingenuous reply, before she attempts to assuage any doubts Corky might have about her motivation by demonstrating its sexual quality. 'You can't believe what you see, but you can believe what you feel', says Violet who, first moistening Corky's finger in her mouth, proceeds to place Corky's hand between her thighs. Violet's invitation and the gesture which accompanies it draw attention to just how artificial things are, both Violet's seemingly heterosexual appearance but also the scene itself: the ploy, the come-on, even the plumpness of the sofa, everything camera-ready for sex. Violet, however, asks Corky to rely not on looks but on the litmus of sexual response, as if the viscous secretions of the body, tested by fingertip, could inspire some further confidence, or even some outcome less predictable than the one that occurs as Corky's slippery progression from first to second base is interrupted by the utterly expected arrival of the excluded Caesar.

Rather than curtailing the thematics of sexual trust, Caesar's entrance merely shifts their terrain from the desirous body to its gendered manifestations. Although the two women quickly resume a quiescent distance and dress, Caesar believes he has disturbed a cheating Violet. He strides aggressively into the room, only to be brought up short. His angry certainty is rescinded with the revelation that the work-clothed figure in the shadowy apartment is a woman, not a man. Caesar's dawning recognition of Corky's sex serves to restore a chauvinist ignorance in the place previously occupied by a mistaken knowledge: he was right about the scene, when he took her masculine gender at its word. The sting, therefore, is that Caesar is caught out both by judging on appearance and failing to do so, since his first impressions, which simply assigned to Corky a masculinity she thus far inhabits, were more accurate in detecting sexual deceit.

Bound continues to transpose the question of heterosexual or homosexual orientation with that of masculine and feminine identification, though in a less than straightforward way. Violet's voluptuous appearance and helpless manner, for instance, signal a passivity that is everywhere belied by her initiations in both the sexual and thriller plots. Corky also plays against type, in bed her Y-fronted masculinity strips down to a sexual receptivity and, in the action sequences, she is patsy to Caesar's more virile intelligence and strength. Judged by diegetic event, not appearance, the thriller plot thus seems to reinforce the lesson Violet had attempted to instil on the make-out couch: handsome is as handsome does, or action overrides image. Butch and femme credentials are given a final shakedown in the action climax when Caesar knocks Corky unconscious a third time, leaving nothing but the money between Violet and himself. Violet holds a handgun on the unarmed Caesar, who stakes his life on knowing Violet better than she knows herself: 'You don't want to shoot me, Vi.' He is wrong, as it happens, and Violet shoots him dead, allowing the film to resolve all its questions about lesbian desire with a finger after all, this one held to the cold steel of a trigger. In *Bound*'s climactic scene, ambivalences that are crucial to the suspense of the film are aggressively closed down in favour of character depth and understanding, and these seemingly cinch tight the case of Violet's sexual loyalty. Caesar is the fall guy here, taking the rap not only for his earlier facile confidence that a fetishized femininity is the inalienable property of heterosexuality, but also for the sexual thriller format itself. Violent though it is, the abstract, designer pulp of Caesar's slow-motion death is oddly lacking in suspense. Where *Bound* elsewhere keeps its audience tautly wired to the intricacies of a plot that seems to invest even the inanimate objects in its vicinity with a capacity for violence and betrayal (telephone, television, porcelain toilet bowl), the final standoff between Violet and Caesar is strangely hesitant, its outcome supported in the mise-en-scene by nothing other than Violet's character motivation, to which it is sole testimony. They stare at each other across a sea of white paint. Violet pauses long enough to offer Caesar the chance to run, but he would rather cajole, seeing in her delay an indecision disallowed by the requirements of the plot, which insists on Violet being one thing, not the other.

Left to the throes of romance, and without the intercession of the mafia deus ex machina, the two women frustrate their own desire. Newly aware that she is not the only one to take up Caesar's place in Violet's bed, Corky, having vacated exactly that spot, deflects Violet's attempt at avowal. The enigmatic, 'I had this image of you inside of me, like a part of me', previously heard as a disembodied voiceover but now sentimentally lodged in Violet's languid figure, meets with a response that suggests Corky's own, less obscure, imagination has been jealously thinking of Violet repeatedly filled by male parts. Sullenly dressing at the bed's edge, Corky's aggression battens down not on her male rivals, Caesar and the unlikely Shelley, but on Violet's doubtful sexuality as neither exclusively heterosexual or homosexual. Sexual compatibility notwithstanding, lesbian desire now becomes a disputed field between the two women. Corky insists that she and Violet are 'different' by the rule that reads sexual availability as identity: having sex with men disqualifies Violet from the ranks of dykes filling the black banquettes of the Watering Hole, the lesbian bar which is Corky's night-time retreat. For Corky, as for Caesar, the name dyke operates metonymically, as does her labrys tattoo, as testimony to acts which are signalled even in their representational absence. Violet, despite her earlier come-on, now holds petulantly to the idea that sexual acts alone can neither confirm nor deny orientation, preferring to think of her time under Caesar as 'work'. Violet's five years with Caesar imply a more than temporal parallel with Corky's time inside prison. Her pre-diegetic jailterm locks Corky in with a fleetingly invoked cell-mate who serves her time for 'being caught'.

In the imaginary women's prison, for which *Caged* (John Cromwell, 1950) provides the cinematic model, the lesbian status of sex acts between, say, Corky and this unnamed woman might be compromised by the mandatory homosociality of the institution. That is, Corky too might have been trapped in a situation in which acts strangely fail to secure identities, an implicit support of Violet's rebuke, 'I think we're more alike than you'd care to admit'. Like many other bedroom arguments, this one is less significant for what it says than what it does not. The subject of the dialogue – while crucial to the thriller plot in so far as it verifies that Corky is not altogether sure of Violet's motives and whether or not she is being worked, like the other occupants of Violet's bed, for some pay-off that is more than, and hence not really, sexual – is countered by the scene's effect, which establishes that the more the two women fight and disagree about sexuality, the more they affirm the extent of their mutual desire. This bedside conversation thus complicates the sexual relation between them, which is here suspended, providing an erotic rift which delays the satisfaction of the film's romantic narrative.

Perhaps perversely, the homosexual lesson *Bound* administers depends less on romantic complication than the thriller narrative, and its associated set pieces, which take over the sexual plot and its spatial and graphic motifs in order to generate the illusion of a lesbian diegesis. Consider the manner in which Violet and Corky's sexual estrangement is bypassed via the brutal sacrifice of Shelley's little finger in the searingly well-lit bathroom of Violet's apartment. The importance of fingers to regimes of truthtelling has already been established in the first sexual hold between Violet and Corky, but now this connection is violently restated as Mickey calmly declares he will ten times ask the whereabouts of the mob's money, counting off each question with a close of the secateurs around each of the digits on Shelley's hands. Likewise, the sound of this torture scene establishes the adjacency of different spaces, a function previously reserved for sexual noise alone. Heard first by Corky who labours in the neighbouring bathroom, Shelley's terror conveyed through the connecting pipes she works on, the scene also distresses Violet who is linked to the torture via her kitchen blender, whose everyday noise and whirlpool action, visually and aurally linked to the white toilet bowl against which Shelley's head is repeatedly smashed, takes up then dissipates the visceral horror of the events in the room through the wall. Mickey graciously suggests Violet leave the apartment and this precipitates her advent next door, miraculous in so far as it occurs without any establishing shots. Violet simply appears in Corky's apartment, the close coordinates of onscreen space being all that is required to suggest their *rapprochement*. Together they remove to a second – straight – bar where, in the safe enclosure of a white banquette, they discuss for the first time Violet's leaving 'the business' and her plan to steal from the mob. The film's plotline, thoroughly hijacked by the thriller scenario, thus keeps live the question of Violet's loyalty, replaying it as the dangerous necessity for trust among thieves. It is this substitution, the way the film has the thriller plot carry and rework its romantic narrative, that enables the resolution of the earlier question about the sexual difference between Corky and Violet, butch and femme. It is only by detouring this thematic concern through the cinematic format of the thriller that *Bound* can achieve satisfactory romantic closure. The lesbian diegesis remains dependent on the graphic violence of the thriller – and, as I will show, its chromatic design – to secure its sexual outcome.

The hybridization of genres that the sexual thriller instantiates is, perhaps, familiar noir territory, but what seems worthy of comment in the context of a film that has been welcomed as an advance in lesbian representation is the way in which this conflation of genres works at the level of image rather than character. Although *Bound* quickly puts Corky and Violet through their sexual paces in several choreographed seduction scenes, the film's closure is certified as lesbian not by this sexual athleticism – spent within the opening half hour – nor by the character development it minimally supports, but by the film's visual style and its repeated distortions of spatial and temporal continuity, most of which are in the service of the thriller format. The romance narrative's girl-gets-girl outcome, however satisfactory, is utterly reliant on the graphic design of the mise-en-scene and the film's formal manipulation of editing devices.

Questions of technique have long haunted cinematic representations of homosexuality. The Wachowski brothers' concern with both sexuality and the conventions of cinematic space comes almost half a century after Hitchcock spliced together formal experimentation and the plot of male perversion in *Rope*. In his formidable discussion of Hitchcock's film, Miller identifies the deniability of homosexuality as symptomatic of not only the film but also the critical discussion that surrounds it. The example of *Rope* reveals a homophobic hermeneutic that raises the possibility of homosexuality within the film's story only to deny it. This denial operates on two levels: as an effect of the connotative system of gay signification that the Hollywood production code necessitates and, less predictably, in the critical discourse addressing the film's formal structure which assumes the homosexual content of the film to be there, though without interest.[5] Hitchcock's film everywhere maintains the forensic deniability of its homosexual subject. Approved by the Hays Office as nowhere disclosing the presence of sex perversion, *Rope*'s dialogue and mise-en-scene (in particular the way its camera angles suggestively frame male bodies in a too-close proximity that recalls the clinch of romance) nonetheless repeatedly work to connote a homosexuality that is nowhere to be found in the film.[6] This second-order invocation of an interdicted topic is signal, not to the failure of the production code but to its peculiar success as a representational order, the enforcing logic of which is to produce homosexuality under a ban. Rather than silence or cancel homosexuality, the code articulates it outside the denotative quarantine of the film's diegesis. This representational logic kept a stranglehold on homosexuality through three decades of Hollywood film production. The administrative order of code-era films required that sex perversion be compulsorily forbidden, yet always illicitly known.[7]

Bound, on the other hand, is evidently interested in the diegetic possibility of lesbianism. That is, it would seem the representational field of *Bound* marks a break with *Rope* in so far as the Wachowskis have the discretionary privilege to make homosexuality their film's thematic and graphic subject. However, that assumption is in many ways false. It suggests that homosexuality is within the one film and without the other, though held in its magnetic vicinity as its interpretative effect. The tact of Hitchcock's film, a tact that is more but never less than its upholding of the production code, is that its homosexual meaningfulness is everywhere maintained as an ignorance, and the perennial lure of *Rope* is the invitation it extends to viewers to align themselves with this knowledge without ever having to claim it. But *Bound* too reveals homosexuality as an interpretative effect of a repre-sentational system, not, of course, the production code, but its Hollywood ally, classical continuity editing. Long after there is any requirement to do so, *Bound* continues, perhaps inevitably, to put cinematic technique in the place of homo-sexuality. This connection is important to trace because it suggests a continuity in homosexual representation which overrides the historical aegis of the production code and enables the illumination of other, less institutional, mechanisms which discipline the performance of male homosexuality and lesbianism in the field of cinematic representation.

Bound repeatedly substitutes graphic meaning in the place of a psychological depth for which it is then mistaken, a cinematic sleight-of-hand for which Hitchcock's thrillers are also known.[8] Familiar from *Rope* as a technical accessory to the production code order that bans direct reference to homosexual content, this same cinematic procedure is detectable in *Bound*'s ostensibly explicit lesbian sex scene, which is most interesting for its refusal of illusionist effect and its blatant recruitment of the camera as sexual prosthetic. Lesbian sex guru Susie Bright's technical consultancy notwithstanding, the sex scene between Gershwin and Tilly suggests that things are, perhaps, much the same as they were in 1948. As we shall see, the preliminary holds of this sexual encounter occur in Corky's red utility truck. The vertical wipe to Corky's apartment releases into the new mise-en-scene a mobile camera which describes a 360-degree orbit around two naked bodies on an already familiar mattress. The camera shot begins at floor level before moving higher and closer into the two figures who provide its orienting centre. The camera tracks the length of Violet's body, past her raised shoulder and haunch, before rounding the foot of the bed. A medium closeup captures from low angle the foreshortened length of Corky's torso, her pelvis lifting against Violet's obstetric hand. The orchestration of the scene synchronizes the sounds of sex with non-diegetic music, both of which are keyed to the stylized progression of the camera whose circumnavigation of the bed is completed on the attainment of a closeup on Corky's face, Violet's finger inserted between her open lips, a softcore placeholder for that earlier wetted finger pressed to unseen depths. Both actions, sex and camerawork, are satiated in a seventy-second take, which then cuts to a bird's-eye shot looking down on the women, now silent, from high above the bed. If this scene can lay any claim to sexual realism, lesbian or otherwise, it would probably rest on the elasticated sheet riding up the corner of the mattress. Everything else is subservient to the exertion of the 360-degree crane, an apparatus shot that is fully invested in the kinaesthetic possibilities of the agile camera and almost indifferent to the requirements of character and narrative.

Bound's indebtedness to *Rope* is most succinctly acknowledged in its title and in the length of white rope that is first seen binding Corky's black-booted ankles as she lies, gagged and unconscious, in the darkened recess of Violet's closet. Of this rope's several returns the last is the most resonant: now lying outside the closet it signals not merely Corky's escape and the start of the final suspenseful sequence, but the film's belated attainment of a narrative present for which Hitchcock's film, and its eponymous object, remains the most condensed of tropes. Like its predecessor, *Bound* foregrounds cinema as a spatial system, a filmic organization of place and time which generates among its effects narrative causality and, less straightforwardly, character motivation. If the 'shooting practice' of *Rope* can be said to be animated by 'the dream of a continuous film', that of *Bound* is doubly invested in the potentialities of continuity as they augment a diegesis that is itself already concerned with a diagnostics of homosexuality.[9] Any attempt to specify the location of homosexuality in *Bound* must, therefore, map two allied systems which between them provide the ground for the emergence of lesbianism within the film's representational field, the parameters of which extend beyond its diegesis. The first system involves the editing conventions which stabilize the connection between cinematic space and narrative temporality, and therefore keep the time and place of plot events intelligible to the viewer. The second system is the graphic or pictorial method by which the film couples the romantic or erotic narrative to the suspense thriller, which provides both the driving momentum of the plot and the mechanism for its thematic resolution.

Scene transitions are the most important element in maintaining the hierarchical relations within these spatial and narrative systems. Consider again *Bound*'s opening scene. Constituting the present moment of the thriller storyline, the closet sequence ends with an inaugural fade, a non-diegetically motivated whiteout which cues in the first of the flashback sequences that will comprise most of the film's plot. The tense present moment of the closet will not be attained until late in screen-time, though it will be reprised twice in the interval, once when another non-diegetic whiteout clears to closeups on the fluttering lids and twitching fingers of Corky's bound figure and a second time when, having been jumped by the more powerful Caesar, a subjectively indexed whiteout signals Corky's fall out of consciousness and the fade-in reveals her lying in the same trussed pose described in the opening shot. The visual cues are strong enough to trigger a recognition for the viewer and, in combination with the sound of Caesar's 'Wake up! Wake up!', a false confidence that the flashbacks have achieved the present moment of the film's start. However, immediately a second whiteout, keyed to Corky's coming-to as water is tossed at her face, reveals her to be lying in an open room alongside an equally restrained Violet, about to be interrogated by Caesar who will stash her inside the closet only when he is interrupted by the buzz of the intercom. The film's forward accelerations are potentially disorienting in so far as these shots graphically signal a temporal simultaneity which is then rescinded by the camera's subsequent enlargement of the mise-en-scene which reveals that plot events still lag behind the film's opening. *Bound*'s pictorial scheme dominates its narrative in this way, flexibly asserting the ability of the image to override then restore the temporal chronology required to support the logical chains of cause and effect that comprise the film's plot.

In the chromatic design of *Bound*, scene transitions cued by white frequently execute reversals or shifts in chronological sequence, whereas changes in location that are realist in effect, spatially distinct and temporally forward in storytime, are initially cued by red. Consider, for instance, the film's deployment of Corky's red utility. A high-angle shot of Corky, her day's work done, climbing into the red Chevy, establishes an exterior outside the apartment building. The '63 Chevy has previously featured as the subject of a dialogue between Corky and Violet when, alone in apartment 1003, Violet introduces herself and the erotic motifs that will be recycled through the romance and thriller narratives. Accordingly connected with coffee and sex, the cab of the truck can legitimately supply the location in which, once Corky is joined by Violet, the women can resume the sex that Caesar's arrival has earlier cut short. Violet's breathless inquiry, 'Do you have a bed some-where?' cues a camera movement upwards through the headspace of the Chevy's cab in a shift which disorientingly converts the roof of the truck into the cross-sectioned floor of Corky's stark bedroom, which appears as a dark horizontal line wiping vertically down the frame. The scene transition signals a conventional ellipsis in time and space – Corky's room, like Johnnie's soon-to-be-wrecked lounge, existing at some unspecified distance from the apartment building that Violet and Caesar call home. More manifest is the aesthetic distance between each location, the heterosexual baroque of Johnnie's bachelor pad being more than miles away from the spare interior and rumpled linen that comprise Corky's lesbian minimalism. The scene transition from truck to bedroom is fully integrated with narrative form, the wipe a placeholder for those events we understand to have occurred in an interim that is nowhere represented: the time it takes to drive across town, the time it takes two women to undress.

After sex, the red Chevy transports us just as efficiently back to the original apartment building. A cut moves storytime and place forward to the parking lot where Corky is seen arriving in the red truck, the morning-afterness of the scene reinforced by the non-diegetic soundtrack which fades out on the disclosure onscreen of the figure of Shelley, clawing at the building's intercom telephone. Shelley's first appearance in the vicinity of the red utility is preliminary to the revelation that he too is a lover of Violet's. His subsequent return to the apartment lot is also linked to the red Chevy – however, in the later scene, the erotic quality of the truck, like that of many other things (most memorably plumbing and fingers), is quickly displaced by an association with violence. Corky stands on the deck of the truck, as a slow-motion point-of-view pan tracks the arrival of a black limousine out of which three mobsters climb. One of them, Johnnie, withdraws a reluctant Shelley from inside the relative safety of the car, then escorts him across the forecourt and back inside the building, delivering him to a violent fate. Now a marked man, Shelley is the male figure on whom the substitution between sex and violence is made, just as Caesar's body will later provide the visual counter on which to switch those things back. Masculine corporeality, in line with *Bound*'s visual codes, stands in for a feminine carnality harder to represent.

Once the mob's torture of Shelley is realized, the film's exploitation of sexual tension will be replaced by a suspense generated in line with the requirements of the thriller, the automotive red now replaced by a wash of blood that will render incarnadine many of the white transitions previously favoured in its plot development. Consider the cut from Corky in white undershirt and Y-fronts, lying against a white sheet in her own apartment, to a paintroller whiting out a wall in the apartment she is renovating. Corky's pose on the bed, and the camera angle from which it is filmed, is restaged in the later sex scene, her frustrated twanging of a Jew's harp now replaced by Violet's ministrations and the acoustics of sex. The temporal expediency of these matches on white are exploited in the opening twenty minutes of the film chiefly to establish the coordinates of the romantic plotline. Once the thriller format takes over, white is stained with red as violence replaces sex as the epistemic nub of the film. The most condensed visual signifier of this transition is that of the white porcelain toilet bowl in apartment 1003 catching droplets of blood and thus becoming its counterpart in the adjacent apartment as the mise-en-scene enlarges to reveal the location of Shelley's torture and his agonized forfeiture of a finger, the fetishized and suitably ungendered body part, which condenses lesbian sex and masculine vulnerability.

Viewers are adept at understanding the causality implied by such graphic devices and the ellipses in time and space these transitions indicate. Together they allow the film's plot sequence (the scenes it depicts for the duration of its screentime, and the order in which they appear) to reference another chronological order of event which we take to be the film's narrative or storyline. Comprised of everything we see and some things we do not, this causal narrative is reconstructed by the viewer who interprets screen events as occurring in different places and at different times. The most sustained and complicated of these sequences is initiated after a reprise of the bound figure in the closet motif. Corky and Violet are caught in the morning light of Corky's studio apartment. Violet describes the events of the night before, cueing a flashback sequence which picks up events previously suspended as her dialogue takes on the status of voiceover narration. Her account of events is supplemented by the images now screened: Caesar irons banknotes late into the night, standing in an unreal room, a laundry of bills fluttering around him on improvised lines. A question from Corky prompts the screening of events further forward: Caesar at his laptop as an automated machine neatly rebinds the mob's money which he counts into a briefcase. The editing foregrounds Corky's reliance on Violet's version of events and restates the issue of trust. However, a subsequent return to Violet and Corky enables a change in narration. Corky, still at the window of her one-room apartment, interrogates Violet for more information, before starting to plan the heist out loud as the image track proceeds to run ahead of the moment of speech and anticipates the events her dialogue describes. The flashforward sequence, which reveals the decoy ploys Violet will enact in order to allow Corky to enter her and Caesar's apartment and take the money, twice returns to the scene in Corky's studio (once to reveal Corky pulling a pearl-handled revolver from beneath her mattress as she counsels Violet, 'Trust me'), and continues to orient itself to the moment of planning until the point where Caesar opens the briefcase to find it full of newsprint. An extreme low-angle shot of Caesar's face tilts and slows his irregular movements against a stable background. The jerky out-of-focus effect, understood as a visual index to his nauseated state, also provides a formal dislocation sufficient to terminate the flashforward sequence. Corky is revealed in the next door apartment, the money beside her, as screen events now mark the suspenseful coincidence of time and space, although these events are still prior to the opening scene of the film. Within an overall though unreliable flashback structure, *Bound*'s technologies of narration and editing move events both ways, reversing and advancing its image track in order to assemble the more compelling plot. Flashbacks and establishing shots are the conventional means film employs to register these spatial and temporal shifts while tracing the causal connections that will retrospectively comprise the coherent story. *Bound*, however, deploys a further series of graphic devices (fades, wipes, visual matches in the mise-en-scene) which also cue spatial and temporal shifts, but which work against this accruing sense of a coherent storytime and storyspace embedded in, though independent of, the film's plot. Even as it unfolds a tightly-wound, causally linked thriller narrative, *Bound* includes moments of formal discontinuity which, far from rescinding the more realist claims of its romance plot, actually secure them.

The film's first whiteout functions in a conventional manner, taking us forward in screentime but backward in storytime to present events which precede Corky's confinement in the closet of the opening shot. The fade-in reveals Corky standing within a deep red interior as a highly distinctive offscreen voice we recognize as one of the non-diegetic voices heard over the earlier scene exhales, 'Hold the elevator', which might be 'Happy Birthday, Mr President' for all the wheezy affect Jennifer Tilly breathes into Violet's voice. The comparison with Marilyn Monroe suggests the vacancy of the acting style the Wachowskis draw from their cast, a style which allows the critical butch and femme difference of the female leads to lodge in nothing more than Tilly's voice and Gershon's pout. The shots which follow establish other coordinates of character and space, though less efficiently. Caesar looks towards the front of the elevator, his back towards the two women. Behind him, as it were, a shot/counter-shot sequence registers a slow exchange of looks between Violet and Corky of which he is unaware. Held in a high-angle shot, the three figures in the lift form a conspicuous triangle, the padded shoulders of Caesar's open overcoat providing a clear apex to the more graphically similar points marked by Corky and Violet's black leather jackets. As Caesar and Violet leave the elevator, we see Corky tilt her head, sideways and down, preliminary to a slow-motion tracking shot on Violet's legs as they move the length of the hallway. The sleazy camera shot, now marked as Corky's gaze, has its alibi in character motivation. Such point-of-view shots are, however, infrequent in *Bound* and the more signature camera set-up is the one which halts Violet's slow walk before a distant apartment doorway (perhaps 1001) some way beyond an exactly similar one in the foreground which Corky will likewise and simultaneously enter (1003). The establishment of the spatial adjacency of the two apartments is no less important to the film's plot than the suggestion of sexual interest between the two women. Prior to the distraction of any onscreen dialogue, the film implicitly links the possibility of same-sex sex with our perception of the synchronicity of cinematic space and time.

An undisguised cut takes us into apartment 1003. A low-level camera runs the length of some buckets on the floor before rising on Corky, in the middle of an empty room. Now stripped of her leather jacket, she stands before a patterned red background, talking into a heavy black telephone. Distracted, she swivels around to listen to the more muffled noises coming from behind a wall whose red paper is now seen in detail. The mobile camera then moves through the space between the figure of Corky and the red background she appears against, carving out a depth which is foreclosed once the flat of the wall has been achieved as the exclusive focus of the frame. The sound cues signal depth and distance but also establish that the wall is paper thin, permeable to noises such as the banging bedhead and male panting that Corky and the viewer currently hear from the as yet unseen bedroom of apartment 1003. The red wallpaper pattern will retain this aural link with heterosexual expenditure, and will be used again to mark the odd contiguity of the two spaces, communicating rooms as it were. These elements of the mise-en-scene, like the one-sided phone conversation that simultaneously explains Corky's presence in the building and suggests the complexities of her past, are fully integrated with the narrative form of the film, defining a coherent storyworld in which plot events can logically occur. The unambiguous delineation of the space of the scene focuses our attention on the information which is crucial to the chain of cause and effect which underwrites both action and character. In this hierarchy, cinematic space defers to narrative, providing the realist backdrop against which motivation can emerge.

In its first appearance, the red wall thus supports the cinematic illusion that apartments 1001 and 1003 are spatially distinct, neighbouring each other in the imagined blueprint of the apartment building which also locates them on a tenth floor, attainable by lift and, as is later necessary to the plot, a vertiginous stairwell. But while the maintenance of this illusion is crucial to the development of the thriller plot (as is the suggestion that sound travels between the two apartments) the film will also include transition shots which dispel the integrity of three-dimensional space by playing against the audience's expectations concerning offscreen space. Consider the next deployment of the red wall motif which occurs after Corky and Violet have had sex. The red Chevy having synchronized the arrival of Corky and Shelley at Violet's apartment building, both ascend to the top floor where Corky and Shelley enter the adjacent apartments in time, as Corky and Violet have earlier done. As in the previous sequence, Corky steps through the white door into the offscreen space of the apartment undergoing renovation. A cut occurs on the white door before the frame is once again filled with the familiar red patterned wallpaper. As before, the smothered sound of panting permeates the red wall. The noise of sex continues to be heard, gaining then falling away in intensity to be succeeded by a female voice whose equally breathy utterance bridges a visual cut from the abstract red pattern to a head and shoulders closeup of Violet, still talking, lying in a bed which abuts what we assume to be the other side of the three-dimensional wall. This 180-degree turnaround is confirmed as the camera pulls back from the bare-shouldered woman to reveal another figure dressing at the bed's edge. The new mise-en-scene is consistent with the sound cues which, having fallen away, lead us to expect the conversational aftermath of sex. However, the dark-haired figure who buttons up furtively at the left of the frame is not the anticipated Shelley but Corky, whom the camera had apparently left in the offscreen space of the other apartment. The unexpected quality of the scene transition, spatially continuous but temporally elliptical is, we might note, compatible with the order of cuts so far established on white or red which denote temporal discontinuities (advances and reversals) in order to facilitate the compression of storytime to plot-time and screen duration.

Indeed, Corky has a way of turning up unexpectedly in onscreen space. After Violet first floats her plan of stealing from the mob, Corky's response, 'I want to see the money', provides an acoustic bridge across a visual cut away from the interior of the Chevy into Violet's apartment. The mobile camera rapidly approaches the red walls of the vestibule, meeting Caesar head-on as he rushes through the door, his white shirt front soaked in Shelley's blood, and across the room to spill the equally stained money into the kitchen sink for the first stage of its literal laundering. Caesar will shortly exit the kitchen, walking to the left and out of frame, leaving Violet standing at the bench looking down on the bloodstained money, as Corky has earlier stood over a sink rinsing white paint through her fingers after their first sexual encounter. Once again, red replaces white, as violence replaces sex. Unannounced, Corky angles into the mise-en-scene from the left and silently takes up a position at Violet's shoulder before a whiteout returns her to the temporally unanchored closet. Such chromatic switches will be increasingly associated with not sex but violence, though they finally provide the terms through which the sexual thematic will be resolved.

The substitution of figures, our discovery of Corky having vacated the position, on top of Violet, we assume to be Shelley's, or the cinematic balance of her arrival in a frame following Caesar's departure, cinches together the film's two narratives, erotic and thriller, establishing that the question of Violet's trustworthiness is indexed to two equally paranoid structures, those of sexual orientation and organized crime. Violet's bisexual capacities notwithstanding, the important information conveyed by Shelley's initial advent in the diegesis is not that Violet is cheating on Corky, but that she is cheating on Caesar with someone inside 'the business'. It is Shelley's insider status, not his gender or putative heterosexuality, that the film exploits. Similarly, the plot of the film is driven by Caesar's brilliant attempts to outstrip criminal knowledges and effectively terminated when the situation calls on him to second-guess Violet's sexuality. In his final scene, adrift in the synchronic time that Corky's slipping of the rope eventually sets ticking, Caesar makes a call in his own favour, judging Violet reluctant to kill him. 'Caesar', warns Violet, 'you don't know shit', before confirming his fatal error. Felled by bullets perforating with red the familiar contours of his white shirtfront, Caesar's mortal arc provides the graphic link *Bound* requires to close down the question of lesbian desire: his body lies in a pool of white paint now washed with a sanguinary tint. Caesar's end is purely cinematic, the bird's-eye camera frames him spreadeagled, bleeding red into a white background. In a final confidence trick, the film offers his splayed and punctured form as visual testimony to that which it could otherwise never establish: Violet's secret and sexualized integrity, the inalienability of her lesbianism.

A non-diegetic whiteout over Caesar's dead body fades to an all-white apartment, an empty closet standing open in a rear corner. There are no other coordinates for reading this space, which could be consequently either apartment 1001 or 1003. An undisguised cut presents Violet and Mickey, the surviving mobster who is charged with hunting down the disappeared Caesar in whose possession the mob's money is assumed to be, standing beside a black car. Plot ends neatly tied off, the family limousine can then be replaced by Corky's new red Chevy. Opened by remote control, the late-model truck allows Corky and Violet, with two million dollars in hand, to climb into the cab and drive out of the retroworld of the film's diegesis and into some other, temporally unbound space where the difference between butch and femme is no difference at all. Corky, windscreen reflections falling across her face, turns to Violet and asks, 'You know the difference between you and me?' The question is doubly disingenuous. Corky and Violet are dressed as they were in the opening elevator scene but, now cropped in medium closeup, their black leather jackets and wayfarers register only their sexual similarity. 'No', says Violet. 'Me neither', replies Corky, before the dark under-carriage of the truck passes over the low-level camera, inaugurating a blackout upon which final credits scroll, there being nothing left to say. The dialogue suggests that the erotic misunderstandings of that earlier bedside argument, which foundered on the homosexual/heterosexual difference between Corky and Violet, have been addressed and resolved; as if the question of Violet's sexual allegiance, whether she goes with men or women, were answered by homicide, by the chill expedient of having her wipe out Caesar. His pulpy, slowmotion death stands as a displaced yet unequivocal testimony to lesbian desire.[10] The same-sex coordinates of the film's closure are enabled, not simply by Caesar's removal from the plot, but by the spectacularity of that withdrawal. Violet's sexual obscurity is resolved, not by the disclosure of sexual clinch or romantic commitment, but by the visual device of mixing white and red.

Cinematic suspense has always exploited this capacity of viewers to see what is not there, but the innovation of *Bound* may well be to suggest that something like this capacity is at play, in our most casual understandings of sexual difference: sexuality, or at least its demarcation as heterosexual or homosexual, is arbitrary, a scam or confidence trick that involves a knowledge augmented by ignorance. Just as the realist space of cinematic action is an illusion generated by the con-ventions of continuity editing, so, perhaps, is sexuality a character effect elicited by the apparatus of the camera and its manipulation of the mise-en-scene. The lesbianism of *Bound*'s characters, like other elements in the mise-en-scene (phones, furniture, floorplans), is foremost and finally a function of the plot. Like *Rope*, *Bound* taps into the double valencies of the sexual thriller. Though separated by five decades and the apparent remission of the production code, in both films the criminal storyline carries the erotic narrative, disguising and supplementing the insufficiencies of its homosexual diegesis. In *Bound*, the proof of lesbianism is cinematically conveyed, not by the choreographed sex scenes which occur within the first twenty minutes of screentime, but by the graphic violence associated with the mafia sting. The thriller plot and its associated technical devices generate the impression of character motivation and depth which the romantic plotline, with its reliance on dialogue and a more restricted visual economy of dress and undress, could never establish unaided. In this way *Bound* inevitably recalls, and inverts, the representational effect Miller discerns in *Rope*: its narrative approaches the subject of lesbianism head-on, yet the film's means of securing homosexual closure is formally oblique, marked less by avowal and disclosure than pictorial displacement and excess. The critical effect of watching *Bound* is not unlike that generated, more homophobically, in the wake of *Rope*: that is, we are convinced we see what is nowhere in evidence. The cinematic sleight goes unnoticed, perhaps, because of our viewerly investments in narrative outcome and closure. We can be relied on to see what we want. *Bound*'s lesbianism is generated in the vicinity of the diegesis as an effect of the film's system of spatial and temporal editing. Violet's sexuality, like Corky's, is cinematic.

Notes

1   D.A. Miller, 'Anal *Rope*', in Diana Fuss (ed.), *Inside/Out: Lesbian Theories, Gay Theories* (London and New York: Routledge, 1991), p. 137.
2   Ellis Hanson (ed.), *Out Takes: Essays on Queer Theory and Film* (Durham, NC and London: Duke University Press, 1999), p. 3.
3   Eve Kosofsky Sedgwick, *Epistemology of the Closet* (Berkeley, CA: University of California Press, 1990).
4   Hanson, *Out Takes*, p. 1.
5   See Miller, 'Anal *Rope*', pp. 121–3.
6   Ibid., p. 130.
7   Equally suggestive for my thinking about *Bound* are two discussions of Otto Preminger's *Laura* (1944) which also align the representational problem of homosexual visualization with contestations between narrative and spectacle in classical cinema. See Robert J. Corber, 'Resisting the lure of the commodity: *Laura* and the spectacle of the gay male body', in *Homosexuality in Cold War America: Resistance and the Crisis of Masculinity* (Durham, NC and London: Duke University Press, 1997), pp. 55–78; and Lee Edelman's 'Imagining the homosexual: *Laura* and the other face of gender', in *Homographesis: Essays in Gay Literary and Cultural Theory* (New York: Routledge, 1994), pp. 192–241.
8   See, for example, Mladen Dolar's 'Hitchcock's objects', in Slavoj Žižek (ed.), *Everything You Always Wanted to Know about Lacan (But Were Afraid to Ask Hitchcock)* (London and New York: Verso, 1992), pp. 31–46.
9   Miller, 'Anal *Rope*', p. 119.
10 The equation assumed between homosexuality and homicide recalls not only *Rope* but far less classical precedents such as *Black Widow* (Bob Rafelson, 1986), *Single White Female* (Barbet Schroeder, 1992) and *Basic Instinct* (Paul Verhoeven, 1992). For an attempt to theorize this tendency to depict lesbianism as a violence against men, see Lynda Hart, *Fatal Women: Lesbian Sexuality and the Mark of Aggression* (London: Routledge, 1994).

Part III

Racialization, queerness and desire

6 Racialized spectacle, exchange relations and the Western in *Johanna d'Arc of Mongolia*

Kristen Whissel

As the spectator watches and is entertained by the travellers in the dining-car sequence in Ulrike Ottinger's film *Johanna d'Arc of Mongolia* (1989), she notices that within the confined space of the coach there is a surplus of spectacle, a dizzying intersection of multiple forms of representation. Lady Windemere (Delphine Seyrig), British anthropologist, narrates the myths upon which Mongolian customs are based; the Kalinka Sisters (Jacinta, Elsa Nabu, Sevimbike Elibay), a 'Georgian Ladies' Combo, mouth tunes as various as the Andrews Sisters' hit Bei Meir Bist Du Schoen and a Russian dirge; American stage actress Fanny Ziegfeld (Gillian Scalici) sings the title song from her latest Broadway performance, *Green Dreams*, following Mickey Katz's (Peter Dem) Yiddish rendition of Al Jolson's Toot, Toot, Tootsie Goodbye. The extensive citation of cultural forms tempts one to read this sequence, as well as Ottinger's entire film, as a celebration of multiculturalism and ethnic difference facilitated by postmodern pastiche. Therese Grisham, for example, reads the film as emphasizing 'singularities over totalities, exchanges between cultures over purity as the basis of culture, and the crucial role minorities and nomadism play in effecting cultural transfer'.[1] Brenda Longfellow reads the film as 'an invitation to [a] phantastical voyage and eroticized encounter with an Other. The narrative subject and the spectator of Ottinger's film do not defend themselves against difference: they let difference in and allow themselves to be transformed in the process'.[2] The cultural transfer and transformation taking place in the diegesis seem to be a result of an avant-garde text inflected by a politics of multiculturalism. I would like to offer a very different reading of this film, one suggesting that *Johanna d'Arc of Mongolia* does not subvert traditionally racist cinematic representations of racial difference. Rather, Ottinger's film participates in the cinema's traditional process of producing, reproducing and organizing historical conceptions of racial and ethnic difference from the position of dominant Anglo-American and northern European culture.

The cinema has traditionally rejected a legalistic definition of race that depends upon 'blood' in favour of a visual production of racial or ethnic difference. Within such a system, 'racial difference' becomes visible through spectacle: an excess of visual signifiers of 'race' that contrast with a relatively non-spectacular representation of Anglo-American and northern European cultures.[3] As I will discuss later, this system of visual organization has allowed the cinema to manage some of the contradictions arising from racial classification by establishing historically variable semiotic criteria for such categorization. Classical Hollywood films, for example, abided by certain codes that determined which characters, despite their legal racial status, could be accommodated within Anglo-western culture and which characters could not. Thus a character's racial identity was determined both by his or her appearance and by participation in certain highly coded behaviours or actions. *Johanna d'Arc of Mongolia* follows the historical trajectory of such classification, but inverts the denigrated value traditionally assigned to racial difference by *overvaluing* it. And it is important to understand that this apparent overvaluation of a previously subordinated category derives from the cultural logic of neo-imperialism. It is this shift, misinterpreted as a break, that accounts for the film's positive critical reception.

Episodes of spectacle structure the film, and are offered up as a means of effecting cultural synthesis. Indeed, the film climaxes with the traveller's participation in a Mongolian summer festival. The participatory logic of Ottinger's racialized spectacle constitutes a movement away from a more explicitly violent classificatory logic typified by the representation of race in Hollywood genres such as the Western. The visualization of race in *Johanna d'Arc of Mongolia* marks a shift in which white Anglo-western 'participation' in racial difference is a point of textual idealization that reflects the contradictory racial politics of what is popularly known as multiculturalism.[4] Spectacle becomes the means through which ethnicity and race are the means by which Anglo-western women *temporarily* and pleasurably participate in racial and ethnic difference. According to this logic, 'racial integration' comes to signify a form of commodity exchange in which the Anglo-western middle class comes to know another culture by sampling its food, dress and art frequently in lieu of understanding the social forces that underpin racism (class relations, patriarchy and imperialism). Under such a system, racial difference takes up a distinct position within capitalism: 'race' is aligned with production in the sense that it is 'performed' for an Anglo-western culture that simply *is* and consumes. The final voiceover of the film indicates the cultural legacy in which we may situate Ottinger's film: we learn that following the travellers' return from Mongolia, Lady Windemere publishes an acclaimed book entitled *7×77: Observations on the Secret History of the Mongols*; Fanny Ziegfeld 'appears in the hit musical *Transmongolian* for two and a half years'; the Kalinkas are awarded the 'coveted Sandstorm Medal with flag and star which distinguishes them as deserving cultural workers in the unremitting struggle for international understanding'; and Johanna and the Princess open an exquisite Mongolian restaurant in Paris. Multiculturalism – which I shall call 'cultural exchange' throughout this essay, simply because this term foregrounds a relationship to capitalism and its uneven exchange relations – ultimately facilitates the production and reproduction of the racial difference in commodity-spectacle forms (the revelatory ethnography, the hit musical, authentic cuisine) for Anglo-western consumption. Herein lies the film's overarching continuity with traditional cinematic representations of racial difference: in order to sustain a fascination with 'foreign' cultures, racialized spectacle must not question the subordinate status of certain groups, and it therefore becomes invested in preserving their peripheral position.

It is in this context that we must reconsider the *mutuality* of exchange and transformation that both Grisham and Longfellow suggest is the linchpin of the film. The film's status as a western phantasy suggests that only after the social relations governing contemporary racial politics have been disavowed can otherwise problematic racial politics be reinscribed in an idealized form. Predictably, this strategy produces a series of contradictions in the film. A conflation of the generic conventions of the travelogue and the ethnographic film allows *Johanna d'Arc of Mongolia* to displace the social formation in which racism has been most problematically circumscribed in recent history: the nation. Thus I agree with Brenda Longfellow that the film works to 'construct a space for the spectator as a space for the heterogeneity'. I also agree that: 'This space is represented not so much as a site of conflicting discursive positions but as an invitation to phantastical voyage and eroticized encounter with an Other.'[5] But, it is crucial that we account for the historical and cultural determinants of such a phantasy in the late twentieth century. Why does this narrative require the westerner to leave her own country to find a 'space for heterogeneity' and to experience an 'eroticized encounter with the Other'?

I would like to suggest that this travel narrative is so pleasurable because it evades the question of racial politics at the national level, which have reached a violent crisis point – including riots, neo-Nazi activity and violence against refugees – in the years preceding and following the film's release. Ottinger relocates and eroticizes racial difference in a distant, pastoral setting: bourgeois travel displaces immigration as the dominant form by which cultural exchange occurs. Moreover, the visual system through which the rest of the filmic phantasy is encoded – the racialized spectacle – displaces the all too familiar and undeniable visibility of a horrific spec-tacularization of race in the popular media of those nations from which the travellers have departed. In the USA, this takes the shape of the representation of African-Americans through the spectacle of poverty, welfare and drug warfare; in Germany, France and Britain, through media scapegoating of guest workers, refugees and postcolonial subjects for economic hardship. In such discourse, racial and ethnic difference are not sites of productivity, but are represented as a parasitic drain on the livelihood of the nation. Needless to say, the media represent Anglo-western participation in this form of racialized spectacle as tragic, not pleasurable; the desire for a 'space of heterogeneity' is in reality a reactionary fear of the encroachment of the ghetto that popular culture tells us threatens the white middle class.

One might respond by arguing that Ottinger's utopia provides a much-needed space in the light of this historical context. Yet this utopic vision maintains visible traces of the historical problem it is trying to escape. That the film smoothes over an Anglo-western fear of dangerous racial difference is clear when the travellers' initial contact with the Mongolians is charged with an anxiety about racially determined violence. When they are taken from the train, Lady Windemere nervously warns her fellow travellers: 'If we obey their laws and customs we will be safe. Hospitality is sacred to them.' Such pleasurable and rewarding subordination to the customs of a foreign ethnicity, which is crucial to the film's exchange phantasy, inverts the dominant position westerners exercise in overseeing the social malintegration of 'foreigners' in their own countries. Ultimately, the thrilling prospect of being temporarily immersed in a foreign culture enables the travellers to pursue their much-discussed 'experience' in a way that they could not have had they remained on board the train or stayed at home. Thus, what begins as a kidnapping becomes a paid vacation at the Mongolians' summer campground. *Johanna d'Arc of Mongolia* might therefore be considered as a late twentieth-century version of the imperialist captivity narrative, in which white Americans and Europeans allow themselves to be subordinated to peripheral cultures temporarily, and to engage in the profitable production of difference once they return home.

In fact, the film's dependence on imperialist discourses that are apparently non-violent but nonetheless constitutive of imperialist culture makes it a pleasurable phantasy about cultural exchange. I would like to show how the aesthetic pleasure produced through displacement depends upon narrative forms that have traditionally provided alibis for western imperialism: the ethnographic film, the discourse of orientalism, and the captivity narrative. To suggest a starting point from within film history, I shall interpret *Johanna d'Arc of Mongolia* through one of the many generic forms the film cites: the Western. I shall identify neither a moral imperative from which Ottinger has strayed, nor an anti-imperialist aesthetic that she might have otherwise followed. Rather, I am interested in the relationship between the cinematic coding of racial difference and the cultural logic of late twentieth-century imperialism: how is this coding masked by the language and visualization of 'difference', 'multiculturalism' and 'exchange'?

In its opening sequences, *Johanna d'Arc of Mongolia* situates itself within the genre of the travelogue and the discourse of what Edward Said has termed orientalism.[6] The film opens in Lady Windemere's luxury car aboard the Trans-Siberian. In voiceover narration, she muses on the history of the railroad. As the camera pans across the Chinese watercolours and ink sketches adorning the walls of the coach – objects that inevitably become a part of orientalizing representations of the East – she thinks, 'In 1581 Yermak Timofeyevich traverses the Urals with his ferocious Cossacks and sees for the first time.' The film posits this crossing as the initiation of Western perception and representation of the 'Orient'. As Lady Windemere's voiceover speaks of 'seeing for the first time', we realize that such originary vision is now impossible, for we are ourselves looking at the exoticized and minimalist images and forms of representation that have become cliched – within the discourse of orientalism, and that subsequently inform any western representation of, in this case, Mongolia. Windemere's narration reinforces this nostalgia for originary vision.

It's always the first time, things read – the imagination – the confrontation with reality. Must imagination shun the encounter with reality, or are they enamoured of each other? Can they form an alliance? Does the encounter transform them? Do they exchange roles? It's always the first time. Yermak Timofeyevich crosses the border line dividing Europe and Asia and beholds for the first time the unending verdant expanses, the myth of the green void.

As the art on the walls suggests, 'reality' is always transformed by the imagination, and the two do change roles: the West's phantasy of the Orient becomes the reality of the East – the inevitable lens through which the Western subject 'sees [it] for the first time'. Thus, as Windemere narrates, the score momentarily changes from nineteenth-century baroque music to oriental chords, signifying the conferring of meaning on the landscape, the pastness of its status as 'void', and the movement from initial perception to the representation. Indeed, Windemere thinks of the pioneers who themselves placed signs on the taiga:

With ingenious means they placed signs in the land of the void. An initial attempt to tame the wilderness with the aid of cultivated nature . . . the written signs altered their colours with the changing seasons and could be seen from great distances. The attempt to place a sign on the void, a mark. . . . Here the fears of the travellers whom the wind otherwise carried unchecked across the endless green plains of the taiga were allayed for the moment. And now, much more than a sign, this line leading directly through the slumbering wilderness. As simply and as easily as you can travel with your finger across the map from Europe to Asia, the Trans-Siberian follows this line.

This 'writing' rids the travellers of the fear of being swallowed into the nothingness, the no-place of the East. These 'natural signs' are replaced by the railroad line that ostensibly unifies the West with the East but that also functions as a borderline sharply delineating these poles. As this scene suggests, the railroad is 'so much more than a sign'; it is the vehicle for an order of signification that organizes East and West into a hierarchical relation. In signifying the necessary distance between East and West, the railroad materializes and sets into motion the binary opposition of 'home' and 'foreign' that structures many of the traditional narrative forms of the cinema: the ethnographic film, the Western, and the travel adventure film.

A rigorous distinction between East and West seems intact when we enter the overcrowded car in which Johanna (Ines Sastre), a young French woman of Asian descent, begins the first leg of her trip. The sequence opens with a shot of Johanna riding in a luggage rack of a car jammed with peasants, livestock and Mongolian soldiers. The segregation of Mongolian and Chinese passengers from the Europeans and Americans in different cars duplicates the East–West dichotomy that structures the discourse of orientalism. The train therefore materializes the West's contradictory notions of space in the East: vast open spaces, a mythologized non-space or a 'void' outside of the train that lies in tension with images of enclosed spaces teeming with the impoverished masses. Lady Windemere's entrance into the car underscores the sense that this scene is filtered through a western imagination. An aria from a Chinese opera coming from Johanna's Walkman scores for the sequence, and the Mongolian soldiers sing along. As Lady Windemere reaches the area immediately beneath Johanna, the train – and the narrative – come to a screeching halt. The camera cuts to a shot of the station outside, which consists of a highly artificial set where a Russian military band plays and peasant women sell their goods. The station is both marketplace and stage: the band, the peasants and the shaman who sells medicinal roots are all excessively costumed and strike staged poses as the frame freezes. Superimposed on the screen is the cast of characters that attempts to account for nearly everyone appearing in the film. The identification of characters as '1 proud goat owner' or '6 sturdy Mongolian wrestlers' in lieu of the actors' and actresses' real (or stage) names suggests that these figures represent cliched characters acting on what Said has called the 'stage' that constitutes the western imaginative geography of the Orient.[7] The list functions as a disruptive device meant to prevent the viewer from reading the representations of the Mongolians as 'true' or 'real'. Although this technique allows Ottinger to avoid essentializing Mongolian culture, it ultimately facilitates a movement in the opposite direction, toward a representation of race through spectacle.[8] This freeze-frame moves the visualization of Mongolia along a trajectory that began with the 'writing on the void' (making legible the visual nothingness of the Asian landscape in which the western traveller fears losing her/himself) to the reproduced objects in the orientalist's collection, to one in which racial difference is produced through a conflation of the hyper-visual and the consumable. Ottinger reproduces Mongolia as spectacle according to this last model as a stage and marketplace produced for consumption by western perception and participation.

The film shifts from the perception of, to participation in, the racialized spectacle by deploying the generic conventions of the Western. Hence, the camera cuts to a conversation between Frau Vohwinkel and Fanny Ziegfeld in the dining car. When Vohwinkel asks, 'You mean by conferring the appearance of objectivity on paternalism, oppression and dependency?' and Fanny replies, 'Yes, the cards were always cunningly stacked against women', the two women cite patriarchy's naturalization. Yet this line of thought is quickly subsumed beneath Fanny's discussion of her latest show. 'Speaking of stacked cards', Fanny begins,

> On Broadway this fall we're launching a new musical, a crazy story about four women . . . Dressed as well-bred ladies, we are a hit in the cities where we appear and take the place by storm. It ends with a stage-coach ambush. We disarm the Terror of Dakota and expose him as a braggart. An amusing Western satire.

Johanna d'Arc of Mongolia is itself 'an amusing Western satire' in which Fanny Ziegfeld plays a role. Fanny's introduction of the Western constitutes a crucial moment in this film. The racial politics of the Western coincides with those of the captivity narrative, the travelogue and the discourse of orientalism. Each narrates an anxiety over the collapse of the imaginary boundaries that separate East from West, home from foreign, and 'whiteness' from 'racial difference'. In order to encompass traces of all three narrative paradigms, the film reverses the formulaic east-to-west geographical and narrative movement of the Western and shuttles the European and American heroines, by railroad, into the heart of Mongolia.

While the dining-car sequence sets a general pattern of spectacle and display that cannot be assigned only to the Mongolians, a crucial difference between the westerners' and the Mongolians' relationship to the visual must be taken into account. Prior to the dining-car sequence, the Anglo-western women are introduced individually through formal devices, such as an interior monologue, that affirm their possession of autonomous subjectivity. Whereas the westerners perform *songs* in the dining-car sequence, the Mongolians, from the moment of their introduction, perform and produce *racial and ethnic difference* for the westerners' pleasurable consumption. Thus, the westerners are not satisfied with seeing one another perform in the dining car. Fanny Ziegfeld claims to have left the US theatre scene 'in order to see something new', and appeases her melancholia over visual 'monotony and monochromy' by singing about 'Green Dreams', suggesting that her *ennui* might be appeased through exposure to 'colour'. Lady Windemere's romanticized vision of eastern femininity and her ethnographic investigation of Mongolian culture situates the Mongolians even more firmly within the context of racial spectacle. Each time the train stops, Windemere seeks picturesque *tableaux-vivants* of eastern women: she describes to Johanna 'a beautiful young Buriat girl with long plaits, even longer than yours . . . wearing a fur frock with colourful embroidery; in her hand a bowl of fiery red kernels, in her left hand a horsehair-whisk to chase away the flies'. Indeed, when she first sees Johanna perched in the luggage rack, she asks her to pose, saying 'Wonderful, wonderful – do stay that way for just a moment. You remind me of that legendary Mongolian princess who could fly over the desert and steppes on her magic sword.'

Significantly, Ottinger uses the same conventions in her cinematic presentation of the Mongolians and alternates between filming the Mongolians in striking, stylized compositions and the conventions of the ethnographic film. Long panning shots produce breathtaking views of the Mongolian landscape, while closeups record the details of a ceremony or the construction of the yurts. The sheer accumulation of cultural details recorded by the camera and narrated by Lady Windemere results in a visual overvaluation of difference. These conventions combine to produce the racialized spectacle, an achievement that is realized through the film's narrative fulfilment of Lady Windemere's desire to 'witness the summer festival of the Mongols and the performances of their famous Geser-Khan epos'. Both Lady Windemere and Ottinger ultimately romanticize Mongolia as an aesthetically compelling living portrait of ethnic and racial difference in a pastoral space outside of the troubled formation of the western nation.

Although we may align Ottinger's vision of Mongolia with Lady Windemere's, Ottinger frequently satirizes older forms of imperialist discourse through her characters, thereby distancing their vision and her own. Her parody of nineteenth-century rational imperialism in the figure of Frau Vohwinkel is perhaps the funniest, yet it fails to take on a critical function because the alternative she offers through Vohwinkel's transformation makes the same shift towards a neo-imperialist model of cultural exchange that governs the general trajectory of the film. Inside Vohwinkel's coach, 'All the signs and symbols of the West's linearity, its sense of its own superiority, detached objectivity, and progress over and against the East' are in working order.[9] The black-and-white photographs of the railway's construction that adorn the walls of her berth are a visible manifestation of her interpretation of the Trans-Siberian as a triumph of modernity and a symbol of progress. As she reads aloud the history of the Trans-Siberian from her *Baedeker* — which she imagines will provide her with 'all the relevant facts behind this greenness' — she marvels:

> When you consider, just the task of organizing, the transportation, food supply, lodging, medicine, sanitary facilities. Back then everything which today is done by machines or calculated by computers had to be performed by engineers and workers. An incredible feat!

A more violent form of such rational progressivism eventually becomes linked to the Russian officer who has a short stay on the train. He is the descendent of one of the 'great reformers' of Russia and founders of the railroad, and the train is conveying him to Kultuk to reinforce the borders dividing East from West: 'Some nomadic families still don't observe the borders and are continually clashing with our soldiers', he says. 'I'm supposed to look after things.' Although the film disavows the Russian officer's militarism, it takes up an uncritical relationship to neo-imperialist cultural practices which, conversely, map consumable 'culture' onto certain marginalized groups, filter racial difference through the lenses of tourism and commodification, and thus set up an idealized form of 'race' that Anglo-western culture is pleased to tolerate.

Infected by Lady Windemere's tendency to understand Mongolian culture as a racialized spectacle, both Frau Vohwinkel and Johanna mistake the ambush for a display of Mongolian culture staged for their visual pleasure. After the camera cuts to the Mongolians outside the train, Johanna asks Lady Windemere, 'Are those the mounted games you were talking about?' In turn, Vohwinkel exclaims, 'Look, a camel caravan. How romantic! How thoughtful to stop here so that we can better observe this exciting spectacle.' This is a moment of irony and intertextuality: between these exclamations, the camera cuts to long shots of bands of Mongolian women emerging on horseback on top of and from behind cliffs, drawing bows and arrows and swords. At this moment, the genres of the Western and the travelogue most forcefully intersect.

The Mongolians evoke the iconography of Native Americans appearing before an ambush in a Western, and the choreographed symmetry of their movements as they draw their swords recalls the image of 'exotic oriental' dances and military exercises. Only after Fanny informs Vohwinkel that they are being ambushed, and only after Lady Windemere gravely explains that 'this is no game', are the naive travellers violently wrenched from the travelogue's scopophilia. Though viewing Mongolia from the train had facilitated Vohwinkel's desire for a safe distance from the Mongolians, it had also insulated Lady Windemere and Johanna from a true travel 'experience'. The shift from travelogue to captivity narrative, and from distance to immersion, is crucial to the film's racial politics. The re-emergence of the West in the figure that was for decades Hollywood's primary representative of racial and ethnic difference forces me to return to the question I posed at the opening of this essay: Why does this phantasy narrative require the Westerner to leave her own country to find a 'space for heterogeneity' and to experience an 'eroticized encounter with the Other'? Whereas earlier I offered a sociological explanation, I would now like to offer an analysis from within film history.

This promise of a pleasurable participation in the racial spectacle constitutes a shift in the representation of race in the cinema. In this respect, *Johanna d'Arc of Mongolia* contributes to, rather than subverts, one of cinema's traditional cultural functions. Racialized spectacle in film in general, and the Western in particular, has historically helped redefine dominant (white) culture and racial difference in moments of social change. That traces of the Western emerge when the travellers are forced into direct contact with the Mongolians is not surprising, for the Western is a genre that most visibly encodes and negotiates race through spectacle. A closer look at a specific example of the Western will help us to understand how *Johanna d'Arc of Mongolia* takes up the racial and sexual politics of that genre.

John Ford's *The Searchers* (1956) performs the historical function of reorganizing racial categories after dramatizing the problem of miscegenation and the absence in American culture of a racially 'pure' whiteness. The film ends with rein-corporation of two characters into the family home despite the fact that they initially represent an intolerable racial mixture. Ford stages the film in 'Texican' territory and in so doing suggests that the liminality of the frontier breaks down the otherwise rigid system of oppositions that structure the Western. Set in the years immediately following the Civil War, the film's anxiety over rape, miscegenation and the genetic determination of race acts as a synecdoche for larger concerns over the redefinition of race in the (newly) United States following the legal abolition of slavery. This anxiety, in turn, marks the era of the Civil Rights movement when the film was produced and released. Just as Ottinger shifts the contemporary problem of 'spaces of [racial] heterogeneity' outside of the national boundaries of Germany and onto a foreign land, Ford displaces his drama onto the margins of the nation, the frontier, and relocates 'race' in the figure of a hypersexual, hyperviolent Native American. Like *Johanna d'Arc of Mongolia*, *The Searchers* resolves its cultural dilemma by redefining the relationship between dominant white culture and peripheral minority cultures by transforming race into spectacle.

The Searchers begins with an ambush of the Edwards' ranch and the kidnapping of white women by a Comanche raiding party. Debbie Edwards' (Natalie Wood) status shifts from an 'object-to-be-recovered' to a 'hunted object' once she reaches child-bearing age while held captive by the Comanche chief, Scar (Harry Brandon). In the mind of Ethan Edwards (John Wayne), she has become Comanche – the racial and cultural opposite of Laurie Jorgensen (Vera Miles), who represents future American domesticity. Or, even worse, she is now Comanche yet still white, which for Ethan is a seemingly intolerable collapsing of differences. Yet by the end of the film, Debbie is reintegrated into the white family home. In this respect, Martin Pawley's (Jeffrey Hunter) status within the film's racial economy – he is an orphan living in the Edwards' household who is one-eighth Comanche – is as important as Debbie's. The film works hard to separate him from his sweetheart, Laurie: Martin returns to her only twice during the seven-year search, and each is nearly married to another during the interim – Martin to a 'pure' Native American and Laurie to a 'pure' Anglo-Saxon. They are reunited only at the end of the film, only after the narrative has reworked the terms of the integration of racial difference into dominant white culture.

The film's project of shifting the criteria for defining race from 'blood' to spectacle is made clear by the film's climax, when Ethan scalps the Comanche chief, Scar. Scalping is a metonymic function of the rape of white women by Scar in the film. The ambush sets off a chain of events that include the rape and scalping of Lucy Wards (Pippa Scott) by the Comanche, and the ensuing revelation that Martin's mother was also scalped by Scar. Scalping exists as an activity that defines one's position as *farther west* than the acceptable liminality of the frontier. The power that the act of scalping has over the visual in this film underscores the idea that the classification of race depends upon spectacle: so horrifying is the image of Lucy's corpse, and so uncanny is the image of the brave who cross-dresses in her clothes (an action that mocks the definition of racial liminality that the film seeks to legitimate), that Ford leaves the viewer to imagine the racialized spectacle of Lucy's death her/himself. Scalping, therefore, represents a racial spectacle that is invoked by the camera and characters, but which is so radically other – or racialized – that it must remain unseen. The invisibility of this negative phantasy of 'going native' is the inverse of white participation in the racialized spectacle that constitutes the phantasy of *Johanna d'Arc of Mongolia*. As I will show below, the hypervisibility of Ottinger's racialized spectacle is enabled by a visual dynamic that allows her travellers to fulfil an idealized phantasy of participating in racial difference without having to go native.

Ethan becomes 'Comanche' only after he scalps Scar. This change in the visual positioning of the white male hero in turn forces a shift in all of the other figures against which it is set in opposition. Following the scalping, Ethan chases Debbie. Shot from inside the opening of a cave, this sequence echoes the famous opening and closing shots of the film in which the frontier is shot from inside the Edwards and Jorgensen households. The incorporation of the landscape into the position of interiority that initially indicated a crucial division between domestic space and the frontier suggests that the terms defining racial difference have shifted. We know from the final shot of the film, in which Ethan approaches and then turns away from the Jorgensen household, that these terms exile him from the white domestic sphere. Furthermore, we must consider the shift in location of American domesticity from the very WASP-ish 'Edwards' household to the Jorgensen household. Despite his northern European descent, Lars Jorgensen is coded as an 'immigrant' by virtue of his very heavy accent and his inability to read and write in English – indeed, Debbie's English, despite her years in captivity, is much clearer than his. The ethnic identity of the Jorgensen family is therefore a step away from 'Anglo-American' on the film's spectrum of racial and ethnic difference. With this shift, Ford seems to suggest that the pure 'Anglo' American household is no longer possible given this necessary (although limited) incorporation of racial difference into dominant white American culture. He thus destroys the Edwards household at the beginning of the film, and replaces it with this immigrant, but nevertheless 'white', home at the end of the film.

Debbie's reintegration is not based solely on Ethan's new status as Comanche; she must also fit into the visual economy of the dominant cultural order. The liminality suggested by the shot from inside the cave corresponds to the hybridity of Debbie's appearance. Her features are Anglo-American, but she wears Native-American style braids and clothing, as well as dark makeup. Yet if we compare her appearance to the group of other captive white women amongst whom Ethan and Martin search for Debbie, the seemingly contradictory nature of the film's racial economy becomes explicable. In contrast to the very orderliness of Debbie's physical appearance and her perfect English, the former captives have dishevelled hair, babble incoherently, and look about with expressions of wide-eyed lunacy. Despite the fact that they appear to be 'whiter' than Debbie (each has comparatively fair skin and hair), their 'savagery' leads Ethan to declare with disgust that they are irretrievably 'Comanche'. Ford suggests that on the surface of Debbie's masquerade there is evidence of a subject whose 'whiteness' is signified by an orderly self that refuses racial spectacle. Thus Debbie is brought back into the domestic sphere because the outward signs of her racial difference or, more precisely, her 'ethnicity', are organized through the language and body of the idealized figure of domestic femininity.

Therefore, it is not Debbie but 'Look' (Beulah Archuletta), the Native American to whom Martin Pawley is unwittingly betrothed, which functions as the term of non-incorporation. The name given to her by Ethan and Martin is fitting, for it is at the level of the spectacle that her exclusion from dominant culture is determined. Her momentary occupation of the space of domesticity designated for Laurie Jorgensen is, in fact, the joke of the film. Look signifies racial difference through her language, costume and body, and her large size corresponds to neither the maternal nor the virginal bodies of the film's idealized figures of white femininity. The slapstick routine that documents the tale of Look's murder – a flashback sequence narrated by Laurie as she reads Martin's letter, punctuated with the belly-laughs of Laurie's suitor – produces the spectacle of her sexual and racial difference. Look is the defining opposite of Laurie and Debbie, the limit of miscegenated domesticity and a signifier of race that cannot be admitted into the Anglo-American domestic sphere. Thus *The Searchers* negotiates the criteria by which an emerging national culture defines itself against racial integration. Similar visual criteria constitute the racial politics of *Johanna d'Arc of Mongolia* and identify both the continuity and difference between this film and Ford's. While *The Searchers* details the terms of integration and non-integration through the violence of the *non-participatory* racialized spectacle, Ottinger's film promises a temporary, pleasurable and profitable participation in racial difference through the participatory racialized spectacle.

Non-participation, distance and anxiety over the integration of racial difference are characteristic of the spectacle of race in relation to constructions of national identity. The contrast between the narrative violence that emerges from the process of defining a white nation with the narrative pleasure that emerges from the process of international 'cultural exchange' is crucial. We must, therefore, understand the logic behind the racialized spectacle in order to understand how *Johanna d'Arc of Mongolia* is complicit with the racial politics of the Western. As I have implied, the Western expresses nostalgia for a time when the frontier represented a liminal national site, when the division between civilization and savagery, frequently marked through racial difference, provided the impetus for the extermination of Native Americans and the resulting affirmation of the authority of Anglo-western culture.

Renato Rosaldo has termed this longing for the other that one has participated in destroying 'imperialist nostalgia', and has theorized the particular subjectivity that such nostalgia accommodates. Speaking of the colonial agent who mourns the transformation of the foreign culture he has violently destroyed, Rosaldo argues, 'The relatively benign character of most nostalgia facilitates imperialist nostalgia's capacity to transform the responsible colonial agent into an innocent bystander.'[10]

Both The Searchers and Johanna d'Arc of Mongolia create a historically situated, nostalgic vision that allows for a doubly invested 'innocence'. A discourse of innocence structures the narratives of both The Searchers (an Indian attack on a vulnerable ranch, atrocities committed against women and children) and Johanna d'Arc of Mongolia (women kidnapped from a train). In the complex overlapping of genres, Johanna d'Arc of Mongolia plays upon the innocence and nostalgia afforded by the Western by transposing the liminal topography of the American frontier and the iconography of the Western to the East. This simultaneous acknowledgement and displacement of a cinematically mythologized national racial politics invests the film with innocence in relation to that problem. Like Ford's displacement of the racial and historical specificity of the Civil Rights movement, Ottinger's double displacement is crucial to the film's function as phantasy. I say 'double' because, on the one hand, the allusion refers to a racial violence that is specifically American, positing the USA, rather than Germany, as a (mythologized) space of racial conflict; on the other hand, the transposition of the cinematic iconography of the Native American signals another displacement through the construction of a narrative space outside the troubled borders of nationality in which a pleasurable confrontation with racial difference can be represented. Traces of the Western enrich the iconography of the Orient by doubly investing in the visual pleasure and reassuring innocence this displacement brings about.

This racialized spectacle is preceded by the nostalgia inscribed in the images and language of Lady Windemere's wistful monologue on 'seeing for the first time' at the opening of the film. Like Rosaldo's imperialist agent, Lady Windemere longs for the moment in which difference of the Orient was first perceived, when the West was poised on the threshold of the imperial era, and when racial difference was simply a pleasurable image held at a distance for the Anglo-western subject. Ottinger's representation of racial difference has its legacy in imperialist nostalgia and the Western, but ultimately derives from the historical context of neo-imperialism. Thus, just as the film cites and then quickly leaves behind Windemere's nostalgia for an irretrievably lost past, so does Ottinger invoke the anxiety-provoking image of the Native American/Mongolian, so that this anxiety can be jettisoned in favour of the pleasurable participatory racialized spectacle. Expecting an encounter with a mythologized Orient from the distance of a train, Ottinger's travellers suddenly find themselves the innocent victims of the sort of captivity narrative found in many Westerns. However, they quickly move from being captives to guests or, more precisely, unwitting participant observers.

Shortly after the women are kidnapped, the Princess Ulan Iga and her all-female court are intercepted on the taiga by the royal court of the Kharatsin, a patriarchal nomadic group that has ambushed and plundered Ulan Iga in the past. It is for this reason that the women were taken from the train, implying that they were originally kidnapped for fairly sinister purposes. Yet this encounter entails a capitulation by patriarchy and, in the words of the Princess, its 'wiles and insidious intrigue'. Having fallen on difficult times since the ambush, the Kharatsin admit to having been driven by 'pride and arrogance' and return the goods, herds and yurts (the mobile houses of the nomadic Mongolians) stolen from Ulan Iga. As Ulan Iga indicates to the women, the subsequent relationship between the westerners and the Mongolians hinges on this capitulation: 'We ambushed you out of necessity. Please be our guests now in this time of plenty and return of good fortune to the yurts', she says. The film playfully suggests that whereas patriarchy initially forces an oppositional relationship between the women, its fall allows them to come together. Likewise, Longfellow's interpretation of the film assumes that the capitulation of patriarchy in the film coincides with a capitulation of racism. Furthermore, she argues that race functions as a substitute for sexual difference in the film's lesbian romances. Joining her argument to one made by B. Ruby Rich, Longfellow suggests that 'race occupies the place vacated by the gender difference in heterosexual coupling'. Racial difference, therefore, becomes a point of desire in the film, leading Longfellow to suggest that '*Johanna d'Arc of Mongolia* repeats the erotic scenario of orientalism, mediating lesbian desire through the desire for a racial/cultural other'.[11] Yet this interpretation fails to account for the film's romantic pairings – Vohwinkel and Fanny, Princess Ulan Iga and Johanna – and seems only to account for Lady Windemere's tendency to romanticize and eroticize Asian femininity. Furthermore, this suggests that in the absence of patriarchy, orientalism ceases to be racist, particularly when mediated by lesbian desire. Although the film encourages this reading, it must be acknowledged that while patriarchy depends upon racism (as we understand from *The Searchers*) and racism is fuelled by patriarchy, the two function differently in both their discursive and material dimensions. Although the racialized spectacle that mediates the encounter between the westerners and the Mongolians is a vestige of the racial politics of the Western, it nevertheless functions in the apparent absence of patriarchy. In fact, the Kharatsin's surrender is a plot device that allows the film to shift away from the captivity narrative to a narrative of cultural exchange. Undoubtedly, this signifies a historical shift in the representation of racial and ethnic difference that depends upon a change in sexual politics. One might simply consider the fact that unlike *The Searchers*, miscegenation is not the cultural anxiety that motivates Ottinger's film. Indeed, the film's phantasy is that of an easy negotiation of racial and ethnic difference by Anglo-western women. In order to fulfil this phantasy, *Johanna d'Arc of Mongolia* depends on *The Searchers'* movement away from a genetic definition of race and its redefinition of racial difference according to visual criteria.

Once again, Vohwinkel's 'misreading' of her situation according to an older narrative paradigm foregrounds the film's racial politics. Following the capitulation, she worries, 'I have no husband, who will pay ransom for me?' Vohwinkel interprets their situation as if it were a captivity narrative. One of the Kalinkas, Moira Orfei, responds, 'But we have all just witnessed an overwhelming steppe-drama. So who wants to speak of time or annoyances?'. Moira Orfei's emphasis on 'drama', as well as the breathtaking shots of the procession of the yurts, the messenger's musical performance and the ensuing bonfire celebration, resituate Mongolia as a stage for cultural exchange. The use of real time, long shots, and a wide-angle lens, lends an ethnographic realism to these dramas which contrasts with the now seemingly inadequate campy artificiality of the dining-car sequence – a realism which suggests that Mongolian culture is, paradoxically, essentially spectacular. And, as the subsequent invitation by Ulan Iga suggests, this racialized spectacle is one in which the travellers may also participate.

Following the Kharatsin's capitulation, participatory spectacles mediate various encounters between the Mongolians and their guests, resulting in varying degrees of threat and pleasure for the westerners. In their capacity as critiques of patriarchal narrative, some of these episodes expose the logic by which the Western and the travelogue/ethnography inscribe femininity as civilization. The most self-reflexive of these episodes involves Frau Vohwinkel, whose character development traces the undoing of her investment in the workings of such narrative logic. After Fanny and Vohwinkel wash their clothes in a creek near the Mongolians' summer camp, Vohwinkel runs a clothes line from her yurt to one of the royal flags posted nearby, and begins to hang her laundry, humming away like the proverbial happy housewife. When a group of Mongolian women nearby see what she is doing, they chase her in circles around the taiga, brandishing burning wood from a nearby fire. This moment of slapstick comedy is, in fact, an ironic citation of the function of white women in the Western as signifiers of domesticity, culture and closure. For the mobile yurts represent not stability and waiting but mobility, not closure but the possibility of unending return: as we find out at the end of the film, European-Mongolian women often return to the yurts each summer 'to preserve in some measure the illusion of a free nomadic life'. After seeing the yurts moving across the taiga for the first time, Fanny Ziegfeld, watchdog for the American appropriation of foreign culture says, 'Now I know where Americans stole the idea of mobile homes.'

The irony of this observation is, of course, the non-mobility of mobile homes, in terms of their function as the static domestic site of the homestead. The laundry outside the yurts therefore presents a double threat to the visual and narrative economy of the film. On the one hand, as a signifier for US domesticity, it threatens to transform the mobility and non-closure of the yurts into the domestic site of the Western, and thus threatens to resurrect the binarism between homestead and Indian camp central to the *non-participatory* racialized spectacle in the Western.

In turn, the resurrected homestead would act as a flag hailing both the male hero's arrival from an offscreen adventure, initiating the inevitable closure that is signalled by his return. Thus, when Lady Windemere says to Johanna, who rides up to the flustered group following the incident, 'Don't do your laundry', Ottinger is not simply making an appeal to the roles women play in film. Rather, this moment should be read as an articulation of the film's self-conscious evolution from western non-participation to participation in the racialized spectacle. I say 'evolution' because the retention of slapstick in the representation of the 'other woman', who poses a (comedic) threat to a white, domestic femininity, recalls the narrative relationship between Look and Laurie Jorgensen in *The Searchers*, and reminds us that the film's racial politics are evolutionary rather than subversive. Just as the non-participatory racialized spectacle maintains a distance between the Anglo-American woman and the woman of colour, the participatory racialized spectacle depends upon the resolution of these two formerly opposed figures. *Johanna d'Arc of Mongolia* does not collapse the opposition, but simply brings these figures together. As I will argue in greater detail below, this reframing maintains a crucial distance that preserves the westerners' self/other or subject/object relation to the Mongolians while it simultaneously allows for the proximity that is required for their participation in the racialized spectacle.

In a later episode involving Frau Vohwinkel, Ottinger critiques the displacement of culturally constructed notions of femininity onto the landscape and parodies this banal narrative convention by literalizing it. Frau Vohwinkel wanders away from the summer camp and enters an underground laministic temple. After performing several rituals, she is 'born' from this subterranean womb-like space through a rupture in the taiga. The money we see pressed into the walls of the temple (to which Vohwinkel contributes her own two marks) underscores the status of this moment as a convention of mass entertainment. Thus, the laman who stages Vohwinkel's rebirth does not possess any *mysterious* power, as Lady Windemere later speculates; rather, his power is the same as the institutional power of the ticket vendor at a movie theatre. Instead, it is Vohwinkel's participation in the commercial form of the ritualized spectacle that enables her 'conversion', eases her anxiety over racial and ethnic difference and helps incorporate her into 'mystical' Mongolian culture. Participation in the commodified racialized spectacle redefines the pleasure of an encounter with difference as that which subtly reinforces the self/other dichotomy while facilitating Anglo-western pleasure in experiencing a form of commercial 'cultural exchange'. The association of this shift to commercialized leisure, and the traces of capital in the ritualized spectacle, precede the cultural logic whereby travellers who temporarily immerse themselves in foreign cultures and thus 'understand' them are awarded coveted national prizes, win lucrative positions on the bestseller list, and perform in smash-hit musicals documenting and reproducing an 'encounter with otherness'.

Later, Ottinger focuses on the inscription of femininity as what Laura Mulvey has termed the 'fetishized spectacle'.[12] In a tight closeup, we see the reflected image of Fanny Ziegfeld's face framed in the tiny mirror of her toilet case, surrounded by compacts, lipsticks and other accoutrements of the fetish. As she shrieks, gurgles and bugs out her eyes, it becomes apparent that we are looking on as she does her acting exercises. When the camera pulls back to a full shot of Fanny at her vanity, her image in the mirror is replaced by the face of a Mongolian woman who peeks through a window, thus reversing the direction of the voyeuristic gaze of the West at the exoticized, orientalized female body. When Fanny turns and directly engages her audience (the camera pulls back to reveal four women at the window), she performs for the giggling Mongolians by putting a cork in her mouth and singing the scale. Fanny's performance parodies the tendency of the ethnographer's camera to transform the mundane routine of its subjects into bizarre ritual: for the moment, Fanny performs her role as racial other. The mirroring achieved by the shot/reverse-shot suggests a moment when mutual understanding and exchange is achieved through an ironic play on the spectacle of femininity and race. Yet, as Fanny tells Vohwinkel in the dining-car sequence, she is to star in an 'amusing Western satire', linking her to the racial politics of the Western. Following her return, she performs in the hit musical *Transmongolian*. The trajectory of Fanny's career seems to track the movement I have suggested is characteristic of this film. That is to say, like Ottinger, Fanny cites and then leaves the Western behind in order to rework the way in which race will function within western cultural productions. Thus the irony and mutuality of the encounter between these two different images of the fetishized spectacle are ultimately subverted by the film's overarching racial politics.

Shot in the style of the ethnographic film (consistent use of the wide-angle lens and the long take), the very long festival sequence is symptomatic of this shift in the representation of race. As the festival games begin, several Mongolian women playfully wage battle with, and ride hobby-horse style on, poles embossed with the images of the Kalinka Sisters. Initially viewing the festival timidly from its periphery, the singers are drawn into participation in the festivities. At this moment, the paradoxical visual dynamics of the participatory spectacle emerge: after the Westerners see themselves participating in this spectacle, it has fulfilled its promise of simultaneous distance from, and participation in, 'race'. The sight of their images moving through the spectacle allows the Kalinkas the contradictory but pleasurable position of being the subject and object of their own gaze: through a 'primitive' reproduction of their images, they are allowed the paradoxical privilege of viewing an image of their participation in the racialized spectacle even before they actually participate in the festivities. The simultaneity of spectatorship and participation affords the westerners a temporal and spatial distance between themselves and the Mongolians. In turn, this spacing gives priority to their position as spectating subjects and consumers, thus foreclosing the possibility that, despite their participation, the westerners will ever actually occupy the spectacularized position of 'race'. Unlike Ethan Edwards, the travellers do not have to go native in order to fulfil the film's phantasy.

While the Mongolians' invitation to join the festivities might also be read as signifying their legendary 'hospitality', we must wonder why the Westerners are incorporated into this spectacle and not the one which immediately precedes it and documents, in similar ethnographic style, a sheep-slaughtering ritual. Like the act of scalping in the Western, animal sacrifices in ethnographic films conflate 'race' with 'primitivism' through the camera's revelation of a hidden, bloody and 'barbaric' ritual. The representation of the careful blood-letting and dissection of the sheep's organs constitutes this sequence as a documentation of what Fatima Tobing Rony terms the 'ethnographic detail'. Tobing Rony argues that culturally specific details (of the body, labour forms, food preparation, dress and so on) were used in turn-of-the-century ethnographic exhibitions and films as a means of producing categories of racial difference. Culturally specific details were to be used as a form of scientific evidence that promised 'to flesh out the classificatory outline of race' and thus to distinguish between that which could be considered racially 'authentic and unauthentic', as well as Anglo-Saxon and non-Anglo-Saxon.[13] The travellers' absence from the slaughter (making Lady Windemere's interpretation unnecessary) allows the scene to remain utterly 'foreign' and hence opaque to the film's spectators. This opacity belies the celebration of cultural exchange that ensues, for the slaughter sequence represents the limit of participation by positing the necessary non-participation of the travellers (and thus the spectators) in a racialized spectacle in which the West cannot tolerate seeing the image of itself. The distance between self and other, home and foreign, East and West, that the participatory racial spectacle seems to collapse is thereby maintained.

The questions of distance, proximity, participation, and exchange that the racialized spectacle invokes are personified in the character of Johanna, for she is both European and Asian, and the choice she must make during the film is initially posited as a choice between identification with East and West – thus the title *Johanna d'Arc of Mongolia*. At the end of the film, Johanna initially decides to stay with the Mongolians, a choice which suggests that during the stay she has found her undisputed origin, her essential ethnic self. Yet in the film's final scene, Johanna rides up to the train on horseback and boards it for return to Europe, offering only the breathless explanation 'Je . . . . Je . . .', an explanation that claims nothing about the essence of that 'I'. What seems to be at stake in the figure of Johanna, who appears by the end of the film in both Levis and traditional Mongolian garb, is a questioning of the notion of racial inauthenticity or liminality that I suggested is at work in *The Searchers*. In *Johanna d'Arc of Mongolia*, liminality initially represents a narrative ideal, for the film seems to suggest that because of her Asian heritage, Johanna moves with the greatest ease between the white Westerners and Mongolians. Johanna's cultural 'inauthenticity' ultimately merges with the positing of a more general Mongolian inauthenticity. When Johanna ambushes the train at the end of the film, she boards the luxury caboose of a Mongolian Princess, with whom Lady Windemere has been invited to stay. When Windemere introduces Johanna to the Princess, the train's whistle drowns out the Princess's name, suggesting that she is representative of all Mongolians. The Princess, dressed in an expensive European suit, then explains to her guests that, 'Many of us return to the yurts only during the summer months in order to preserve in some measure the illusion of the free nomadic life.' Ottinger's film retroactively posits itself as a sort of textual farce that points up an expectation of authenticity – for this moment suggests that the Princess and the Mongolians may be as 'western' as Windemere, Vohwinkel and Johanna.

It is not my intention to suggest that Ottinger's film suppresses the possibility of a Mongolian authenticity, or that positing racial or cultural 'essence' is a valuable political project. Rather, the playful inauthenticity aligned with Mongolian allows Anglo-western culture to maintain a psychic distance between itself and racial difference. As bell hooks and Richard Dyer have both argued, authentic 'whiteness' is understood as being without race, the absence of colour.[14] Defining racial authenticity is a historical process that must be constantly renewed, as *The Searchers* does in order to account for and contain Anglo-American anxiety over the permeability of the category of whiteness in the face of social change. Whereas in *The Searchers* miscegenation provokes murderous horror (Ethan's initial reaction to Debbie) or barely hidden contempt (his initial reaction to Martin), mixture and inauthenticity affords pleasure in *Johanna d'Arc of Mongolia*. The revelation of the Princess's Westernness retroactively suggests that Mongolian inauthenticity has been the condition of possibility for white western participation in the racialized spectacle. As the Princess's new costume – a Chanel suit – suggests, this inauthenticity depends upon a mediation of 'race' by capitalism; she thus embodies the West's phantasy that racial difference can be transformed into a market for the white middle class. Again, this idea is reinforced by the absence of Western participation in the sheep sacrifice, which we might now read as the return of the film's repressed, as a representation or reminder of the scene of difference from which the travellers have fled – the violent scenes of racial politics and racialized poverty at home. Thus *Johanna d'Arc of Mongolia* ultimately preserves a sense of Anglo-western authenticity as that which ultimately remains outside of race – for the signifiers of whiteness are never playfully deconstructed. Although we can say that the Princess and Johanna 'masquerade' to a certain extent, we never see Lady Windemere in Mongolian garb, and she never appears to be performing racial difference. While Vohwinkel stays behind in Mongolia, her 'conversion' – announced in voiceover at the end of the film – has the status of a joke. Like the travellers' participation in the summer festival, it is contained within the safety of the commodity form of the participatory racialized spectacle. And just as the signifiers of whiteness allow Debbie to return to the domestic sphere, Johanna's position in the film's racial economy is determined by the signifiers of difference: whereas she begins the trip on the side of the consumption of the racialized spectacle, she is realigned with its production for Anglo-western consumption upon returning to Paris. Rather than winning an award for international understanding, Johanna becomes a waitress in the Princess's exquisite Mongolian restaurant – an establishment, we are told, which Lady Windemere is reputed to frequent. The character who momentarily represented an idealized figure of, in Grisham's words, 'cultural transfer', is ultimately aligned by the film's racial politics on the side of the racialized spectacle and cultural exchange. Johanna and the Princess are the conduits of cultural exchange to the extent that they represent the promise of importing from without a pleasurable – commodifiable – form of cultural difference into a national context in which racial politics remain the politics of racism.

One could argue that through its formal self-reflexivity, playful artificiality, and generic pastiche, *Johanna d'Arc of Mongolia* reveals itself as a text that critically interrogates the very problems I have been discussing. Yet, if this were the case, would the film not then depend upon spectators of fairly privileged position – like the travellers themselves – who already have a working knowledge of, for example, generic conventions and the discourse of orientalism? This would seem to be required in order for 'textual subversion' to take place and for the film to fulfil its critical mission. And if the film's spectators mirror the position of the travellers, is the pleasure offered by *Johanna d'Arc of Mongolia* not the same pleasure offered by the racialized spectacle – namely, the phantasy of an encounter with racial difference that is mediated by the commodity form of the spectacle? Before we decide the film is subversive, we must ask whether or not the film produces knowledge about the social and cultural context in which it emerged and, if so, at what level? Given that the film's point of idealization is a pleasurable integration of racial difference, we must ask how this idealization functions at a point in history when racial politics are in crisis. The film's dependence upon narratives traditionally associated with imperialist discourses, and the disavowals it must make in order to produce its phantasy, point to the importance of the social and cultural relations the film's narrative displaces: the persistent problem of racism within national borders. A critical reading of *Johanna d'Arc of Mongolia* must, therefore, begin by examining the historical need to produce an idealized model of cultural exchange.

Notes

1   Therese Grisham, 'Twentieth century *theatrum mundi*: Ulrike Ottinger's *Johanna d'Arc of Mongolia*', *Wide Angle*, vol. 14, no. 2 (1992), p. 26.

2   Brenda Longfellow, 'Lesbian phantasy and the Other woman in Ottinger's *Johanna d'Arc of Mongolia*', *Screen*, vol. 34, no. 2 (1993), p. 35.

3   See Richard Dyer, 'White', *Screen*, vol. 29, no. 4 (1998) for a discussion of whiteness.

4   For a critique of this concept, see Hazel Carby, 'Multicultural wars', in Michelle Wallace and Gina Dent (eds), *Black Popular Culture* (Seattle, WA: Bay Press, 1992), pp. 187–99.

5   Longfellow, 'Lesbian phantasy and the Other woman', p. 135.

6   Edward Said, *Orientalism* (New York: Vintage, 1979).

7   Said, *Orientalism*, p. 63.

8   The concept of the racial spectacle owes much to bell hooks' analysis of the commodification of race in 'Eating the Other', in *Black Looks: Race and Representation* (Boston, MA: South End Press, 1992).

9   Grisham, 'Twentieth century *theatrum mundi*', p. 35.

10 Renato Rosaldo, 'Imperialist nostalgia', *Representations*, no. 25 (Spring 1989), pp. 107–22.

11 Longfellow, 'Lesbian phantasy and the Other woman', p. 135.

12 Laura Mulvey, 'Visual pleasure and narrative cinema', in Bill Nichols (ed.), *Movies and Methods*, Volume 11 (Berkeley, CA: University of California Press, 1985), pp. 305–15.

13 Fatima Tobing Rony, 'Those who squat and those who sit: the iconography of race in the 1895 films of Felix-Louis Regnault', *Camera Obscura*, vol. 29 (January 1992), pp. 263–89.

14 bell hooks, *Black Looks: Race and Representation*, pp. 12–13; Dyer, 'White'.

7   From Nazi whore to good German mother: revisiting resistance in the Holocaust film

Julia Erhart

The debate over how best to represent the past as well as the difficulties involved in doing so has animated countless German film projects since the 1962 Oberhausen manifesto.[1] Some of these, such as *Germany, Pale Mother* (Helma Sanders-Brahms, 1980), *Peppermint Peace* (Marianne Rosenbaum, 1982) and *The Hunger Years* (Jutta Brückner, 1979), have focused on women's experiences, showing how women simultaneously were agents within, and victims of, the ideologies and practices of National Socialism and its immediate historical aftermath.[2] While such work has productively broadened the terms of the discussion and interrupted the masculinist tenor of the dialogue, it has tended to identify the heterosexually oriented family as the single most important determinant of women's lives. In this essay I want to explore the new questions which emerge when the past is shown from the point of view of two lesbian characters. Although much has been written about 'the lesbian' in cinema, little has been written about the cultural function of that figure within specific national cinemas, or within films about actual historical events.[3] What new pressures are brought to bear on notions such as resistance and collaboration when performed by lesbian characters? What changes does the Holocaust film undergo when imaged through the generic parameters of the lesbian love story?

Until recently there existed only one production from Germany or elsewhere that dealt with the issue of the Holocaust from a lesbian perspective. A French–German coproduction whose release was timed to coincide with the forty-year anniversary of the end of the war,[4] *November Moon* (Alexandra von Grote, 1985) is formally a relatively straightforward period drama. The film is about two women, a Frenchwoman and a German Jewish expatriate, who meet and fall in love in Paris before the war. Once war breaks out, the women flee the city to the un-occupied zone in the south, where November, the Jewish woman, is captured by the SS, raped and sent to work in a brothel. With the help of a sympathetic German officer, who later on in the film is executed for having assisted her, she manages to escape from the brothel and make her way back to Paris and to her lover, Férial. The events that take place following November's return to Paris are, to my mind, what distinguish the film as a specifically feminist and lesbian interpretation of the Occupation. In Paris, while November remains in hiding in the small apartment, rations grow thin and an anxious Férial resourcefully resumes a friendship with the film's most complex supporting character, a collaborator named Marcel.[5] Agreeing to become his paramour as well as secretary at the pro-fascist newspaper where he works, Férial effectively remakes herself overnight as Nazi sympathizer and as heterosexual. In so far as the two women are not found out, the ruse is more or less successful; at least until the end of the war, when Férial is denounced and punished by her nationalist French neighbours who of course know nothing of her Jewish woman lover. In the very last scene of the film, in what would otherwise be a celebratory moment, Férial is dragged from her home, where she is drinking champagne with her lover, to a city square. There her head is shaved and she is assaulted with insults of 'Nazi whore' and 'Nazi slut'.

As a feminist film, *November Moon* is clearly invested in disrupting the opposition between public history (stereotypically considered to be important solely to men) and private stories (thought significant mostly to women). Eschewing large-scale depictions of great, historical events – France's entry into the war; the commencement of the Occupation; the arrival of the Allies in Normandy, and so on – the film renders such occurrences as fragments of information that are exchanged principally between the women characters. Though the movie includes one shot of fighting at the front, it is so brief in duration (fifteen seconds) and so decontextualized from neighbouring scenes that it appears out of place. As my summary of the film's plot should show, von Grote's central aim is to re-cast the issue of collaboration from a feminist and, moreover, anti-homophobic point of view – that is, in a way that acknowledges the existence of historical lesbian relationships. In doing so, the film works to counter *a posteriori* the accusations that historically were levied at women who had engaged in (or who it was thought, had engaged in) relations with occupying officers or soldiers. The clandestine relationship between Férial and her lover is an exemplar of but one of the 'unseen' components of women's experience that, hypothetically, would have justified cooperation with the occupying forces. As such, the representation of that relationship is a polemic aimed at those who would, or did, pass judgement because of hearsay or gossip, asking them retrospectively to reflect on the certainty of their perceptions. At the same time, given that the relationship is a lesbian one, it is also a corrective to a historically located homophobia that prohibited the 'seeing' of non-heterosexual romantic liaisons. In the film's logic, the non-seeing of lesbianism is what the fascists do: to 'not see' is at the very least to produce a view of political activism that is inaccurate, if not actually reactionary. The final shot of the film, a closeup of November in the city square trying to comfort her battered lover, is an indication of the inadequacy of November's presence within the frame, and indeed within the story, to counter the violence. In an attempt to right the historical record, the film challenges society's double standard that acknowledges some forms of presence but not others.

A 1997 BBC documentary rehearses many of the issues raised in von Grote's film, in a nonfictional context. Based on a book, *Aimee and Jaguar*, published in 1994 by the German feminist writer Erica Fischer, *Love Story* (d. Catrine Clay) is about a real relationship that occurred between two women in wartime Berlin. Like the couple in *November Moon*, Felice Schragenheim and Lilly Wust stand at polar ends of the political and ethnic spectrum: Felice was a Jewish lesbian who was active in the German underground and who stayed alive by passing as a non-Jew, while Lilly, mother of four boys and 1942 recipient of the Maternal Cross for exemplary mothering, was the wife of a German officer and, by some people's accounts, the ideal Nazi mother. Although she separated herself from her husband's politics and ultimately threw her unqualified support behind her lover – divorcing her husband and helping Felice in her political work – Lilly was initially feared by many of Felice's friends, who suspected her of upholding fascist ideals. I shall discuss these issues in some detail later, but for the moment, it is sufficient to say that while the concerns of Felice's friends eventually proved unfounded, the political and cultural differences between the women were strategic for Felice: by her own devising and on the advice of several friends, Felice decided to live with Lilly in part because she thought that no one would ever suspect a recipient of the Maternal Cross to be harbouring a Jew.

Like *November Moon*, the 1997 documentary complicates and amplifies conventional categories of realist historical storytelling, such as heroism, humanitarianism, courageousness and so on, rather than simply showing women performing tasks that men have typically been shown to do. Like the feature film, the documentary aligns political or ethical correctness with homosexuality, retroactively expanding the scope of the former by associating it with the latter. In the logic of the two films, 'fascist' and 'homosexual' are mutually exclusive identities, an idea that departs significantly from what is seen earlier in art films such as *The Conformist* (Bernardo Bertolucci, Italy/France/West Germany, 1970) but which emerges in other feminist films of the decade, such as Liliana Cavani's *The Berlin Affair* (Italy, 1985) and Karoly Makk's *Another Way* (Hungary, 1982). Both films critique conventional understandings of resistance, which, at least in the case of France, have typically functioned to foreclose upon the construction of women as worthy social actors and have distracted national interest from the fact of French collaboration.[6] Although *November Moon* features a minor character who is a member of the French Resistance (Férial's brother), there is not a single scene of him in that context; overall, the film does not seem especially interested in either him or his work. While there is no shortage of feature films about the Resistance, including at least one which depicts women Resistance fighters (*Blanche et Marie* [Jacques Renard, France, 1985]) and one which deconstructs the achievements of the Resistance (*Armée des ombres* [Jean-Pierre Melville, France,

1969]), to my knowledge there have not yet been any that have achieved this from a feminist point of view.[7]

What distinguishes both *November Moon* and *Love Story* is precisely such a perspective, that is, a criticism of the differential logic which recognizes and validates certain forms of resistance over others. For example, while *November Moon*'s male collaborator, Marcel, aims to cross the border into Germany once the Allies arrive, that option is not open to the female character, Férial. In this film, the mapping of political treachery on to sexual licentiousness via the term 'Nazi whore' is a product of the same inequity that allows Marcel to make a midnight-hour escape while Férial is roundly humiliated. And, although the progressive-thinking Férial is as disgusted by the Nazis as is her Resistance fighter brother, he alone is able to vent his outrage through the masculinist and socially sanctioned mode of voluntary conscription. Though *Love Story* makes this point implicitly rather than explicitly, resistance here is likewise principally an act carried out by women in a world that is predominantly homosocial. Only one of the five major characters of the story, Gerd Ehrlich, is male, and not one of the key women characters, who include Ulla Schaaf and Elenai Predski-Kramer in addition to Lilly and Felice, is visibly linked to a male partner. Like *November Moon*, *Love Story* considerably broadens the definition of resistance, including everything from the theft of identification cards to Felice's passing as a non-Jew to the very act of 'reckless living' carried out by both Felice and Lilly.

Although *Love Story* does not centre on the issue of collaboration in the same way as *November Moon*, it highlights related acts of duplicity and masquerade, showing both to be important to the women's survival.[8] Central to the narratives of both films is a cross-ethnic relationship in which the Jewish woman is protected by the actions of her lover, which appear to be one thing (pro-fascist) but in fact are resolutely the opposite. That each of the non-Jewish leading characters, Férial and Lilly, functions as two things at once – lover and protector of a persecuted subject, what Alison Owings would call a 'righteous gentile',[9] and secretary at a pro-Nazi paper in Férial's case, or model Nazi mother in Lilly's – raises issues at the heart of Holocaust studies: what counts as resistance, what counts as collaboration, are there 'rules' to resistance and is there only one right way to act, in Abigail Rosenthal's words, an 'appropriate way to undergo one's Holocaust'?[10]

At one end of the continuum is the view, authored by Hannah Arendt and developed by Raul Hilberg, that only those actions that directly stemmed or stayed the Nazi advance constitute resistance – such as, for example, that of the woman prisoner who grabbed the SS officer's gun and shot him, even though it cost her her own life, or the work of underground organizations.[11] At the other end are those such as survivor Terence Des Pres, who argues that, within the camps or ghettoes, the act of surviving itself qualifies as resistance, regardless of how the survivor did or did not cooperate. Roger Gottlieb's definition embraces those of both Hilberg and Des Pres, in that resistance reflects the situational difference that varies from one context to another.[12] For Gottlieb, resistance is a relational concept that is determined according to the circumstances in which the persecuted subject finds him or herself.[13] In other words, if it is the religious aspect of identity that is deemed offensive, then public prayer, regardless of the outcome, would qualify as resistance. If it is physical survival, then escape by any means necessary would count. As the principal threat in both films is that of discovery, in Gottlieb's definition the act of remaining disguised (in *Love Story*) or hidden (in *November Moon*) would qualify as resistance.

Above all, what emerges in both films is an idea of resistance that pivots upon the sexual: enacted principally by women, each act is facilitated by a character's successful apprehension and flaunting of the codes of normative femininity. From Férial's performance of a Nazi-sympathizer to Felice's construction of herself as a non-Jew, to Lilly's appearance as the quintessential Nazi mother – not one of the women is precisely what she appears to be. As I have suggested, in both films survival is achieved by the dissemination of the suggestion that the non-Jewish women are other than they are. In both, the success of political mimicry is contingent upon their masquerade of sexuality that Germans and collaborationist French do not question. Only by imitating the conventions of heterosexuality is Férial credible as a Nazi-sympathizer; it is largely because of her status as a 'good German (Nazi) mother' that Lilly's activism can remain undetected. The mimicry of normative sex/gender relations that would appear purely capitulative, is paradoxically what makes oppositional activity possible.

For Homi Bhabha, mimicry is a form of fetishism enacted by the colonized against the colonizer that helps mediate the disempowering and expropriative effects of colonization. Represented in both the stereotype and in the anglicized-but-not-English colonial subject, mimicry involves the apprehension of the cultural codes of the colonizer, including dress, manners and language, by the colonized subject.[14] What Edward Said would call a median category that emerges from colonial discourse,[15] mimicry both controls a perceived threat to the established order and has the transformative effect of changing the look of colonial surveillance into the distanced and 'displacing gaze of the disciplined'.[16] An agonistic attitude that allows for different forms of agency than earlier metaphors of domination, mimicry produces the colonized as a presence rather than as the purely negative or repressed double of the colonizer.[17]

Although the racial, industrial and other differences between the colonial territories, about which Bhabha writes, and Europe in the 1940s might seem to invalidate my invocation of him in this context, there are structural commonalities between his map and the territories I am describing that are helpful to my thinking about the strategies available. In *Love Story*, reference is repeatedly made to the contradiction between the apparently fascist and anti-fascist components of Lilly's personality. Although in 1981 she was awarded the Federal Service Cross for her wartime anti-fascism, surviving acquaintances recall her uttering anti-Semitic remarks, and testify to the existence in the living room of her home of a bronze relief of Hitler. In talking-head footage with the film's director, Lilly Wust not surprisingly denies such charges, blaming her reputation on the fact that she was married to a German officer. While acknowledging people's contradictory memories of her, the voice of the film comes down firmly on the side of Lilly's anti-fascism, undercutting negative references to her politics by naming her the 'supposed Nazi' and ending with the unequivocal statement that 'the woman once suspected of being a Nazi, turned out to be the very opposite'.

My point here is not to pass judgement on the details of Lilly's wartime politics, but to demonstrate how they function in the world of the historical story. Regardless of 'what' Lilly 'was', the suspicions about her politics prove strategic, for Felice and for herself as Felice's safeguard. Talking-head footage from a friend, Ulla, directly links Lilly's reputation to the safety Felice enjoyed. Estimating the reasons Felice trusted she would be safe at Lilly's house, she states, 'Lilly was known as a bit of a Nazi. No-one would suspect her of hiding a Jew. So Felice moved in and stayed.' The significance of Lilly's doubled identity – her being 'a bit of' a Nazi – is further evident in a description of Lilly's grilling by the Gestapo, during which she denied knowing Felice was Jewish. As the camera lingers on a photograph of Lilly with her young boys, the voiceover relates that the Gestapo believed her, 'because they couldn't imagine that a good German mother with four fine sons would harbour a Jew'.

The two-sidedness that characterizes Lilly's identity also characterizes the women's demeanour as a couple. While the film informs us of their awareness of the danger they were both constantly in, it also relates how they travelled confidently around the city, visiting friends in cafés, cycling around, going everywhere together, in short, conducting themselves, as a friend Elenai describes it, 'as though there were no danger'. Although under other circumstances reports of such conduct would bring viewers pleasure, because viewers imagine the risks involved, Elenai's narration induces apprehension. Lilly's description of how she and Felice took particular pleasure from going to the hotel across from Hitler's headquarters, the Kaiserhof, has more or less this effect. 'It was bursting with SS uniforms!' she says, almost triumphantly, in a way that leaves viewers cringing. What is finally apparent from Ulla's, Elenai's and Lilly's testimonies is a split in Lilly's identity and in the couple's actions that, on the one hand, expresses extraordinary vulnerability and, on the other, exudes confidence and authority – in short, proper Aryan Germanness.

The trope of two-sidedness is also apparent in *November Moon*, in which each intercultural exchange has two contradictory meanings, an obvious or capitulative one for the occupying forces, and a coded or oppositional signification for the French and the Jews. In each case, the (in)ability to see the 'code' or covert meaning turns upon the reader's dependence on the stereotype in his or her interpretive process. While November and viewers are aware that Férial's acceptance of the job at the pro-fascist paper is intended to divert attention from her household, Marcel and his German colleagues are blinded by her coquettish manner, unable to see beyond the masquerade of heterosexuality that she performs. A scene in which Férial appears to dance for the benefit of the Nazis and their French collaborationist friends demonstrates the doubled significance of her actions, that is only partially legible by the Germans but fully visible to viewers. On the night before the Nazi defeat, Férial accompanies Marcel and some of his friends to a bar. Not responding to the men's overt interest in her, Férial dances, not with them, but alone, by herself, in the middle of the room. Whereas the bar patrons read the dreamy, exuberant smile on her face as evidence of heterosexual, narcissistic pleasure in being looked at, viewers recall an earlier lesbian scene in the movie, where before the war Férial and November danced together in a café in front of an initially indifferent but ultimately irate Parisian audience – a scene which concluded with the women's hasty departure from the establishment. Because the film's viewers remember the earlier dancing scene, they know that Férial's thoughts are, indeed, not with the Nazi onlookers in this latter scene, but with her lover who waits for her, with whom she will celebrate later that night. Because of stylistic commonalities between the two dancing scenes – such as muted lighting, a relay of closeups on the café patrons' faces, the dancer(s)' expressions of enjoyment and their patent disregard for the patrons' stares – the analogy between the first homophobic set of viewers and this second fascist set could not be clearer. In both scenes, the implication is that there is a good deal more going on in the heads of the dancers or dancer than the other patrons are able to grasp: the first dancing scene marks the beginning of a lesbian love affair, whose existence patrons either do not see or cannot comprehend, while the second scene coincides with the arrival of the Allies in Normandy – the consequences of which are comprehensible to Férial, but not to the Nazis. Especially in the latter scene, there is considerably more power in being looked at than the classical understanding of the voyeurism has led us to expect:[18] precisely by not returning the invasive gazes of the onlookers, Férial is able to maintain her doubled status, to remain unavailable to the bar patrons.

The scene in which the Gestapo search Férial's apartment likewise manifests a doubled complex of meanings. Key to the working of the scene is the preceding one in which Férial, tipped off about the search, hurriedly helps November to leave the apartment and spend the night elsewhere. When the Gestapo finally appear, viewers, who know what is at stake but also that the object of the search has flown the proverbial coop, perceive Férial's feigned nonchalance to be highly ironic. While her petulance about cooperating can pass as the legitimate outrage of someone with her 'connections' being the subject of a search, viewers have a different opinion. Férial's reluctance to carry out the officer's demand to disclose the contents of November's (by now empty) hiding place under the couch seems to ridicule the entire operation. While Férial's question, 'How could anyone hide in the bottom of the couch?', strikes the officer as merely rhetorical, viewers hear an additional meaning.

In cinematic terms, the doubled meaning of Férial's performance is conveyed throughout the movie via a distinct, repeated framing and blocking technique that is employed in nearly all the encounters between Férial and Marcel. Each encounter between the two is initiated by a lingering shot of Férial turned away from Marcel with her face hidden from him but fully visible to viewers. For example, in two encounters, she walks beyond him, deeper into the room (in their first encounter when she approaches him for a job) or towards a window (when they meet at her apartment); two other scenes show Férial seated at a desk in the foreground, directly facing the camera, typing dictation, as Marcel paces behind her in the background of the frame. In each of these scenes, the camera pauses for a few seconds as she stares away from him. Clearly, such shots generate tension and uncertainty as to whether Férial will continue to maintain her masquerade, and what is most interesting is precisely that Férial's face does not betray her; even when Marcel's dictation becomes violently anti-Semitic, she continues to appear detached.

While Férial is *November Moon*'s most blatant mimic, other characters in the film also engage in this practice. For example, a supporting character, Chantal, one-time lover of November's father and owner of the local bistro, passes as pro-Nazi by bantering casually and flirtatiously with her German patrons. Whereas the Germans equate Chantal's hospitality with 'natural' 'French' *joie de vivre*, viewers know that the purpose of her solicitousness is to deflect attention from the fraudulent industry she is involved in (at night she switches labels between costly and inexpensive wines) and from her harbouring of Férial's brother, the Resistance fighter. The doubled meaning in her telling of a La Fontaine fable in which she disparagingly but indirectly compares the Germans to ants – the subtlety of which, like Férial's masquerade, is lost on her bar patrons – exemplifies her ability to challenge the Germans' authority, to make a mockery of them.[19]

If, in Bhabha's overtly Lacanian formulation, 'the recognition of sexual difference . . . is disavowed by the fixation on an object that masks the difference and restores the original presence',[20] certainly the fixation on Férial's 'hetero-sexuality', Chantal's 'Frenchness', and Lilly's 'Nazi' maternal abilities can hide the recognition of anti-fascist and, in Férial's and Lilly's cases, lesbian difference that is also at issue. I am arguing that Chantal, Lilly and Férial are able to play up, and therefore play off, the stereotype that is described in Bhabha's argument in order to forward their own libidinal and political projects. The female characters' sexuality that the Germans interpret as genuine is a construction or a perform-ance of the stereotypical that returns the men to an illusionary 'point of total identification', a place of misconstrued certainty where no questions can be asked.[21] Férial's mimicry of heterosexuality, Chantal's mimicry of Frenchness, and Lilly's mimicry of a 'good German mother' make of all three a kind of fetish for the

Germans, restoring to them the security of ideal relations during wartime, and thereby deflecting attention from the women's oppositional work.[22]

So ultimately, the alignment of both *November Moon* and *Love Story* with other critical discourses about lesbianism is an ambivalent one. On the one hand, as I have discussed, both films call for the increased visibility of lesbian relationships, citing invisibility as a central characteristic of homophobic representations of lesbianism. But on the other, both also recognize the mimicry of non-lesbian subject positions as strategic in specific historical circumstances. In so doing, regardless of the makers' claims, the films work as critiques of dominant critical and popular discourses which blankety cede the moral or ethical high ground to the lesbian who is 'most out', regardless of the cultural or historical context.

It is important to remind readers that the mimics I am discussing are not the Jewish subjects in the stories but rather the non-Jews – Lilly and Férial. If we agree with Bhabha's idea that power is constitutive of a range of subjects, then we must wonder about the effects, upon the Jewish female characters in each film, of the non-Jew's undertaking to be the fetish herself. I would argue that what occurs when Férial and Lilly become the fetish is that November and Felice no longer need to 'be' it, and can cease being the amputated subject Bhabha describes.[23]

I shall now pursue this matter of the representation of the relationship between the Jewish and the non-Jewish characters through a discussion of the generic parameters of the films. In spite of the fact that *Love Story* is technically a non-fiction film, both it and *November Moon* employ elements of two genres – the lesbian love story and the history film. Of the latter genre, Marcia Landy has argued that both elite and popular representations of the past are permeated with the formal properties and narrative elements of melodrama.[24] In history films, moments of considerable national or cultural significance are transmitted through the generic components of melodramatic fiction – for example, large- and small-scale betrayals; threats to individual and group welfare; subterfuge both successful and unsuccessful; reversals of fortune; changes of heart; reconciliation on personal and large-scale levels; and so on. Like other significant cultural projects, the matter of *Vergangenheitsbewältigung*, or coming-to-terms-with-the-past, is rehearsed in the history film via the dramatized relationships between individuals who are often of opposing class or cultural or ethnic groups. For instance, in *The Night Porter* (Liliana Cavani, Italy, 1974), Max, the ex-Nazi hotel employee, and Lucia, the wife of an American conductor and concentration camp survivor, play and replay the events of the past in a shifting representation of a chain of subjects, with Lucia alternatively standing for 'women, who could stand for victims, who could stand for Jews', and so on.[25]

Interestingly, one of the more popular tropes within contemporary lesbian and gay cinema, and I would say within lesbian and gay love stories especially, is that of the interracial or inter-ethnic romance. Films such as *The Watermelon Woman* (Cheryl Dunye, US, 1995), *Young Soul Rebels* (Isaac Julien, UK, 1990), and the aforementioned *The Berlin Affair* in particular have explored issues of racial difference from within the context of a gay or lesbian love story.[26] Ruby Rich has suggested that within queer cinema, racial difference can function in much the same way that sexual difference works within the hegemonic heterosexual love story.[27] If we agree with Rich, we then need to examine the function of such a trope in films about real historical events. While both *November Moon* and *Love Story* point to the possibility of reconciliation, Felice's arrest and subsequent deportation in 1944 by the Gestapo necessarily make the narrating of reconciliation in the latter film somewhat monologic, attributing the fruits of wartime effort solely to Lilly Wust, who, as I mentioned, in the 1980s received the Federal Service Cross for humanitarianism. The point is not to blame the film for Felice's absence which is, after all, a historical fact, but to consider what a more dialogic representation would look like. *November Moon* offers such a representation. In the remainder of this essay, I want to look in some detail at how von Grote translates a historically specific cultural project, that is, *Vergangenheitsbewältigung*, into a fictional affair between two characters. *November Moon* represents reconciliation as a linguistic rather than an administrative project that is achieved, not through the passing of laws, but performatively through language. As I intend to show, coming to terms with the past is contingent on the fact of the persecuted, Jewish subject becoming a speaking being.

The opening shots of *November Moon* show an adult Jewish man telling a fable to a very young girl, who turns out to be his daughter, November. The scene is a flashback, recollected on the eve of the Second World War by the adult November, twenty or so years after she originally heard the fable as a child. What occasioned the original telling was the event of November's mother's death; the story her father tells is a Talmud legend about what happens to children just before they are born. As her father told it, an angel kisses children so that they will 'forget' everything that life will bring. In the flashback, he says:

> Before they are born their whole life unfolds before them, and also their death. But no one could live knowing when or how they are to die. So God sent an angel and with that kiss, they are able to forget everything about life and death.

Interestingly, for a film whose cultural project is to amplify contemporary awareness of Occupation and the Holocaust, the fable insists less on the importance of knowing than on the pain involved in having to know: were one aware of all that is in store, it would be impossible to summon either the hope or strength to continue to live. Not to know, in the logic of the legend, is to inhabit a more livable state – as did, for example, Eve, to invoke another parochial tale, before the tasting of the apple. Having to know – or in the case of survivors, such as Abraham Bomba in *Shoah* (Claude Lanzmann, France, 1985), having to remember – is almost as difficult and painful as the initial historical experience.

The issue of foreknowledge has been a nagging one for survivor historians and others attempting to make sense of the devastating effects of war, in particular the racial policies of National Socialism. Lack of awareness of the seriousness and extent of the draconian measures associated with the Final Solution has dominated explanations of both Jewish inability to resist and Allied failure to intervene. Allegations of Allied anti-Semitism, on the one hand, and Jewish 'passivity', on the other, though clearly differing in tenor, aim and effect, have both been assuaged by the notion that not enough was known in time to make a difference. Some publicizing of historical evidence to the contrary, such as that demonstrating early Allied knowledge of the camps and ghettoes for instance, has productively and significantly shifted the terms of the debate from the failure-to-know to the failure-to-act. For example, the Washington DC, Holocaust Museum's documentation of the US decision against bombing Auschwitz well after the camp's purpose was known, and in spite of pleas from Jewish groups to do so, is only the most recent and well-publicized example of such a shift. The issue of Jewish non-resistance is, not surprisingly, more complex. While most historians are in agreement as to the overwhelming paucity of options available, particularly after the 1942 Wahnsee Conference, stereotypes of Jewish 'denial' and 'docility' have been difficult to overcome. How Jews simultaneously knew of, and continued to participate in, their own extermination is the question animating the chapter entitled 'Soliciting the cooperation of the victims' in Zygmunt Bauman's seminal sociological study of the *Judenräte* – the Jewish leaders who administered the ghettoes, acting as a link between them and the outside world.[28] Rather than re-asking the unanswerable – if people had known, could it have been stopped? – Bauman examines the conditions that produced the possibility for certain actions to occur in spite of what was or was not known. Although focused on differently positioned historical subjects possessing distinctive forms of agency, what both the Museum panel and Bauman's study in particular explore is the nebulous area between knowing and not knowing, that is, the type of knowledge apprehension that involves both knowing and disavowal. If people had known, could it have been stopped? The significance of Bauman's argument turns upon his displacing of this question.

At the risk of, first, exculpating those who knew the extent of the genocide, had means to intercede, and did not take steps to do so and, second, disrespecting the memory of those such as Warsaw Ghetto leader Adam Czerniakow who figured the extent of the horror in light of his own meagre interventionist capacities and subsequently made the rational choice to end his own life,[29] I would like to suggest that the fantasy of a knowledge-suspending angel might be of strategic importance to a fictional character such as November. Confronted with seemingly insurmountable odds with no means to act, foreknowledge, for the German-Jewish refugee, would be an encumbrance to which the sole rational response would be suicide, as it was for Czerniakow and undoubtedly countless others less well-known than he. For November as a Jew, the angel's kiss would constitute not an espousal of inaction but a strategic disavowal, a suspension of knowledge of the certainty of a violent and annihilating future. Not an evacuation of agency, the kiss would be a suspension of knowledge necessary to go on living.[30] In psychoanalytic terms, the kiss would function in a manner similar to the concept of the fetish, which arrests the process of knowing in the moment just prior to the subject's realization of knowledge too painful to bear.[31]

As the film does not return to the opening scene of the father's telling of the legend, it could be said that *November Moon* re-performs the very act of repression that the fable itself seems to advocate – at least, until a very important moment towards the end of the story. In a film full of verbal references to the history of the record – the Spanish Civil War, Germany's invasion of Poland, the French armistice, Liberation – the moment when Férial learns of her mother's death is one of the most intimate. The scene opens abruptly with a tight closeup on the faces of November and Férial; firmly held by November, Férial sobs and tries to make sense of the suddenness of the event. How will she arrange for the funeral? How is she to contact her brother? In an effort to try to comfort Férial, November recalls the story her father told her a long time ago, at the time of her own mother's death. Speaking his words to Férial, she repeats out loud the story of the angel that is spoken by her father at the beginning of the film. Her exact words are: 'Before we are born, we know everything that will come to pass in our lives, even our death. But since no one could live, not even for one second, knowing all this, God sent down an angel who kisses us on the forehead before we are born into the world, so that we may forget everything.'

Although the death of Férial's mother is merely the first in a series of climactic circumstances that mark a turning point in the narrative and push it towards resolution, the incident seems arbitrary in a film which is otherwise extremely economical in its depiction of the domestic. The mother's death, which we do not see, whose cause is only briefly referred to and not entirely clear, seems narratively unnecessary to the film, which, in the few moments that follow, will be wholly concerned with resolving the occurrences of the war's end. The function of the mother's death is to provide November with a chance to tell, or rather re-tell, the story of the angel.

A character whose structural and, in 1940s parlance, racial position in the story leaves her little room for physical agency, November spends most of the film literally and metaphorically on the run, reacting to the actions and decisions of those with more power and freedom of movement than she. When she is not shown running from or being brutalized by the Germans, November is dependent on the mercy and will of others, such as Férial and Férial's mother, spending much of the time physically confined, for example in a barn in the unoccupied zone, or in the hiding place in the underpart of the couch. Although the film permits her an occasional gesture of defiance, she largely exists as a fugitive who must remain out of sight and away from the light of day, and, most importantly, silent. Throughout much of *November Moon*, November's access to verbal agency or voice and the power of analysis is limited and ineffective. Although the beginning of the film opens with the image of her, suggesting that this will be her story, the first words spoken are not hers but those of her father. In the scene where the two women first meet, November is harassed by a set of anti-Semitic boys, but it is Férial who appears, vocally intervenes, and escorts November away. Whereas Férial on two occasions verbally acknowledges her relationship with November (in a scene with her brother, and in a scene with her mother), November never speaks about it directly. In sum, whereas Férial is allowed the luxury of analysis and commentary, November, for the most part, only silently reacts. Even the film's title, that would seem intended to address her, dispossesses her: 'November Moon' is not a name she has created, but is in fact a nickname made up by Férial's brother.

In the chapter on *Shoah* in her book on the subject of witnessing, Shoshana Felman writes of the contest between interviewer and witness over breaking the silence on the subject of the Holocaust. The difficulty for both the witness and for those who were not there in speaking about the Holocaust derives from the 'pact' of silence struck between the historical event and its witness: as long as the witness remains silent, there is no event to be spoken about; as long as the horror is not revealed, there need not be, need not have been, a witness.[32] Thus Lanzmann's accomplishment, in Felman's thinking, is to force what many survivors regard as unspeakable events to be discussed. Lanzmann's success derives from his polite disrespect for codes that would preserve both the privacy of the survivor and the sacredness of the events; his objective is primarily to get the witness to speak. Accordingly, he starts slowly, attentive to the tiniest detail – 'What were the [gas] vans like?', 'What colour?' – before hedging more difficult questions – 'How did you feel when you saw all these naked women arriving with children [into the gas chamber]?' In doing so, Lanzmann 'desacrilizes' the historical circumstances and deflates their paralysing power, which does not erase it, but rather releases it. He thereby establishes a powerful, public, and institutionalized forum for voices that did not previously have one, a way for survivors of the experiences of ghettoization and internment to 'own' their own stories, speak them in the first person.

In *November Moon*, November's telling of the Talmud legend to Férial allows her to own what had previously only been spoken to her as a child by another, and, crucially, to locate herself as agent and subject proper of the story. There are four signs that indicate this important shift: first, she tells the story, that is, it is her voice that is heard telling it, not that of her father; second, the story is told in the present tense, not recollected (she originally recalls it in a flashback); third, she tells the story in the first person plural, using 'we' (her father had told it in the third person); and fourth, in this new telling, she occupies the position of the angel-agent as opposed to the object, the one receiving the kiss. Brushing back the hair on Férial's forehead as she relates the story, looking as if she would kiss Férial, November becomes the agent of a narrative that had previously signalled her historical dispossession, constructed her as the forgetter. What this second telling of the story does is allow her to redeem a part of her past upon which her ability to face the future depended and, henceforth, depends. At stake in the re-telling of the angel story is not just the temporal frame of its utterance, the past, but the temporal frame of its enunciation, which is the present. With the recovery of the angel story, November's past is assumed, released, and made available for the present and indeed for the future. With November's assumption of the first person plural pronoun, she identifies herself with the children of the story, and, by extension, with the collective subject-victims of the Holocaust. No longer simply the recipient of the story, November becomes, most importantly, with this re-telling, its transmitter. While the first telling, occurring on the eve of the war, coincided with the beginning of a historic loss whose proportions need no empha-sizing, the second telling, heard at the war's end, marks not just the possibility of cultural survival but of cultural continuation. And the kiss? As it occurs between two historically adversarial bodies – Jew : non-Jew; subjugator : subjugated – the kiss could signal a tentative reconciliation, at least between Férial and November, and potentially between the different audiences that they symbolically stand in for.

Like nearly all shots of Férial and November in the film, the women are imaged throughout the angel/kiss sequence in an intimate two-shot. From the women's first encounter after they flee the anti-Semitic boys, to various scenes of them in the south of France, to shots of them in bed – they are nearly always depicted together in the frame, rather than isolated in alternating shots as they would be in shot/reverse-shot sequences. Although there are several meanings we could ascribe to this stylistic choice, the most obvious is that it engenders a sense of unity between the characters. The fact that the two-shot is not employed for other characters in the film suggests furthermore that it is specific to November and Férial as a lesbian couple. This stylistic configuration, and the fact that the kiss takes place between two women, signals finally the need for women, feminists and lesbians to participate in the process of coming to terms with the past. What is suggested by the final scene, where Férial is denounced as a collaborator and cruelly humiliated by her neighbours, is that the burden of historical reckoning and accountability has not dissipated, but shifted. No longer a scenario that pits perpetrators against victims, the final scene points to the need to cast a wider net around the issue of historical responsibility that too frequently has congealed upon two binary oppositions.

I am grateful to Claudia Cantañeda, Yvonne Keller and Terri Mesbah for their helpful comments on earlier drafts of this essay.

Notes

1   Yet cinematic efforts to make sense of German participation date back much farther, to *The Murderers are Among Us* (Wolfgang Staudte, 1946).

2   The matter of women's participation in contemporary German cinema has received considerable attention. See Julia Knight, *Women and the New German Cinema* (London: Verso, 1992); Barbara Kosta, *Recasting Autobiography: Women's Counterfictions in Contemporary German Literature and Film* (Ithaca, NY: Cornell University Press, 1994); Susan E. Linville, *Feminism, Film, Fascism: Women's Auto-Biographical Film in Postwar Germany* (Austin, TX: University of Texas Press, 1998); Richard W. McCormick, *Politics of the Self: Feminism and the Postmodern in West German Literature and Film* (Princeton, NJ: Princeton University Press, 1991); Renate Mührmann, *Die Frau mit der Kamera: Filmemacherinnen in der Bundesrepublik Deutschland. Situation, Perspektiven, 10 exemplarische Lebensläufe* (Munich: Carl Hanser, 1980); Ingeborg Majer O'Sickey and Ingeborg von Zadow (eds), *Triangulated Visions: Women in Recent German Cinema* (Albany, NY: SUNY Press, 1998); Gabriele Weinberger, *Nazi Germany and its Aftermath in Women Directors' Autobiographical Films of the Late 1970s: in the Murderer's House* (San Francisco, CA: Mellon Research University Press, 1992).

3   Exceptions would be anthologies, such as Stephen Bourne, *Brief Encounters: Lesbians and Gays in British Cinema, 1930–1971* (London: Cassell, 1996) and Keith Howes, *Broadcasting it: an Encyclopedia of Homosexuality on Film, Radio and TV in the UK 1923–1993* (London: Cassell, 1993). The issue of gay male representation within national cinemas has received more thorough consideration. See, for instance, essays in Paul Julian Smith, *Laws of Desire: Questions of Homosexuality in Spanish Writing and Film: 1950–1990* (New York: Oxford University Press, 1992); Chris Berry, *A Bit on the Side: East-West Topographies of Desire* (Sydney: Empress Publications, 1994); Owen Heathcote (ed.), *Gay Signatures: Gay and Lesbian Theory. Fiction and Film in France, 1945–1995* (Berg: Oxford, 1998).

4   Heiko Rosner, 'Review of *November Moon*', *Film-echo Filmwoche 4*, vol. 5, no. 24 (January 1986), p. 27.

5   Although reviews of the film were mixed, one aspect that was well received, even by people who did not especially like the film, was the representation of the ambivalence of life under Occupation. See Marli Feldvofl, *Novembermond, EPD Film*, vol. 3, no. 2 (February 1986), p. 31; Margret Köhler, 'Filme von Frauen', *Medien*, vol. 29, no. 2 (1985), pp. 76–82; Rosner, 'Review of *November Moon*'. Two supporting characters in particular stood out – one of whom was the collaborator, Marcel (see Feldvofl, *Novembermond*; Köhler, 'Filme von Frauen').

6   That the first Frenchman was not convicted of crimes against humanity until April of 1994 would seem to be an indication of the national reluctance to acknowledge pro-Nazi activity. Cf. Serge Klarsfeld, 'Slaughter of the innocents', *New York Times*, 25 January 1995, p. A19.

7   Although overall there exist fewer films about German or German-language resistance movements than about movements in other countries, interestingly there are at least two feminist films about efforts in Germany and Austria respectively. *Five Last Days* (Percy Adlon, 1982) focuses on the five days prior to the execution of Sophie Scholl, one of the leaders of the student-led anti-government groups. *The White Rose. A Minute*

of Darkness Does Not Blind Us (Susanne Zanke, 1986) is based on the life and memoirs of the Austrian resister Grete Schütte Luhotzky.

8 Seen through the eyes of her unknowing French neighbours, Férial's apparent fall from outspoken antagonist of fascism to 'Nazi whore' would function, in Dominick LaCapra's words, 'transferentially' for contemporary subjects for whom guilt and atonement are pressing issues. See 'Representing the Holocaust: reflections on the historians debate', in Saul Friedlander (ed.), *Probing the Limits of Representation: Nazism and the 'Final Solution'* (Cambridge, MA: Harvard University Press, 1992), pp. 106–27. On this question, see also Eric L. Santner, 'History beyond the pleasure principle', in Friedlander, *Probing the Limits*, pp. 143–54.

9 Alison Owings, *Frauen: Women Recall the Third Reich* (New Brunswick, NJ: Rutgers University Press, 1993), p. 432.

10 Abigail Rosenthal, 'The right way to act: indicting the victims', in Roger S. Gottlieb (ed.), *Thinking the Unthinkable: Meanings of the Holocaust* (New York: Paulist Press, 1990), p. 138.

11 Hannah Arendt, *Origins of Totalitarianism* (London: Allen, 1962).

12 Terence Des Pres, 'Us and them', in Gottlieb (ed.), *Thinking the Unthinkable*, pp. 109–25.

13 Rober S. Gottlieb, 'The concept of resistance: Jewish resistance during the Holocaust', in Gottlieb (ed.), *Thinking the Unthinkable*, p. 329.

14 Homi Bhabha, *The Location of Culture* (New York: Routledge, 1994), p. 87.

15 Quoted in ibid., p. 73.

16 Ibid., p. 89.

17 Ibid., p. 88.

18 I refer here to the initial characterization of cinematic visual pleasure/labour as unexceptionally oppressive to women. The canonical text is Laura Mulvey's 'Visual pleasure and narrative cinema', *Screen*, vol. 16, no. 3 (1975), pp. 6–18.

19 And indeed, the film even allows (some of) the Germans to appear equivocal in their loyalty to Nazism, as is the case with the petty officer who facilitates November's escape from the brothel. The ambiguity of this character is further reinforced by a sympathetic (and I believe quite radical) identification that the film sets up between him and November, via a dissolve from a closeup of his face, as he is executed.

20 Bhabha, *The Location of Culture*, p. 74.

21 Ibid., p. 76.

22 Although some would argue that mimicry would be impossible for Jews in the context of the Holocaust, where the aim was not fetishism but annihilation, it may help to remind readers that the subjects of the two films I am discussing differ significantly from films whose sole focus is the substance of the Final Solution, that is, those set in camps or ghettoes, in terms of the respective representation of the matters and practices of anti-Semitism. While the spectre of discovery/deportment looms over both stories, annihilation is not the central subject of either film. Although both films are obviously interested in the topic of anti-Semitism, this is largely because it is a technology for Occupation (in *November Moon*'s case), or (in *Love Story*'s) as it constructs the life of underground Jews and their associates.

23 Throughout Bhabha's writing that I have referred to, there is a more than occasional ambiguity as to who is the subject of the colonial gesture, the one that we might term

the colonizer, or the one which might be called the subjugated. This ambiguity would seem strategic for Bhabha: like the psychoanalytic paradigms from which he borrows, colonialism is not a uni-directional subject-forming process but rather a 'scene' in which each of the subjects is co-implicated and mutually constitutive.

24   Marcia Landy, *Cinematic Uses of the Past* (Minneapolis, MN: University of Minnesota Press, 1996), p. 17.

25   Marguerite Waller, 'Signifying the Holocaust: Liliana Cavani's *Portiere di Notté*, in Laura Pietropaolo and Ada Testaferri (eds), *Feminisms in the Cinema* (Bloomington, IN: Indiana University Press, 1995), p. 215.

26   And indeed, lesbian and gay American cinema in the 1990s saw several films featuring such a trope. See for example, *The Detta* (Ira Sachs, 1996), *Parallel Sons* (John Young, 1994), *Rescuing Desire* (Adam Rogers, 1995) and *Out of Season* (Jeanette Buck, 1998).

27   B. Ruby Rich, 'When difference is (more than) skin deep', in Martha Gever, John Greyson and Pratibha Parmar (eds), *Queer Looks: Perspectives on Lesbian and Gay Film and Video* (New York: Routledge, 1993), pp. 318–39.

28   Zygmunt Bauman, *Modernity and the Holocaust* (Ithaca, NY: Cornell University Press, 1989).

29   The minutiae surrounding Czerniakow's oscillation between hope and denial, on the one hand, and deep despair, on the other, that eventually resulted in his final decision, are preserved and available to contemporary readers. See Raul Hilberg, Stanislaw Staron and Josef Kermisz (eds), *The Warsaw Diary of Adam Czerniakow: Prelude to Doom*, trans. Stanislaw Staron and the staff of Yad Vashem (New York: Stein, 1979).

30   A comparable process would appear to be taking place at the end of Toni Morrison's *Beloved*, which concludes with the words, 'it was not a story to pass on'. As November's 'forgetting' is always only a kind of temporary stand-in for the act of 'remembering', Morrison's 'pass on', which means both to 'repeat' and to 'let go', also has at once a doubled and, it would seem, mutually excluding signification. *Beloved: a Novel* (New York: Knopf, 1987).

31   The idea that one should have to forget in order to begin – or rather that there is already something to forget before one begins to begin – seems a profoundly iconoclastic notion, in that it undermines the conventional relation of the present to the future and subverts the idea of time as unidirectional, continuous, regular and unique. The value of a non-progressional temporality has obsessed a considerable number of scholars, from Proust to Bergson to Hayden White to Walter Benjamin: like *November Moon*, Benjamin's work is also memorable for, among other things, an angel – specifically the angel of history that appears in 'Theses on the philosophy of history', in Hannah Arendt (ed.), *Illuminations*, trans. Harry Zohn (New York: Schocken, 1969), pp. 255–64.

32   And it is for this reason that Felman designates the Holocaust as an 'event-without-a-witness', Shoshana Felman and Dori Laub, *Testimony: Crises of Witnessing in Literature, Psychoanalysis and History* (New York: Routledge, 1992), p. 219.

8 The autoethnographic performance: reading Richard Fung's queer hybridity

José Muñoz

In the Caribbean we are all performers
Antonio Benítez-Rojo

Are Queens born or made? The royal visit sequence of Richard Fung's *My Mother's Place* (1991) undoes the either/or bind that such a question produces. A sequence from the film's beginning narrates a moment when the pasty spectre of a monarch born to the throne helps to formulate an entirely different type of queen. A flickering sound and image connotes an 8 mm camera, the technology used before the advent of amateur video cameras. A long black car leads a procession as school children, mostly black girls and boys wearing white or light blue uniforms, look on. At the centre of the procession we can easily identify the British Queen. The voiceover narration sets the scene:

> Under the watchful eyes of the priests we stand for ages on the side walk, burning up in our school uniforms. Then quickly they pass, and all you see is a long white glove making a slow choppy motion. We wave the little flags we were given and fall back into class. White socks on our arms my sister and I practice the royal wave at home. After Trinidad and Tobago got our independence in 1962 Senghor, Salessi and Indira Ghandi also made visits. We were given school holidays just like we got for the Queen and Princess Margaret, but my mother never took pictures of them.

The young Chinese Trinidadian's identification with the Queen is extremely complicated. Practising the royal wave, in this instance, is an important example of a brand of dissidence that Homi Bhabha has defined as 'colonial mimicry': 'mimicry emerges as the representation of a difference that is itself a process of disavowal. Mimicry is thus the sign of the double articulation; a complex strategy of reform, regulation and discipline, which "appropriates" the other as it visualizes power.'[1] The modalities of difference that inform this royal gesture are not only structured around the colonized/colonizer divide but also a gay/straight one.

This moment of proto-drag 'flaunting' not only displays an ambivalence to empire and the protocols of colonial pedagogy, but also reacts against the forced gender prescriptions that such systems reproduce. This mode of mimicry is theatrical inasmuch as it mimes and renders hyperbolic the symbolic ritual that it is relying upon. This brief 'visualization' of power is representative of Fung's cultural performance. Fung's video 'visualizes' the workings of power in ethnographic and pornographic films, two discourses that assign subjects like Fung, colonized, coloured and queer, the status of terminally 'other' object. Many of the performances that Fung produces are powerful disidentifications with these othering discourses.

Eve Kosofsky Sedgwick recently defined the term 'queer' as a *practice* that develops for queer children as

> the ability to attach intently to a few cultural objects, objects of high or popular culture or both, objects whose meaning seemed mysterious, excessive or oblique in relation to the codes most readily available to us, [which] became a prime resource for survival. We needed for there to be sites where meanings didn't line up tidily with each other, and we learn to invest these sites with fascination and love.[2]

Thus to perform queerness is to constantly disidentify; to constantly find oneself thriving on sites where meaning does not properly 'line up'. This is equally true of hybridity, another modality where meaning or identifications do not properly line up. The postcolonial hybrid is a subject whose identity practices are structured around an ambivalent relationship to the signs of empire and the signs of the 'native', a subject who occupies a space between the West and the rest.

This is not to say that the terms 'hybridity' and 'queerness' are free of problems. In a recent article Ella Shohat attempts to temper the celebratory aura that currently envelops the word 'hybridity':

> As a descriptive catch all term, 'hybridity' *per se* fails to discriminate between diverse modalities of hybridity, for example, forced assimilation, internalized self-rejection, political co-optation, social conformism, cultural mimicry, and creative transcendence.[3]

It would be dangerous to collapse together the different modalities of hybridity we encounter in the first world and its neo-colonial territories, and in the various diasporas to which the diversity of ethnically marked people belong. Queerness, too, has the capacity to flatten difference in the name of coalition. Scholars working with these anti-essentialist models of identity need to resist the urge to give in to crypto-essentialist understandings of these terms that eventually position them as universal identificatory sites of struggle. Despite some of the more problematic uses of the individual terms 'hybridity' and 'queerness', I take the risk of melding them when discussing the work of cultural producers such as Fung because hybridity helps one understand how queer lives are fragmented into various identity bits: some of them adjacent, some of them complementary, some of them antagonistic. The hybrid – and terms that can be roughly theorized as equivalents, such as the Creole or the Mestizo – are paradigms that help us account for the complexities and impossibilities of identity, but except for a certain degree of dependence on institutional frames, what a subject can do from her or his position of hybridity is, basically, open-ended. The important point here is that identity practices such as queerness and hybridity are not a priori sites of contestation but, instead, spaces of productivity where identity's fragmentary nature is accepted and negotiated. It is my understanding that these practices of identification inform the reflexivity of Fung's work.

The concept of hybridity has also been engaged by theorists outside of the field of postcolonial or critical race studies. Bruno Latour, the French philosopher of science, has recently put forth that the hybrid is a concept that must be understood as central to the story of modernity. Latour contends that the moderns, the denizens and builders of modernity, are known not for individual breakthroughs such as the invention of humanism, the emergences of the sciences, the secularization and modernization of the world, but instead with the conjoined structure of these historical movements. Latour writes:

> The essential point of the modern constitution is that it renders the work of mediation that assembles hybrids invisible, unthinkable, unrepresentable. Does this lack of representation limit the work of mediation in any way? No, for the modern world would immediately cease to function. Like all other collectives it lives on that blending. On the contrary (and here the beauty of the mechanism comes to light), *the modern constitution allows the expanded proliferation of the hybrids whose existence, whose very possibility, it denies.*[4]

Latour's formulation explains the way in which modern culture produces hybrids while at the same time attempting to elide or erase the representation or signs of hybridity. I want to suggest that Latour's formulation might also give us further insight into empire's panicked response to the hybrids it continuously produces. Empire's institutions, like colonial pedagogy, are in no small part responsible for the proliferation of hybrid identities, but it is in colonialism's very nature to delineate clearly between the West and the rest. Its terms do not allow for the inbetween status of hybridity. We might thus understand the work of hybrid cultural producers such as Fung as a making visible of the mediations that attempt to render hybridity invisible and unthinkable: in both *My Mother's Place* and *Chinese*

Characters (1986), Fung works to make hybridity and its process comprehensible and visible.

Fredric Jameson has recently contended that, 'The visual is essentially pornographic, which is to say it has its end in rapt, mindless fascination.'[5] But some visuals are more pornographic than others. The epistemological affinity of ethnography and pornography has been explained in 'Ethnography, pornography and the discourses of power', Bill Nichols's, Christian Hansen's and Catherine Needham's mapping of various ways in which the two regimes of ethnography and pornography share a similar discourse of dominance.[6] Both discourses are teleologically cognate in so far as they both strive for the achievement of epistemological utopias where the 'Other' and knowledge of the 'Other' can be mastered and contained. Ethnotopia can be characterized as a world of limitless observation, where 'we know them', while pornotopia is a world where 'we have them', 'a world of lust unlimited'.[7] At the end of that essay the authors are unable to imagine a new symbolic regime or practice where these genres can be reformulated differently, in ways that actively attempt to avoid the imperialist or exploitative vicissitudes of these cinematic genres. My project here is to explicate the ways in which Richard Fung's work invites the viewer to push this imagining further. Fung challenges the formal protocols of such genres through the repetition and radical reinterpretation of such stock characters as the 'native informant'[8] and the racialized body in porn. I will be considering two of Fung's videos, *My Mother's Place* and *Chinese Characters*. The former tape traces the Fung family's migratory history in the Asian diaspora through a series of interviews with Rita Fung, the artist's mother, while the latter considers the role of the eroticized Asian Other in the discourse of gay male pornography.

A consideration of the performativity of Fung's production sheds valuable light on his project. Reiteration and citation are the most easily identifiable characteristics of this mode of performativity. I will suggest that by its use of such strategies as voiceover monologues, found familial objects such as home movie footage, and the technique of video keying, Fung's work deploys a practice of performativity that repeats and cites, *with a difference*, the generic fictions of the native Other in ethnography and the Asian 'bottom'[9] in fetishizing, North American, speciality porn. The definition of 'performative' I am producing is not meant as an overarching one, but as a working definition designed to deal with the specificity of Fung's productions. This operative understanding of performativity is informed, to some degree, by the work of Judith Butler in her most recent book *Bodies that Matter: on the Discursive Limits of Sex*. Butler explains that if a performative succeeds,

> that action echoes prior actions, and accumulates the force of authority through the repetition or citation of a prior authoritative set of practices. What this means then, is that a performative 'works' to the extent that it draws on and covers over the constitutive conventions by which it is mobilized.[10]

In this quotation Butler is answering a rhetorical question put forward by Jacques Derrida when he considers whether or not a performative would work if it did not 'repeat a "coded" or iterable utterance . . . if it were not identifiable in some way as a "citation"?'[11] Butler, in her analysis, is in agreement with Derrida as she understands a performative as working only if it taps into the force of its site of citation, the original that is being repeated, while it draws on and, in time, covers the conventions that it will ultimately undermine. While Butler's essay is concerned specifically with the performative charge of queerness, its ability to redo and challenge the conventions of heterosexual normativity, it can also explicate the workings of *various* 'minority' identifications. Homi Bhabha defines the power of performance in the postcolonial world as the '"sign of the present" the performativity of discursive practice, the *recits* of the everyday, the repetition of the empirical, the ethics of self enactment'.[12] The repetition of the quotidian in Bhabha, like citation and repetition in Butler, elucidates Fung's own ethics of self-enactment.

Fung's performances work as 'autoethnography', inserting a subjective, performative, often combative, 'native I' into ethnographic film's detached discourse and gay male pornography's colonizing use of the Asian male body. I will be suggesting that through acts such as postcolonial mimicry and the emergence of a hybridized and queerly reflexive performance practice, the social and symbolic economy that regulates otherness can be offset.

The movement of personal histories into a public sphere is typical of autoethnography. Françoise Lionnet describes the way in which autoethnography functions in written cultural production as '[a] scepticism about writing the self, the auto-biography, turning it into the allegory of the ethnographic project that self consciously moves from the general to the particular to the general'.[13] These movements from general to specific, and various shades inbetween, punctuate Fung's work. Lionnet, in her study of folk anthropologist and novelist Zora Neale Hurston, conceives of autoethnography as a mode of cultural performance. She explains that autoethnography is a 'text/performance' and 'transcends pedestrian notions of referentiality, for the staging of the event is part of the process of "passing on", elaborating cultural forms, which are not static and inviolable but dynamically involved in the creation of culture itself'.[14] The creation of culture in this style of performance is always already braided to the production of self in autoethnography in so far as culture itself is the field in which this 'figural anthropology' of the self comes to pass.[15]

Mary Louise Pratt has also recently employed the term 'autoethnography' in her study of travel writing on the imperial frontier. In this study, Pratt lucidly outlines the differences between ethnography and autoethnography:

> I use these terms [autoethnography and autoethnographic expression] to refer to instances in which colonized subjects undertake to represent themselves in

ways which engage with the colonizer's own terms. If ethnographic texts are a means in which Europeans represent to themselves their (usually subjugated) others, autoethnographic texts are those the others construct in response to or in dialogue with those metropolitan representations.[16]

Conventional video and documentary style can, in the case of Fung and in the light of Pratt's definition, be understood as the 'colonizer's terms' that are being used to address the metropolitan form. But in Fung's case these terms work to address more than just the metropolitan form and the colonizer. The terms are also meant to speak to the colonized in a voice that is doubly authorized, both by the metropolitan form and subaltern speech. I am not proposing an explanation where form and content are disentangled. More accurately, I mean to imply the metropolitan form is inflected by the power of subaltern speech and the same is equally true in reverse. Fung's cultural work elucidates a certain imbrication – that the metropolitan form needs the colonial 'other' to function. Autoethnography is a strategy that seeks to disrupt the hierarchical economy of colonial images and representations by making visible the presence of subaltern energies and urgencies *in* metropolitan culture. Autoethnography worries easy binarisms such as colonized and the colonizer or subaltern and metropolitan by presenting subaltern speech through the channels and pathways of metropolitan representational systems.

Lionnet's and Pratt's theorizations are useful tools in understanding the tradition of autobiographical film that has flourished in North America since 1968.[17] The practice of combining evidentiary sound/image cinema with narratives of personal history has been especially prevalent in video documentary production since the advent of widespread independent video production in the late 1960s. Video technology provided disenfranchised sectors of the public sphere with inexpensive and mobile means to produce alternative media. Video documentary practices were adopted by many different minority communities that we might understand as counter-publics. Native Americans, African-Americans, Asians, Latina/os, feminists, gays and lesbians all made considerable contributions to the field of documentary video. In the 1980s, AIDS/HIV activist groups such as ACT-UP made use of this technology and the practices of documentary in politically adroit ways.[18]

We might consider this modality as an intensification of what Jim Lane has called the 'personal as political trend' in post 1960s autobiographical film.[19] Lane registers a diminishing production of overtly political cinema in the face of what he understands as the more privatized identity politics of the 1970s and 1980s. Such a dichotomy would be of little use when considering trends in video production, a medium which has always found political relevance precisely in the politics of identity and different minority communities.

This strain of autobiographical documentary is best illustrated in recent work by numerous queer video artists. Fung's practice shares an autoethnographic impulse with the work of Sadie Benning and the late Marlon Riggs, to identify only two examples from a larger field. Riggs excavated an African-American gay male image that has been elided in the history of both black communities and queer communities.[20] Benning's confessional experimental videos produce an interesting ethnography of white queer youth culture.[21] In both these examples the artists inhabit their videos as subjects who articulate their cultural location through their own subcultural performances as others: poetic teen angst monologues in the case of Benning, and from Riggs, vibrant snap diva virtuosity that includes, but is not limited to, dance, music and monologues.

This queer trend that I am identifying is in many ways an effort to reclaim the past and put it in direct relationship with the present. Autoethnography is not interested in searching for some lost and essential experience, because it understands the relationship that subjects have with their own pasts as complicated yet necessary fictions. Stuart Hall provides a formulation that addresses this complicated relationship between one's identity and one's past:

> Far from being eternally fixed in some essentialized past, they [identities] are subject to the continuous play of history, culture and power. Far from being grounded in a mere 'recovery' of the past, which is waiting to be found and which, when found, will secure our sense of ourselves into eternity, identities are the names we give to the different ways in which we are positioned by, and position our selves within, narratives of the past.[22]

A subject is not locating her or his essential history by researching a racial or cultural past; what is to be located is in fact just one more identity bit that constitutes the matrix which is hybridity.

This relationship between a past and present identity is articulated through a voiceover near the end of *My Mother's Place*, when Fung explains that his mother: 'connects me to a past I would have no other way of knowing. And in this sea of whiteness, of friends, enemies and strangers, I look at her and know who I am.' The past that his mother makes available to Fung is not an essentialized racial past but instead a necessary fiction of the past that grounds the video artist in the present.

Fung's relationship with and love for his mother are at the centre of *My Mother's Place*. The video paints an endearing portrait of Rita Fung as a woman who came of age during colonialism and took her identifications with the colonial paradigm with her to the moment of decolonization. It is shot in Canada and Trinidad and is composed of a series of 'interviews' and recollections that form a decidedly personal register. This video portrait of his mother is a queer son's attempt to reconstruct and better understand his identity formation through equally powerful identifications, counter-identifications and disidentifications with his mother and her own unique relationship to the signs of colonization. The tape relies on its documentary subject's ability to tell her own story in a witty and captivating fashion.

The opening of *My Mother's Place* includes a section subtitled 'Reading instructions'. This depicts a sequence of women, mostly academics and activists, mostly women of colour, sitting in a chair in front of a black background on which photographs of different women's faces are projected. After the women pronounce on various critical issues including imperialism, gender, political action and exile, the screen is filled with captions that loosely define the cluster of talking heads on the screen. The descriptions include: teacher, writer, sociologist, arts administrator, feminist, poet, Jamaican, English, Indian, friends. The visual text is accompanied by Fung's voiceover saying 'these women have never met my mother'. This 'not lining-up' of sound and image is not meant to undermine any of the women's interviews. More nearly it speaks to the ways in which identification with neither his mother nor with his academic friends and colleagues suffices. This moment where things do not line up is a moment of reflexivity that is informed by and through the process of queerness *and* hybridity. It is a moment where hybridity is not a fixed positionality but a survival strategy that is essential for both queers and postcolonial subjects who are subject to the violence that institutional structures reproduce.

This scepticism and ambivalence which Lionnet identifies as being characteristic of autoethnography can be located throughout Fung's project. Fung employs various tactics to complicate and undermine his own discourse. During a sequence towards the middle of the video the artist once again employs home movie footage. The 8 mm home video instantly achieves a texture reminiscent of childhood. In viewing the section from the tape the spectator becomes aware of the ways in which the videomaker supplies contradictory information on three different levels: the visual image, the voiceover and the written text which appears on the screen. The visual image shows a young Rita Fung strolling the garden in her 1950s-style *Good Housekeeping* dress and red pillbox hat. She does not look directly at the camera. Her stride is calm and relaxed. There is a cut and Rita Fung reappears, her back to the camera as she walks off, holding the hand of a little boy. The little boy is wearing a white button-down oxford and black slacks. He holds on tightly to his mother's hand. The next cut shows both mother and son smiling and walking towards the camera. This is the first view the spectator has of the narrator. The voiceover scene matches the image by narrating a family history:

> It's Sunday after Mass. Dressed in satin, she looks like the woman in the *Good Housekeeping* magazine that arrives from the States. During the week she is off to work while I go to school. She wears a pencil behind her right ear and her desk is near the Coke machine. When she is not at the shop she is washing clothes, cooking, sitting on a box in the garden, cutters in hand, weeding. In the evening she is making poppy sauce or making cookies to sell. We dropped six cookies at a time in a plastic bag while we watched *Gunsmoke* on TV. When I bring home forms from school she puts 'housewife' down as occupation.

The women in *Good Housekeeping* are housewives. In the afternoon they wait at home to serve cookies and milk to their children. Mom was never home when I got home from school.

When this segment of narration concludes, the flickering sound of home projector fades and is replaced by the film's nondiegetic score. Text appears over the image of young Richard and Rita Fung. It reads: 'These pictures show more about my family's desire than how we actually lived.' The voiceover narration then continues: 'But in all the family pictures this is the only shot that shows what I remember.' The image that follows this statement is of a young Richard wearing shorts and T-shirt, still holding onto his mother's hand as they both dance. A new title is superimposed over the image and this text responds to the last bit of narration by explaining: 'We're doing the twist.' The next image shows an uncoordinated little Richard dancing and jumping barefoot in his backyard. He looks directly at the camera and sticks his tongue out. His manner is wild and effeminate. The narrator then introduces the last instalment of text in this segment by saying: 'And me, well you can see from these pictures that I was just an ordinary boy doing ordinary boy things.' The screen is then once again covered with text. The story superimposed over the image is one that is familiar to many children who showed cross-dressing tendencies in early childhood: 'One day Mom caught me in one of her dresses and threatened to put me out in the street. . . . I was scared but it didn't stop me.'

When Fung betrays the visual image as a totally imaginary ideal that was more about his parents' fantasy life than about what really happened he is refusing the colonial fantasy of assimilation that his family's home movies articulated. In this scene, and throughout *My Mother's Place*, the 'Queen's English' is spoken by a mimic man, a subject who has interpolated the mark of colonial power into his discourse but through repetition is able to disarticulate these traditional discourses of authority. The term coined by Bhabha to describe the condition of the colonized subject, 'not quite/not white', aptly depicts the overall effect of the 'all-American' home movie footage. The statements disseminated through the visual text are directly connected with Fung's then proto-queer identity as an effeminate boy, the type of queer child which Sedgwick describes as a subject for whom meaning does not neatly line up. He was not, as his voiceover suggested, 'an ordinary boy doing ordinary boy things', he was, in fact, a wonderfully swishy little boy who, among other things, liked to dress in his mother's *Good Housekeeping* style dresses, liked the fictional moms on television who baked cookies for their children. I would also suggest that we might understand the actual storytelling practice of the film, the not-lining-up of image, sound and text, as something that is decidedly queer about Fung's production. This not-lining-up of image and sound is a deviation from traditional documentary, which is chiefly concerned with sound and image marching together as a tool of authorization. The not-lining-up strategy was employed in different ways in Fung's earlier videotape *Chinese Characters*, achieving similar disidentificatory effects. While the two tapes deal with vastly different subjects they nonetheless, on the level of process and practice, share significant strategical manoeuvres that once again are indebted to a predominantly queer wave in documentary production.

The reassertions of agency that Fung displays in *My Mother's Place*, the way in which he claims the natives' authority in the ethnographic project, are not entirely different from those that are achieved in *Chinese Characters*. This videotape performs an intervention in the field of mainstream pornography by adding an Asian male *presence* where it has routinely been excluded. This experimental documentary interviews gay Asian men about their relationships to pornography. The documentary subjects reflect upon the way in which pornography helped mould them as desiring subjects. The tape also includes a narrative sequence in which a young Asian man penetrates the white gay male field of pornography by being video-keyed into an early porn loop.

The mainstream gay pornography that has dominated the market, produced by California-based companies such as Catalina, Falcon and Vivid Video, has contributed to a somewhat standardized image of the porn performer. It is paradoxical that the promise of pornotopia, the promise of lust *unlimited*, desire without restriction, is performed by a model who generally conforms to a certain rigid set of physical and racial characteristics. This standardized porn model is a paler shade of white and hairless, and he is usually young and muscled. He is the blueprint that is later visualized infinitely at gay male identity hubs such as gyms and dance clubs. The mainstream porn image, throughout the late 1980s and early 1990s, continued to evolve into an all too familiar clean-shaven Anglo twenty-something clone. While the pornography with which Fung interacts in his interventionist video performances is not quite as homogenized as today's pornography, the porn loops he riffs upon still display the trace of this white normative sex clone. The point here is not to moralize upon how such an image might be harmful, since it is my belief that it is a futile project to deliberate on the negativity or positivity of images within representational fields.[23] Instead, it is far more useful to note the ways in which Fung transfigures porn through his practices. His video production illuminates the normative logics of porn productions by deploying, through an act of postcolonial mimicry, a disidentification with a popularized ideal: the Asian gay male body. Fung's disidentification with the generic and racially inflected protocols of porn opens up a space that breaks down the coherence of white domination in the gay male erotic imaginary. This disidentification accesses possibilities, through the unlikely vehicle of the Orientialized body, that are ultimately sex and pornography positive, but nonetheless rooted in a struggle to free up the ethnocentric conceit that dominates the category of the erotic in the pornographic imaginary.

By 'ethnocentric conceit' I mean the troubling propensity of representing standardized white male beauty as a norm, and the tendency in erotic representation to figure non-white men as exotic kink.

It is important to note here the powerful connection between gay male porn and gay male culture. Richard Dyer, in an often-cited essay on gay male pornographic production, has pointed out that gay male pornography is analogous to gay male sexuality in more general terms.[24] Understanding pornography as an analogue to broader aspects of gay male culture makes even more sense today, as pornography, during this second decade of the AIDS pandemic, is one of the only completely safe and sex-positive, identity-affirming spaces/practices left to gay men. Fung's critique of porn, or the one that is being offered here, should not be understood as antipornographic; rather, by unveiling the ethnocentric bias at work in the pornographic imaginary that is collectively produced by the porn industry, we can better understand the larger problem of white normativity and racism within North American gay male culture.

In her essay 'The she-man: postmodern bi-sexed performance in film and video', Chris Straayer has recently described the process of this re-enacting of historically denied agency in Fung's work. She explains that, 'Fung uses technology to intervene in conventional positioning. First he video-keys himself into a pornographic film where he then poses as the lure for a desiring "stud".'[25] Straayer's description is evocative of the way in which the terrain of pornography becomes a 'contact zone',[26] one in which the ideological (visualized in Fung's technological reinsertion into the representational field) and the epistemological (pornography's need to carnally know the Other) collide.

The ideological effect I am referring to is visible in a scene from *Chinese Characters* where an actual Chinese character is video-keyed into an exclusively white gay male porn film. The Asian male body, after being keyed into the grainy seventies porn loop, proceeds to take what seems like a leisurely stroll in an outdoor sex scene. The act of taking a leisurely walk is designed to connote casual tourism. The touristic pose taken here is quite different from the usual options available to gay men of colour in the pornography industry. This performatively reappropriates the position of the white male subject who can touristically gaze at minority bodies in such tapes as *Orient Express* (1990), *Latin from Manhattan* (1992) or *Blackshaft* (1993).[27] The newly subjectivized Other who has been walking through this scene then comes face to face with a character from this porn loop. The white male reaches out to the Asian male who, by the particular generic protocols of this vanilla porn subgenre, would be excluded from that symbolic field. Donning a 'traditional' dome-shaped Asian field worker's hat, the Asian male subject plays with his own nipples as he then materializes in a California poolside orgy. Such a performance of autoeroticism, within a symbolic field such as the 1970s white male porn loop, realigns and disrupts the dominant stereotype in so far as it portrays the Asian male body not as the perpetually passive bottom who depends on the white male top, but instead as a subject who can enjoy scopic pleasure in white objects while at the same time producing his own pleasure.

Fung later, in a print essay, deals with the marginal genre of interracial porn, especially tapes featuring Asian men.[28] In this essay Fung explains that the Asian male body in interracial videotapes is almost always cast as the passive bottom who depends on the white male top to get off. I find it significant that this inquiry into interracial porn follows an initial engagement with porn's exclusionary and racially biased image hierarchy (the critique that *Chinese Characters* produces). Within the logic of porn, a subfield such as racially integrated or exclusively non-white tapes are roughly equivalent to other modalities of kink such as bondage, sado-masochism, shaving and so on. The point here is that, due to white normativity of the pornotopic field, race *counts* as a different sexual practice (that is, doing sadomasochism, doing Asians). Thus race, like sadomasochism, is essentially a performance. An observation of Fung's practices reveals that the Asian men in his tapes essentially repeat Orientalized performances with a difference through the video insertions and interviews they perform in the tape.

Chinese Characters narrates another cultural collision through different repre-sentational strategies. What seems like a traditional Chinese folk tale is first heard as the camera lyrically surveys what appears to be a Chinese garden. When the visual image abruptly cuts to a full body shot of an Asian man trying on different outfits, the nondiegetic 'traditional' Chinese music is replaced by a disco soundtrack that signifies one has entered a gay male subculture. For a brief period we continue to hear the folk tale with the disco soundtrack. When the folk tale expires we hear the soundtrack of a porn trailer that announces the name of recognizable white porn performers/icons, such as Al Parker. The announcer's voice produces a typical raunchy rap that eventually fades as a techno-disco beat rises in volume. The Asian man finally chooses his outfit and commences his cruise. The filaments of the artist's hybridized identity, in this brief sequence, are embodied in sound and performance. The gay man's body literally bridges these different sound messages: traditional Chinese music, the heavy accent of a Chinese–American retelling what seems to be an ancient fable, the voice of the white porn announcer as he describes the hot action, and the techno-beat that eventually emerges as the score for the gay man's cruise. On the level of the visual, the fact that the subject is dressing during the scene identifies it as a moment of queer hybrid self-*fashioning*. Both the performances of drag and striptease are referenced during this sequence. Rather than taking off his clothing, as in the traditional striptease (the process of revealing an 'authentic' self), the Asian male about to commence his cruise continuously dresses and redresses, enacting a kind of counter-striptease that does not fetishize a material body but instead mediates on the ways in which, through costume and perform-ance, one continuously *makes* a self. Each outfit that is tried on displays a different modality of being queer; all the ensembles depict different positions on a gay male subcultural spectrum. All of it is disguise and the sequence itself works as a catalogue of various queer modalities of self-presentation.

Of these different disguises, the Orientalized body is one of the most important. Fung's critique is not simply aimed at the exclusion of Asians from pornographic video and, in turn, other aspects of a modern gay lifeworld. It is also, through a mode of mimicry that I understand as disidentificatory, a challenge to the limited and racist understandings of the gay male body in pornography. Orientalism is a powerful critical term first coined by Edward Said in his influential study of that name. There Said described Orientalism as 'a style of thought that is based on an ontological and epistemological division made between "the Orient" and (most of the time) "the Occident"'.[29] The totalizing implications of Said's theory have, over the last decade, been critiqued by many scholars. Bhabha, in perhaps the most famous of these challenges to Said's analysis of Orientalism, points to the ambiv-alence of power in colonial discourse, arguing that Said's narrative of Orientalism posited all agency and power on the side of the 'Occident', ignoring the ways in which the colonized might gain access to power and enact self against and within the colonial paradigm.[30] Recently, Lisa Lowe has made a significant contribution to the development of the theoretical discourse on Orientalism by further describing the phenomenon with a special attention to its nuanced workings:

> I do not construct a master narrative or a singular history of orientalism, whether of influence or of comparison. Rather, I argue for a conception of orientalism as heterogeneous and contradictory; to this end I observe, on the one hand, that orientalisms consist of uneven orientalist situations across different cultural and historical sites, and on the other, that each of these orientalisms is internally complex and unstable. My textual readings give particular attention to those junctures at which narratives of gendered, racial, national and class differences complicate and interrupt the narrative of orientalism, as well as to the points at which orientalism is refunctioned and rearticulated against itself.[31]

Fung's engagement with Orientalism can be understood to operate in a similar way to Lowe's. Orientalism in *Chinese Characters*, like the signs of colonial power in *My Mother's Place*, are refunctioned by Fung's disidentification with these cultural referents. Disidentification is the performative re-citation of the stereotypical Asian bottom in porn, and the trappings of colonial culture. In this instance, we have a useful example of the way in which disidentification engages and recycles popular forms with a difference. Fung's strategy of disidentification reappropriates an ambivalent yet highly charged set of images – those representing the queer Asian body in porn – and remakes them in a fashion that explores and outlines the critical ambivalences that make this image a vexing site of identification and desire for Asian gay men and other spectators/consumers with antiracist political positions.

The erotic is not demonized but instead used as a site for critical engagement. Documentary, in the case of Fung's production, is reflexive practice inasmuch as it aims to rearticulate dominant culture and document a history of the other, an orientalized other that remakes otherness as a strategy of enacting the self that is undermined and limited by orientalist and colonialist discourses.

Specific scenes, postcolonial or decolonized spaces such as Fung's Trinidad or the Asian community in Toronto, enable these sorts of rearticulations by functioning as contact zones, locations of hybridity that, because their location is liminal, allow for new social formations that are not as easily available at empire's centre.

The Caribbean basin is an appropriate setting for *My Mother's Place* in that it is a 'contact zone', a space where the echoes of colonial encounters still echo in the contemporary sound produced by the historically and culturally disjunctive situation of temporal and spatial copresence that is understood as the postcolonial moment.

Pratt elaborates one of the most well-developed theories of contact zones. For Pratt, the 'contact' component of contact zone is defined as a perspective:

> A 'contact' perspective emphasizes how subjects are constituted in and by their relations to each other. It treats the relations among colonizers and colonized, or travelers and 'travelees', not in terms of separateness or apartheid, but in terms of copresence, interaction, interlocking understanding and practice, often within radically asymmetrical relations of power.[32]

For Pratt, a contact zone is both a location and a different path to thinking about asymmetries of power and the workings of the colonizer/colonized mechanism. Both videotapes I have analysed in this essay, stage copresences which are essentially instances of contact: the contact between a colonized queer boy (and his mother) with the signs of empire and imperialism such as the Queen, *Good Housekeeping* magazine and *Gunsmoke* in *My Mother's Place*, and, in the case of *Chinese Characters*, the contact between the Asian male body in pornotopia and the whiteness of the industry that either relegates him to the status of perpetual bottom or excludes him altogether.

It would also be important to situate the artist's own geography in this study of contact zones. Fung's Trinidad is considered a contact zone par excellence in part because its colonial struggle has been well documented by postcolonial thinkers, such as C.L.R. James, who have written famous accounts of the island's history of colonization.[33] Fung's status as Asian in a primarily black and white colonial situation further contributes to Fung's postcolonial identity. An Asian in such a setting, like an Asian in the already subcultural field of (white-dominated) gay male culture, is at least doubly a minority and doubly fragmented from the vantage point of dominant culture. Canada, on the other hand, has not received extensive consideration as a postcolonial space.[34] A settler colony, Canada is positioned as a somewhat ambiguous postcolonial site. Canada, for example, is an importer of US pornography. It is therefore, on the level of the erotic imaginary, colonized by a US erotic image hierarchy.[35] I want to suggest that the geographical location of Fung's production is significant when considering the hybridity of his representational strategies. Fung's *place*, in Canada, Trinidad, gay male culture, documentary practice, ethnography, pornography, the Caribbean and Asian diasporas, is not quite fixed, thus this work is uniquely concentrated on issues of place and displacement.

Furthermore, these zones are all productive spaces of hybridization where complex and ambivalent *American* identities are produced. The process by which these hybrid identity practices are manufactured is one that we can understand as syncretism. Many Latin American and US Latino critics have used the term not only to explicate a complex system of cultural expressions but also to describe the general character of the Caribbean. The Cuban theorist of postmodernism, Antonio Benítez-Rojo uses the term supersyncretism, which for him arises from the collision of European, African and Asian components within the plantation. For Benítez-Rojo the phenomenon of supersyncretism is at its most visible when one considers performance:

> If I were to have to put it in a word I would say performance. But performance not only in terms of scenic interpretation but also in terms of the execution of a ritual. That is the 'certain way' in which two Negro women who conjured away the apocalypse were walking. In this 'certain kind of way' there is expressed the mystic or magical (if you like) loam of civilizations that contributed to the formation of Caribbean culture.[36]

Benítez-Rojo's description is disturbing in so far as it reproduces its own form of Orientalism by fetishizing the conjuring culture of Cuban Santería and its mostly black and often female practitioners in a passing lyrical mention. There is, nonetheless, a useful refunctioning of this formulation. Instead of Benítez-Rojo's example I want to consider the acts that Fung narrates: the way in which a proto-queer Chinese Trinidadian boy with a sock on his hand mimics the Queen's wave, a gesture that is quite literally the hailing call of empire. Fung's videos are especially significant in that through such acts and performances they index, reflect upon and are reflexive of some of the most energized topics and debates confronting various discourses such as cultural studies, anthropology, queer theory and performance studies. In the end, white sock sheathed over his hybrid's hand like a magical prophylactic, protecting him from the disciplinary effect of colonial power, the queer gesture of Fung's wave deconstructs and ruptures the white mythologies of ethnotopia and pornotopia.[37]

I would like to thank Jane Gaines, Katie Kent, Mandy Merck, Eve Kosofsky Sedgwick, Gustavus Stadler and Sasha Torres for their suggestions on earlier versions of this article.

Notes

1   Homi K. Bhabha, *The Location of Culture* (New York and London: Routledge, 1993), p. 86.

2   Eve Kosofsky Sedgwick, *Tendencies* (Durham, NC: Duke University Press, 1993), p. 3.

3   Ella Shohat, 'Note on the post-colonial', *Social Text*, nos 31/32 (1992), p. 110.

4   Bruno Latour, *We Have Never Been Modern*, trans. Catherine Porter (Cambridge, MA: Harvard University Press, 1993), p. 34.

5   Fredric Jameson, *Signatures of the Visible* (New York and London: Routledge, 1992), p. 1.

6   This co-authored essay appears in Nichols' collection *Representing Reality: Issues and Concepts in Documentary* (Bloomington and Indianapolis, IN: Indiana University Press, 1992), pp. 201–28.

7   For further discussion of 'Pornotopia' see Linda Williams, *Hardcore: Power, Pleasure and the Frenzy of the 'Visible'* (Berkeley and Los Angeles, CA: University of California Press, 1989).

8   The idea of the 'native informant' has been discredited in contemporary anthropology and is now only written within scare quotes. The idea of indigenous people serving as informants to first world ethnographers has been critiqued throughout anthropology, critical theory and postcolonial studies.

9   In contemporary queer culture, 'top' and 'bottom' are words used to describe people's sexual proclivities. Women or men who prefer to be penetrated in the economy of sexual acts are bottoms, while those whose identification is connected with acts of penetration are usually referred to as tops. The words top and bottom do not capture the totality of one's sexual disposition but instead work as a sort of cultural shorthand. Asian gay men, as I will explain later in this article, are stereotypically labelled as strictly bottoms in the erotic image hierarchy of North American gay porn.

10 Judith Butler, *Bodies that Matter: on the Discursive Limits of Sex* (New York and London: Routledge, 1993), pp. 226–7.

11 Jacques Derrida, *Limited Inc.*, trans. Samuel Weber and Jeffery Mehlman (Evanston, IL: Northwestern University Press, 1988), p. 18.

12 Bhabha, *The Location of Culture*, p. 245.

13 Françoise Linnet, *Autobiographical Voices: Race, Gender and Self-Portraiture* (Ithaca, NY and London: Cornell University Press, 1989), pp. 99–100.

14 Ibid., p. 102.

15 This phrase is developed in the work of Michel Serres, *The Parasite*, trans. Lawrence R. Schehr (Baltimore, MD: Johns Hopkins University Press, 1982), p. 6.

16 Mary Louise Pratt, *Under Imperial Eyes: Travel Writing and Transculturation* (New York and London: Routledge, 1992), pp. 6–7.

17 Jim Lane has recently argued for the utility of literary theories of autobiography when considering the historical and theoretical underpinnings of autobiographical film. Lane's

article also provides a good gloss of the autobiographical film after 1968. See 'Notes on theory and the autobiographical documentary film in America', *Wide Angle*, vol. 15, no. 3 (1993), pp. 21–36.

18 For a historical overview of documentary video see Deirdre Boyle, 'A brief history of American documentary video', in Doug Hall and Sally Jo Fifer (eds), *Illuminating Video: an Essential Guide to Video Art* (New York: Aperture Bay Area Video Coalition, 1990), pp. 51–70. Boyle's most significant elision in the summary is the omission of gay, lesbian, queer and HIV/AIDS activist video documentary.

19 Lane, 'Notes on theory'.

20 See Marcos Becquer, 'Snap!thology and other discursive practices in *Tongues Untied*', *Wide Angle*, vol. 13, no. 2 (1992) for a fine reading of Riggs' black and queer performance and production.

21 Chris Holmlund has recently discussed Benning's videos as autoethnographies. 'When autobiography meets ethnography and girl meets girl: the "Dyke Docs" of Sadie Benning and Su Friedrich', unpublished manuscript, presented at Visible Evidence, Duke University, September 1993.

22 Stuart Hall, 'Cultural identity and cinematic representations', in Mbye Cham (ed.), *Ex-Iles: Essays on Caribbean Cinema* (Trenton, NJ: African World Press Inc., 1992), p. 133.

23 Michelle Wallace has argued forcefully against the trend to produce negative/positive critiques in critical race theory in her book *Invisibility Blues: from Pop to Theory* (New York and London: Verso, 1990), pp. 1–13.

24 Richard Dyer, 'Male gay porn: coming to terms', *Jump Cut*, no. 30 (1985), pp. 27–8.

25 Chris Straayer, 'The she-man: postmodern bi-sexed performance in the film and video', *Screen*, vol. 31, no. 3 (1990), p. 272. See Chapter 11 in this volume.

26 The term 'contact zone' is borrowed from Pratt's study, *Under Imperial Eyes*, pp. 6–7.

27 This tradition of white male spectators, firmly positioned in a superior hierarchical position, dates back to the very first photographic male pornography. A recent article on six gay male pornographic photographs, retrieved from the Kinsey Institute for Research in Sex, Gender and Reproduction, identifies an orientalist motif in the images of two men with turbans and 'Oriental' robes, having oral and anal sex in front of the artificial backdrop of exoticized palm trees. The article's author argues that Orientalism has long occupied an important position in gay male pornography. Todd D. Smith, 'Gay male pornography and the east: re-orienting the Orient', *History of Photography*, vol. 18, no. 1 (1994).

28 See Fung, 'Looking for my penis: the eroticized Asian in gay video porn', in *How Do I Look?: Queer Film and Video* (Seattle, WA: Bay Press, 1991), pp. 145–60. In this essay Fung explains an orientalism that Edward Said's seminal study could not imagine. Fung surveys the different racist constructions of Asian men that dominate gay male pornography, and tentatively imagines a pornography that affirms rather than appropriates Asian male sexuality.

29 Edward Said, *Orientalism* (New York: Random House, 1979), pp. 2–3.

30 Homi K. Bhabha, 'The other question: the stereotype of colonial discourse', *Screen*, vol. 24, no. 6 (1983), reprinted in Bhabha, *The Location of Culture*. A recent article by Tom Hastings offers the most interesting and sustained critique of the heterosexist blindspots in Said's study. 'Said's Orientalism and the discourse of (hetero)sexuality', *Canadian Review of American Studies*, vol. 23, no. 1 (1992), p. 130.

31   Lisa Lowe, *Critical Terrains: French and British Orientalisms* (Ithaca, NY and London: Cornell University Press, 1991), p. 5.

32   Pratt, *Under Imperial Eyes*, p. 7.

33   See, for example, C.L.R. James, *Beyond a Boundary* (London: Stanley Paul & Co., 1963).

34   Vijay Mishra and Bob Hodge touch upon Canada's ambiguous postcolonial status in their co-authored essay 'What is post(-)colonialism?', *Textual Practices*, vol. 15, no. 3 (1991), pp. 339–414. Canada is also covered in Bill Ashcroft, Gareth Griffiths and Helen Tiffin's important primer *The Empire Writes Back: Theory and Practice in Post-Colonial Literatures* (London and New York: Routledge, 1989).

35   The colonization of Canada's 'French-other', Québec, by a decidedly North American (here meant to include Anglo-Canadian and mainstream US) culture has been touched upon by Robert Schwartzwald in his essay 'Fear of federasty: Québec's inverted fictions', in Hortense Spillers (ed.), *Comparative American Identities: Race, Sex, and Nationality in the Modern Text* (New York: Routledge, 1991), p. 181. Fung's Asian queer community can be understood as another 'Other-Canada' that experiences a cultural colonization under the sign of North America.

36   Antonio Benítez-Rojo, *The Repeating Island: the Caribbean and the Postmodern Perspective*, trans. James E. Maranisis (Durham, NC: Duke University Press, 1992), p. 11.

37   Fung's videos are available through Video Data Bank, School of the Art Institute of Chicago, 112 South Michigan Avenue Suite 312, Chicago, Illinois 60603. Tel. 312 345 3550.

Part IV

Queer bodies and histories

9 Space, time, auteurity and the queer male body: the film adaptations of Robert Lepage

Peter Dickinson

> What constitutes the crystal-image is the most fundamental operation of time: since the past is constituted not after the present that it was but at the same time, time has to split itself in two at each moment as present and past, which differ from each other in nature, or, what amounts to the same thing, it has split the present in two heterogeneous directions, one of which is launched towards the future while the other falls into the past. . . . In fact the crystal constantly exchanges the two distinct images which constitute it, the actual image of the present which passes and the virtual image of the past which is preserved: distinct and yet indiscernible, and all the more indiscernible because distinct, because we do not know which is one and which is the other. This is unequal exchange, or the point of indiscernibility, the mutual image.[1]

In the scholarship on the films of Robert Lepage, a dominant critical paradigm has emerged to complement the academic focus on his theatre. Drawing primarily on the work of Gilles Deleuze, and making frequent comparisons to Alain Resnais and Alfred Hitchcock, critics have elaborated a whole taxonomy of space-time collapses – parallel montage, flashbacks and films-within-films – that work to absorb and sustain the past within the present in Lepage's cinematic representations of memory.[2] Such effects are, in turn, often linked to questions of authority, or the lack thereof. For, as Henry A. Garrity points out, the reconstructed past in Lepage's films is essentially a *de-* or *un*authorized one, lacking an identifiable narrator, in the sense that the edits used to evoke the past on screen are more often than not the result of Deleuzian 'irrational' cuts, which cannot be tied to a diegetic character's actual sensory-motor recognition but only to extradiegetic, or virtual, representation, what Deleuze calls the 'recollection-image'.[3] Neither can these recollection-images be tied to a stable point of view, other, that is, than that provided by the omniscient camera.[4] This is, perhaps, another way of saying that if Lepage's films, by virtue of their status as mediated texts generally and 'adaptations' more specifically, lack an author (in the Barthesian sense), they do at least have an auteur.

In this essay, I examine the intersection of auteurism and adaptation in Lepage's cinema by focusing on the transposition of images of the queer male body from his theatrical source texts to their filmed adaptations.[5] While perhaps not as visibly or politically 'out' as fellow Québécois theatre contemporaries René-Daniel Dubois and Michel Marc Bouchard, both of whom have seen their most famous (and famously gay) plays adapted memorably for the screen, neither does Lepage make a secret of his homosexuality. Moreover, his theatrical creations are filled with all manner of queer characters and images of same-sex eroticism. Curiously, however, in Lepage's first four films such characters and images are either largely absent or, in the case of *Le Confessionnal* (1995), so overlain with the symbolic weight of internalized guilt and dysfunction as to be borderline homophobic. It is possible to interpret such changes as Lepage's concession to the more mainstream audience tastes that govern the film industry. Likewise, one can see this as a necessary consequence of what, after Deleuze, we might call the collision of 'two distinct images' of the Québec cinematic imaginary, where past memories of political, social and religious repression continue to haunt present representations of gender and sexuality. At the same time, however, I would argue that the changes also point significantly to Lepage's own *self*-adaptation from theatre to film director.

What is at stake here is that, as film auteur, Lepage is arguably able to control his cinematic narratives more vigilantly than his theatrical ones, most of which were created collaboratively with his Théâtre Repère and Ex Machina troupes, or with cowriters such as Marie Brassard, and which Lepage has famously argued are never 'finished', because they are always evolving and being adapted in the neces-sarily evanescent and non-repeatable context of the performance moment. However, when it comes to the filmic artefact, and representations of the queer male body recorded (or not recorded) therein, a degree of auteurity necessarily accrues by virtue of each film's temporal positioning after, and thus definitive recording of, each play's constitutive images. Or, to put this in the terms out-lined by Deleuze in the epigraph to this essay, the image moves from the 'virtuality' of the past (those once fleeting and now lost moments of theatrical inspiration, rehearsal and performance) to the 'actuality' of the present, where it can be ceaselessly and unchangeably replayed in the temporal and spatial moment of apprehension that constitutes the film's projection. What I am interested in exploring in this essay, then, is the 'unequal exchange', the 'point of indiscernibility' that occurs in the 'crystallization' of images of the queer male body in Lepage's translation of, and surveillance over, his (and others') stage narratives as they are adapted into screen narratives. Because many of these images reflect a highly ambivalent – and atemporal – intersection of the religious and the secular, the political and the personal, the social and the familial in Lepage's work, attention must also be paid to the mutuality of the sexual symbolic and the national symbolic in much Québécois cinema.

Thus, before going on to my queer reading of Lepage's films, it is first important to note how any such reading is inherently governed by a larger, and largely psychoanalytic, cultural discourse in Québec, which has repeatedly recuperated filmic representations of homosexuality within a framework of Québec's arrested development and English Canada's social dominance. Here, I am alluding to a very influential 1987 article by Gilles Thérien, which argues that representations of same-sexuality in films by Micheline Lanctôt (*Sonatine* [1984]), Jean Beaudin (*Mario* [1984]), Léa Pool (*Anne Trister* [1986]) and Yves Simoneau (*Pouvoir intime* [1986]), among others, are in fact restagings of Québec's permanent identity crisis, where the child of the Quiet Revolution, alienated, but unable to completely cathect her/himself from, a patriarchal family environment, displaces this power dynamic onto a 'falsely feminine' idealization of a person of the same sex (who stands in for English Canada).[6] While Thérien's argument, and the homophobic pre-suppositions underpinning it, have been succinctly and efficiently deconstructed by critics such as Robert Schwartzwald and Bill Marshall,[7] this has not stopped others from applying its analytical paradigms to an endless catalogue of films not discussed by Thérien, including, in Martin Lefebvre's case, *Le Confessionnal*. As Lefebvre notes, the scenario described by Thérien 'completely overlaps with Marc's situation in Lepage's film':[8] Marc (Patrick Goyette), unable to reconcile his feelings of bitterness for his recently deceased 'adoptive' father, allows himself to fall back into a homosexual relationship with the ex-priest-turned-federal diplomat Massicotte (Jean-Louis Millette), who drags Marc to Japan on government business. Significantly, it is here, in this foreign country, that Marc commits suicide, death 'the only possible outcome for he who can't accept domination yet refuses to challenge it'.[9]

While I find much in Lefebvre's reading of *Le Confessionnal* to be convincing, this last point is less so. Indeed, the problem with conscripting the queer male as a signifier of failed or unrealized national identity in Québécois cultural production generally, and the corpus of Lepage's films more specifically, is that that signifier very often ends up a corpse. In an illuminating article on Hitchcock's frequent film adaptations of drama, Alenka Zupančič notes that '*Every time cinematic and theatre realities coincide*, every time cinematic and theatre narratives overlap, *there is a corpse.*'[10] André Loiselle has recently explored the pertinence of this insight to Jean Beaudin's 1992 adaptation of Dubois's play *Being at Home with Claude* and John Greyson's 1996 adaptation of Bouchard's play *Lilies (Les Feluettes)*.[11] One could just as easily apply this insight to the films of Lepage, each one an adaptation of a theatrical narrative in some fundamental way, each one featuring, however obliquely (as in the case of *Nô* [1998]), a corpse. My argument in the rest of this essay, then, is that the corpse-as-signifier in Lepage's films, even when not literally embodied/discarnated by the queer male, is nevertheless tied to the 'death' of certain important homosexual significations in Lepage's source-texts, and that such auteurial revisionism has important implications for the gendered reception of both his cinematic *and* his theatrical narratives, as well as for a Deleuzian reading of Québec's national imaginary more generally.

As an adaptation, *Le Confessionnal* is multiply complex: not only does it contain characters from Lepage's first great theatrical triumph, *The Dragons' Trilogy* (chief among them protagonist Pierre Lamontagne), it also consciously quotes and incorporates scenes from Hitchcock's *I Confess* (1953), itself an adaptation of a 1902 stage play, *Nos deux consciences*, by French playwright Paul Anthelme. Finally, *Le Confessionnal* is also an anachronistic and anamorphic sequel to Lepage's next great theatrical project, *The Seven Streams of the River Ota*, which concludes by placing the eastern-identified Pierre in Japan.

Lepage has described the character of Pierre Lamontagne as his 'alter ego', a 'linking character' who makes connections between the various threads of Lepage's theatrical and cinematic narratives, and between those narratives and the audience: 'His naive approach towards the events he encounters reflects the spectator's position.'[12] Lepage goes on to admit that 'Over the course of his incarnations, the character developed a few inconsistencies.'[13] Thus, *Le Confessionnal* begins with Pierre (Lothaire Bluteau) returning from China, where he had gone to study calligraphy, in 1989. *Seven Streams*, however, ends with the character (here renamed Pierre Maltais) arriving in Japan in 1995 to study *butoh* dance, an Orientalist elision which makes one question Lepage's statement that his 'fascination with Japan began when [he] was sufficiently mature to be able to distinguish it from China'.[14] Similarly, it is worth noting that the fluidly bisexual Pierre of *Seven Streams* (who seduces not only David Yamashita, but also, it's implied, his mother, Hanako) is, as we shall see, straightened out, or at the very least *de*sexualized, in *Le Confessionnal*.[15]

Le Confessionnal's opening shots gesture towards the disjunctive spatio-temporal poetics that govern the film as a whole. Following a Hitchcockian establishing shot of the Pont de Québec, there is a cut to shots of the 1953 premiere of Hitchcock's *I Confess* at Québec City's grand Capitol cinema. Here, the space of our present tense viewing of *Le Confessionnal* starts to merge with the pastness of Lepage's fictional intradiegetic spectators' viewing of Hitchcock's film, Pierre's voiceover recalling, as the camera focuses on his mother, Françoise's (Marie Gignac) swollen belly, that there were actually three Lamontagnes attending the screening that night. In the next scene, the now-adult Pierre arrives home to attend the funeral of his father, Paul-Émile (François Papineau), who has died after a long battle with diabetes. Thereafter, the film cuts back and forth between the 'present' diegesis of 1989 and the 'past' diegesis of 1952. The 1989 narrative concerns Pierre's attempts to reconnect with his estranged adopted brother Marc, who works as a male prostitute. The 1952 narrative details the pregnancy and eventual suicide of Marc's unmarried birth mother, Rachel (Suzanne Clément), Françoise's younger sister.

The diplomat Massicotte provides the link between the film's past and present narratives. In flashbacks to 1952, we learn that a much younger Massicotte (Normand Daneau) actually began his working life as a priest, serving the church in Québec City where Hitchcock (Ron Burrage) and his crew are preparing to shoot scenes for *I Confess* under the guidance of Hitchcock's harried assistant (Kristin Scott Thomas), and where Rachel also works as *a femme de ménage*. No longer able to hide her pregnancy, Rachel is dismissed from her job, but not before confessing to the young Massicotte that Paul-Émile is her unborn baby's father. Unable to break the seal of confession, and with Rachel unwilling to confirm otherwise, Massicotte is in turn removed from his post after suspicions are aroused in the congregation that he is Rachel's lover. The two storylines converge in a double denouement that features several cuts between parallel scenes in both time-frames, the closing titles and the final shot of the Chateau Frontenac at the end of the 1953 screening of *I Confess* mirroring Pierre's apprehension of the 'truth' about his family in Massicotte's room at the same hotel at the end of *Le Confessionnal*.

Having shown how this narrative can be recuperated allegorically into the larger heteronormative story of Québec's national identity crisis, I shall now examine the queer male character's key symbolic role as the 'fall guy' within that story, concentrating in particular on how his body is framed and disciplined by the quasipanoptical composition of several of Lepage's shots. In this regard, it is first important to point out that the two queer characters in Lepage's film are introduced to the spectator via their positioning within lofty spaces. Massicotte occupies a grand suite in one of the turrets of the Chateau Frontenac, outside of which Pierre first spies his brother. And when the brothers finally talk properly face to face, following their encounter at the sauna (described below), the meeting takes place in the revolving restaurant atop the Hilton, which has a 360-degree view of the city.

These associations, ironically, far from signalling the queer character's reverse panopticism, his ability to return and thereby subvert the minoritizing gaze of heteronormativity, actually position him metonymically even further as the disciplined object of that gaze. In order to understand this, we need to examine more carefully the scene at the gay sauna, where Pierre finally tracks down Marc. The scene begins at dusk, with an exterior shot of the nondescript, opaquely windowed building, isolated on a lonely and deserted expanse of street. Pierre enters the frame, pausing to look sideways along the street before crossing it to enter the building. But for the absence of the requisitely suspenseful music and maybe some lower-key lighting, it is a classic film noir sequence, one usually meant to bestir anxiety in the viewer for the detective-hero who has come to investigate a mysterious lead: who on earth would come here; what dangers lurk behind those doors? In the lobby Pierre is greeted by a wary front desk clerk, who surveys his scrutiny of the Tom of Finland drawings and the sign-in list with mild disdain, commenting to Pierre that no one in their right mind would use their real name

Figure 9.1
Pierre (Lothaire Bluteau) makes his way through
the sauna. *Le Confessionnal* (Robert Lepage,
1995). Courtesy of Cinémaginaire.

Figure 9.2
Marc (Patrick Goyette) in foetal position.
Le Confessionnal (Robert Lepage, 1995).
Courtesy of Cinémaginaire.

at a gay sauna – a reminder of the continued need for anonymity in a queer sexual space still subject to raids by the police. Hence the double coding of the goldfish bowl on the clerk's counter, into which Pierre peers upon entering the sauna: placing oneself on display inside such a space is potentially subject to exterior surveillance as well. As if to bear this out, once Pierre has found his room and changed into his towel, the camera begins to track his search for Marc from an overhead angle, pulling back panoptically to reveal, through the wire mesh atop their cubicles, all that the men are getting up to (which is not much, admittedly) below (Figure 9.1). The guarantee of anonymity no longer holds in this space. The queer male body, even when it does not want to be found out, will be exposed and put on display by Lepage's all-seeing camera, as when, at the end of this scene, the outline of Marc's naked body emerges from the steam to be framed alongside his brother's towelled one in the doorway to the shower area.

Lepage's panoptical framing of this gay sauna scene might not seem so significant were it not for the fact that he employs a similar overhead camera angle three more times throughout the course of the film; each time it is Marc's body being framed by the shot (Figures 9.2–9.4). The first instance takes place at the same sauna; Marc has retreated there after being told by Pierre in the previous scene that, according to a nosy aunt, the reason Rachel killed herself was because the father of her baby was a priest. Again, the camera is looking down through the grille atop a cubicle, this time capturing a naked Marc curled up in the foetal position. The second instance occurs in the limousine that will take Marc and Massicotte to the airport and their flight to Japan; there, in the back seat, with the camera looking down through the open sun roof, Massicotte prepares to correct Pierre's previous misinformation, and tell Marc the truth about his parentage.

Figure 9.3
Massicotte (Jean-Louis Millette, and Marc
(Patrick Goyette) outside the motel.
Le Confessional (Robert Lepage, 1995).
Courtesy of Cinémaginaire.

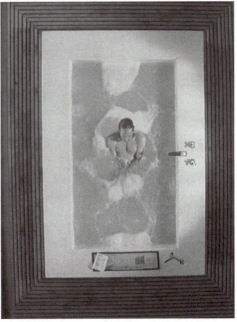

Figure 9.4
Marc's suicide. *Le Confessionnal* (Robert Lepage,
1995). Courtesy of Cinémaginaire.

The last of these overhead shots records Marc's suicide in Japan; standing up in
the sunken bathtub, the blood from his slashed wrists trickling down his body,
Marc falls backwards into the water, and the camera tracks back quickly to reveal
an aerial shot of his submersion just as the jacuzzi jets begin and the water starts
turning red. All three shots occur just after or just prior to Marc receiving crucial
information about his family, and about his own place within that sphere; their
combined imagistic weight adds up to a positioning of the queer male as forever
outside – *even when inside* – the bourgeois family, to the point of Marc's ultimate
self-disciplining of his own body through the act of suicide.

Something similar happens in terms of Massicotte's association with another
Foucauldian space of sexual self-disciplining, namely the confession box.[16] Early
on in the film, during one of the 1952 flashback scenes, Massicotte is shown hearing
Rachel's confession. The young priest is receiving news that, like the information
received by Montgomery Clift's Father Logan from the killer, Keller, in *I Confess*,
he must keep secret because of the seal of the confessional, but that, paradoxically,
will have the effect of framing each priest for a crime he did not commit. This
points to how the confessional, far from being a space that disciplines the congregation (as its prominent presence within the nave of most churches is meant
to), in this case serves to frame and discipline Massicotte, his extended time within

its confines with a now visibly pregnant Rachel coming to serve as evidence, in the congregation's mind, of his guilt-by-association. The grille that separates Rachel from Father Massicotte in the confessional box, like the grille above the cubicles in the gay sauna, becomes a symbol of the social constraints faced by the queer male when placed in the context of a later flashback scene. Massicotte, under pressure from his clerical superiors to resign, visits Rachel at home to beg her to reveal that he is not the father of her child. Rachel refuses to let him in, and he is forced to speak to her through the grille of the doorframe. It is a striking visual representation of Massicotte's own imprisonment and a reminder, within the context of what the audience knows about him from the 1989 narrative, that there would be another way for him to prove to the congregation that he is not Rachel's lover: by declaring that he is homosexual.

Of course, it is really no choice at all. Either way, Massicotte would be forced to leave the priesthood. In this respect, Lepage's film represents, as Garrity suggests, a far more 'ruthless' updating of Hitchcock's film, in which 'the self-contained Jansenistic priest of *I Confess* who escapes punishment despite his own inaction is transformed by Lepage into one who suffers humiliation and degradation, never succeeding in rehabilitating himself with his church or parishioners'.[17] This is a reminder that there is another queer male 'framed' within Lepage's film: Montgomery Clift. Although he appears as Father Logan only in one brief excerpted scene from *I Confess*, the flashing of his name on the screen-within-the-screen at the start of Lepage's film necessarily interpolates him as a crucial absent presence throughout *Le Confessionnal*. As Deleuze notes at one point in his discussion of the crystal-image, the film within the film 'has often been linked to the consideration of a surveillance, an investigation, a revenge, a conspiracy, a plot'.[18] In the case of Clift's role as the tortured priest in *I Confess*, who is not only unable to declare his innocence of murder but who is also unable to return the love of the female protagonist, Anne Baxter, one site of surveillance must necessarily be the actor's own sexuality. Clift's equally tortured life offscreen is a reminder that the closet is as powerful a space of self-disciplining as the confessional. That Lepage consigns to the closet the queer male protagonist of the play that inspired his next film thus bears further analysis.

Lepage's second film, *Le Polygraphe* (1997), is based on the play of the same name he cowrote and costarred in alongside longtime collaborator Marie Brassard. It premiered in Québec City in a French-language production directed by Lepage in May 1988. The play was subsequently produced in an English translation in Toronto in February 1990. It is this latter version which Lepage chose to have tour the world, as well as to be published.[19] For the film version, however, Lepage reverted to French dialogue, but not before radically revisioning and revising the original script.

The play focuses on the complex interrelationships between three characters. David is a criminologist who escaped from East Berlin and now works at a forensics institute in Montreal. He meets Lucie, an actress from Québec City, when they witness a suicide in a Metro station. Lucie has just been cast as the murder victim in a film based on an actual unsolved case, for which François, her gay neighbour, remains the prime suspect. François maintains that he is innocent, and has taken a lie detector test to prove it, but the police assert that the results were inconclusive, and their continued harassment, together with their failure to find the real murderer, eventually drive him to take his own life (also by jumping in front of a subway train). Meanwhile, the audience learns that David has his own secrets: not only did he leave a former lover behind when he escaped to the West, but, in the play's penultimate scene, it is revealed that he was the one who both administered the polygraph to François *and* planted the seeds of doubt within him about the validity of his testimony.

Early on in the play, David boldly states that 'the body never lies',[20] although what Michael Sidnell has identified as the 'instrumental' operations of 'somatic truth' in this play relate as much – if not more – to what sexual acts François voluntarily chooses to have performed upon his own body as they do to what was involuntarily visited upon the body of the murder victim, Marie-Claire Légaré, whom we are told was raped before being repeatedly stabbed.[21] That is, the play version of *Le Polygraphe* makes it clear that François, who is both gay and a masochist, is the subject of a police investigation in part because of his perceived 'criminal' sexuality, and that his feelings of self-doubt derive in no small measure from the shame he is made to feel in confessing to the police – and, tangentially, to Lucie – the pleasure he gets from pain. This autocritique is largely absent from Lepage's film adaptation, which shifts the hermeneutics of truth, as applied to the queer male body, from detection to cover-up.

To this end, the all-important polygraph scene, which closes the play, opens the film, a temporal relocation that spatially abstracts the forensic thrust of the action that follows. Specifically, Lepage uses the opening credit sequence to capture, with diagnostic precision, François's (Patrick Goyette) head, torso, arms and fingers being attached to all manner of wires and electrodes (Figure 9.5), as well as, through time lapse dissolves, the prosthetic record of his responses to the questions put to him by the technician Hans (James Hyndman). We later learn that Hans is an old friend of Christof (Peter Stormare), the film's reworked version of the David character from the play. What is significant about how this scene has been adapted for film, apart from who is asking the questions this time round and the fact that Lepage once again employs a series of overhead shots to frame François's body, is that the audience not only witnesses François's self-declaration of innocence at the start of the film's narrative diegesis (rather than at the close of the play's), but in effect has 'objective' corroboration of this in the form of the polygraph needle's steady and unwavering movement over the printout being monitored by Hans. Whereas in the play the audience is left to wonder about the *othered* François's innocence or guilt until the very end, Lepage's film works to solicit spectators'

Figure 9.5 François (Patrick Goyette) taped to the polygraph machine. *Le Polygraphe*
(Robert Lepage, 1997). Courtesy of Ex Aequo Films.

identification with the character from its opening frames, thereby transferring
the weight of narrative suspense to the question of who *other* than François is
responsible for Marie-Claire's (Marie-Christine Le Huu) murder. Here, again, the
presence of a film within a film serves as an important 'mode of the crystal-image'.[22]
And yet, while the scenes documenting the making, editing and broadcast of Judith's
(Josée Deschènes) film about Marie-Claire's murder do, in the end, resolve the
generic conspiracy at the heart of Lepage's crime drama – by revealing, eventually,
the identity of the murderer – they also perpetuate further conspiracies relating
to gender by confirming that the only alibi François ever needed was his
heterosexuality.

Among the changes made in the film version of *Le Polygraphe*, is the addition of
a back story absent from the play that informs the spectator that not only were
François and Marie-Claire lovers who had quarrelled the night of her murder, but
that while she was seeking comfort from her best friend, Judith, he was getting
drunk in a bar, allowing himself to be picked up by Marie-Claire's sister, Claude
(Maria de Medeiros), with whom he had had a previous affair. In scenes of double
parallel montage near its conclusion, the film cuts from Judith and François talking
about the night of the murder in her Montreal editing studio to Lucie (Marie
Brassard) showing Claude the empty apartment of François in Québec City, and
from shots of Judith's film's ultimately false intradiegetic reconstruction of the
murder (she blames the police) to Claude's flashbacks of what really happened:

in a fit of jealousy she had stabbed her sister and set fire to her apartment. In other words, in the film François's relative gender normativity gets him off, relative in the sense that the film does at the very least indicate that the erotic basis of François and Marie-Claire's relationship was partially informed by S/M sexual practices.

In a scene just prior to François's departure for Montreal, Lucie confronts him in his bathroom about what she has learned about his relationship with Marie-Claire during the making of Judith's film; he tells her that she does not know everything, and proceeds to blindfold her and tie her hands to the washbasin with a leather belt (Figure 9.6). He then says that he sometimes tied up Marie-Claire when they made love, before hitting and breaking the bathroom mirror in rage. And yet, even here, the scene is presented as a relatively sanitized version of the one from the play upon which it is based, not least because of the hiding, or covering up, of the queer male body, as well as the transferring of the belt from a signifier of male masochism to one of male sadism. In the play, François explains to Lucie that one of the functions of the belt is as a device for auto-asphyxiation during masturbation. He then ties Lucie, like her screen surrogate, to the washbasin. However, in the ensuing dialogue he informs Lucie that, in the case of his own sexual practices, he is invariably the person being tied up. Furthermore, this confession to Lucie, delivered in French, is simultaneously translated for the audience into English by David, who, it soon becomes clear, is actually reading from a transcript of François's police interrogation in connection with the murder of Marie-Claire. By contrast, in Lepage's film version of *Le Polygraphe* we never witness François divulging his sexual secrets to anyone other than Lucie, and even then they serve not so much to demonstrate his vulnerability as to confirm his power.

Figure 9.6 François (Patrick Goyette) ties Lucie (Marie Brassard) to the washbasin, *Le Polygraphe* (Robert Lepage, 1997). Courtesy of Ex Aequo Films.

Figure 9.7
François (Patrick Goyette) in the bath.
Le Polygraphe (Robert Lepage, 1997).
Courtesy of Ex Aequo Films.

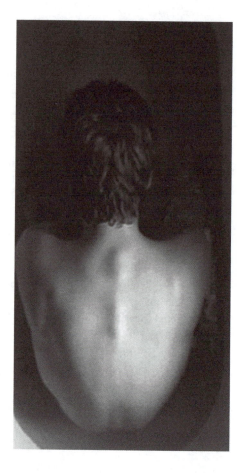

   In the end, the queer male body in *Le Polygraphe* is most hidden when it is most exposed. It is important to note that in addition to the insertion of the crucial back story noted above, there are several key shots of actor Patrick Goyette's back in the film. In this, *Le Polygraphe* is linked metonymically to *Le Confessionnal* not only through the casting of Goyette in the respective roles of François and Marc, but also in terms of how, in both films, the actor's naked body is framed by the camera. Just as in *Le Confessionnal* Lepage uses a series of panoptical top shots during key scenes featuring Marc, so he shoots François from above not only during the opening polygraph/credit sequence, but also during another scene early on in *Le Polygraphe*. François is in the bath, bent forward with his head between his knees, so that all we see of his body is the smooth and unblemished expanse of his naked back (Figure 9.7). The camera lingers clinically, forensically, as if searching for something embedded upon the skin, a scratch or bump or bruise that might betray a secret that evaded detection by the polygraph machine. But the François of Lepage's film has nothing to hide, unlike, say, Christof, who bears the burden of guilt in the film *vis-à-vis* a betrayal of heteronormativity when we discover that the wife he abandoned in East Berlin has committed suicide now that the Wall has come down. And unlike the François of Lepage's play, whom we witness, in a scene titled 'The Flesh', entering a 'crowded gay bar', being 'propositioned to have sex in a private room', kneeling against a wall, removing 'his shirt . . . his belt . . . which he gives away': 'He turns his back, and unzips his pants. As he is beaten, with each sound of the whiplash, François physically recoils against the wall. La petite morte and collapse, finally, the exchange is finished. Satisfied, soul weary, François gathers his clothes and his shreds of self-esteem.'[23]

A comparison of the play and film versions of *Le Polygraphe* yields two very different images of François. Both solicit the (male) viewer's gaze, but whereas the screen François invites identification (including erotic identification), the stage François effects only alienation. How can this phenomenon be explained? One way is in terms of gender, with the theatrical representation of the queer male body's excessive 'anti-naturalness' and passive acquiescence to the performed lie distancing the (stage) actor from the (stage) role, and with the cinematic representation of the straight male body's proximate 'realism' and active mastery of the embodied truth making obsolete the distinction between (social) actor and (social) role. In other words, heterosexuality is not dependent upon illusion or artifice: it just exists. So too with cinema, and another way of explaining the differences between the two François is in terms of the form or *medium* of the representation of each's body. As Steven Shaviro has noted in discussing the differences between theatre and film, whereas theatrical spectatorship depends for its effect on 'the physical presence of the actors' bodies in space', cinematic spectatorship replaces bodies with images, physical space with virtual space, presence with absence:

> Film's virtual images do not correspond to anything actually present, but as images, or as sensations, they affect me in a manner that does not leave room for any suspension of my response. . . . The cinematic image, in its violent more-than-presence, is at the same time immediately an absence: a distance too great to allow for dialectical interchange or for any sort of possession.[24]

Given Shaviro's comments, it is hardly surprising that a reading of the shifting representations of the queer male body in Lepage's third film, *Nô*, should likewise depend on looking at how that body has been fatally disposed of in the process of adaptation from stage to screen. Shot with super-16 mm film in seventeen days, *Nô* is based on Section 5 ('The Words') of *The Seven Streams of the River Ota*. The play, which in its epic entirety comprises seven parts staged over seven successive hours, was developed collaboratively over a three-year period with the members of Ex Machina, and subsequently toured to more than twenty-five different locations around the world. Its plot spans fifty years, moves back and forth in time and space between Japan, the United States and Europe, incorporates over fifty different speaking roles in four different languages (English, French, Japanese and German), and employs all manner of meta-representational devices to foreground the processes of spectatorship and cultural mediation. Even more boldly, *Seven Streams* also attempts to make political and historical sense of such cataclysmic world events as the Holocaust, the bombing of Hiroshima and AIDS in terms of a recurring set of aesthetic oppositions: between East and West, life and death, tragedy and comedy, masculine and feminine.

Wisely, Lepage narrowed his scope for the eighty-five-minute *Nô*. In the film, he has chosen to focus on Sophie (Anne-Marie Cadieux), a Québécoise actress starring in a production of a Feydeau farce as part of Canada's cultural programme at the 1970 World's Fair in Osaka, Japan. Sophie, with the aid of Hanako (Marie Brassard), a blind Japanese translator attached to the show, has just learned she is pregnant. She is not sure if the father is her costar, François-Xavier (Éric Bernier), or her boyfriend, Michel (Alexis Martin), a writer who, back in Montreal, has suddenly been thrust into the thick of the October Crisis thanks to an unexpected visit by radical friends intent on planting a bomb. While Sophie finds herself embroiled in her own bedroom farce when she drunkenly sleeps with Walter (Richard Fréchette), the Canadian cultural attache in Tokyo, Michel labours over the wording of the political message that will be attached to his friends' bomb, whose detonator, he soon discovers, has been incorrectly set. The two narratives, whose temporal and spatial distinctiveness had previously been signposted by having the scenes in Montreal filmed in black and white and the scenes in Japan in colour, merge during a key scene in which Sophie, returning from Japan to discover only rubble where her home once stood, is arrested by Agents Bélanger (Tony Conte) and Ménard (Jules Philip), plain-clothes detectives who had been keeping her and Michel's apartment under surveillance. Not only does the shift from black and white to colour that occurs during the middle of this scene chromatically connect the intradiegetic media footage of the 1980 Québec referendum results that follows in the film's epilogue with similar intradiegetic footage of Pierre Trudeau being interviewed about introducing the War Measures Act to deal with the FLQ in the 1970s used at the start of the film; its resulting focalization of the spectator's gaze on the blood flowing down Sophie's legs as a result of the miscarriage brought on by her arrest serves as a syntagma that connects the various overlapping discourses of nationalism and sexuality throughout the film (Figure 9.8).

In an earlier scene in the film, the police officers arresting Sophie are explicitly depicted as duplicitous, not only in terms of their collaboration with the state by spying on their nationalist brothers but also in terms of attempting to hide the true nature of their domestic *ménage*. Staking out Michel and Sophie's apartment from what they believe is an unoccupied apartment across the street, the police are interrupted by the landlady, who wants to show the place to a pair of prospective tenants. While Bélanger attempts to keep her at bay by blocking the door, Ménard quickly hides their surveillance equipment on the floor, covering it with the

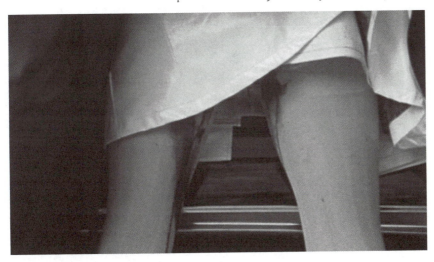

Figure 9.8 Sophie (Anne-Marie Cadieux) miscarries as she is arrested by Bélanger (Tony
Conte) and Ménard (Jules Philip). *Nô* (Robert Lepage, 1998). Courtesy of
Ex Aequo Films.

roll-out cot from the sofabed, upon which he promptly installs himself in a languor-
ous pose (Figure 9.9). This is how Lepage and André Morency's script describes
the ensuing shot sequence:

> Pushing against [Bélanger], the landlady enters energetically and stops just as
> quickly when she sees the other police officer stretched out on the hide-a-
> bed. Believing she's dealing with a homosexual couple, she gives them a dirty
> look. Under the same impression about the sexual identity of the cops, the
> visitors, themselves homosexuals, exchange knowing looks, attempting to
> establish a complicity that singularly embarrasses the representatives of the
> forces of order.[25]

The scene, like most in the film, is played for laughs, and in a social satire of the
sort directed here by Lepage one should be wary of critiquing broad stereotypes
employed for comic effect. Still, within the context of the long-entrenched symbolic
associations of homosexuality in Québécois culture that I have been sketching
throughout this essay, it is hard not to take away a familiar message. The queer
male body being overwritten with/by the 'forces of order' in this scene means,
concomitantly, that it cannot also be linked with the forces of revolution and change.
Hence the image of a gay couple blithely out shopping for an apartment while all
around them the world is exploding. This also explains why the queer 'self-
abortion', that in some senses constitutes Sophie's miscarriage at the hands of these
same police officers, is in cinematic terms absolutely necessary.[26]

Figure 9.9 Ménard (Jules Philip) is interrupted by the concierge (Natalie D'Anjou). *Nô*
(Robert Lepage, 1998). Courtesy of Ex Aequo Films.

I do not wish to indict Lepage for his failure to produce positive images of
queerness here or elsewhere in his cinema. Rather, to come back to the ambivalent
heterogeneity of Deleuze's time-image, I want to suggest that the virtual traces of
national memory in Lepage's films, and Québécois cinema generally, are in part
sustained by a willed sexual amnesia in the actual present, whereby a 'teleological
vision' of progress paradoxically preserves a heteronormative link between past
repression and future liberation. Here, it is worth examining more closely the
conclusion of *Nô*, which flashes forward from October 1970 to 20 May 1980, the
night of Québec's first referendum on sovereignty-association. As Sophie and a
newly yuppified Michel watch dispiritedly the television results confirming a victory
for the 'No' side, Michel expounds upon his theory that 'people with a collective
project are always a little disadvantaged next to people who don't have a project.
. . . The idea is that it always takes more energy to change political institutions,
social institutions than . . . to do nothing'.[27] To Sophie's response that the 'common
project' of the No side in the referendum must surely be the idea of a unified
Canada, Michel scoffs that 'It's a bit static as a project, isn't it?'.[28] He then suggests
that perhaps he and Sophie need a common project, something that looks to
'posterity', something like a child. Incredulous, Sophie asks him whether he would
have considered that a worthy 'common project' ten years earlier, at the start of
their relationship. Michel replies that it wouldn't have been the same thing ten
years ago: 'we were occupied with changing the world. . . . Times have changed.'[29]
The scene ends with Sophie – who clearly intends not to tell Michel about her
earlier failed pregnancy – gradually acceding to Michel's increasingly amorous
arguments, assenting to the idea of a baby in an escalating series of percentages –

she goes from being 40.5% sure, to 49%, to 50%, and then finally 50.5% – that mirror the closeness of the numbers for and against sovereignty in Québec's second referendum.

Indeed, it is impossible not to read this scene in light of the events of 1995. The film's release date of 1998, combined with the appearance of Jean Chrétien as a talking head on some of the television footage shown of the 1980 referendum, ensures that Sophie and Michel's conversation will resonate with both Québécois and English-Canadian audiences. Not least because of the discourse surrounding reproduction that emerged over the course of the 1995 campaign, with sovereigntist leaders such as Lucien Bouchard and Jacques Parizeau urging *pure laîne* Québécois to do their bit to reverse the plummeting provincial birthrate in order to offset, among other things, the inevitable antinationalist consequences of 'les votes eth-niques' and, by extension, 'les votes *fédérastes*'.[30] This confluence of discourses of racial and sexual difference within the context of Québec self-determination leads us back to *The Seven Streams of the River Ota* and explains, paradoxically, why Sophie's miscarriage is, in some respects, inevitable.

In the narrative universe of the play, the child that results from Sophie's pregnancy is both a born *fédéraste* and a future queer libertine, the product of his mother's drunken liaison with the Canadian diplomatic toady Walter, and, as such, voracious in his pursuit and consumption of new experiences and pleasures, different cultures and genders. Indeed, when he should be back in Québec performing his nationalist duty by voting in the referendum, the Pierre of *Seven Streams* is actually in Japan learning to dance like a woman: one of the last images we see in the play is of him dressed in a Japanese wedding kimono, his face covered in white makeup, '[performing] a butoh dance in which a woman moves gracefully, then experiences a moment of terror and pain'.[31] Is it any wonder that such an image is excised from the film version of *Nô*? In the 'common project' that is the Québec national imaginary, the queer male body is, fundamentally, disposable. Like the Oriental body, it functions as an arrested Other against which to measure the normative progress of an autonomous selfhood; but, also like the Oriental body, it is, in the end, unassimilable. This, to some extent, explains the fate of the queer male body in Lepage's next film, *Possible Worlds* (2000).

Possible Worlds opens with the camera focusing, from the inside, on a window cleaner (Griffith Brewer) who is busy washing, from the outside, the floor-to-ceiling windows of a trendy condominium loft. As the soap suds are gradually wiped away by the deft strokes of his squeegee, the window cleaner is able to see inside the condo, whereupon he makes a shocking discovery: the dead body of its owner splayed across the sofa. We then cut to the arrival of Detective Berkley (Sean McCann) at the scene, who learns from his partner, Williams (Rick Miller), who the murder victim is – George Barber (Tom McCamus), a successful stockbroker – as well as what makes this particular crime so gruesome: the killer has neatly sawn off the top part of his victim's skull and absconded with the brain. Although

Lepage's fourth film, *Possible Worlds* is his first shot in English. And, while the film is based on a previously staged work of drama, it is not, this time, one by Lepage. Instead, he is adapting John Mighton's 1992 play of the same name. However, a brief analysis of the plot and structure of Mighton's play reveals some familiar Lepage themes, including the paralleling and overlapping of different temporal and spatial realms, the mourning of a lost love object, and the unravelling of a mystery whose solution is in some fundamental sense beyond imagination.

In the case of *Possible Worlds*, this mystery concerns not just who stole George's brain and why, but also the exact nature of his relationship with his wife Joyce (Tilda Swinton). To summarize, both the play and film, like all of Lepage's films, follow two (at the very least) separate narrative temporalities, flashing back from the opening scene described above to trace the initial meeting, courtship and, it is briefly suggested, subsequent estrangement of George and Joyce. But even here, in the flashback narrative, there are further diegetic layers. In one version of events, George and Joyce meet in the cafeteria of the hospital where she works as a research biologist, or rather re-meet, as it soon becomes clear that they are from the same small town in Northern Ontario. In another possible scenario that both theatre and film audiences witness, the couple meet in a crowded downtown bar, as a coquettish Joyce, who now seems to work as a stockbroker in the same office as George, aggressively pursues a liaison. These scenes, and others documenting further stages in the couple's twin relationships, are repeated throughout the play and film, dramatizing what George describes to Joyce at one point as the metaphysical romance of human interconnection, that 'each of us exists in an infinite number of possible worlds'.[32] Meanwhile, in the present tense of the crime narrative, the play and film's other couple, Berkley and Williams, who kibbutz, cajole and generally annoy each other like an old married couple, trace the theft of George's brain to a Doctor Penfield, renamed Doctor Keiber in the film (Gabriel Gascon), a neurologist who has been stockpiling the cerebella of very intelligent and powerful people as a way of 'extracting information from them'.[33] As Penfield puts it to Berkley early on in the play: 'Everything you think, Inspector, even the most trivial fantasy, leaves a trace, a disturbance in that field. I'm trying to learn how to control those disturbances.'[34]

What, one might ask, has any of this to do with representations of the queer male body? Arguably nothing and everything. That is, George's fantasies of heterosexual happiness with Joyce, who may or may not be the same 'wife' whom George repeatedly claims died three years ago in another of his possible lives, would depend, following from Judith Butler's theories of gender melancholia, on the trace signs of another 'disturbing' fantasy that he has repudiated, namely homosexuality. In other words, Doctor Penfield/Keiber might not be the only one trying to 'control' George's imagination. George's own obsessive replaying of his life with Joyce – which is only ever presented as but one of a number of *possible* scenarios – might betray certain anxieties around the equally possible 'fictiveness' of his presumed heterosexual gender. But what images of the queer male body are there in Lepage's film to support such a claim? None other, I would argue, than that of George's corpse.

Monique Wittig has argued that 'the straight mind continues to affirm that incest, and not homosexuality, represents its major interdiction. Thus, when thought by the straight mind, homosexuality is nothing but heterosexuality'.[35] Likewise, Butler has theorized normative heterosexual gender identification as a kind of melancholia in which unresolved same-sex desire is internalized as a prohibition that precedes the incest taboo.[36] Homosexuality, in other words, is, to use terminology borrowed from two other classic essays by Wittig, nothing more than a 'fiction', but a necessary one, whose symbolic otherness helps constitute and maintain the 'heterosexual contract'.[37] Structuring the various versions of George and Joyce's marriage contract throughout Lepage's film is another 'possible world', another window of gender identification, made available to the spectator in its opening minutes. As Detectives Berkley and Williams circle George's corpse looking for evidence and a motive for the crime, and thus policing to a certain extent our generic reading of the scene, Lepage's camera swoops down from the upper reaches of the loft, lingering almost pornographically over the body of actor Tom McCamus, splayed across the back of his sofa, shirt front open to the waist, a look of absolute ecstasy on his face (Figure 9.10). In short, George is made into an object of desire for the viewer, even if only clinical desire, *and regardless of the gender of that viewer*. And here our screen surrogates are none other than the homothetical couple of Berkley and Williams, whose close inspection of George's body, the camera makes clear, is lovingly professional. If, in Butler's and Wittig's

Figure 9.10 George (Tom McCamus) found dead at the film's start. *Possible Worlds*
(Robert Lepage, 2000). Courtesy of Ex Aequo Films.

readings of Freudian and Lacanian psychoanalysis, homosexual cathexis must precede ego identification and the successful resolution of the Oedipus complex, then this is the scene in Lepage's film that performs most spectacularly that rupture, and that perforce haunts our reading of all subsequent images in the film, especially those involving George.

To this end, it is important to note that the opening image of George's body draped provocatively across his sofa is repeated once more in the film; this time, however, George wakes up, to the realization that he is merely suffering from a massive hangover, and that he has just slept with Joyce #2, the stockbroker. Moreover, consider the opening scene as I have discussed it in relation to the speech by Joyce #1 that closes both the play and the film:

> The word 'not' is really magical. I could describe something and say – 'But it's *not* that, it's something more' – and you'd know what I meant. It's a way of getting around our ignorance. . . . We say 'Things might not have been the way they are', and feel free or uneasy. But there's really nothing behind it. Just a bunch of ghostly possibilities. Because, in the end, everything simply is.[38]

My argument about the absent presence of images of the queer male body in Lepage's film adaptation of *Possible Worlds* likewise coalesces around this interdictive word. Homosexuality is what is 'not' in our culture; it's the ghost in the machine of the 'heterosexual matrix' generally, but also of the matrix of cinema more specifically.[39] In other words, take away the straight mind and what you are left with is the queer body. Arguably, this is what we are left with in Lepage's most recent film. Only this time, that body is incarnated on screen by the auteur himself.

Winner of the FIPRESCI International Critics Prize in the Panorama Series at the 2004 Berlin International Film Festival and a Canadian Genie Award for Best Adapted Screenplay, Lepage's fifth film, *La Face Cachée de la Lune* (2003), is shot in high-definition video. An adaptation of his award-winning solo play of the same name, the film is set against the backdrop of the US–Soviet space race and current investigations into extraterrestrial life. Jumping back and forth in time between the 1950s and the present day, the narrative through-line concerns the complicated relationship between two Québec City brothers, Philippe and André (both played by Lepage), and their different responses to the death of their mother (played in flashbacks by a mute Anne-Marie Cadieux). Not only is *La Face* Lepage's most personal memorial film to date (the impetus for the source play came from the death of his own mother), and not only does it mark his debut as an actor in one of his own films, it also sees Lepage, as director, consciously quoting from his previous work. Indeed, one important scene crucially revises and reorients the scopic regime of queer male images on offer in Lepage's previous films. Let me conclude this essay by very briefly explaining how this works.

The theme of narcissism runs throughout *La Face*. Most prominently, it serves as the theoretical cornerstone of Philippe's twice-rejected PhD thesis in the philosophy of science, which argues that the US and Soviet space programmes were fuelled not by the desire to seek out and explore new worlds, but rather to claim and remake those worlds in each country's national and ideological image. As for Philippe's own self-image, it has been shaped by childhood memories and battered by adult failures. Still living in the old family apartment, surrounded by his dead mother's clothes and shoes, he is unkempt and socially inept, reduced to taking on a series of menial and underpaid jobs while he revises his thesis. Even his one shot at academic stardom he manages to sabotage; having been invited to present his research at a conference in Moscow, he sleeps through his scheduled panel. Meanwhile, younger brother André could not be more different. A self-absorbed and pompous weatherman, he lives in a trendy and well-appointed new condo overlooking the harbour with his equally well-appointed boyfriend, Carl (Marco Poulin). André is the stereotyped embodiment of gay male narcissism, obsessed with surface appearances – his own and others'. However, just when it looks like Lepage is in danger of recycling classic homophobic tropes from Hollywood cinema, he inverts this process by exposing his own body to the minoritizing gaze of the camera.

In a very funny scene midway through the film, Philippe, having put in a desultory workout at a local gym, suddenly finds himself sharing a sauna with Carl. Never having met his brother's boyfriend, Philippe misinterprets Carl's friendly grin and casually provocative legs-splayed pose as a cruise, and rapidly rushes to declare his heterosexual credentials. It is only at this point that Carl reveals his own identity, noting that he immediately recognized Philippe as André's brother owing to the family resemblance. Thereafter, the two men fall into a casual conversation about work, with Philippe surprised at Carl's interest in his research. What I find most interesting about this scene is how it subtly revises the epistemology of surveillance that governs the sauna scene in *Le Confessionnal*. Not only is it the straight male who is required to out himself in this space, but it is his body which is subjected to both Carl's and the camera's voyeuristic gaze (see Figure 9.11). That the body is here framed in medium closeups and a shot/reverse-shot sequence of edits, rather than via the overhead tracking shots used in *Le Confessionnal*, also forces us to consider exactly who is policing whom in *La Face*. In the sexualized space of the sauna, Philippe's overweight, out-of-shape and pale straight body, when juxtaposed against Carl's tauter, tanned, tattooed, and pierced queer one, cannot help but be found wanting.

Moreover, both Philippe and André are played by Lepage himself, who has openly acknowledged his, at times painful, alienation from his own body (he suffers from alopecia, resulting in a complete hair loss), which would seem to authorize a re-evaluation of all of his screen images of the male body. In this regard, consider

Figure 9.11 Philippe (Robert Lepage), and Carl (Marco Poulin) talk in the sauna.
La Face cachée de la Lune (Robert Lepage, 2003). Courtesy of Ex Aequo
Films.

La Face's memorable closing shot. In it, Philippe's/Lepage's body 'floats', courtesy
of blue screen technology and the director's own surprising physical agility, up
out of the Moscow airport lounge where he awaits his return flight to Canada, and
into the stratosphere. For me, its orbit, like Deleuze's crystal-image, splits time
in two, launching Lepage's queer male body into a future as yet indiscernible but
fundamentally free, at least in my estimation, of the weight of its hitherto overdetermined nationalist inscriptions.

Notes

1   Gilles Deleuze, *Cinema 2: the Time-Image*, trans. Hugh Tomlinson and Robert Galeta
    (Minneapolis, MN: University of Minnesota Press, 1989), p. 81.
2   See Bill Marshall, *Quebec National Cinema* (Montreal: McGill-Queen's University Press,
    2001); Henry A. Garrity, 'Robert Lepage's cinema of time and space', in Joseph I.
    Donohoe and Jane M. Koustas (eds), *Theater sans Frontières: Essays on the Dramatic Universe
    of Robert Lepage* (East Lansing, MI: Michigan State University Press, 2000), pp. 95–107;
    Martin Lefebvre, 'A sense of time and place: the chronotope in *I Confess* and *Le
    Confessionnal*', *Quebec Studies*, no. 26 (Fall 1998/Winter 1999), pp. 88–98; Aleksandar
    Dundjerovic, *The Cinema of Robert Lepage: the Poetics of Memory* (London: Wallflower
    Press, 2003).
3   See Garrity, 'Robert Lepage's cinema of time and space', pp. 102, 105–6; on
    Deleuze's definition of the 'recollection-image', see his *Cinema 2*, p. 54.
4   On how the presence of a narrator need not be a precondition of narration in film,
    and on how film narration 'presupposes a perceiver, but not any sender, of a message,

see David Bordwell, *Narration in the Fiction Film* (Madison, WI: University of Wisconsin Press, 1985), p. 62.

5   In an earlier version of this essay, I had used the word 'gay' instead of 'queer' in formulating the argument that follows. However, as one of the anonymous readers of the essay noted, this presupposes a somewhat essentialist conception of male homosexual identity formation (and deformation) that is belied both by the theoretical framework of the essay itself, and by the imaging of several of the sexually polymorphous characters in Lepage's films. At the same time, it might be argued that 'gay' is one of the signifiers lost in translation of his 'queer' male bodies from stage to screen.

6   See Gilles Thérien, 'Cinéma québécois: la difficile conquête de l'altérité'. *Littérature*, no. 66 (1987), pp. 101–14.

7   See Robert Schwartzwald, '"Symbolic" homosexuality, "false feminine", and the problematics of identity in Québec', in Michael Warner (ed.), *Fear of a Queer Planet: Queer Politics and Social Theory* (Minneapolis, MN: University of Minnesota Press, 1993), pp. 264–99: Marshall, *Quebec National Cinema*, pp. 129 ff.

8   Lefebvre, 'A sense of time and place', p. 96.

9   Ibid.

10   Alenka Zupančič, 'A perfect place to die: theatre in Hitchcock's films', in Slavoj Žižek (ed.), *Everything You Always Wanted to Know about Lacan (But Were Afraid to Ask Hitchcock)* (London: Verso, 1992), p. 80. Italics in original.

11   See André Loiselle, 'Cinema, theatre and red gushing blood in Jean Beaudin's *Being at Home with Claude*', *Canadian Journal of Film Studies*, vol. 5, no. 2 (1996), pp. 17–33; and 'The corpse lies in *Lilies*: the stage, the screen, and the dead body', *Essays on Canadian Writing*, no. 76 (2002), pp. 117–38.

12   Robert Lapage, with Rémy Charest, *Connecting Flights*, trans. Wanda Romer Taylor (London: Methuen, 1997), pp. 33–4.

13   Ibid., p. 35.

14   Ibid., p. 42.

15   It is important to note that any reading of Pierre's screen sexuality necessarily overlaps with such extradiegetic considerations as Bluteau's own sexuality and his previous acting roles. Again, as a reviewer of this essay put it, Bluteau, 'although fiercely private, may well have a personal identity that matches his onscreen queer personae in such new queer films as *Bent*, *Orlando*, and *I Shot Andy Warhol*, but his public persona, as well an his onscreen sensibility in such films as *Black Robe* and *Jésus de Montréal*, are basically asexual, and the character of Pierre surely appropriates that asexual aura'.

16   Obviously, my reading of Lepage's panoptical camera and the disciplined queer male body in *Le Confessional* owes much to Foucault's analysis of the Benthamite panopticon in *Discipline and Punish: the Birth of the Prison*, trans. Alan Sheridan (New York: Pantheon, 1977). In the first volume of *The History of Sexuality*, Foucault famously reads the seventeenth-century confession as one of the sites of the production of a discourse of sexuality, arguing that this 'unrelenting system of confession' puts 'sex into discourse' by '[compelling] individuals to articulate their sexual peculiarity – no matter how extreme'; see Michel Foucault, *The History of Sexuality, Volume 1: an Introduction*, trans. Robert Hurley (New York: Vintage, 1990), p. 61.

17 Garrity, 'Robert Lepage's cinema of time and space', p. 103.

18 Deleuze, *Cinema 2*, p. 77.

19 See Marie Brassard and Robert Lepage, *Polygraph*, trans. Gyllian Raby, in Alan Filewod (ed.), *The CTR Anthology: Fifteen Plays from Canadian Theatre Review* (Toronto: University of Toronto Press, 1993).

20 Ibid., p. 652.

21 See Michael Sidnell, 'Polygraph; somatic truth and the art of presence', *Canadian Theatre Review*, no. 64 (Fall 1990), pp. 45–8.

22 Deleuze, *Cinema 2*, p. 77.

23 Brassard and Lepage, *Polygraph*, pp. 657–8. Ellipses in original.

24 Steven Shaviro, *The Cinematic Body* (Minneapolis, MN: University of Minnesota Press, 1993), pp. 44, 46.

25 Robert Lepage and André Morency, *Nô* (Laval and Montreal: Les 400 Coups/Alliance Vivafilm, 1998), p. 57. My translation.

26 Christopher Gittings reads Lepage's cut 'from a low-angled close-up shot of blood running down the inside of Sophie's legs to Sophie and Michel watching television coverage of the results of the May 1980 Referendum' somewhat differently, arguing that it constitutes Lepage's 'rather heavy-handed point about the failure of Québécois separatists to carry the embryonic Québec nation to full term'. See Christopher Gittings, *Canadian National Cinema* (New York: Routledge, 2002), p. 191.

27 Lepage and Morency, *Nô*, p. 87. My translation.

28 Ibid. My translation.

29 Ibid., p. 89. My translation.

30 In an important article examining the 'tragic resiliency' of various homophobic tropes that have helped fuel a 'profound sexual anxiety in Québec's anticolonial discourse', Robert Schwartzwald has analysed the jokes about 'fédérastes' that routinely appeared in the back pages of the journal *parti pris* in the 1960s. As Schwartzwald explains, *parti pris*'s punning link between federalism and pederasty implies that Québec's national self-interests have been perverted and corrupted by a predatory and ultimately non-productive English-Canadian system. See his 'Fear of federasty: Québec's inverted fictions', in Hortense J. Spillers (ed.), *Comparative American Identities: Race, Sex, and Nationality in the Modern Text* (New York: Routledge, 1991), pp. 176, 178.

31 Robert Lepage and Ex Machina, *The Seven Streams of the River Ota* (London: Methuen, 1996), p. 147.

32 John Mighton, *Possible Worlds* (Toronto: Playwrights Canada Press, 1988), p. 23.

33 Ibid., p. 27.

34 Ibid., p. 26.

35 Monique Wittig, 'The straight mind', in *The Straight Mind and Other Essays* (Boston, MA: Beacon Press, 1992), p. 28.

36 See Judith Butler, *Gender Trouble: Feminism and the Subversion of Identity* (New York: Routledge, 1990), pp. 63 ff; *Bodies That Matter: On the Discursive Limits of 'Sex'* (New York: Routledge, 1993), pp 235–6 ff; *Antigone's Claim: Kinship Between Life and Death* (New York: Columbia University Press, 2001).

37 Wittig, 'The mark of gender', pp. 76–89, and 'On the social contract', in *The Straight Mind and Other Essays*, pp. 33–45.

38 Mighton, *Possible Worlds*, p. 74.
39 On the 'heterosexual matrix', see Butler, *Gender Trouble*, pp. 35–78. On the specific ghosting of lesbianism in modern literary and cinematic culture, Terry Castle and Patricia White have both written perceptively. See Terry Castle, *The Apparitional Lesbian: Female Homosexuality and Modern Culture* (New York: Colombia University Press, 1993); Patricia White, *UnInvited: Classical Hollywood Cinema and Lesbian Representability* (Bloomington, IN: Indiana University Press, 1999).

10 The suspended spectacle of history: the tableau vivant in Derek Jarman's *Caravaggio*

James Tweedie

In the mid-1980s Caravaggio's work experienced a renaissance, as a major exhibition at New York's Metropolitan Museum in 1985 and a series of critical studies returned the artist to the centre of European and American art historical discourse. A new generation of artists and critics was forced to reconsider the painter's relevance, after an era dominated by minimalism and abstract expressionism, to the broader social project of discovering alternative histories of the early modern world. Debates among artists and critics surrounding the Metropolitan exhibition asked whether Caravaggio is 'our contemporary'[1] and a tutor figure for the successors of abstract expressionism;[2] or a poor draughtsman with a worse disposition, whose revival merely confirms that 'three hundred and seventy-five years have not dimmed [his work's] power to be showy, pushy, and hollow';[3] or one of the last exponents of a tradition of artistic craftsmanship, which, far from contemporary, 'sadly is now past beyond recall'.[4] Despite the vast separation in time between Caravaggio's late sixteenth-century and early seventeenth-century Italy and the moment of his revival, his artwork and biography were conscripted into a variety of contemporary struggles: his work became a corrective to formal impasses in abstract and neo-avant-garde art, and his life a model of rebellion and resistance important to revisionist histories of the early modern era. While professional *Caravaggisti* debated the merits of the few biographical sources concerning his sexuality, other scholars searched for gay shibboleths, for an anachronistically queer iconography scattered throughout his paintings.[5] Although consideration of Caravaggio's sexuality will always involve a certain amount of speculation, his paintings often revolve around sexually inviting or challenging glances and gestures and incorporate an iconography associated with homoerotic subcultures of his time. Caravaggio's Victorious Cupid (*c.* 1601–2), writes one art historian, may preserve the 'slender thread of a rudimentary "homosexual tradition"' and mark 'the culmination and swan song of openly homosexual expression' in the baroque era.[6] As recent critics have suggested, Caravaggio also inserts authorial signatures and self-portraits – including two as decapitated heads – into paintings that seem otherwise unconcerned with autobiography, establishing himself as one of the most self-revelatory of mannerist and baroque artists. For Leo Bersani and Ulysse Dutoit, conjecture about Caravaggio's sexual identity is unfortunate, no matter how well-founded, because it deprives the paintings of their 'intractably enigmatic quality'.[7] They argue that 'Caravaggio's enigmatic bodies have not yet been domesticated by sexual – perhaps even gendered – identities'.[8] But in comments on the conjectural nature of his screenplay for *Caravaggio* (1986), Derek Jarman emphasizes the interplay of biography and fiction in both his film and its necessarily ambiguous sources: 'The narrative of the film is constructed from the paintings. If it is fiction, it is the fiction of the paintings.'[9] Given Caravaggio's penchant for self-revelation in his paintings, and given the paucity of other biographical information, those images become crucial testimony, ultimately producing a speculative account of the artist's life, but a 'fiction' grounded in the paintings. What is permissible in reconstructing the life of Caravaggio and what lessons his biography offers the present depend largely upon whether or not the paintings themselves count as historical documents and, if they do, whether or not history can incorporate those images without subordinating them to the texts they either bolster or contradict.

In Jarman's *Caravaggio* the tableau vivant serves as the medium for a history based on images; it becomes an interface between art and history, film and painting, the present and the past. One legacy of the political modernism of the 1970s was the assertion that politics originates in a bold and decisive break from the past; but Jarman's cinema acknowledges the impossibility, even undesirability, of that break for artists and activists hoping to discover and insert themselves within a community of opposition. Rather than rehearse the concerns of political modernism, *Caravaggio* posits the tableau vivant – a force of suspension and possible reorientation, a quotation that foregrounds difference as well as repetition, a medium of historical return that never sloughs off the mediating presence of actual bodies – as a successor to the ideology of the break. The foundational representational problem for Jarman's filmmaking is how to resolve the formal politics of political modernism and the exigencies of the present, in particular an oppositional queer politics centred on the archaeology of past identity formations and a genealogy of the present. The film's destruction of the organic, mimetic diegesis is reminiscent of similar tendencies in political modernism, but Jarman also establishes identification as a compelling aesthetic model, and alternates between extremes of distanciation and intimacy.[10] In Jarman's mode of identity politics – specifically, queer activism during the height of the AIDS crisis and under Thatcherite governance – the rediscovery of identities submerged beneath dominant histories and a genealogy of current subcultures becomes an explosive political project.[11] Resistance has a history, the film suggests, though that history may remain obscured by centuries of accumulated discourses. The film reanimates gestures suspended on canvas since the cusp of the seventeenth century, subjecting those movements to the retrospective gaze of history and the prospective gaze of contemporary queer movements, joining the paradoxically future-oriented return to art history designed to recuperate Caravaggio for contemporary art and politics. The film reflects what might be called a mannerist sense of history, a recognition of, and struggle with, a past at once insistently present and necessarily estranged. It incorporates formal strategies of political modernism while infusing history into this formula, becoming a form of modernism with hindsight, with a historical dimension that allows for a return both to and of the past.

Benjamin writes that the 'authenticity of a thing is the essence of all that is transmissible from its beginning, ranging from its substantive duration to its testimony to the history which it has experienced'.[12] But what constitutes the origin of a work of art, and how does it transmit its history? The historical project in *Caravaggio* centres on a succession of tableaux vivants because through these histrionic copies it alludes to a qualitatively different moment in the social life of art objects, when the artwork existed only as a work in progress. These tableaux shown on screen exist not as a conduit for the ostensible subject matter of the painting, the narrative announced in titles or museum placards, but instead initiate a speculative recreation of their immediate conditions of production. *Caravaggio* departs from one of the most conventional genres – the life of the absolute artist – and foregoes formal, biographical, iconographic or narrative modes of 'reading' pictures. Instead it focuses on the production of pictures, recreating them in studio settings to afford access to the moment at which a welter of social and economic forces, identities and desires were inscribed on canvas. Each tableau becomes a microcosm of Rome's sexual, economic and power relations, as the city's elite insinuate themselves into the lives of Caravaggio and his friends and therefore into the studio of the painter. Jarman uses the tableau vivant to suspend and expand time just before the completion of the painting, before the drama of the studio concluded in a completed picture and dissipated over centuries of interpretation. Just as linguistics provided the operative metaphor when critics in the 1970s reconstituted the 'language' of images, *Caravaggio* provides a realization of the project Joan Copjec alludes to when she exhorts us to become 'literate in desire'.[13] The tableaux in Jarman's *Caravaggio* derive their power not from the privileged signifiers on their frames, but from the more intimate circumstances of the studio: the moment when the life of the artist – a story of both desire and the effect of power on that desire – was depicted on canvas.

But the narrative of Jarman's *Caravaggio* would be difficult to discern from standard biographical information on the artist, such as it is. Little is known about the life of Caravaggio because he left few of the written records normally used in the reconstruction of lives on the cusp of the seventeenth century. The primary contemporaneous documents of his life are police records, which hint at a narrative of habitual criminality, beginning with the peccadilloes of his youth, escalating gradually through an almost annual appearance before the magistrates for crimes such as a fight over a plate of artichokes, and culminating with the murder of Ranuccio Tommasoni – a crime which caused the artist to flee Rome in 1606, dying on the run four years later. Contemporary journalistic accounts and letters and later biographies confirm many of the salient facts, in particular the more sensational details of this well-documented fight: 'it has been a long time since we have had a dispute in Rome such as the one that took place on Sunday in Campomarzo between the painter Michelangelo da Caravaggio and a certain Ranuccio', reads one of the surviving primary sources.[14] The film is most remarkable in its frequent departure from the well-known narrative of crimes and misdemeanours, a narrative that conforms very closely to romantic myths of the menacing artist in the Rimbaud mould, whose unstable behaviour bespeaks the peculiarity of an 'artistic sensibility'. Later biographers and critics have been forced to reconcile these salacious official accounts and the sketchy but intriguing story they imply, with the alternative eloquence of the primary extant autobiographical record: Caravaggio's paintings. A history of the completed canvases, of their exchange and ownership, is less schematic than the necessarily speculative biography, but that history only tangentially relates to the artist and his mode of production. The well-known biblical and classical tales related in the paintings also reveal little about the artist himself. The stories predate Caravaggio by centuries and he often rendered them in a contemporary idiom, clothing his characters in the garb of sixteenth-century Roman commoners and removing all of the conventional trappings of antiquity, escaping as far as possible the tyranny of stylistic and hermeneutic traditions enveloping those oft-painted stories. A formal account of styles, of Caravaggio's break with classicism and experiments with mannerism, also reveals little about the life of the artist, in the studio and elsewhere. The warp and woof of art and commerce, styles and subjects, intersect with the canvas at various moments; but they can say little about Caravaggio himself beyond the strictly limited sphere of artistic patronage and the economics of art, the purely formal realm of individual and period style, or the usually uniform templates of iconography. Adhering only to the most authentic and incontrovertible evidence, Caravaggio's biography devolves into the story recorded and propagated by the official public discourse of police records and buyers and sellers of art.

Yet as Michael Fried argues in his 1997 essay on Caravaggio's often concealed and disguised self-portraits, many of Caravaggio's paintings contain lingering traces of the artist himself and hint at the particularities of his mode of production. Fried suggests, for example, that Caravaggio's Boy Bitten By a Lizard (*c.* 1596–7) is figured in the act of painting a self-portrait, of swiveling between a mirror and a canvas arranged at right angles, constructing a triangle, with the canvas and mirror offering two different takes on the artist/subject who occupies the third side.[15] The eponymous boy's expression of shock is also a record of the painter's own discomfort at discovering the difference between the mirror image and the self-representation – in essence, having seen himself in his mirror or canvas, as though for the first time. De Certeau suggests that this dynamic of identification and estrangement became a signature theme in baroque art because 'probably no era was more conversant with the ruses of the image'.[16] He writes that figurative representations became exercises in catoptromancy, or divination through mirrors, with the reflection representing not the imaginary fullness of identity but a 'doubling of the ego'. The mirror image enacts a complex process of dispersal whose stages de Certeau describes as follows:

> What I see in the image of the other is me; I am not here where I am but elsewhere, in the mirror representing the absent other, and I didn't know it: this was the iconic theme of those years. The other who appears to me through vision is an unknown me.[17]

Fried's essay on Caravaggio also hinges on the expressions of shock and misrecognition that disfigure the artist's self-portraits and then on the artist's compulsion to inscribe himself on canvas despite these obvious misgivings. In most modern studies of the artist's work, Fried writes:

> What by and large has not been recognized is that Caravaggio is one of those rare painters . . . whose paintings must be understood as evoking a primary, even primordial, relationship to the painter himself, who afterwards is succeeded, but never quite supplanted, by other viewers, by the viewer in general, in a word, by us.[18]

Jarman's film takes this proposition literally: it searches for the submerged autobiography inscribed on those canvases and reconstructs from these primary extant autobiographical records the 'primordial' relationship between Caravaggio and his work. If Caravaggio indeed inscribed so many traces of himself on his canvases, if scenes drawn from biblical sources include the face or telltale gestures of the artist, the obvious but ultimately unanswerable question is 'Why?'. Jarman responds first with another question, asking why the paintings resort to strategies of obscurity and deferral. He echoes Foucault's observation on the possibility of subversion even within the rules of relatively circumscribed and inhospitable regimes:

> The successes of history belong to those who are capable of seizing these rules, to replace those who had used them, to disguise themselves so as to pervert them, invert their meaning, and redirect them against those who had initially imposed them: controlling this complex mechanism, they will make it function so as to overcome the rulers through their own rules.[19]

The director suggests that his starting point in the construction of the narrative was 'a reading of the paintings' themselves, particularly Caravaggio's late depiction of David holding the head of Goliath, with its self-portrait as a decapitated head, and his Beheading of John the Baptist (1608), with a statement of incrimination and responsibility inscribed in the martyred saint's dripping blood: 'I, Michelangelo, did this.'[20] From these seminal facts, Jarman expands the film into a work of immanent picture theory, as it offers a 'reading' of the desire inscribed in this and other works and reconstructs a partial narrative to locate those desires. In a draft of his 'Theses on the philosophy of history', Benjamin wrote that:

> The past has deposited in it images, which one could compare to those captured by a light-sensitive plate. Only the future has developers at its disposal which are strong enough to allow the image to come to light in all its details.[21]

The representational problem at the core of Jarman's *Caravaggio* is how to materialize these vestiges of an unrealized past.

Frank Stella's Charles Eliot Norton Lectures at Harvard in 1983–4, which centred on Caravaggio's relevance to a generation of artists dealing with the institutionalization of abstract art, advanced a related thesis about the importance of the studio setting to an understanding of Caravaggio's art. For Stella, Caravaggio's belated re-emergence affords an opportunity to appropriate his unique response to a classical tradition and his experimentation with mannerism in new contexts as a panacea to the excesses and limitations of postwar art. Stella's Norton Lectures and the subsequent published version, descriptively entitled *Working Space*,[22] offer a more formalist parallel to Jarman's own project, as both elaborate a speculative relationship to Caravaggio and make contemporary an artist from a radically different historical era. Despite the differences between Stella's early minimalism and Jarman's more politically oriented farrago of styles, Stella's Caravaggio bears a close resemblance to Jarman's. Both Stella's critical appreciation in the lectures and Jarman's film biography centre on 'working space' in several senses of the term. And because of his keen attention to the details of how a fellow artist worked, how the manipulations of the studio translated into shapes and colours on canvas, Stella moves backward in time from the frozen canvas to the configuration of models, the originary tableaux vivants, that became the Caravaggio paintings passed on through the centuries.

Beyond its repeated comparisons between Caravaggio's work and that of present-day abstract artists, Stella's book also reflects a fascination with the workings of the studio, and in particular the arrangement of artist and model that allowed Caravaggio to realize a complex framework of bodies. In critical accounts roughly contemporaneous with the paintings themselves, Giovanni Baglione writes that Caravaggio's innovative chiaroscuro lighting derived in part from his peculiar configuration of models in the studio, as he lit scenes from above, through a skylight placed strategically in the ceiling. But Stella also provides a speculative reconstruction of the studio space, suggesting that the artist would situate himself between the canvas and the models, swiveling towards, then away from, the people recreating a dramatic scene before, then behind, him. Thus 'Caravaggio would be in the center of his universe, orchestrating the twin realities of pictoriality – subject and object – while his model/actors reveled in the immortalization of their own performance, watching themselves in Caravaggio's canvas mirror'.[23] If Stella's hypothesis is correct, then Caravaggio could have painted from carefully arranged tableaux vivants whose theatrical performance preceded the 'original' canvas.[24] For this reason the scene depicted on canvas becomes more than captured stillness, its players more than forms and shadows; the studio is transformed into a performance space, with the canvas akin to a reflective surface, or more accurately, a device for recording those patterns of light. Using the same metaphor – the mirror that 'retains the image' – that Bazin upholds as an essential characteristic of cinema,[25] Stella envisions the canvas almost as a protocinematic apparatus, capturing an event unfolding in time and promising immortality for those posing, though that event remains fossilized in sheets and layers, in a palimpsest rather than cinema's serial succession of frames. Stella praises Caravaggio's paintings for their ability to construct a pictorial space where this drama of the studio can unfold: first through his violation of the viewer's space by projecting an object or gestures forward in the composition, thereby breaking the plane of the picture; and second by delimiting that depth with a vague, unrealized backdrop, a conscious circumscription of Albertian perspective. Having identified a crisis in abstraction in his own era, a crisis attributable to an obsession with colour and surface, Stella beckons toward Caravaggio's canvases as a model for escaping the tyranny of pure surface. Caravaggio not only created 'a kind of pictoriality that had not existed before', he also 'changed the way artists would have to think about themselves and their work. He made the studio into a place of magic and mystery, a cathedral of the self.'[26] As Stella's fantastic and mystifying language attests, these spaces are always imagined and hypothetical in retrospect. But the juxtaposition of these two spaces, the studio and the canvas, posits Stella's 'working space' as the site where the personal intersects with the materiality of the medium, where the necessarily ephemeral inscribes itself upon the potentially enduring, where the past is translated into a present suspended in emergence. Of the paintings in the Contarelli Chapel, he writes: 'Even though we know it is not possible, we sense that we are close to the moment when these paintings were made. We feel that we want to leave the church immediately; we would like to locate the place and fix the moment where and when these paintings were made.'[27] That moment of production, when the space of the studio enters that of the canvas, is also the object of the beholder's desire in Stella's account: it is something we 'would like to locate . . . and fix', something 'close' but always elusive, something endlessly receding before us. This moment is also the subject of Jarman's film, and the tableau vivant becomes its means of representation.

Stella's book does not advance a new argument about Caravaggio's treatment of space; this discussion of pictorial space was standard commentary in the earliest monographs on the subject, particularly in Friedlaender's *Caravaggio Studies*, written thirty years before Stella's lectures. When Jarman first undertook the project for *Caravaggio*, he read Friedlaender's book, and perhaps incorporated the argument about pictorial space into his filmmaking practice.[28] But while Friedlaender argues that Caravaggio's work gestures always towards an *hors champ*, a transcendent sphere where the artist's lingering religiosity could reside, Stella focuses on the space inside the bounds of the canvas and on the 'cathedral' an individual artist constructs there. Jarman performs one further transformation. For him the studio is not only a place where the artist inscribes the self on canvas, it is also a social space; at once an escape from, and a microcosm of, the social forces at work outside that seeming refuge. Jarman and cinematographer Gabriel Beristain have received praise from most reviewers for the faithful rendering of Caravaggio's lighting and modelled figures, but with its depthless dimensions the film also recalls Caravaggiesque space, as the artist infamous for his refusal or inability to master Albertian perspectival paradigms also evokes a strictly limited, forward-reaching rather than infinitely receding space. This 'authenticity' is due, in part, to the exigencies of production: the film was made for half a million pounds in six weeks in a warehouse in the Isle of Dogs, London, and as a result features no Italian landscape. But this construction of intimate, domestic, bodily space also introduces the film's thematics from the outset. Within that space *Caravaggio* presents tableaux vivants designed to reinsert the personal, the body and the social sphere into the masterpiece whose timeless canonicity depends on the suppression of such ephemera.

In the periods of their utmost popularity, critics evaluated performances of tableaux vivants according to strict criteria: their precision in reproducing a familiar work of art; their faithfulness to an original; their capacity to evoke the presence of that original despite the distance of a country or continent. When constructed in accordance with these standards, the tableau vivant copies paintings, embodies inaccessible artworks, performs scenes from literary classics, or composes a compressed theatrical miniature, approximating under adverse conditions the sort of dramatic action best captured in full throttle on stage. The tableau as em-bodied masterpiece succeeds when it defers to the original, when it remains faithful to its source, when it basks in the aura of art. These paintings on tour once served as an early museum without walls, affording access to otherwise sequestered or distant works of art. Goethe, for example, wrote enthusiastically about the dramatic attitudes of Emma Lyon as an embodiment of his theory of performance. The attitude begins to mould the body into an imitation of a classical prototype, and 'by performing the classical body, one can bring an effective gravity, a "celestial" aspect to the event. By imitating the fibre of antiquity's statues, the performer is able to elevate her work and evoke awe and wonder from her audience'.[29]

This variation on the tableau vivant allows the performer to become 'a classical statue brought to life, a revitalized antiquity'.[30] But it also reinforces through repetition an already prevalent conception of a particular cultural heritage. It reinscribes the boundaries of that heritage by inhabiting the artworks that bear repeating for two overlapping and ultimately indistinguishable reasons: because of their intrinsic worth and because they 'belong' to their audience and performers. As the actors inhabit a tableau vivant and the audience recognizes its allusion, the original also inhabits them, constituting them as an audience through those very acts of repetition and recognition. The performance of the tableau vivant becomes an exercise in the installation and indoctrination of cultural heritage and an occasion for the conspicuous display of cultural capital.

But despite, or even because of its belated, ancillary relationship to more established art forms, the tableau vivant can also exploit its difference to construct a hybrid between art and commentary. It can capitalize on its definitionally pre-scribed departure from an ideal by emphasizing its difference, highlighting its constitutive falsity until it verges on the camp or the grotesque. It becomes both a means of revenge on the ideal that remains the exclusive right of the original and a celebration of the copy precisely because it marks the limits, and ultimately the failure and collapse, of that ideal. Benjamin's book on the *Trauerspiel* foregrounds the use of tableaux on the baroque stage, arguing that beyond their stunning visual impact, their capacity for raw spectacle, these stilled and assiduously arranged bodies occupy a crucial position within the thematic and aesthetic structures of baroque drama. According to a study cited by Benjamin, the *Trauerspiel* becomes virtually synonymous with the tableau vivant, with the former presenting a succession of still scenes modelled after paintings. A *Trauerspiel*, writes its author, is 'an allegorical painting executed with living figures, and with changes of scene. The spoken word makes no pretence to be dialogue; it is only a commentary on the images, spoken by the images themselves'.[31] While they foreground their status as quotations from canonical works of European art, the tableaux vivants in *Caravaggio* also become mourning plays for the history elided in the translation of experience to canvas. In the process, these camp and grotesque tableaux high-light the extravagance of their often elaborately posed and constructed sources; they insinuate themselves back into their sources, unveiling the constitutive excess, the inherent falsity always present in the ideal and the original. They exact revenge by exposing the penchant for excess in the more established media and canonical artworks imperfectly approximated. Jean-François Lyotard invokes a potentially transgressive variation on the tableau vivant in his 1973 essay 'Acinema', which considers alternative strategies available to filmmakers at the outset of post-modernity and gestures towards 'two directions', 'two seemingly contradictory currents' energizing 'whatever is intense in painting today' and the 'truly active forms of experimental and underground cinema'.[32] Lyotard identifies these 'poles' as 'immobility and excessive movement', and he cites the tableau vivant as one example of postmodern immobility, situates cinematic 'abstraction' at the opposite pole, and anticipates a 'libidinal' cinema able to match the 'drift of desire' that characterizes the work of his most revered artists. Jarman's *Caravaggio* originates in the unlikely pairing of art history and the 'drift of desire' and becomes a speculative history of desire's static traces.

Caravaggio opens with a closeup of the artist's head, in a deathly aspect, with one eye closed and the other fixed in a distant stare that recalls the decapitated head in David with the Head of Goliath (*c*. 1609–10), the self-portrait conflating death and desire that sparked Jarman's interest in the submerged biography hinted at in this and other pictures. A beginning that foreshadows the death of the title character is obviously a privileged moment in a narrative, and this premonition recalls Geoffrey Hartman's theory of narratological ends and beginnings: 'Stories begin with something . . . that means too much', he writes.[33] In 'The voice of the shuttle' he elaborates a rhetorical figure from Sophocles into a more general theory of 'poetical and figurative speech' and, ultimately, narrative structure, when he writes that all literature occupies the space between 'overspecified ends and indeterminate middles'.[34] This model also serves as the narrative structure of *Caravaggio* as a whole, as the story follows a dilatory path through discrete moments in the painter's life, always leading towards the inescapable historical fact of Caravaggio's early death on a beach at Porto Ercole. Immediately after Caravaggio's deathly counten-ance disappears from the screen, the film translates this structural principle, this demarcation of overdetermined poles surrounding an elided middle, into spatial terms. In the left foreground his assistant, Jerusaleme, sits carving wood at an out-of-focus table that threatens to spill over into the viewing space, to pierce the plane of the screen. In the right background, lying in a bed placed against a mottled grey back wall, Caravaggio marks the furthest extent of the film's depth of field (Figure 10.1). In the foreground, the beginning, the mute act of creativity, and craftsmanship; in the background, the death of the artist, the event that anchors his elusive biography in an overarching historical narrative. The camera distorts in this opening shot, as the empty room provides no waymarks to allow for steady passage between these two poles; depth perception is impossible, as it would be with Caravaggio's one-eyed visage. And in between these two characters, spaces and times, lies the elided middle where the rest of the film occurs. Like the painter whose biography it narrates, the film pries apart these two planes and creates a middle space where the action literally *takes place*.

Caravaggio's paintings have been praised and criticized for their tendency to transform sacred stories into genre scenes, for their rendering of the most charged moments of biblical history in a domestic idiom. They present a series of epiphanic moments in everyday settings, situating scenes of revelation in a manger or tavern. These humbled stories take place within an equally humble space that foregoes the illusions of infinite regress and intersects with the viewer's world through a

Figure 10.1 Caravaggio (Derek Jarman, 1986) BFI production

contiguity with the viewing space. This distinction between the system of Albertian perspective and Caravaggio's forward projection recalls Newton's discourse on 'absolute' and 'relative' spaces. Newton writes:

> Absolute space in its own nature, without relation to anything external, remains always similar and immovable. Relative space is some moveable dimension or measure of the absolute spaces; which our senses determine by its position to bodies; and which is commonly taken for immovable space.[35]

The space of Jarman's *Caravaggio* asserts the triumph of the body and the relative space it defines, inviting the viewer's involvement not through incorporation into a larger system, but by transforming the space of the film into the human, bodily space of the audience. 'Effective history', writes Foucault, 'shortens its vision to those things nearest to it – the body, the nervous system, nutrition, digestion, and energies';[36] and the film's presentation of history focuses primarily on these more mundane activities and the locations in which they unfold. The manufactured depth of the filmic image often constructs an illusion of enlightenment, an illusion that knowledge abides somewhere in these protracted spaces, waiting to be discovered. Bersani and Dutoit emphasize that Caravaggio's aversion to Albertian space signals a departure from paradigms centred on knowledge and an embrace of 'the relationality that constitutes the human as we know it'.[37] 'Art illuminates relationality by provisionally, and heuristically, immobilizing relations', they write.[38] The space in *Caravaggio* occupies the opposite extreme from the Albertian model and its promise of knowledge in depth. The film's chronically foreclosed space advertises the absence of knowledge immediately accessible by scanning or by farther receding into the visual field, suggesting that the film's answers exist in another locus altogether, in the bodily and relational space where the action unfolds. The principal characters reinforce this foregrounding of relational space by appearing to ignore the presence of the camera as they enter and exit the frame not through theatrical wings but from the space behind the camera. Lena, for example, enters the film during the boxing match between Ranuccio and the bartender, and she appears first as a hand, implying a body that extends somewhere out into the viewing space. And perhaps more than any character, Jerusaleme seems oblivious to the presence of the camera and the integrity of the frame; he exists in a network of relations with the film's other characters and a space that extends not back into the image but from the foreground forward. Rather than supply knowledge according to the framing and spatial priorities of the apparatus, each of these bodies is a phenomenon of relationality.

This emphasis on relative space and relations among bodies also translates into a concern with the everyday economy of art production, as the demands of patrons and the power structures of the larger society are implicated in the life of the studio. Jerusaleme, a mute boy adopted by the artist to serve as an assistant and the only completely fictional character in Jarman's account, supports the domestic economy of artistic production, as he grinds pigments and mixes the paints, a form of silent participation all the more poignant because portraits of the artist at work too often elide this role. As Benjamin writes in his 'Theses on the philosophy of history', cultural treasures 'owe their existence not only to the efforts of the great minds and talents who have created them, but also to the anonymous toil of their contemporaries'.[39] One peril of the simulacrum is its separation from the individuals and the labour that produced it; the danger is less the absence of an original than a denial of origins. *Caravaggio* situates the labour of artistic production at the centre of art historical discourse, countering the threat of sourceless simulation with yet another copy, the tableau vivant, whose embodiments emphasize that the painting is not mechanically or digitally simulated but *made*. Jerusaleme's presence beside the tableau vivant locates the 'voice' of these anonymous contributors somewhere outside the dominant linguistic order, in an alternative signifying system to which the body serves as the primary ingress. Alternating and in tension with the mocking superficiality of its mise-en-scene, so riddled with anachronisms and the trappings of 1980s bourgeois existence, the exigencies of Caravaggio's daily work also assume an important position in the film, especially through his relationship with Jerusaleme. Because the tableau vivant exists in several tenses at once – in the present of the performance, in the past viewed through historical representation, and in the future perfect, through which characters overlap with the paintings and historical figures that will have been – it allows the work that produced the painting to coincide with a premonition of the final product.

Those overlapping time frames signal Jarman's departure from Stella's model of the Caravaggiesque studio: not only a cathedral of the self, the studio is also a workshop, a space where the exigencies of art, desire and commerce intertwine in the simultaneously social and personal act of artistic production. The simultaneousness inherent in the tableau is revealed most explicitly when Cardinal Del Monte enters the studio to examine a work in progress and causes the models to snigger. Acting as the Cardinal's surrogate and therefore implicating himself in the systems of power at work in this mode of production, Caravaggio bellows, 'You are paid to be still'. And in the most explicit visualization of the convergence of money, power, desire and art, Caravaggio literally feeds coins to Ranuccio as he poses for The Martyrdom of St Matthew (1599–1600). Ranuccio is at once the model for Matthew's executioner in the unfinished picture, a desired and desiring subject, and the recipient of funds funnelled through the artist into the production of a work of art, investment and propaganda. The model thus exists at the site where these several narratives converge, and it is impossible to extricate one of those functions at any discrete moment. And Caravaggio himself fills a similarly complex multiplicity of roles, all constructed and produced within the discourses of power everywhere enveloping him. With the canvases all becoming the property of someone else and the models becoming hired hands, the paintings themselves reflect this sense of alienation. If these paintings are supposed to serve as an avenue into a submerged biography of the artist, they reveal instead the labyrinth of discourses surrounding and converging in each work of art. If these paintings are meant to afford access to an elusive, originary moment in the social life of the artwork, they instead reveal that what 'is found at the historical beginning of things is not the inviolable identity of their origin; it is the dissension of things. It is disparity'.[40] As Caravaggio incorporates blood into the surface of his canvases, as Ranuccio's pounding of his head against a prison wall is juxtaposed with the artist pounding his head against a canvas, as the dead body of Lena is used as a model for the Death of the Virgin (c. 1605–6), the extremity of the artist's attempts to overcome that alienation becomes apparent. The tableau vivant exists in a liminal state, with its living figures suspended among the vitality of the theatrical and the stilling of life on canvas and the eventual crystallization of the art object: the tableau vivant is always also a *tableau mourant*. Only the artist's literal incorporation of bodies in the painting can mark them as irrevocably his. And if, as Foucault writes, genealogy is charged with exposing 'the body totally imprinted by history and the process of history's destruction of the body', *Caravaggio* also lays bare the artist's desperate attempts to inscribe traces of that body into those seemingly impermeable official discourses.[41]

This economic exchange between Caravaggio and Ranuccio also introduces the film's peculiar pattern of editing, which replicates the triangular configuration of characters introduced in the earliest moments. In the scene where Caravaggio first sees Ranuccio and Lena at the boxing match, a succession of closeups – each of the lovers, then Caravaggio – culminates not in the expected closeup of Ranuccio, but in a medium-shot of Ranuccio and Lena, into which Caravaggio strolls from behind the camera, creating a triangle centred on the money offered to the victorious fighter. After the introduction of the basic structure, the film continues its radical departure from shot/reverse-shot patterns, usually through some triangulation of that bipolar standard. As Caravaggio and Jerusaleme clean Lena's body, for example, the progression of shots alternates between closeups of the members of the love triangle and medium shots of the artist caressing the body. As other characters interpolate themselves into the orbit of these relationships – as Ranuccio is displaced by Scipione Borghese, for example – a new triangle is constructed – with Borghese and Caravaggio the new pair of rivals. Or when Pipo enters the narrative, establishing herself as rival to Lena, she replicates her rival's infatuation with Caravaggio's money and art. This pattern of editing begins to resemble the structural principles elaborated by René Girard in *Deceit, Desire and the Novel*, in which he posits triangular desire as the ur-principle of the novelistic regime.[42] For Girard, despite romantic insistence on the autonomy of desire, on the direct connection between a desiring subject and its object, desire is always defined '*according to Another*' and '*opposed to this desire according to Oneself* that most of us pride ourselves on enjoying'.[43] Girard's term for that other is a 'mediator', and the demonstrated interest of this figure serves to foment desire, to render the object 'infinitely desirable'. And as that mediator becomes more of an obstacle to any ultimate fulfillment, 'envy, jealousy and rivalry' begin to complicate the narrative, as every bout of jealousy 'contains an element of fascination with the insolent rival'.[44] These passions, according to Stendhal, are the quintessential 'modern emotions', the traces of 'the centrifugal movement of an ego powerless to desire by itself'.[45] 'Vanity, copy, imitation' become the 'key-words' to describe all manifestations of desire, because the very notion of mediation calls into question the possibility of an originary desire existing somewhere in an individual or collective past.[46] Girard writes that:

> Recapturing the past is recapturing the original impression beneath the opinion of others which hides it; it is to recognize that this opinion is not one's own. It is to understand that the process of mediation creates a very vivid impression of autonomy and spontaneity precisely when we are no longer autonomous and spontaneous.[47]

The story that fills the domestic space of *Caravaggio* is just this tale of triangulated desire, of a craving that, far from autonomous, is always subordinated to ubiquitous, insistent and socially constructed rivalries between lovers. But because rivalry is always a social phenomenon, because the 'mediator' always situates triangulated desire in a context of social struggle, Girard's theory remains rooted in history despite its simultaneous allusion to basic psychological forces. Emotions can be 'modern', he suggests, and are always subject to manipulation and transformation over time.

Caravaggio attempts to situate this triangular desire in a specific social and economic context, as its first instance literally revolves around money: Lena, Caravaggio and Ranuccio stand around and gawk at the winnings the last earned for his victory in the boxing match. Subsequent rivalries also result from concerns with money, prestige and power, as when Caravaggio asserts his economic power over Ranuccio, sparking an explicit debate about the financial aspects of desire. After the first session of Ranuccio posing for The Martyrdom of St Matthew, Lena accuses him of falling in love with the artist; 'I'm in love with his money', Ranuccio responds. After she becomes the mistress of Scipione Borghese, nephew to the Pope, Lena taunts Ranuccio with the prospect that her children will be 'rich beyond avarice'. Ranuccio then responds with the film's first murder, and Caravaggio in turn kills Ranuccio. Much commentary on the film attempts to reconstruct the motivations for, and theoretical ramifications of, this sequence of violent actions, because this chain of murders, incited by ultimately failed transactions of desire and money, hints at a tragic aftermath for the homosexual desire figured in the film and for the woman posited as a useful but expendable handmaiden to desire. Lena's brutal death and aestheticized burial underscore her status first as a token of exchange used to up the ante of desire between the two men, and then as an ornament, celebrated only after death has rendered her a pliant aesthetic object rather than a defiant subject.[48] But the film also posits a proximate cause of the resort to murder of friends and lovers: a resented mediation and a commodified desire that reduce all relationships to inferior copies of an imagined ideal, and therefore a sense of alienation permeating the most intimate levels of human interaction. *Caravaggio* displaces questions of what constitutes an essential homosexual or heterosexual desire because such inquiries often revolve around an imagined paragon of desire, relegating each particular manifestation to the status of mere copy. Instead the film asserts that all desire is a copy constituted through imitation, and it celebrates the possibilities of a desire imagined as a copy rather than an essence: desire would then consist of an absolute openness in a network of relationality rather than the futile pursuit of an illusory original. The tragedies in *Caravaggio* are produced not by a failure to achieve the standards of an imagined and idealized model, but by the political and economic strictures that tangle that web of relations and foreclose the movements of desire. Lynne Tillman argues that Caravaggio's murder of Ranuccio proclaims his refusal to 'love over this dead woman's body';[49] and more generally this violence marks the momentarily deferred struggle for a desire founded on openness rather than erasure. The 'ego powerless to desire by itself', an always inadequately realized copy of an illusory essence, is displaced by 'the centrifugal movement of an ego', the endlessly overlapping and replicating figures of triangular desire. The aspiration towards an original and ideal subjectivity is replaced by an accumulation of manners.

If triangular desire underlies the basic editing pattern, and if each vertex of the triangle expresses its own brand of mediated desire, what do we make of scenes where this triangulation also includes a painting? What purpose does the canvas serve in this ongoing narrative of mediated desire? Does the painting reflect or transform, imitate or resuscitate, the desire that it purports to reproduce? The most remarkable instance of this action is the three-minute sequence of shots when Caravaggio has finished (or is just finishing) his painting of Victorious Cupid, also called Amor Vincit Omnia or Profane Love (Figure 10.2). The painting becomes an important presence in this succession of gazes (Figures 10.3–10.5). With no dialogue, the scene consists largely of an exchange of glances between Pipo, Caravaggio and the picture's wide-eyed, Dionysian boy-angel, who seems almost to beg for equal participation in this interchange of desire.[50] Writing of the painted portrait in cinema, Marc Vernet argues that the picture's

> impermeable permanence makes it into a representation of the Ideal, of its imposing mystery, of its inexhaustible secret. The portrait would thus serve to represent that which, once approached, can never be left behind. It comes to signify, iconically, the obsession of desire, the obsession of duty. The character's mouth is always closed, participating in a mute order, yet always with open eyes, to play the role of a sentinel waiting close-mouthed for the answer to a question.[51]

With no answer forthcoming, the picture ultimately becomes a figure for the 'unattainable'.[52] But the triangular interchange of glances between the artist, the tableau vivant and the painting complicates this formula, as the film alternates among the scanning eyes of the artist and tableau and the equally dynamic gaze inscribed on canvas. From the perspective of the artist, lying in a state of almost post-coital relaxation, the painting could serve as a model for one narrative of Caravaggio's life: it bespeaks a narrative of cupidity and Bacchanalian excess, one in keeping with the known facts of his biography. Earlier in the film, Caravaggio's voiceover admits as much, as he says, 'I painted myself as Bacchus and took on his fate'; and in a pun on the role-playing implied in human 'character', he adds, 'man's character is his fate'. But because it partakes in this triangular drama of the studio, and because it introduces a discrepancy between the completed picture and a profilmic reality, the scene also invites other readings. It invites a comparison, first of all, with the model whose likeness it is supposed to reflect but by design does not. It therefore reveals the artifice of the studio, the process by which a woman with propped-up wings becomes, through an act of transformative gender performance, Cupid materialized in paint. But the camera also transfigures the subject of the painting, fragmenting it, destroying the imaginary wholeness provided in a museum context. By virtue of the closeup on its eerily active eyes, the painting becomes more than a 'detour for the gaze' that the painted portrait in cinema normally invites;[53] instead,

Figures 10.2–10.5
Caravaggio (Derek Jarman, 1986)
BFI production

in a quixotic and utopian gesture, this lingering closeup imagines a face that usurps the power of the gaze, and a mouth with the power to speak. Roland Barthes writes at the beginning of *Camera Lucida* that he happened upon a photograph of Napoleon's younger brother, 'and I realized then, with an amazement I have not been able to lessen since: "I am looking at the eyes that looked at the emperor".'[54] Lingering on the eyes of the angel, alternating between that gaze and the personal drama performed in the studio, the film suggests that Caravaggio's paintings offer a similar connection to an artist who predates the advent of photography: these eyes bring us as near to the artist as posterity, endowed only with the power of retrospection, can see.

But as Benjamin writes in his essay on Baudelaire, 'The deeper the remoteness which a glance has to overcome, the stronger will be the spell that is apt to emanate from the gaze'.[55] Despite a distance of centuries between the artist and the present-day spectator, and despite the objectified presence of the painted subject, Caravaggio's paintings remain haunted by a gaze. And like the ghostly presence in Derrida's reading of *Hamlet*,

> this spectral *someone other looks at us*, we feel ourselves being looked at by it, outside of any synchrony, even before and beyond any look on our part, according to an absolute anteriority (which may be on the order of a generation, of more than one generation) and asymmetry, according to an absolutely unmasterable disproportion.[56]

People 'inhabit' what they produce in a manner akin to haunting, writes Derrida, and the process of haunting becomes a form of personification.[57] By returning to the moment of inscription, when the canvas is not yet (or just) finished, the scene also evokes an earlier and qualitatively different phase in the social life of art objects. Caravaggio's Profane Love, like the other canvases recreated on screen, fans out the elided moment between the inception of the painting and its release into a commercial sphere, inserting that moment into the precipitate narrative of the artist's life. In these moments the tableau vivant becomes a force of expansion as well as suspension; more than merely holding narrative in abeyance, the tableau engages with the possibilities hidden on the canvases, invisible in public records, and therefore 'hidden from history'.[58] Like Caravaggio's hidden self-portraits, this painting invites the beholder to take the place of the artist who produced it and, within the larger studio and social contexts provided throughout the film, to imagine the communities in which he moved, to uncover his various objects of desire and the proscriptions against that desire. Jarman's comments on the film frame the project in the dual contexts of queer historiography and contemporary queer political mobilization, linking each to the other.[59] And this archaeology of the artist's identity, this almost desperate search for the submerged story of Caravaggio's sexuality establishes these early modern models of resistance as a contribution to contemporary oppositional politics. If unmediated desire occupies an unattainable position with the advent of the modern era, Profane Love represents the survival of desire in the systems of simulated, bought, and sold desire. With Cupid balancing acrobatically over the musical instruments, books and building materials scattered at his feet the detritus of a culture playfully subverted – the painting presents its 'victorious' subject as a transcendent figure. Jarman's film ascribes that power of transcendence to the scene enacted before the canvas, to the gender performance and playful, boundary-crossing desire cryptically inscribed in paint. This victorious cupid, whose ancient arrows provoke the oldest form of exogenous desire, also inspires Stendahl's modern emotions'; but 'vanity, copy, imitation' become indicators of success rather than degeneration.

The painting that forms the still centre of this complex scene is particularly significant in Caravaggio's oeuvre because, as Howard Hibbard points out, 'it most clearly exhibits his confrontation with Michelangelo's achievement, a compound of admiration and almost childish rebellion'.[60] But 'there may well have been more than rivalry or rebellion moiling in Caravaggio's mind when he created these Michelangelesque images', he suggests.[61] Victorious Cupid recasts the master's idealized male nudes as a more earthy, sexualized figure, thus establishing 'a pro-found identification . . . with a great artist of the past whom Caravaggio must have believed to have been homosexual'.[62] The same combination of rivalry and identification marks Jarman's relationship with Caravaggio in his film. Jarman's film disrupts and dismembers the paintings included in the film, as it attempts to renovate these now well-known and widely circulated images through a directed tour of the canvas and the uniquely cinematic project used to reveal their submerged autobiography. In the era of cinematic homage, an undertheorized mutation of the simulacrum, *Caravaggio* rejects the currency of cultural capital and resists the temptation to quote without commentary and critique. Yet underlying this rebellion against inherited images runs a strain of profound identification with Caravaggio, particularly with the artist's own attempts to rework the usual subjects, inserting markers of his own sexual identity into canvases targeted for appropriation and into a longer hermeneutic tradition. With a trace of rebellion Jarman enlists Caravaggio in the paradoxical project of writing a prehistory of contemporary queer resistance. Antonio Negri has argued that the problem of social change is 'to think the new in the total absence of its conditions'.[63] Political modernism, like previous manifestations of the avant garde, encountered a similar problem even as it preached the value of a break with ideologies of the past. Jarman's film returns to Caravaggio's work with the hope of finding the new buried somewhere in the past, or, more precisely, because traces of the past exist on the canvases themselves, hidden in plain sight.

Girard's model of triangular desire is useful again because his foundational work on internal mediation, the mediation of a literary master or model, has also inspired later work on the status of art in a condition of belatedness. Girard begins with an extended quotation from *Don Quixote*, from a passage where the would-be knight errant, using the analogy of literary and artistic models, explains to Sancho how to venture closest to perfection in their vocation:

> I think . . . that, when a painter wants to become famous for his art he tries to imitate the originals of the best masters he knows; the same rule applies to the most important jobs or exercises which contribute to the embellishment of republics. . . . In the same way Amadis was the pole, the star, the sun for brave and amorous knights, and we others who fight under the banner of love and chivalry should imitate him. Thus, my friend Sancho, I reckon that whoever imitates him best will come closest to perfect chivalry.[64]

The paradox underlying Jarman's art of imitation is that it both foregrounds its artifice and its inadequacy as reproduction through a parade of excessive images, and situates these ultra-contemporary interventions within an expansive history of artifice. This duality of orientation begins with an ostentatious rejection of classical Hollywood cinema and its illusions, a refusal of mimetic mythology most evident in *Caravaggio*'s anachronistic props – a calculator, typewriter, scooter and tractor, along with nouvelle cuisine and immediately dated 1980s clothing – that identify *Caravaggio*'s baroque era as a historically and logically impossible one and there-fore a self-conscious construction rather than an organic reproduction or mirror of reality. The film exists within a temporal dimension closer to Jean-Luc Nancy's 'unbound time' than to the chronologies of conventional history.[65] In Jarman's filmmaking this anachronism is intimately intertwined with an overarching political project: the development of oppositional communities and filmmaking practices in a Thatcherite moment when the manipulation of a national past and its histories and images remains an integral strategy in a conservative ideological programme.[66] Much of Jarman's oeuvre – from *Jubilee* (1977) to *The Last of England* (1987), from *The Tempest* (1979) to *Edward II* (1991) – can be read as an attempt to destabilize that burgeoning and exclusionary identity by overwriting Britain's cultural institu-tions with both estranging, graffiti-like visual excess and an untimely history that puts the lie to dominant constructions of that national past. Strategies of distanciation coexist with attempts to establish alternative forms of identification. *Caravaggio*'s moments of estrangement are at the same time markers of alternative history of both Caravaggio's time and Jarman's. The film's obtrusive and anachronistic but oddly familiar props can also be seen as an attempt at a signature, as an attempt to solidify the film's connection to Jarman's own time and place, as a more playful alternative to the flesh and blood that his Caravaggio incorporates into the canvas. Camp acting plays a similar role in the film, as minor players often perform in hyperbolic fashion, both destroying the film's illusion-ism and establishing a link between Jarman's time and Caravaggio's: the film's repeated, knowing, sexualized glances mirror those of Caravaggio's camped-up Cupid in *Profane Love*, and beckon towards the trail of gay shibboleths in both Jarman and Caravaggio.[67] The distancing strategies of political modernism have become at the same time strategies to spark identification, particularly among a queer subculture of viewers.

Other Jarman films betray more ambivalence about his own influences because even those who fought against their times can succumb to the potentially more powerful force of nostalgia. Graffiti scrawled during the Paris uprisings of 1968 declared 'art is dead, don't eat its corpse', an admonition to steer clear of a rotting heritage, but also, as Benjamin might have added, an exhortation to preserve evidence that might later prove the best witness to its own demise.[68] Jarman's ambivalence emerges most provocatively in the opening moments of *The Last of England*, when Spring, a young squatter living amidst piles of rubble in a landscape postapocalyptic and postindustrial, first tramples on, then simulates sex with, Caravaggio's *Profane Love*. As Benjamin writes, 'visions of the frenzy of destruction, in which all earthly things collapse into a heap of ruins . . . reveal the limit set upon allegorical contemplation, rather than its ideal quality'.[69] *The Last of England* bridles at the restrictions of *Caravaggio*'s allegories, its confinement to a world of corpses and contemplation of desire in the abstract. Jarman's millennial film riddled with haunting images of power violently exerted and victims huddled together in their powerlessness, posits Spring's resistance as a double-edged sword: while rebelling against the power structures that seemingly everywhere oppress, he also destroys records of earlier acts of resistance, relegating Caravaggio's attempt to rework and transcend the culture scattered at Cupid's feet to just another piece of rubble. Spring's desperate, purely sexual advances towards the artwork reflect a poverty of critical tools at his disposal: his only means of accessing the image are the either/or of indiscriminate destruction of, or rapt fascination with, the image. But *Caravaggio*'s tableaux return these to the archive of images through an act of critical reincorporation. The film alludes to, but transforms, the Death of Marat, Jacques-Louis David's painting of the revolutionary who died while penning a political tract in his bathtub.[70] In the film the Jacobin becomes a rival painter and hostile critic searching for the most acerbic phrases to attack Caravaggio, just as David's neoclassicism is founded upon an implicit critique and abandonment of Caravaggio, an abject figure for his anti-Albertian construction of space and his search for a contemporary idiom to renovate and transmit biblical tales. The tableau with Cardinal Del Monte as Caravaggio's St Jerome Writing becomes a knowing wink at the subject's inadequacy in such an exalted role, his corruption clashing with the stores of wisdom scattered on his desk. These two quotations seem anomalous in the film because they contrast dramatically with the seriousness of the studio reanimations of other Caravaggio masterpieces. They allude to famous tableaux as vehicles for trivial commentaries on trivial characters. Flat and still, these images are the filmic equivalents of the glossy magazine that Baglione carries around to demonstrate the limitations of Caravaggio's work to anyone willing to look. Divorced from the moment of their production, these quotations advertise their status as vacuous simulacra, as consumable and disposable objects devoid of the context present elsewhere, in the tableaux that provide evidence of the artist's production process and the craftsmanship it entails.

Rather than peddle Caravaggio's pictures in a display of cultural capital, the film foregrounds the superficiality of uncritical homage and quotation, emphasizing their complicity in systems of commodification. Its tableaux vivants instead represent an act of critical hermeneutics; they exist not merely for the sake of allusion, but as part of a renovation of the image through a uniquely cinematic project. If a canvas with 'I, Michelangelo, did this' sparked the filmmaker's interest in the project, *Caravaggio* emphasizes the verb as well as the subject, positing the act of making as an integral part of the personality embodied in the film. Shown as works in progress, within the studio, the tableaux transform their original canvases into protocinematic devices used to record gestures, motion, labour, even the duration of their own creation. Jarman rereads Caravaggio's paintings as early avatars of Deleuze's opsigns and chronosigns. They not only, as Stella says, 'telescope art history',[71] they also represent a struggle against the temporal and spatial constraints of the medium. The film becomes a search for the palimpsest implied in the layering process of painting, the process Henri-Georges Clouzot reveals in *Le Mystère Picasso / The Picasso Mystery* (1956), an earlier attempt to capture on film the elusive method of an artist. Centring on the production of the artwork, *Caravaggio* also provides a tentative answer to W.J.T. Mitchell's vexing and ultimately unanswerable question about the nature of pictorial 'language' and 'desire': 'What do pictures really want?', he asks.[72] The cumulative subject of Jarman's film is the mass of information that the paintings themselves cannot tell: the story, at once economic and formal and biographical, of their own production. The film presents the unrepresentable history of the moment of production, of the spaces, stories and desires elided in the conventional life of the artist or even on the surface of the canvases themselves. Perhaps pictorial desire is not unlike human desire in this respect: perhaps pictures, too, hope most of all to reveal their lost histories, what they have witnessed, what is beneath the surface; but are forced to do so only with the surfaces that become their interface with the world and crystallize into a world in themselves. The tableau vivant reconstructs those static surfaces, transforming the stability of being into a process of becoming. They exist in what Deleuze calls the pure form of time, the infinitive form of the event, a synthesis of virtual past and virtual future that combines what has already happened and what will happen.[73]

The film ends by returning to the closeup of Caravaggio's face that opened the film, with the artist reduced to the status of corpse and the earlier carnivalesque atmosphere dampened into mourning. Yet as Benjamin writes of the atmosphere of mourning and the omnipresent corpses around which the *Trauerspiel* revolves, these dead bodies expire, then linger on stage because

> the allegorization of the physis can only be carried through in all its vigour in respect of the corpse. And the characters of the *Trauerspiel* die, because it is only thus, as corpses, that they can enter into the homeland of allegory. It is not for the sake of immortality that they meet their end, but for the sake of the corpse. . . . The corpse becomes quite simply the pre-eminent emblematic property. . . . The apotheoses are barely conceivable without it.[74]

The lifeless body of Caravaggio bookends the film because that corpse embodies precisely what is absent from images and from histories based on texts and pictures. The film presents a biography of Caravaggio, but not one based on his police records or his patronage but his body. The self-portraits inscribed by Caravaggio onto canvas continue to haunt the paintings because they gesture towards a record of the body otherwise inaccessible to history. These spectral bodies are the object of *Caravaggio*'s hauntology. The film's final corpse becomes the crux of an allegory for the film's historical project because, while it mirrors the body of Caravaggio, it also marks the failure of representation necessarily devoid of the desires that constitute the body. In the published version of *The Last of England*, Jarman describes the acts of filmmaking and viewing as akin to archaeology:

> My world is in fragments, smashed in pieces so fine I doubt I will ever reassemble them. So I scramble in the rubbish, an archaeologist who stumbles across a buried film. An archaeologist who projects his own private world along a beam of light into the arena, till all goes dark at the end of the performance, and we go home. . . . An artist is engaged in a dig.[75]

That digging takes place on a small scale, in intimate sites. Jarman's film recasts Caravaggio as a precursor in that project, as an artist who counters the eventual appropriation of his canvases by inscribing indelibly upon them both self-portraits and group portraits of friends, transforming monumental artworks into artefacts of his immediate personal, domestic and social surroundings. The reconstructive process in *Caravaggio* becomes a search for those lost desires and ultimately unrecoverable bodies, and the excavation wills them into being precisely as an object of inquiry. Jarman enlists Caravaggio as a model of an artist who likewise constructed within grand biblical and historical narratives, within his own enveloping economic context – in short, within the dominant discourses of his society – a small space where a cohort of artists and friends could together contribute to a covert history of desire. In his 'Introduction' to the second volume of the *Realms of Memory* series, Pierre Nora defines 'tradition' as 'memory that has become historically aware of itself'.[76] Jarman constructs the past in a different manner: the tradition invoked in *Caravaggio* is memory that has become aware of the difference in itself.

Near the beginning of the film, Jerusaleme picks up the shield bearing Caravaggio's Medusa, stares into its petrifying gaze, then prances around the studio, flashing the Medusa at the artist. Caravaggio then scoops up the boy, looks into the face of Medusa and laughs. This exchange of glances with Medusa exemplifies a strategy used throughout the film, as the artist returns to an emblem from the past, a mixture of abjection and the mythology deployed to contain it, and discovers difference that might otherwise have remained obscure. Nietzsche famously likened his concept of eternal return to the head of Medusa, venturing in his notebooks that 'the great thought' also resembled a '*Head of Medusa*: all the world's features petrify, a congealed death-throe'.[77] Yet, as Derrida points out, Nietzsche's proposed hymn to Medusa also recognizes the laughter and sense of injustice with which she accepts her banishment. The identification with the abjection of Medusa appears as early as antiquity and from the defiant, aggrieved Medusa of Shelley[78] to the laughing, almost joyful version of Hélène Cixous,[79] the countenance of Medusa has represented both abjection solidified through myth and the possibility of a jubilant escape from myth. What simultaneously frightens and attracts in the engagement with Medusa is immobility itself and its escape from the repetitions of myth. The tableau vivant also operates through a kind of Medusa effect, feigning immobility in order to avoid the eternal repetition of the same. To see Medusa through the lens of myth crystallizes the viewer into a pattern of eternal return; but in that instant of paralysis the repetition of myth also ceases, if only momentarily. To see the tableau through the lens of heritage merely reiterates that heritage with all its limitations; but within its moment of uncanny immobility other possibilities emerge. Daryl Hine captures the possibilities of Medusa and myth in his poem Tableau Vivant:

Perseus on an ornamental charger,
German work, sixteenth century,
Hovering above the slumbering Medusa
Like a buzzing fly or a mosquito
On beaten, golden wings. His head averted
From her agate gaze. In his right hand
A sword, in his left a mirror.

Helmeted by night, slipshod by darkness.
Wondering where to strike. She looks asleep
As if dreaming of petrified forests,
Monumental dryads, stone leaves, stone limbs,
Or of the mate that she will never meet
Who will look into her eyes and live.[80]

Jerome McGann argues that 'this poem is, among other things, a brief allegory about what has happened to western art between the sixteenth century and our own day', with Shelley's invented lover for Medusa the harbinger of a monumental change in thinking about Medusa, and Hine's poem 'as far from Shelley as Shelley is from the sixteenth century'.[81] What distinguishes these lines is a fascination with the moment just before Perseus slays Medusa, as the poet deviates from a narrative of heroic action and focuses instead on the vacillation that precedes it. The moment of hesitation becomes a flash of possibility. The poem's title, Tableau Vivant, underscores the connection between the momentarily immobilized tableau and this indecision before the act that forever cements Medusa's place in myth. The purpose of modern art, writes Adorno, is to 'teach the petrified forms how to dance by singing them their own song'; but modernity veils those paralysed forms behind an illusion of movement and innovation. The tableau vivant stills bodies to display that stupefaction, and then to petrify the viewer, allowing for the return of difference, leading to 'a discovery of the joints and sutures in the stone. So that the statues – the forms, the fetishes – do finally creak into motion'.[82] The past turned to stone, the tableau vivant in Jarman's *Caravaggio* also echoes with haunting voices, with the songs of those momentarily stilled bodies who have gazed at Medusa and lived.

Notes

1   James Gardner, 'Is Caravaggio our contemporary?', *Commentary*, June 1985, pp. 55–61.

2   Frank Stella, 'Caravaggio', *The New York Times Magazine*, 3 February 1985, p. 1.

3   Sanford Schwartz, 'Not happy to be here', *The New Yorker*, 2 September 1985, p. 75.

4   Gardner, 'Is Caravaggio our contemporary?', p. 55.

5   For an iconographic approach to the artist's biography, see Adrienne Von Lates, 'Caravaggio's peaches and academic puns', *Word and Image*, vol. 11, no. 1 (1995), pp. 55–60. For an overview of the debates about the artist's sexuality and an attempt to rebut Hibbard's argument, see Creighton E. Gilbert, *Caravaggio and His Two Cardinals* (University Park, PA: Pennsylvania State University Press, 1995) pp. 191–238.

6   James M. Saslow, *Pictures and Passions: a History of Homosexuality in the Visual Arts* (New York: Viking, 1999), pp. 116–17.

7   Leo Bersani and Ulysse Dutoit, *Caravaggio's Secrets* (Cambridge, MA: MIT Press, 1998), p. 13.

8   Ibid.

9   Derek Jarman, *Derek Jarman's* Caravaggio: *the Complete Film Script and Commentaries* (London: Thames & Hudson, 1986), p. 75.

10   Terence Davies, Bill Douglas, Isaac Julien and Sally Potter are some of the British filmmakers who pursued related projects in the 1980s.

11   In 1987 the Local Government Bill passed by Parliament included a provision, known as Clause 28, prohibiting the 'promotion of homosexuality' and forbidding schools from teaching 'the acceptability of homosexuality as a pretended family relationship'. For a discussion of the relationship between Jarman's cinema and queer politics in

the 1980s, see Chris Lippard and Guy Johnson, 'Private practice, public health: the politics of sickness and the films of Derek Jarman', in Lester Friedman (ed.) *Fires Were Started: British Cinema and Thatcherism* (London: UCL Press, 1993), p. 292.

12   Walter Benjamin, *Illuminations*, ed. Hannah Arendt, trans. Harry Zohn (New York: Schocken books, 1968), p. 221.

13   Joan Copjec, *Read My Desire: Lacan Against the Historicists* (Cambridge, MA: MIT Press, 1994).

14   Howard Hibbard, *Caravaggio* (New York: Harper & Row, 1983), p. 206.

15   Michael Fried, 'Thoughts on Caravaggio', *Critical Inquiry*, vol. 24, no. 1 (1997), pp. 18–19.

16   Michel de Certeau, *The Mystic Fable: Volume One, The Sixteenth and Seventeenth Centuries*, trans. Michael B. Smith (Chicago, IL: University of Chicago Press, 1992), p. 276.

17   Ibid.

18   Fried, 'Thoughts on Caravaggio', p. 21.

19   Michel Foucault, 'Nietzsche, genealogy, history', trans. Donald F. Bouchard and Sherry Simon, in Paul Rabinow (ed.), *The Foucault Reader* (New York: Pantheon Books, 1984), p. 86.

20   Derek Jarman, *Dancing Ledge*, ed. Shaun Allen (London: Quartet Books, 1991), p. 14.

21   Quoted in Eduardo Cadava, *Words of Light: Theses on the Photography of History* (Princeton, NJ: Princeton University Press, 1997), pp. 86–7. In their description of the act of transporting Caravaggio's paintings into the anachronistic context of a film, Jarman's diaries echo Benjamin: 'I'm certain they will survive in the hurly burly of the modern world – only by making Caravaggio a contemporary will we see how revolutionary a painter he was.' Jarman, *Dancing Ledge*, p. 24.

22   Frank Stella, *Working Space the Charles Eliot Norton Lectures, 1983–4* (Cambridge, MA: Harvard University Press, 1986).

23   Ibid., p. 18.

24   Caravaggio's mode of painting would then have resembled that of the fictional artist Tonnere in Pierre Klossowski's *The Revocation of the Edict of Nantes*. See *Roberte ce soir and The Revocation of the Edict of Nantes*, trans. Austryn Wainhouse (New York: Grove Press, 1969), p. 99.

25   André Bazin, *What is Cinema?*, ed. and trans. Hugh Gray (Berkeley, CA: University of California Press, 1967), p.97.

26   Stella, *Working Space*, pp. 4, 12.

27   Ibid., p. 17.

28   Jarman's comments on the film cite Friedlaender's book as an important source in his research into the life and work of Caravaggio. See Walter Friedlaender, *Caravaggio Studies* (Princeton, NJ: Princeton University Press, 1955).

29   Volker Schachenmayr, 'Emma Lyon, the attitude, and Goethean performance theory', *New Theatre Quarterly*, vol. 13, no. 1 (1997), p. 6.

30   Ibid.

31   Walter Benjamin, *The Origin of German Tragic Drama*, trans. John Osborne (London: Verso, 1998), p. 195.

32   Jean-François Lyotard, 'Acinema', trans. Paisley N. Livingston, in Philip Rosen (ed.), *Narrative, Apparatus, Ideology: a Film Theory Reader* (New York: Columbia University Press, 1986), p. 351.

33   Geoffrey Hartman, 'The voice of the shuttle: literature from the point of view of language', *The Fate of Reading and Other Essays* (Chicago, IL: University of Chicago Press, 1975), p. 352.

34   Ibid., p. 339.

35   Quoted in W.J.T. Mitchell, 'Spatial form in literature: toward a general theory', in Mitchell (ed.), *The Language of Images* (Chicago, IL: University of Chicago Press, 1980), p. 275.

36   Foucault, 'Nietzsche, genealogy, history', p.89.

37   Bersani and Dutoit, *Caravaggio's Secrets*, p. 40.

38   Ibid., p.72.

39   Benjamin, *Illuminations*, p. 256.

40   Foucault, 'Nietzsche, genealogy, history', p. 79.

41   Ibid., p. 83.

42   René Girard, *Deceit, Desire, and the Novel: Self and Other in Literary Structure* (Baltimore, MD: Johns Hopkins University Press, 1976). Timothy Murray notes the relationship between the love triangle represented in Caravaggio and the paradigm set forth in Girard's study. He also compares Girard's model with that proposed by Luce Irigaray, who suggests that woman becomes the abject element in these diagrams of triangular desire because she serves as a token and provocation of male desire while being denied desire herself. See Murray, *Like a Film Ideological Fantasy on Screen, Camera, and Canvas* (New York: Routledge, 1993), p. 134.

43   Girard, *Deceit, Desire and the Novel*, p. 4 (emphasis in original).

44   Ibid., p. 12.

45   Ibid., p. 15.

46   Ibid., p. 29.

47   Ibid., p. 38.

48   Murray's essay on the film outlines the possible ramifications of these violent actions. See Murray, *Like a Film*, pp. 134–42.

49   Lynn Tillman, 'Love Story', *Art in America*, vol. 75, no. 1 (1987), p. 23.

50   Jarman's screenplay details the production problems associated with this scene, as no casting agencies would allow child actors to play the part of Cupid in a tableau vivant based on Caravaggio's painting. Ultimately, a fully-clothed Dawn Archibald assumed the role of Cupid, emphasizing the disparity rather than identity between model and finished painting. See Jarman, *Derek Jarman's Caravaggio*, p. 75.

51   Marc Vernet, 'Irrepressible gaze', *Iris*, nos 14–15 (1992), p. 10.

52   Ibid., p. 14.

53   Dominique Païni. 'A detour for the gaze', *Iris*, nos 14–15 (1992), p. 5.

54   Roland Barthes, *Camera Lucida*, trans. Richard Howard (New York: Hill & Wang, 1981), p. 3.

55   Benjamin, *Illuminations*, p. 190.

56   Jacques Derrida, *Specters of Marx: the State of the Debt, the Work of Mourning, and the New International*, trans. Peggy Kamuf (London: Routledge, 1994), p. 7.

57   Ibid., p. 158.

58   See Martin Bauml Duberman, Martha Vicinus and George Chauncey, Jr (eds), *Hidden from History: Reclaiming the Gay and Lesbian Past* (New York: NAL Books, 1989).

59   For Jarman's discussion of Caravaggio's transformation into 'the most homosexual of painters', despite a relentlessly 'hostile environment', see Jarman, *Dancing Ledge*, pp. 21–4.

60   Hibbard, *Caravaggio*, p. 155.

61   Ibid., p. 159.

62   Ibid.

63   Antonio Negri, 'Notes on the evolution of the thought of the later Althusser', in Antonio Callari and David F. Ruccio (eds), *Postmodern Materialism and the Future of Marxist Theory: Essays in the Althusserian Tradition* (Hanover, NH: Wesleyan University Press, 1996), p. 54.

64   Quoted in Girard, *Deceit, Desire, and the Novel*, p. 1.

65   Jean-Luc Nancy, *The Sense of the World*, trans. Jeffrey Librett (Minneapolis, MN: University of Minnesota Press, 1997), p. 142.

66   See Andrew Higson, 'Representing the national past: nostalgia and pastiche in the heritage film', in Friedman (ed.), *Fires Were Started*.

67   See, for example, Von Lates, 'Caravaggio's peaches and academic puns'.

68   Angelo Quattrocchi and Tom Nairn, *The Beginning of the End, France, May 1968: What Happened, Why It Happened* (London: Panther, 1968), p. 39.

69   Benjamin, *The Origins of German Tragic Drama*, p. 232.

70   In his screenplay for *Caravaggio*, Jarman criticizes David for reintroducing a 'scientific' element to painting, thereby reducing the image to the grids imposed upon it. See Jarman, *Derek Jarman's* Caravaggio, p. 45.

71   Stella, 'Caravaggio', p. 39.

72   W.J.T. Mitchell, *Picture Theory* (Chicago, IL: University of Chicago Press, 1994), pp. 71–82.

73   Gilles Deleuze, *Difference and Repetition*, trans. Paul Patton (New York: Columbia University Press, 1994), pp. 86–91.

74   Benjamin, *The Origins of German Tragic Drama*, pp. 217–19.

75   Derek Jarman, *The Last of England*, ed. David L. Hirst (London: Constable, 1987).

76   Pierre Nora, 'Introduction', *Realms of Memory: the Construction of the French Past*, Volume II, trans. Arthur Goldhammer (New York: Columbia University Press, 1997), p. ix.

77   Quoted in David Farrell Krell, *Postponements: Women, Sensuality and Death in Nietzsche* (Bloomington, IN: Indiana University Press, 1986), p. 69.

78   Percy Bysshe Shelley, 'On the Medusa of Leonardo da Vinci'. A hypertext edition of this poem edited by Neil Fraistat and Melissa Jo Sites can be found at URL: http://www.rc.umd.edu/editions/shelley/medusa/medcover.html (4 August 2003).

79   See Hélène Cixous, *La Risa de la Medusa* (Barcelona: Direccion General de La Mujer, 2001).

80   Daryl Hine, *Minutes* (New York: Atheneum, 1968), p. 45.

81   Jermone J. McGann, 'The beauty of the Medusa: a study in romantic literary iconology', *Studies in Romanticism*, vol. 11, no. 1 (1972), p. 24.

82   Quoted in T.J. Clark, 'Origins of the present crisis', *New Left Review*, no. 2 (March–April 2000), p. 91.

11 The She-man: postmodern bi-sexed performance in film and video[1]

Chris Straayer

Cinema's double standard regarding nudity has fixed opposing modes of sexual signification for women and men. Certain makeup and costume styles have conventionally coded a woman's surface as sexual and announced her sex. At the same time, also conventionally, her sex has a relatively high chance of being displayed explicitly at another time in the movie. The eventual availability of her breasts and other sexual areas as cinematic rewards have insured, by temporal contiguity, the essential content of her 'mask'.

In contrast, the historic absence from view of the penis in cinema has allowed the male body an independence from sexual anatomical verification. It is his charging about that has identified a male film character as male, yet it is his penis that has invested him with the cultural right to charge about – the signifier *in absentia*. Richard Dyer and Peter Lehman have written about the difficulty of maintaining the penis-phallus alliance in case the penis is seen onscreen.[2] In actuality, the penis (man's hidden 'nature') cannot compare to the phallus (man's cultural power). It is the generic narrative threat of bodily exposure, as much as his 'feminization' via costume, that has 'emasculated' the male crossdresser, i.e., castrated his symbolic phallus, in temporary transvestite films such as *Some Like It Hot* (1959, Billy Wilder) and *Tootsie* (1982, Sidney Pollack).[3] At the level of performance, feminine garb ironically both accentuates the male's secondary sex characteristics, thus signalling his 'nature', and keeps his genital biology out of view.

What I want to emphasize here is that, in classical cinema representation, female sexuality is actually present both in the masquerade of femininity and in the female body, whereas male sexuality is doubly absent. It is present on the male body but remains unseen and therefore unavailable. When symbolized as the phallus, power displaces sexuality rather than delivers it. It is this 'visible difference' that (although traditionally undermined by comic constructions) allows the male crossdresser the *potential* for an intense double-signification of sexuality, containing both macho male sexuality via the unseen penis, and female sexuality displaced onto visible display via masquerade.

This potential is most evidenced by a contemporary phenomenon in popular culture that contests the traditional conditions and compromises of crossdressing in mass media — the appropriation of female coding by a male performer as a straightforward empowering device, rather than an emasculating comic ploy. This transgressive figure, which I term the She-man, is glaringly bi-sexed rather than obscurely androgynous or merely bisexual. Rather than undergoing a downward gender mobility, he has enlarged himself with feminine gender *and* female sexuality.

In *Mother Camp* Esther Newton relates the drag queen's reliance on visible contradictions, as opposed to the transvestite's attempt to pass as the other sex.[4] Laying bare his feminine masquerade by baring a hairy chest, the drag queen makes obvious the superficiality and arbitrariness of gender costuming. But in *Pink Flamingos* (John Waters, 1972), a 'transbreastite' squeezes this contradiction onto the body, disrupting sexual as well as gender signification. The sight of 'his' hormonally produced breasts is followed by 'his' exposed penis, an incongruity that outgrows its own binary opposition.

In *The Rocky Horror Picture Show* (Jim Sharman, 1975), bisexual, transsexual Dr Frank N. Furter (Tim Curry) makes lipstick look macho and undulates a black garter belt in aggressive, seductive exhibitionism. In *Pink Flamingos*, a nude male dancer executes anal acrobatics with phallic nerve and Medusan humour, and Divine puts a steak between her legs to simultaneously parody the rhetoric of women as meat and embody the taboo of menstruation, thus pushing the transgression of sex beyond anatomy to physiology. In *La Ley de Deseo/Law of Desire* (Pedro Almodóvar, 1987), the 'slutty', male-to-female transsexual Tina (played by a woman – Carmen Maura), under a jet of water and clinging dress, harks back to a classical harlot, then later outslugs a policeman like a 'real' man – or a real 'woman'. In *Shadey* (Philip Saville, 1987), Oliver (Anthony Sher), a 'woman trapped in a man's body', is stabbed in the testicles with a kitchen knife and responds with a look of *jouissance*.

Today, sex role stereotypes are 'up for grabs'. The attitude of Tina Turner's What's Love Got To Do With It? has reversed the sexual expressivity (cries of sexual oppression) once embodied in Janis Joplin's screeching romantic masochism. And, in her One Man Show, Grace Jones' 'feeling like a woman, looking like a man', gives a new bodily relevance to Marlene Dietrich's transvestism/persona. In *Consuming Passions*, Judith Williamson describes the firm, narrow-hipped, boyish body of transsexual Tula (who appears in the Smirnoff Loch Ness advert) as a contemporary blueprint for women – 'the male form as the ideal for females' according to the body image industry of modelling, photography, and fashion.[5] In the era of music television, both Boy George and Michael Jackson make louder *scenes* as Boy-Girls.

Rather than diminishing his phallic power, or amplifying it via a contrast with weakness, female coding inserts additional strength into the She-man. The male

Figure 11.1
The Rocky Horror Picture
Show: publicity still,
Jim Sharman, 1975,
courtesy RCA Records

body's 'staying power' remains unchallenged by feminine dress, makeup and gestures which, in media, have become one and the same with female sexuality. More indexical than symbolic, the feminine costume utilizes conventions of spatial and temporal contiguity to actually deliver its referent. Much as the bulge in Tim Curry's corset indexes his male sex, the determined geometry of his bra and garters bestows a female anatomy on him. The power of the She-man, then, is expressly sexual.

An obvious question now arises as to the origins of this feminine power. Is not the phallus the dominant signifier, which defines woman by her lack? Is not the penis the dominant sexual signifier, reigning by virtue of a proclaimed anatomical visibility (which nevertheless remains hidden in media except for pornography's privileged ejaculation shot) that supports its own invisible visibility with an exaggerated persona – the Freudian phallic symbol?

Writing about second generation Victorian women who were presumed to be empty of sexuality, Esther Newton has argued that male clothing served as a means for women to proclaim their *de facto* sexuality:

> The bourgeois woman's sexuality proper was confined to its reproductive function; the uterus was its organ. But as for lust, 'the major current in Victorian sexual ideology declared that women were passionless and asexual, the passive objects of male sexual desire . . .' Sex was seen as phallic, by which I mean that, conceptually, sex could only occur in the presence of an imperial and imperious penis.[6]

Thus the signification of sexuality was under male control. Ironically, women had to declare/display their own active libidos through male clothing codes.

How then is the contemporary She-man sexually empowered by female coding? How did female imagery come to signify sexuality and power? Since the Victorian age, major shifts in sexual positions have occurred, partly as a result of sexology, sexual liberation, and the feminist and gay movements. Whether 'on our backs' or 'off our backs', our female sexual responses and desires are now seen as powerful. No longer only feared, female sexuality is envied.

Ironically, cinema's sexual imaging of woman is also partly responsible for making possible a representation of femaleness as sexual power. Following a long history of visual representations that established woman's body as the conventional marker of sexual difference, cinema made this body the carrier of sexuality in both the film's visuals and narrative. Woman's image because the visible site of sexuality that was obtained by the male hero, i.e., male sexuality was projected onto, represented by and obtainable through her body. Although quite different than the Victorian woman who announced her sexuality via the male image, woman's 'sexual' image in classical cinema similarly potentiated an involuted image of sexual power.

The most forceful paradigms for active female sexuality – which deconstruct involution and assert realignment – are found in contemporary women's performance art where artists boldly expose their bodies for purposes of direct address. Such bodily discourse constructs both a new 'speaking subject' position and an aesthetics of female sexual presence. Two concepts relating to the She-man's origin can be narrativized. In practice, however, the two seem inseparable. The first is the story of the phallic femme which evolves from the feminine masquerade; the second story is that of the Medusan femme which evolves from the female body. These are the two powers that are appropriated by the She-man and merge in his/her signifying formation. Feminism and feminist artists, rather

than popular culture and She-men performers, must be credited for this
empowerment of the feminine.

A first narrative might be that, in the late 1960s and early 1970s, second-wave
feminists (in dress-for-success suits) abandoned 'femininity', disrupting feminine
signification to steal the phallus, which, soon afterwards, they laterally passed on
to self-conscious feminist femmes (in leather miniskirts). Thus, they created, via
a process quite the reverse of fetishism, the phallic-femme whose phallus was locked
into a revived feminine mode of signification. To steal it back, the male performer
now assumes a post-feminist drag. When successful, he becomes the She-man, his
phallic power marked in the feminine.

   Early in the present feminist era, Lynda Benglis attacked the art world's
discrimination against women with a self-portrait in *Artforum* (December 1974) in
which she 'props' a dildo onto her nude body. Thus she effectively identified the
phallus as the basic qualification for artistic success and explicitly collapsed the
phallus with the penis – via body/object/photo collage art.

Figure 11.2
Lynda Benglis 'Posed
with instrument' photo
by Arth-Gordon
(courtesy of Lynda
Benglis, 1974)

Now, in the 'post-feminist' era,[7] women spike their hair to match their heels, a generation of daughters dons fifties pink lipstick to 'talk back' to the silence imposed on their mothers, crosses hang purple from ears instead of pearl from necks – i.e., skirts are worn (and torn) self-reflexively. Now, when a male character stalks the night 'as a woman' the effect is not a classic comedy of misidentity, but a drama of the phallic prostitute – the gigolo.

In 'Film and the masquerade', Mary Ann Doane describes the feminine masquerade as a distancing device:

> The masquerade, in flaunting femininity, holds it at a distance. Womanliness is a mask which can be worn or removed. The masquerade's resistance to patriarchal positioning would therefore lie in its denial of the production of femininity as closeness, as presence-to-itself, as, precisely, imagistic. The transvestite adopts the sexuality of the other – the woman becomes a man in order to attain the necessary distance from the image. Masquerade, on the other hand, involves a realignment of femininity, the recovery, or more accurately, simulation, of the missing gap or distance. To masquerade is to manufacture a lack in the form of a certain distance between oneself and one's image. . . .
>
> The very fact that we can speak of a woman 'using' her sex or 'using' her body for particular gains is highly significant – it is not that a man cannot use his body in this way but that he doesn't have to. The masquerade doubles representation; it is constituted by a hyperbolisation of the accoutrements of femininity.[8]

Through an excess of femininity, then, woman stands back from her image in order to read it better. The pertinent question to this discussion is where does woman's 'sexuality' reside in this improbable separation – in the cultural construction of femininity which she now consciously manipulates as a 'persona', or in some nature within her but beyond her reading? This question parallels the situation of women in language. Can women better speak by parodying patriarchal language (Benglis's phallic femme), or by narrating their own sexual bodies (the Medusan femme)?

A second process, which can be postulated to explain the feminine power that the She-man usurps, spans this distance between culture and nature. Vagina envy, as evidenced in some She-men, suggests that female sexuality is challenging the phallus's position as the dominant signifier. In her early feminist performance *Interior Scroll* (1975), Carolee Schneemann defended the suitability of personal experience as material for art by reading a 'diary' scroll (with)drawn from her vagina.[9] Thus she asserted the female body to be a producer of meaning.

Female sexuality is now neither simply the sign of lack, as Laura Mulvey has identified it, inciting castration anxiety and thus necessitating fetishization and

Figure 11.3
Carolee Schneemann
performing *Interior Scroll*,
photo by Anthony
McCall, 1975
(Courtesy of the artists)

narrative punishment, nor a generator of signs within Levi-Strauss's parameters.[10] It is, rather, a primary signifier erupting into culture like a volcano in the suburbs. Like the laughing Medusa, described by Hélène Cixous,[11] who haughtily displays her sex to men's horrified reactions, the Medusan femme provides a paradigm for an empowering bodily address. Furthermore, this 'imagined' figure exerts a specifically feminine body-signifying process – a multiplying, questioning, digressing, fragmenting language that corresponds to the indefinable plurality of female sexuality spread over a woman's body – described by Luce Irigaray:

> So woman does not have a sex organ? She has at least two of them, but they are not identifiable as ones. Indeed she has many more. Her sexuality, always at least double, goes even further: it is *plural*. Is this the way culture is seeking to characterize itself now? . . .
>
> *[W]oman has sex organs more or less everywhere*. She finds pleasure almost anywhere. Even if we refrain from invoking the hystericization of her entire body, the geography of her pleasure is far more diversified, more multiple in

its differences, more complex, more subtle, than is commonly imagined – in an imaginary rather too narrowly focused on sameness. . . .

Thus what [women] desire is precisely nothing, and at the same time everything. Always something more and something else besides that *one* – sexual organ, for example – that you give them, attribute to them. Their desire is often interpreted, and feared, as a sort of insatiable hunger, a voracity that will swallow you whole. Whereas it really involves a different economy more than anything else, one that upsets the linearity of a project, undermines the goal-object of a desire, diffuses the polarization toward a single pleasure, disconcerts fidelity to a single discourse . . .[12]

Finally rebelling against the symbolic order, contemporary sexual culture demands a 'plural' sight/site that can be seen *and* felt. The phallus, a mere abstraction which hides the organ which might go limp, is a holdover from the Victorian age. Today's Medusan femme expresses her sexuality with her entire body, spreading and kicking her legs to join the postmodern laughter.

In 'Form and female authorship in music video', Lisa Lewis has written about the opportunity afforded to female musicians by the music video form. Not only does their singing role suggest authorship and assign narrative importance to them, but they are able via performance strategies to express gender-specific attitudes or viewpoints. She states:

Female musicians are actively participating in making the music video form work in their interest, to assert their authority as producers of culture and to air their views on female genderhood. The generic emphasis in music video on using the song as a soundtrack, together with the centrality of the musician's image in the video, formally support the construction of female authorship. . . .

Many female musicians have proved to be quite adept at manipulating elements of visual performance in their video act, thereby utilizing music video as an additional authorship tool. In What's Love Got To Do With It?, the gestures, eye contact with the camera and with other characters, and the walking style of Tina Turner add up to a powerful and aggressive on-screen presence.[13]

This new visual music format requires specific performance talents from male musicians as well. As Richard Goldstein states in 'Tube rock: how music video is changing music', they have to learn to communicate with their bodies:

Tube rock forces musicians to act. Not that they haven't been acting since Jerry Lee Lewis learned to stomp on a piano and Chuck Berry essayed his first duckwalk; but on MTV, musicians have to emote the way matinee idols once did if they're to establish the kind of contact tube rockers covet – the heightened typology of a classic movie star. What once made a rock performer powerful – the ability to move an arena with broad gesture and precision timing – has been supplanted by a new strategy: the performer must project in close-up.[14]

Because of their different relations to bodily expression, then, females and males have adjusted differently to the music video form. While MTV's emphasis on body and presence seems to have provided women performers an avenue for gaining authorship, males have attempted to 'master' the facial expression of sensuality as well as the language of exhibitionism, efforts which have themselves recast gender and asked new questions about sexuality. As Simon Frith writes in *Music for Pleasure*:

> The most important effect of gender-bending was to focus the problem of sexuality onto males. In pop, the question became, unusually, what do men want? And as masculinity became a packaging problem, then so did masculine desire. . . . On video, music can be mediated through the body directly.[15]

These passages from three authors suggest that the music video form has produced new positions for both female and male performers. These repositionings often result in ambiguous reversals, such as that evident in two Bananarama videos, I Can't Help It and Love in the First Degree. In each video, the three female vocalists sing in the first person, to the camera/viewers as well as to a male 'you' within the fictional performance space. In each, the male body is exploited as visual object at the same time as lyrics admit female dependency. 'I can't help it', Bananarama sings as a shirtless male dances. 'I'm captivated by your honey. Move your body. I need you. I won't give up'. Similarly, as a group of males dance in prison-striped briefs and crop-tops, the 'fully dressed' female Bananarama trio sings, 'Only you can set me free'. As one of these singers shakes a dancer's head and then pushes him away, they continue, 'cause I'm guilty of love in the first degree'. The men's bare legs contrast strikingly with the women's covered legs. The number ends with the men down on their hands and knees.

This 'nouveau' reversal of subjectivity and exhibitionism between female and male performers incorporates ambiguity to satisfy multiple audience identifications and desires. When the She-man collects all this ambiguity on 'his' body, subjectivity and exhibitionism reverberate in a contradictory assemblage of gender and sexual codes. In this case the male performer adopts sexualized female body language to achieve a powerful exhibitionistic subjectivity.

What happens, then, when the male – metaphoric possessor of the dominant, if out-of-style, signifier – exercises his prerogative to appropriate the phallic femme's masquerade or the Medusan body? He finds himself a split personality, a schizo-phrenic sign, a media image combining disbelief and an aesthetic of his-teric, richocheting signifiers – a She-man, whose sexual power depends not on the ostensibly stable male body but on embraced incongruity. He finds himself the site of a nervous breakdown, the utter collapse of the most basic structuring device, i.e., male/female binary opposition, into postmodern irrelevance.

The She-man's performance engulfs and rewrites the conventional heterosexual narrative, suturing the viewer into unending alterations of absence and presence, desire and pleasure. First we see a woman. Where's the man? Then we see a man. Where's the woman? Simultaneously we are given the pleasures of reading conventionally and subverting convention. The woman *is* the man. The She-man is the shot-reverse shot. Performance is the nouveau narrative.

The particularly postmodern sexual imagery of the She-man is especially prevalent in youth music culture. Ironically, a discussion of the She-man in music videos and video art calls for a return to modernist concerns. For two reasons, the video medium is especially suitable for the She-man's scheme. Historically, video art has shown an affinity with performance art, perhaps because of what Rosalind Krauss called the medium's property of narcissism.[16] Second, as Douglas Davis has pointed out, the experience of viewing the small video monitor contains its own particular physicality that seems appropriate for performance.[17]

Rather than being swept away by film's large screen, video viewers maintain a sense of their own physicality. Instead of identifying with some larger-than-life idealized (Lacanian) 'mirror' image, video viewers experience the medium's (McLuhanesque) tactility, or its subtle existentialism as Davis describes it. When they do use it as a mirror, as Krauss suggests, it is not to mistake themselves for ideal images, but to check their makeup.

Video's mobile viewers, whether in their living rooms or in dance bars, are less likely to feel that they are dreaming than cruising. Video music especially benefits from the viewing logistics of the medium, engaging viewers in a physical/rhythmic identification. Rather than an empty vessel for emphatic identification, the performer is a surrogate dance partner. Very often this is reinforced by a per-formance aesthetics of movement – the artist's continual movement interacts with and against the editing and camera movement.[18]

An examination of several independent video artworks and commercial music videos will demonstrate the above ideas. A variety of ways in which She-men appropriate the female can be enumerated by focusing on performance and bodily imagery rather than narrative or music.

John Scarlett-Davis's *A Trip Through the Wardrobes of the Mind* (5 minutes, colour, 1983, UK) displays gender bending as a *style* played out in dress, hair style, gestures

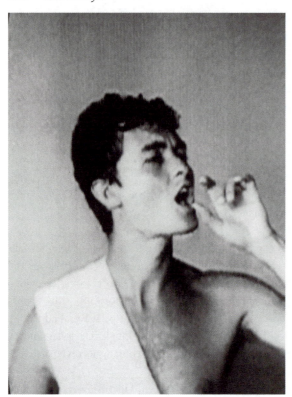

Figure 11.4
The Kipling Trilogy: Perils
of Pedagogy (Greyson,
Canada, 1984)

and the body. Sex is essentially coopted by style, resulting in the sexy rather than the sexual. A series of characters in a gender-range of fashions strike poses and perform dances while glancing at the camera/audience. A young man in a black leather vest kisses the tattoo on his shoulder. Another young man in a skirt paints a triangle on his stomach.

In John Greyson's *The Kipling Trilogy: Perils of Pedagogy* (5 minutes, colour, 1984, Canada), the 'female's' position as object of the erotic gaze is appropriated by a young male character who flounts himself exhibitionistically before the camera and another character – his male mentor. This implies a connection between the desire usually directed at women and a desire directed at both male and female youth. In a typically gay pantomime, this boy appropriates a woman's voice, assisted technologically as her song (To Sir With Love) is slowed down to lower the pitch. Similarly, by camera positioning, the boy is turned on his side, i.e., technologically 'laid'.

In Richard Fung's *Chinese Characters* (21 minutes, colour, 1986, Canada), the male artist video-keys himself into a clip from a pornographic film where he poses as the lure for a desiring stud. His presence as both performer and character

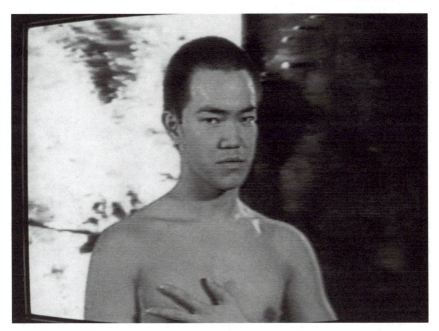

Figure 11.5 Chinese Characters (Fung, Canada, 1986)

constructs two different identificatory positions for us. Elsewhere in the tape, he tells how he learned to make appropriate sounds during sex by listening to women in porn movies. A generic emphasis on the porn stud's large penis is juxtaposed with the artist/character's emphatic fondling of his own nipples. Hardcore pornography is the only genre that consistently shows the penis. Its convention of large penises can be 'seen' as an attempt to uphold the phallus in the realm of the physical. Performance and technology collaborate in this tape to create a She-man whose breasts are the visual equivalent of the porn star's 'cock'.

In his music video *Boys Keep Swinging*, David Bowie appears as lead singer as well as (in drag) three backup female singers. As a man he sings, 'Nothing stands in your way when you're a boy. . . . Other boys check you out. . . . You get a girl. . . . Boys keep swinging. Boys always work it out'. As the female chorus, he echoes himself with, 'Boys!' The video ends, not on the handsome Bowie in suit and tie, but with each of the three female singers walking forward on a stage. The first two dramatically remove their wigs and smear their lipstick with the backs of their hands as if attempting to wipe it off. The third is an older female character who walks slowly with a cane. Rather than following the actions of the other two, she blows a kiss to the camera/audience, that ensuring an open ending to this already ambiguous declaration about gender.

In the music video *Walk Like a Man*, Divine achieves the most complete gender/sexual transformation – via costume, makeup, gestures, and look

Figure 11.6 Divine in *Walk Like a Man*

'suggestive' of Mae West.[19] As Divine stands on a wagon/car singing, swinging and whipping her imaginary horses, the camera places viewers in the position of the missing horses. Combined with the video medium's maintenance of the viewer physicality, this situates them well for her whipping. The diegetic audience encourages viewer to 'join in' the song, yet when we do, we enter into camp S&M theatre.

The examples of appropriation in these video works demonstrate a tentative collapse of the phallic femme and the Medusan femme on the male body. Female sexuality originally carried either by the masquerade or by the body abandons these boundaries to slip back and forth between the male body and his masquerade, constantly threatening to engulf and dissolve him. For example, Divine's costume is a masquerade that generates a womb on/in his/her body.

Interestingly, a trace of masculinity is deliberately maintained in all these works, as if this threatened engulfment necessitates the shy penis to peek out: under his dress, the man in *A Trip Through the Wardrobe of the Mind* wears pants. In *Perils of Pedagogy*, the penis of the flirting, feminized boy is once shown and once indexed by a bulge in his undershorts. The eroticization of nipples supplements rather than displaces the 'masculinized' anatomy of the 'well-endowed' porn star in *Chinese Characters*. Though triply female, Bowie's drag personas ostensibly serve to back up the real Bowie – the GQ male. As Divine swings her hips, a cut-in shot briefly focuses on a male masturbatory gesture she enacts with horses' reins.

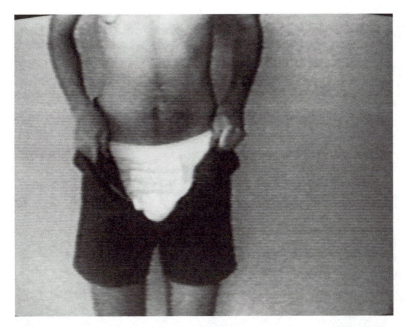

Figure 11.7 The Kipling Trilogy: Perils of Pedagogy (Greyson, Canada, 1984)

It can be argued that via mechanisms of 'the look', the young male (gigolo) in *Perils of Pedagogy* is 'womanized'. Furthermore, his receiving body 'is emphasized when he points at his open mouth and turns over to offer his ass'. However, these receiving gestures are balanced by the presence of the penis. This co-presence, or balance, creates the internal distance which establishes his image as bi-sexed rather than transsexual. This internal distance insures both masculinity and femininity.

Divines very corporality, the accenting of her stomach by the 'outline' design of her costume, tends to posit the woman in his/her body. By not showing his/her anatomy, he moves his image from transvestite to transsexual. The rapid editing between different subject-camera distances mimics a *fort-da* game, which, combined with her whipping action, suggests Divine also as the phallic mother in relation to the audience.[20]

Examples of She-man imagery in several additional music videos will further demonstrate the construction of this bi-sexed figure. In Dead or Alive's, Save You All My Kisses, the lead (male) singer appears extremely androgynous but emanates a distinctly feminine sexual energy. This sexuality is both emphasized and kept separate by a silver codpiece prominently shown during a vertical track up his/her body. Also signalling maleness is his Adam's apple. Coexisting female signals include his/her dominatrix whip and long, obviously styled hair. Dressed in black leather jacket and tights, he/she walks, dances and sings in front of a wire fence while a gang of boys climb the fence attempting to get at him/her. Their enthusiastic

Figure 11.8 Save You All My Kisses, Dead or Alive

Figure 11.9 Mike Monroe, Hanoi Rocks

approach displays much ambivalence – they seem both attracted to and repelled by him/her. At times their postures and glances seem to signify lust, but at other times they seem to be mocking him/her. While one holds and swings his baseball bat in a way that threatens a fag-bashing, another rips open his t-shirt as if stripping for him/her. A male alter-ego is also present, also dressed in black leather and resembling his female counterpart except that he wears more masculine pants, presents a more masculine posture, and carries a baseball bat. Again it is unclear whether he is attracted to 'her' or threatening to attack 'her'. The contradictory reactions of this diegetic audience emphasize and confirm the She-man as simultaneously female and male.

It should be noted that, although gay audiences may have more to gain from the She-man's radical display of gender *and* sex constructions, the She-man is not a gay figure, nor an effeminate male, nor a hermaphrodite. The She-man, as enacted by both gay and straight performers, is a fully functional figuration signifying woman/man.

This uncompromising ambiguity of the She-man, created by simultaneous female and male presence, also exists in Mike Monroe of Hanoi Rocks. During a

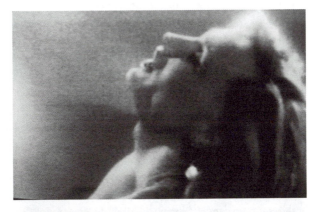

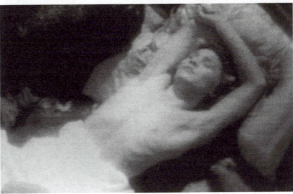

Figures 11.10–11.11
Marilyn in *Cry and Be Free*

performance of Taxi Driver, he seems to combine two sexes without neutralizing them. As he performs both male and female gestures – in makeup and androgynous clothing – a doubling of sexes occurs which increases sexuality and produces a bi-sexed rather than bisexual image.

In *Cry and Be Free*, Marilyn uses cross-gender movements – a sort of Barbra Streisand positioning of head and shoulders – that epitomize her progression of the masquerade beyond costume and makeup to gestures and posturing. This is a progression which is basic to the She-man's 'upgrading' of transvestism from gender-crossing to sex-crossing. The eroticization of Marilyn's bare male breasts by movements of reclining and arching in combination with 'her' female-coded diverted glances make visual the concept of a woman in a man's body.

Finally, Swans' video *A Screw* uses a split screen and mirrored imagery to produce a receptive openness in a male body, particularly at the sites of mouth, abdomen and buttocks. The vagina imagery made obvious in *A Screw* is also hinted at in some other of the video artworks and music videos discussed here, e.g., in *A Trip Through the Wardrobes of the Mind*, when the young male paints a triangle on his bare stomach. Like Divine in *Walk Like a Man*, the She-man in *A Screw* creates a womb on/in his body; however, the *Videodrome*-like vaginal imagery here has a rougher aggressivity than that created by Divine's frilly dress.

In *The Desire to Desire*, an analysis of 1940s women's films, Mary Ann Doane identifies proper makeup and dress as indicators of a woman's stable narcissism.[21] Should that makeup be smeared or that dress torn, the woman is marked with the pathetic condition of impaired narcissism – either too much self-love, or the audacious desiring (otherising) of another.

Narcissism becomes quite different, however, when two sexes are present in the same body – which can signal both heterosexual coupling and bisexuality. When Mike Monroe sweats through his makeup, it seems like a return of the male and signals a *successful* narcissism. Doane has argued a predilection in women for tactility and overidentification, in contrast to men's affinity to voyeurism and fetishism which both require distance.[22] By invalidating the concept of distance as separation, Mike Monroe's narcissistically bi-sexed figure makes overidentification a mute point.

Psycho-sexologists have long referred to penis envy in women and described women's clitoris as an undeveloped penis. Women have been positioned alongside boys, their 'lack' diminishing them and disqualifying them for adulthood. Traditionally, when crossdressing, they achieved boyishness rather than manliness.

The obvious question for future investigation on this subject is: is there a complementary bi-sexed figure, a reverse of the She-man, built from woman's body and man's masquerade? I think not. Because female sexuality is conventionally imaged and indexed by the female masquerade, and because the male 'costume' conventionally serves to mask rather than index male (genital) sexuality, there is no appropriation mechanism by which a 'he-woman' could be produced via masquerade alone. Even more than the She-man's use of gesture to make transvestism physical, the incorporation of action is essential for a woman performer's successful sex crossing. In order to construct an empowerment and achieve a transgression similar to those of the She-man, women would need to entirely disrupt the *men act* and *women appear* sex roles described by John Berger.[23] In short, without also appropriating 'male action', women's transvestism fails to achieve the double sexuality of the She-man.

The portrait of Madonna which appeared on the cover of the June 1990 issue of *Interview* magazine successfully employs reversal, contradiction, *and action* to disrupt gender and sex. Wearing dark lipstick, exaggerated eyelashes, fishnet stockings, hot pants and a polka dotted blouse with bell-shaped collar and cuffs, Madonna thrusts forward her pelvis, grabs her crotch, and squeezes her thigh muscle in a gesture that young men often use playfully to suggest a gigantic-sized penis. Madonna's 'girlish' clowning around both mocks machismo and use of the penis. By plagiarizing a male fantasy, she ironically reassigns and complicates penis envy.

Annie Lennox of Eurythmics deliberately recalls/retains the female masquerade, when crossdressing, via her bright red lipstick – which, even on young girls, signals adult female sexuality. This lipstick sexualizes her image while her *act* of wearing

Figure 11.12
Annie Lennox
(courtesy of RCA
Records)

a suit (rather than the mere presence of a suit) pushes it towards a bi-sexed image. Her assertive masculine behaviour – speech, gestures, and posture – 'invests' the suit with transgressive power. Similarly, when Lily Tomlin impersonates her character Tommy Velour, a working class, Italian nightclub singer, 'her' sexual come-ons to 'girls' in the audience validate and sexualize the hair on 'his' chest. These sexual actions make Tomlin's act more transgressive than the image of Katharine Hepburn wearing a false moustache in *Sylvia Scarlett* (1935, George Cukor) or Julie Andrews wearing a suit in *Victor/Victoria* (1982, Blake Edwards).

Woman's 'counterpart' to the She-man would likely require appropriation of male sexual prerogatives in two areas/actions. First, she needs to trespass the boundaries of sexual segregation relating to pornography and sexual information, erotica, expression of libido, and sexual joking. (Here we might think of Mae West as groundbreaking.) Second, she must aggressively expose the untamed sexual imagery of her body. For instance, her unruly mature pubic hair contrasts sharply with the image of female genitals in conventional pornography, where shaving or partially shaving pubic hair converts a physical characteristic into masquerade and constructs an (ageist) image of feminine youth. Instead of a he-woman, this transgressive figure might better be termed the 'She-bitch'. In contrast to the She-man's image-actions (actions on images), the She-bitch would perform action-images (images containing action).

Indeed, it is from the arena of avant-garde performance that the She-bitch will likely emerge. Following the taboo-breaking work of performance artists such as Lynda Benglis and Carolee Schneemann, Karen Finley appropriates male prerogatives in her 'id-speak' performances. Dirty talk/dirty acts such as I Like to Smell the Gas Passed from your Ass, I'm an Ass Man, and Don't Hang the Angel use the language of pornography for radical 'feminine' misbehaviour.[24] Another ripe for action figure, which I have termed the 'nouveau lesbian butch', is the contemporary lesbian who self-consciously deconstructs/constructs the male body via transgressive sexual prostheses and practices.[25] Whether such avant-garde/underground trangressions will ever be reflected in mainstream culture (as the She-man is to a limited degree) will no doubt depend on economic determinants as well as on the media's ability to negotiate/package the She-butch's sexual subjectivity in a way that does not directly challenge society's prevailing concept of passive/image/woman.

Currently, the She-man is the most transgressive signifier of sexuality in play, evident in popular music culture as well as underground film and experimental video. This figure suggests the collapse of the phallus as the dominant signifier and its replacement by a new empowered female sexuality which cannot be reduced to boyishness. Such evidence of the phallic femme's effectivity and the Medusan femme's signifying power signals a She-butch on the horizon/edge. Although he/she is him/herself an obvious result of male prerogative, the She-man's dependency on female sexuality for his/her power is also obvious. More importantly, the

She-man disrupts the very concept of male–female discontinuity. Via his/her appropriations of femininity, the She-man not only achieves a postmodern dismantling of gender and sex differences but also adopts a *greater* sexuality.

Notes

1 The core of this chapter was originally presented at a Television and Postmodernism seminar at the University of Wisconsin-Milwaukee Center for Twentieth Century Studies in 1988. Slightly different versions occur in my dissertation, *Sexual Subjects: Signification, Viewership, and Pleasure in Film and Video* (Northwestern University, 1989), and in Jane Gaines (ed.), *Classical Hollywood Narrative: the Paradigm Wars* (Durham, NC: Duke University Press, 1992), pp. 203–25.

2 Richard Dyer, 'Male sexuality in the media', in Andy Metcalf and Martin Humphries (eds), *The Sexuality of Men* (London: Pluto Press, 1985), pp. 28–43; Peter Lehman, 'In the realm of the senses: desire, power, and the representation of the male body', *Genders 2* (Summer 1988).

3 In 'Redressing the natural: the temporary transvestite film'; (Chapter 6 of my dissertation cited above), I identify and analyse this subgenre of crossdressing films.

4 Esther Newton, *Mother Camp: Female Impersonators in America* (Chicago Press, 1972), pp. 97–111. For additional discussion of drag in relation to crossdressing and transvestism, see Chapter 6 of my dissertation.

5 Judith Williamson, *Consuming Passions: the Dynamics of Popular Culture* (New York: Marion Boyars, 1986).

6 Esther Newton, 'The mythic mannish lesbian: Radclyffe Hall and the new woman', *Signs*, vol. 9, no. 4 (1984), p. 561. Newton's internal quote is cited by her as: George Chauncey, Fr., 'From sexual inversion to homosexuality: medicine and the changing conceptualization of female deviance', *Salmagundi*, nos 58–9 (Fall 1982–Winter 1983), pp. 114–45, esp. 117.

7 By using this term 'post-feminist', I do not wish to imply that we have given up on or moved past feminism. Rather, with its permeation throughout American culture, it is now possible for feminist practice to be taken for granted and feminist thought quoted as rhetoric. When dogma approaches kitsch, perhaps only humour provides the necessary distance and self-reflexivity to combat stasis.

8 Mary Ann Doane, 'Film and the masquerade: theorising the female spectator', *Screen*, vol. 23, nos 3–4 (1982), pp. 81–2.

9 A photograph of this performance can be found in Moira Roth (ed.), *The Amazing Decade: Women and Performance Art in America 1970-1980* (Los Angeles, CA: Astro Arts, 1983), p. 15.

10 See Laura Mulvey, 'Visual pleasure and narrative cinema', *Screen*, vol. 16, no. 3 (1975), pp. 6–18 and Claude Levi-Strauss, *The Raw and the Cooked*, trans. John and Doreen Weightman (New York: Harper & Row, publishers, 1975).

11 Woman writing her sexual body is a thematic concern throughout Hélène Cixous's work. See 'The laugh of the Medusa', in Elaine Marks and Isabelle Courtivron (eds), *New French Feminisms*, (New York: Schocken Books, 1981), and 'Castration or decapitation', trans. Annette Kuhn, *Signs* 7, no. 1 (1981), pp. 41–55.

12   Luce Irigaray, *This Sex Which is Not One*, trans. Catherine Porter and Carolyn Burke (Ithaca, NY: Cornell University Press, 1985), pp. 23–33.

13   Lisa Lewis, 'Form and female authorship in music video', in Caren Deming and Samuel Becker (eds), *Media in Society: Readings in Mass Communication* (Glenview, IL: Scott, Foresman and Company, 1988), pp. 140, 143.

14   Richard Goldstein, 'Tube Rock: how music video is changing music', in Caren Deming and Samuel Becker (eds), *Media in Society*, pp. 50–1.

15   Simon Frith, *Music for Pleasure* (Cambridge: Polity Press, 1988), pp. 166, 167.

16   Rosalind Krauss, 'Video: the aesthetics of narcissism', in Gregory Battock (ed.), *New Artists Video* (New York: E.P. Dutton, 1978), pp. 43–64.

17   Douglas Davis, 'Filmgoing/videogoing: making distinctions', in *Artculture: Essays on the Post-modern* (New York: Harper & Row, Publishers, 1977), pp. 79–84.

18   A good example of this is the Communards, Never Can Say Good-bye in which constant sweeping camera movements 'bring' viewers to the singers/stars, and swirling camera movements incorporate both stars and viewers into a large group of dancers. The stars are both centre and part of the dynamic social group. This accomplishes a 'live and let live' solidarity in which it no longer matters if one is gay or straight as long as he/she can dance. (The Communards are openly gay: the diegetic audience is composed primarily of heterosexual couplings, though the rapid pace achieved by cinematography and editing fragments this.)

19   Parker Tyler raises the interesting question of who is imitating whom between Mae West and the drag queen. 'Miss West's reaction to comments that connected her with female impersonators . . . was reported as the boast that, of course, she "knew that female impersonators imitated her". It is often hard, as everyone knows, to establish primacy of claims to originality, whether actually asserted or only indicated statistically. Perhaps one ought simply to say that Miss West's style as a woman fully qualifies her – as it always did – to be a Mother Superior of the Faggots' (Parker Tyler, *Screening the Sexes: Homosexuality in the Movies* (New York: Holt, Rinehart & Winston, 1972), p. 1). This question is quite relevant to my evaluation of the She-man (in the conclusion of this chapter) as a new and separate entity that transcends/abandons any original male agency.

20   See Jane Gallop, *The Daughter's Seduction: Feminism and Psychoanalysis* (Ithaca, NY: Cornell University Press, 1982) for an elaboration of the concept of phallic mother.

21   Mary Ann Doane, *The Desire to Desire: the Woman's Film of the 1940s* (Bloomington, IN: Indiana University Press, 1987).

22   See Doane, 'Film and the masquerade' and *The Desire to Desire*.

23   John Berger, Sven Blomberg, Chris Fox, Michael Dibb and Richard Hollis, *Ways of Seeing* (London: British Broadcasting Corporation, 1972), p. 47.

24   C. Carr, 'Unspeakable practices, unnatural acts: the taboo art of Karen Finley', *The Village Voice*, 24 June 1986, pp. 17–20.

25   Chris Straayer, 'The lesbian butch image: appropriation or intervention', unpublished paper presented at the 1990 Society for Cinema Studies Conference. See also, Chris Straayer, *Deviant Bodies: Sexual Re-orientations in Film and Video* (New York: Columbia University Press, 1996), pp. 271–87.

Part V

The *Boys Don't Cry* debate

12 Pass/fail

Michele Aaron

Boys Don't Cry (Kimberly Peirce, 1999) is a tale of passing, of Teena Brandon's passing as a heterosexual male, as Brandon Teena. Like other biographical accounts of the transgendered experience, it tells of an individual's 'natural' and necessary assumption of the appearance and identity of the 'opposite' sex. Indeed, the film contains numerous details which attach it to this 'outlaw' heritage: the protagonist's rescripting of 'his' past; allusions to medical intervention; a postscript thanking the transgendered community.[1] But it is as a fictionalization of this true and tragic tale that *Boys Don't Cry* demands interpretation within the context of film theory, and that passing becomes so telling a strategy not only for enacting the performativity of gender, but for divulging the knowingness or complicity at the heart of spectatorship.

It is in response to its generic and mainstream appeal, and *not* to Brandon's transgendered status, that *Boys* is to be considered here as, ostensibly, a crossdressing or transvestite film. Such films feature a central character disguising him- or herself as the opposite sex, and fulfil a set of similar characteristics with regard to narrative structure and thematic concerns.[2] Like them, *Boys* builds from the initial assumption of disguise to its grand public disclosure; it prioritizes a love story, and (more inclusively than most) it is '*about* the fixity or otherwise of gender identity'.[3] As will be shown, this film reinvents the basic formula, and most significantly in terms of the disavowal of spectatorial implication which is central to the genre.

Primarily comedies, crossdressing films, such as *Some Like It Hot* (Billy Wilder, 1959), *Victor/Victoria* (Blake Edwards, 1982) and *Mrs Doubtfire* (Chris Columbus, 1993), derive their effect from the slapstick, sexually suggestive or supposedly absurd scenarios resulting from the central character's 'mistaken' identity, that is, from the gap between the character's passing within the diegesis and the audience's privileged position of knowledge (being in on the disguise). Fuelled by heterosexual imperatives, the narratives progress towards the climactic disclosure of the protagonist's 'true' identity. Simultaneously, the narrations repeatedly remind the spectator of this real identity, through the transparency of their disguise (Cary Grant/Henri in *I was a Male War Bride* [Howard Hawks, 1949]); the dropping of the disguise afforded by co-conspirators (Tony Curtis/Josephine and Jack Lemmon/Daphne in *Some Like it Hot* [Billy Wilder, 1959]); or by the involuntary intrusion of an 'innate' gender (Anshel admiring the china in *Yentl* [Barbra Streisand, 1982]). But why does the spectator need reminding? On the one hand, such reminders reinforce the essentialism of gender even if the protagonists' (relatively) easy disguise confirmed its performativity. On the other hand, they make safe the gender play and, especially, the homoerotic implications arising from it. For some, therefore, the genre is insidiously conservative. It exploits transgression only to heighten the return to order, or, as Annette Kuhn writes, it 'problematise[s] gender identity and sexual difference . . . only to confirm the absoluteness of both'.[4] For others, it offers a rare and radical space for gender and sexual ambiguity – that is, for queerness – within the most mainstream of products. These reminders, then, these disruptions to passing, represent the spectator's disavowal of queerness: they both deny and acknowledge, contain and permit, the queer by-products of crossdressing. They halt the illusion, but in so doing they guarantee its full affect (and if this sounds awfully like the machinations of spectatorship in general, it does so deliberately). In this way, passing is shown to be intimately linked with failing to pass within the spectatorial experience of the crossdressing film. While *Boys* exploits a similar dynamic between passing and failing, their relationship is at once more pervasive, more explicit, and more fraught with liability.

Like these predecessors, *Boys* is, inevitably, about the spectacle of transvestism: despite its new queer cinema sensibility and elegiac thoughtfulness, it is Hilary Swank's crossdressed success, her 'stellar stunt performance' as Brandon, which made the film an international hit and garnered her an Oscar, among numerous other awards.[5] Indeed, it was not so much Brandon's as Swank's passing as a man that was at stake in the reception of *Boys*, and she more than merely passed, she got gold. If her apparational femininity at the Academy Awards ceremony sniffed of mainstream recuperation (here finally was that 'original' identity: the pre-disguise girl missing from the film's start), it did, nevertheless, consolidate the breadth and ease of gender performativity.[6] It also served to reiterate the absence of those essentialist details and disclaimers from the film itself. While *Boys* is suffused with reminders of Brandon's disguise, these work to *avow* queerness and, despite the film's sensationalist appeal, they extend spectatorial implication within the sexual (and social) workings of the diegesis rather than seal it off.

Brandon's true identity, that is, his transgendered identity, is ever-present to the spectator. Brandon is not so much trying to pass as someone else as trying to be 'him' self. Passing is not, therefore, a means to an end, as in the comedies, but the end itself. In general terms, in the spectator's constant awareness of Brandon's ambiguous identity – in the simultaneity of he and she – passing *is* failing: the reassuring distance between these 'events' (and the spectator's experience of them) dissolves. In addition, in the film passing is tinged with the threat of punishment, symbolized by the speeding ticket and court summons stalking Teena, and reverberating on from Cousin Lonny's (Matt McGrath) warning about Falls City: 'You know they shoot faggots down there.' It is always, then, haunted by failure as well. On a more local level, however, the fact that there is no before-Brandon for the spectator to 'forget', no essential singular gender to intervene into the narrative illusion, means the narrative reminders of disguise serve other purposes.

There are two key moments where Brandon's biology disrupts his passing: when Brandon's period starts, and when Lana (Chloë Sevigny) views his cleavage. Both of these are reminders of the physical: Brandon's breasts and bleeding index sex characteristics and not gender. Thus, the film suggests, the body joins with the Law as the (contested) arbiters of identity. *Boys* will later offer the ultimate statement on the separation of gender from anatomy in the climactic scene of public disclosure where John (Peter Sarsgaard) and Tom (Brendan Sexton III) force down Brandon's underwear. Rather than reifying Brandon's essential identity as John intends, Lana responds to John's taunts of 'look at your little boyfriend' with 'leave *him* alone'. The significance of this response is stressed as the frame seems to freeze, and a fantasy sequence begins which reifies instead the distinction between gender and sex, as the divested Brandon splits from and stares at a clothed Brandon standing watching behind the other witnesses. The tableau has an eerie but obvious resemblance to the crucifixion of Christ: a semi-clad, brightly lit Brandon has an arm over the shoulders of Tom and John on either side of him; Lana kneels below him looking up; a small audience gazes on. The composition's purpose is to invoke not the simple martyrdom of Christ/Brandon but the complicity of the spectators (both inside and outside the frame).

The two earlier reminders of disguise are used to underline rather than undermine the queerness of the encounters between the central couple, as well as Lana's and the spectator's consciousness of it. The shot of Brandon grappling with a box of tampons at a store is held just too long for the approaching Lana not to see what he's doing, or, at least, for us to think this is so. She may have been, as she confesses, 'so wasted', but Lana knows that store well – she's on first-name terms with the teller, and she directs another customer to the beer at the back. Escorted home by Brandon, as their interaction gets more flirtatious she turns to look at him and says: 'Wait a minute, what's your name again?' When Lana views Brandon's cleavage during sex, she does seem confused: she stares at the impression of his penis in his jeans, touches it gingerly, scrutinizes his hairless chin . . . and then forgets the whole thing and resumes their love-making. That she subsequently lies to her friends, saying that following sex she and Brandon took off their clothes and went swimming, testifies to her wittingness. Lana definitely knows. And she knows to keep it quiet.

In *Boys* these reminders also serve to unsettle the spectators' fixed position of superior knowledge about Brandon's identity; their supposedly sharp contrast to the duped characters. As a shift in privileged perspective, this occurs most emphatically when we share Lana's point of view in spying Brandon's breasts. In being made aware of the characters' suppressed knowledge about Brandon, the spectator joins them as a community of witnesses to Brandon's passing/failing. What is more, the concurrence of the heterosexual and homosexual implications arising from the crossdressed figure is explicitly conveyed here through Lana, who comes to represent the spectator's own inevitably unfixed or queer response to the crossdressed figure in general and to Brandon in particular.[7] The queer implication of 'knowing' about Brandon is not only declared in every rejection of homosexuality in *Boys* (from Teena's 'I'm not a dyke' to Lana's 'I'm not a lesbian') but is also inscribed on the surface of the film. Candace (Alicia Goranson) having discovered Brandon's disguise, comes to confront Lana, who is high and lying on her back on a spinning roundabout in a park. In a composition reminiscent of a certain sexual configuration (and one that occurred earlier when, similarly, Lana declared to Brandon she was 'in a trance'), Candace is framed centrally between Lana's open legs. It is not just that Lana is exposed as having a woman in that position, but that Candace, Brandon's earlier admirer, is also exposed, also queerly configured.

The awareness of Brandon's identity is not set up solely through Lana. In an early scene, Lana's mother (Jeanetta Arnette) beckons him over, peers at his face, and feels his smooth skin. As she does so, John looks on, squinting with similar suspicions. The scene is reminiscent of one found in *Yentl* where an old woman caresses the crossdresser's cheeks. Where her response, 'so young', is a convincing answer to the lack of hair growth, Lana's mother's exclamation at Brandon's handsomeness is not. That the old woman in *Yentl* has trouble seeing emphasizes Mom's voluntary sightlessness. In a similar vein, Brandon is not the only character straying from the idealization of gender (at the same time, however, only Brandon is 'so handsome' – although this is, as Pidduck suggests, as much to do with class as with gender[8]). Chloë Sevigny as Lana is far from the 'gangly' youth of J. Hoberman's description,[9] but, instead, her downy fleshiness is in sharp contrast to the lithe hairlessness of Brandon, or as Xan Brooks suggests: 'her heavy-jawed beauty contrasts nicely with Swank's more refined, aquiline looks and further blurs the tale's gender roles'.[10] Meanwhile Tom, with his pubescent flourish of facial hair, and John, doe-eyed and long-lashed, cuddly yet sociopathic, further promote the film's deliberate inscription of a spectrum of gender expression.

Neither is Brandon singled out in his irregularity. John's and Tom's excited embraces immediately after raping Brandon confirm their homosociality and an alternative network of implicated queerness. Brandon might, as he puts it, 'have this weirdness', but he is not alone. Tom is a self-mutilating ex-con with a pyromaniac past and John, Tom tells us, has 'no impulse control . . . that's what the doctors say'. It could also be argued that there is a sense of an otherworldliness to Falls City which is conjured as general, as shared; grounded in the inclusivity of objects rather than the fleetingness of John's good moods or Brandon's life. This sense is created by a sci-fi quality which permeates *Boys*, from the cinematographic distortion of light, and time – periods of day and night are shown passing at warp speed – in the film's images of factories with the smoke and metallic splendour of space-stations, and of parked cars with the luminosity of flying saucers. These are not just the stoned aesthetics of a 'surreal dreamscape',[11] but, in their allusions to the iconography of popular sci-fi they mean to invoke a community of aliens and dreamers, and to invoke it specifically for the spectator who oversees these extra-diegetic connections. Just in case these allusions aren't clear: not only is the drunken Mom discovered in front of a black and white sci-fi television programme, upon which the camera lingers, but Lana, in her last moment of hopefulness, wishes that she and Brandon could just 'beam' themselves out into the beautiful blue yonder.

Boys avoids rigid categories, ready answers or the supposition of singular responsibility. As Brooks argues, 'the perpetrators are never demonised as brutish monsters' and neither is Brandon 'a simple martyr',[12] but the film's anti-exclusivity goes much further than muddying the distinction between good and bad. Indeed, it is precisely around the apportioning of responsibility or, rather, the opening up of implication, that *Boys* seems so interesting and so important a film. Where in the crossdressing comedies the relationship between passing and failing reeked of reassurances for the no-less titillated spectator, in *Boys* their interaction constructs and confirms the knowingness, the implication, of *all* those witnessing Brandon's activities.

Notes

1 Jay Prosser, 'No place like home: the transgendered narrative of Leslie Feinberg's *Stone Butch Blues*', *Modern Fiction Studies*, vol. 41, nos 3–4 (1995), p. 503.

2 For discussions of generic characteristics, see Annette Kuhn, *The Power of the Image: Essays on Representation and Sexuality* (London: Routledge & Kegan Paul, 1985), pp. 48–73; Chris Straayer, 'Redressing the "natural": the temporary transvestite film', in Barry Keith Grant (ed.), *Film Genre Reader II* (Austin, TX: University of Texas Press, 1995) pp. 402–27.

3 Kuhn, *The Power of the Image*, p. 55 (emphasis in original).

4 Ibid., p. 57.

5 J. Hoberman, 'Use your illusion', *The Village Voice* (29 September–5 October 1999), http://www.villagevoice.com/issues.9939/hoberman.shtml. Swank received her Oscar on 26 March 2000. She also won the following, for best actress: BSFC award, BFCA award, CFCA award, Silver Hugo award, DFWFCA award, FFCC, Golden Globe, Golden Satellite award, Independent Spirit award, Sierra Award, NBR, FIPRESCI, LAFCA. See the Internet Movie Database for details of these awards: http://www.us.imdb.com/.

6 This breadth, and its queerness, is even more apparent in Chloë Sevigny's role as a stone butch in *If These Walls Could Talk 2: 1972* (Martha Coolidge, 2000).

7 See Straayer, 'Redressing the "natural"', for a useful discussion of how these opposing desires interact within the mainstream transvestite film by way of the 'paradoxical kiss'.

8   Julianne Pidduck, 'Risk and queer spectatorship', debate on *Boys Don't Cry*, *Screen*, this volume, Chapter 13, pp. 265–71.

9   Hoberman, 'Use your illusion'.

10   Xan Brooks, 'Review of *Boys Don't Cry*, *Sight and Sound* (April 2000), p. 44.

11   Pidduck, 'Risk and queer spectatorship', p. 99.

12   Brooks, 'Review of *Boys Don't Cry*', p. 44.

13 Risk and queer spectatorship

Julianne Pidduck

I first saw *Boys Don't Cry* (Kimberly Peirce, 1999) the night it opened at the Glasgow Film Theatre. This was something of an occasion: an Oscar-nominated work of 'new queer cinema',[1] for which local 'queers'[2] (predominantly lesbians) turned out in force. That night there was a frisson in the air arising in part from a queer erotics sheltered by this cosmopolitan city, but this urban bravado was edged with risk. Queer cultural events always remind me of the high stakes, the symbolic, affective and corporeal risk of queer representation itself. Nowhere is this more evident than with *Boys Don't Cry*. Peirce's film transforms the last few weeks of Brandon Teena's life into the stuff of legend, and Hilary Swank brings him back to life as an androgynous pin-up boy. Cinema traffics in identification, desire and mythology, and *Boys* plays on these powers, mobilizing a tangle of allegiances.[3] While Michele Aaron discusses 'the knowingness and complicity at the heart of spectatorship',[4] I would like to raise some of the distortions of allegiance across differences of location, class, gender and sexuality. Further, the irreducible 'real' violence haunting this 'gold-getting' crossover new queer cinema film highlights the affective and corporeal risks of spectatorship.

Based on events that took place in Nebraska in 1993, *Boys* is, from the first, haunted by the real-life Brandon's bleak fate. The film projects fictionalized fragments of biography through a stylized hyperrealism, drawing the viewer into the corporeal, emotional and desiring flow of the protagonist's experience. Peirce uses the generic frame of the road movie to broaden the scope of address from 'document' to 'entertainment'. The road movie's iconography, thematics and narrative structure impress a cultural legibility onto the residue of a life. In the process, Brandon Teena is transformed into an icon, a quintessential outsider whose transgressive choices are understood against the backdrop of the flat Midwestern landscape. The emotional power and problematic address of *Boys* spring from the tension between the dynamic mythology of the road movie and the persistent actuality of Brandon Teena's death.

Brandon is introduced in a big closeup while his cousin Lonny cuts his hair, short. Peirce comments:

> Knowing Brandon was destroyed for not being understood, I needed to bring
> him to life in a way that was universally understandable. [I did] that by creating
> a unified event, by having him stand in front of the mirror getting ready to
> go out. Gay or straight, male or female, you understand that.[5]

This is a stock 'makeover' scene of the crossdressing film, but as Aaron demonstrates, the film eschews the 'heterosexual imperatives' lurking within many such
narratives.[6] In the closeup, a privileged point of cinematic identification, we are
offered Swank's face first, her wide grin calculated to win over the audience.
Although the film does not second-guess its hero's choice diegetically, the film
inevitably relies on Swank's bravura performance as a bankable Hollywood actress.
And it is this underlying (extra-diegetic) guarantee of Swank-as-Brandon's delicate
features and fragile *female* body underneath the cowboy garb that ultimately will
ensure the mainstream audience's sympathy.

On an intertextual reading, the closeup is haunted by the actual Brandon. The
closeup rubs up against the residue of photographs widely reproduced in news
reports, on the internet, or in the documentary *The Brandon Teena Story* (Susan
Muska and Gréta Olafsdóttir, 1998). Roland Barthes suggests that 'however "life-
like" we strive to make it, Photography is . . . a figuration of the motionless and
made-up face beneath which we see the dead'.[7] *Boys* is littered with photographs:
Brandon carries snapshots in his dufflebag,[8] polaroid snapshots mark the romance
with Lana, and Brandon ritually burns photos after the rape. An intertextual
shadowplay between Brandon's and Swank's faces juxtaposes the fragmented record
of lived experience and the conventions of fiction – and a more existential tension
between the stasis of death ('Brandon' glimpsed only in truncated moments) and
the dynamic intensities of cinema. As a leavener to the tale's brutality, Peirce
incorporates the iconography and implied mobility of the road movie. From his
initial makeover, Brandon becomes a dashing, sensitive outsider. His roller-skating
date marvels that he seems like he's from somewhere else, 'some place beautiful'.
The audience is drawn into Brandon's outlaw game of risk, of getting away with
something dangerous and fine. Kissing a girl, narrowly escaping a beating or
worse in Lincoln, Brandon's speedy state of mind is communicated through scenes
of driving fast, almost floating – and in landscapes shot in time-lapse photography
streaked with the light of passing cars. The soundtrack chooses otherworldly
synthesizers over the realism of ambient sound (no cheerful chirping crickets here!),
and country music adds a note of romantic yearning ('the bluest eyes in Texas are
haunting me tonight'). Reminiscent of the dreamscapes of Gus Van Sant's *My Own
Private Idaho* (1991), Peirce uses driving sequences and landscapes to suggest the
escapist power of fantasy.

Boys follows on the heels of a cycle of 1990s feminist and queer-themed road
movies, including *Thelma and Louise* (Ridley Scott, 1991), and *Leaving Normal* (Edward

Zwick, 1992), *The Living End* (Gregg Araki, 1992), *To Wang Foo, Thanks for Everything! Julie Newmar* (Beeban Kidron, 1995), *My Own Private Idaho, Even Cowgirls Get the Blues* (Gus Van Sant, 1994), *The Adventures of Priscilla, Queen of the Desert* (Stephan Elliott, 1994) and *Happy Together* (Wong Kar-Wai, 1997). These offset the road movie's masculinist hegemony, but to what degree does this generic frame allow for different stories to emerge? A self-proclaimed 'sexual identity crisis' at the root of his social alienation, Brandon is a beautiful drifter who waxes poetic about heading down the road. But as the dangerous psychodrama builds, the viewer can only watch with rising frustration: in a genre that turns on the thematics of mobility and escape, why doesn't Brandon leave? The overt answer lies in Brandon's relationship with Lana (Chloë Sevigny). This complexly poignant love story nimbly negotiates anxiety about Brandon's body, as Lana's knowing disavowal allows her to choose a gentle lover who may 'take her away from all this'. Tragically, class curtails the characters' horizons, defeating the transcendence of fantasy and the transformative powers of love. This exchange between Lana and Brandon reveals the gap between the mythology of the road and the lived social space of working-class Falls City:

> Brandon: You are one cranky girl.
> Lana: Yeah, well you'd be cranky too Mr 'I'm going to Memphis-Graceland-Tennessee' when you're stuck in a town where there's nothing to do but bumper ski and chase bats everyday of your evil fucking life.
> Brandon: Hey, I've been bored my whole life.
> Lana: Is that why you let John tie you to the back of a truck and drag you around like a dog?
> Brandon: No, I just thought that's what guys do around here.

Symptomatic of the schism within the fabric of the film, the romantic impulse of trysts by moonlight and time-lapse photography of clouds scudding across the plains is on a collision course with the frenetic boredom of trailer parks, bonfires and beer-sodden tensions that may ignite into violence at any moment. Manohla Dargis notes that 'the road defines the space between town and country. It is an empty expanse, a tabula rasa, the last true frontier'.[9] If this blank expanse invites projection, the brutality of *Boys* connects with a widespread cultural articulation of small-town middle America with 'trailer trash' anomie, intolerance and murder.[10] This image recurs in such diverse films as *Deliverance* (John Boorman, 1972), *Wild at Heart* (David Lynch, 1990), *True Romance* (Tony Scott, 1993), *Natural Born Killers* (Oliver Stone, 1994), *From Dusk Till Dawn* (Robert Rodriguez, 1996), *Fargo* (Joel Coen, 1996), *Sling Blade* (Billy Bob Thornton, 1996) – not to mention a plethora of horror films from *The Texas Chainsaw Massacre* (Tobe Hooper, 1974) to George A. Romero's zombie trilogy that characterize 'white trash' as monstrous killing machines or disposable human waste. To specify the (primarily middle-class and urban) international audience of the new queer cinema, it could be argued that a cycle of recent queer-themed (if not necessarily authored) films (*Fun* [Raphal Zielinski 1994], *Butterfly Kiss* [Michael Winterbottom, 1995], *The Living End*, and even *Idaho*, *Priscilla* and *Happy Together*) designate the tabula rasa of the road as a liminal 'elsewhere' for the exploration of violence and queer sexuality.[11]

Subtle performances by Chloë Sevigny (Lana), Peter Sarsgaard (John) and Brendan Sexton III (Tom)[12] distinguish *Boys* from this tendency to flatten the geographical specificity of middle America and the humanity of its occupants.[13] What comes across is not only small-mindedness and hatred, but the warmth, humour, fears and desires of the characters around Brandon. The film is particularly eloquent in its treatment of masculinity and violence. Bumper-skiing – a truck roaring round and round in a cloud of dust – crystallizes a 'redneck' ethos, a dead-end frenetic motion steeped in desperate bravado and brutality. From the bar-room brawl to the bumper-skiing scene to the heady chase along the 'dustless highway', from Tom's self-mutilation to John's mounting jealousy over Brandon's seduction of Lana, the film relates a series of painfully slow, erotically charged and increasingly violent challenges between John, Tom and Brandon. At the centre of this vortex is the ethereal Brandon who, with his 'movie-star good looks', enigmatic body, a certain luminosity in the way his face is shot, promises to transcend the limitations of working-class masculinity.

As the film careers toward its terrible finale, the film's 'devil may care' dynamism increasingly shifts to gritty, claustrophobic interiors, captured in tight, edgy hand-held camerawork, in the emotionally charged violation prefacing the rape, Brandon is pinioned, weeping, in a tiny bathroom as John and Tom examine his genitals. Tom's first sudden punch to the jaw snaps Brandon's delicate neck around, breaking any residual veneer of comradeship. The terrible humiliation of this moment is marked by two still shots, like snapshots. First, Tom, John and Brandon are frozen motionless in a medium-shot. Cut to a reverse-shot with Lana and Lana's mother (Jeanetta Arnette) and Brandon himself dissociated, watching. These stills mark a break in the flow of the film, a point of no return. This is the moment where, as Aaron suggests, Brandon's 'passing' fails.[14] Steve Neale suggests that masculinity is encoded into film language through control of the gaze and the physical dominance of space.[15] In the film's latter moments, Brandon is successively cornered and stripped of his already-tenuous access to the masculine privileges of mobility and to Lana's body.

From this surreal break, the film switches into flashback to portray the rape. The diegetic Brandon is doubly violated – both as self-identified male forced into sexual submission as a woman, and through the brutal police interrogation. Cinematic rape scenes present situations of extreme emotional danger. Onscreen rape can symbolically repeat the violation either by facilitating sadistic identification with the rapist, or traumatic identification with the victim.[16] Further, as Anneke Smelik suggests, the rape of a film's protagonist can annihilate the subjectivity that offers the primary point of identification.[17] Peirce negotiates this horrific moment by anchoring the narration in Brandon's voice and point-of-view. (Some viewers will recognize that the interview is based on the transcript of Brandon Teena's actual police interview. In using these transcripts, the film allows the silenced voice of the actual Brandon to narrate his story, retroactively.) Tom and John take Brandon to a deserted oil refinery, harshly lit with neon blues and greens. An extreme long-shot in slow motion distances us from the action as John picks up Brandon bodily and throws him into the back seat. John's attack is spliced into Brandon's account with four brutal closeups that flash on the screen like fragments of memory too painful to recall in its entirety. Tom's rape is depicted in greater detail. Shirt torn off, the camera holds on an excruciating sustained shot of Brandon's bruised face in profile, his thin, bare shoulders racked with the brutal thrusting motion from behind.

Effectively, the viewer is asked to experience the rape from the victim's point of view. The film invites political, emotional and corporeal allegiances linked to known and imagined risk, especially for female and/or queer viewers. An allegiance with Brandon's outsider status aligns the viewer with Brandon's initial exhilaration at his transgressive success as a boy, drawing us through to the film's disturbing finale. Actual attacks, threats and near misses, a familiarity with the continuum of hatred and violence, can intensify the disturbing recognition ('that could have been me') of watching such an event, especially an account of a 'true story', on screen. However, I would maintain that, as Brandon's boy's garb is torn away, it is the violation of Swank's lithe, recognizably female body that commands a much more 'universal' pathos. According to western representational codes of gender violence, the explicit beating and kicking of a woman's body (particularly a young, pretty, white, middle-class woman's body) is taboo. Watching this film as a feminist and a lesbian, in a queer context, I was torn between the recognition of Brandon as a gender outlaw, and a corporeal affinity with Swank-as-Brandon's residual 'female' body, both in the rape scenes, and in the erotic encounters with Lana. Aaron convincingly argues that the film privileges a 'queer' reading that can separate sex and gender.[18] However, in the film's concluding scenes, such a fluid reading is confronted by John and Tom's violent re-imposition of Brandon's 'femininity', and by Swank's insistent physicality.

In this dense weave of diegetic and spectatorial risk, betrayals and violations, there is one more to mention. The violation and annihilation of the protagonist as object of desire and identification stretches the generic frame of cinema-as-entertainment. Writing about the Western (a close cousin to the road movie), Richard Slotkin has argued that 'the myth of regeneration through violence became the structuring metaphor of the American experience'.[19] Confounding the road movie's preferred tempo of mobility and bravado, Brandon does not exit driving fast, in a shower of bullets. Landscapes and roads are deployed throughout *Boys* to contain the omnipresence of 'real' violence within the generic promise of 'regeneration'. Immediately before Tom and John first seize Brandon, there is a cut to a fantasy sequence: Lana says to Brandon, 'Look how beautiful it is. We can just beam ourselves out there', as she gestures to an imagined psychedelic sky sequence with the clouds rushing by. And again, after the murder, there is a landscape shot of a pink and strangely tranquil dawn, followed by a brief shot of Lana driving; accompanying these shots is Brandon's voiceover of his last love letter to Lana, 'I love you always and forever'. These closing clues signify, variably, the Western landscape ensuring regeneration; the power of true love to transcend even death; and ongoing possibility of escape. But given the resounding absence of the 'real' Brandon from the Nebraska landscape (the stasis of death), the film's ultimate return to generic requirements of mobility and transcendence is troubling.

As a crossover work of the new queer cinema and as an example of an increasing filmic and televisual trend towards the blurring of 'document' and 'drama', *Boys* is an important and provocative film. By highlighting risk, I have sought to foreground ethical issues about how the irretrievable 'raw material' of human experience (both pleasure and pain) is formed into preset narrative and generic patterns. The notion of life and death as 'haunting' the frame of entertainment insists on a limit to the pleasures of spectatorship as complicity or allegiance.

Notes

1   This term was coined by B. Ruby Rich in an article of that title in *Sight and Sound* (September 1992), pp. 30–4. In a recent update to that article, Rich suggests (controversially) that *Boys*, 'not about a lesbian at all', falls outside the remit of 'new queer cinema'. See 'Queer and present danger', *Sight and Sound*, vol. 10, no. 3 (2000), pp. 22–5.

2   I use the term 'queer' as an inclusive shorthand to suggest an affective and political affinity among lesbians, gay men, bisexual and transgendered people. Clearly, this term raises difficulties of assumed sameness, some of which are addressed below, and some of which exceed the scope of this essay.

3   I use the term 'allegiance' rather than identification advisedly, to suggest a recognition rooted partly in social experience.

4   Michele Aaron, 'Pass/fail', debate on *Boys Don't Cry*, this volume, Chapter 12, pp. 259–64.

5   Danny Leigh, 'Boy wonder', interview with Kimberly Peirce, *Sight and Sound*, vol. 10, no. 3 (2000), p. 18.

6   Aaron, 'Pass/fail', p. 259.

7   Roland Barthes, *Camera Lucida* (New York: Noonday Press, 1981), pp. 31–2. Barthes's idiosyncratic 'phenomenology', highlighting photography as 'contingency, singularity, risk' and 'irreducible affect', informs my analysis.

8   Among these is an image of Swank in a gangster outfit copied from an oft-reproduced portrait of the real Brandon Teena.

9   Cited in Steven Cohan and Ina Rae Hark (eds), 'Introduction', in *The Road Movie Book* (London: Routledge, 1997), p. 1.

10 As a case in point, the documentary *The Brandon Teena Story* begins wryly with a shot of a road sign: 'Nebraska . . . the good life'; this image is juxtaposed with three gunshots.

11 Victoria E. Johnson discusses the persistent stigma attached to the American Midwest as a counterpoint to urban 'lesbian chic' in 'This is no "Dayton chic": the abject Midwest in *Ellen and Roseanne*', Society for Cinema Studies conference paper, Chicago, March 2000.

12 For Peirce's discussion of class and performance, see http://www.foxsearchlight.com/boysdon'tcry/prod.html.

13 Clearly, each of the films and cycles mentioned has insights, complexities and angle of critique that fall outside of this essay. For an analysis of the road movie see Cohan and Hark (eds), *The Road Movie Book*.

14 Aaron 'Pass/fail', p. 261.

15 Steve Neale, 'Masculinity as spectacle', *Screen*, vol. 24, no. 6, pp. 2–16.

16 For instance, see the sociological analysis of female spectatorship and *The Accused* (Jonathan Kaplan, 1988) in Philip Schlesinger, R. Emerson Dobash, Russell P. Dobash and C. Kay Weaver, *Women Viewing Violence* (London: British Film Institute 1992), pp. 127–63. See also Anneke Smelik's insightful treatment of Marion Hansel's and Marleen Gorris's films in *And the Mirror Cracked: Feminist Cinema and Film Theory* (Houndmills: Macmillan Press, 1998), pp. 56–9.

17 Smelik, *And the Mirror Cracked*, pp. 66–78.

18 Aaron, 'Pass/fail'.

19 Richard Slotkin, *Regeneration Through Violence* (Middletown, CT: Wesleyan University Press, 1973), p. 5.

14 Girls still cry

Patricia White

> What is this love we have for the invert, boy or girl? It was they who were spoken
> of in every romance that we ever read. . . . For in the girl it is the prince, and in
> the boy it is the girl that makes a prince a prince, and not a man.
>
> Djuna Barnes[1]

An insistent link between the invert or transgendered figure and the romance genre
is forged in *Boys Don't Cry* (Kimberly Peirce, 1999), the independent narrative
film based on the events leading to twenty-one-year-old Brandon Teena's rape and
subsequent murder on New Year's Eve, 1993. Besides an eerie lighting and sound
scheme that seem to envelop the film's desolate Falls City, Nebraska setting in an
electrical haze – a motif highlighted now and again with speeded-up shots of traffic
and power lines – Peirce's film does not answer to Djuna Barnes's lesbian modernist
legacy on the level of baroque style. On the level of narrative, the film is also
functional. In true-crime or biopic fashion, *Boys* sweeps inevitably – even, cruelly,
satisfyingly – to its foregone conclusion, preserving tragic unity and eliciting pathos.
But the film's transgendered hero (played by Hilary Swank) seems to be Barnes's
'prince' incarnate, and the anguished female desire that *Boys* encompasses within
an authorial/spectatorial 'we' would not be out of place in Barnes's fiction.

If I say female desire, it is not because I am disavowing Brandon's transgendered
identity. It is because for me the centring subjectivity of the film belongs to
Brandon's lover, Lana Tisdel (Chloë Sevigny). Brandon is present in most of the
film's scenes (with important exceptions): Lana is not, and there are many events
that she does not observe. But whether Brandon is fucking up, desiring or desirable, he is seen from a perspective that could be Lana's. We do not experience
his passing as a man as a deception, and I do not think this is only because we
witness his gleeful self-fashioning in the film's first scene (complete with hair-
cut and crotch stuffing). For when Lana 'finds out' much later, she does not
feel betrayed. The film enunciates a 'we' who share 'this love . . . for the invert',
extending from teenage girl to audience through numerous narrational cues. For
example, the optical point of view that opens the film – Brandon's gaze caught in

his rear view mirror as he speeds away from a cop – is answered in the film's last shot by Lana's gaze ahead as she finally drives away from Falls City. The narrative throughline provided by Lana and Brandon's romance has angered some commentators looking for a more documentary fidelity to the circumstances and context of Brandon's life and death. But the strategy makes Lana's desire and way of seeing count. Brandon's wish for an 'elsewhere' becomes hers and ours. In an early scene at a roller rink in Lincoln, Brandon's date tells him, 'You don't look like you are from around here.' He teases out her idea of where she thinks he does come from: 'Someplace beautiful.' Brandon's world is strewn with cliches, and disavowals, but like the bubble-gum-machine-quality ring he gives to Lana, they signify something beautiful.

Feminist psychoanalytic readings of the process of film spectatorship have analysed the gendered dimensions of the fetishism and disavowal its pleasures require. Not only is the viewer's suspension of disbelief necessary to enjoy the film illusion, but 'his' spectatorial desire is also affirmed specifically by disavowing female lack.[2] Fetishism as a mastery of castration anxiety is an inadequate account of *female* visual pleasure, many feminist theorists have pointed out. *Boys* offers a chance to revisit issues of spectatorship and fetishism in relation to a quite literal scenario of genital (in)difference. Brandon may experience lack in his own body (in the remarkable scene of his stripping and exposure, the film portrays a second, intact Brandon looking on from the periphery), but for him girls are complete – and completely captivating. Brandon's (clean-shaven, small-boned, teen-magazine heartthrob) gender fiction sustains Lana's fantasy. When Brandon's persecutors force him to prove his sex to Lana, she tells him to keep his pants on: 'Think about it. I *know* you're a guy', she insists.[3] *Boys* marks a convergence of queer, feminist and what I would like to call (for reasons that will become clear) girl-viewer optics.

Fetishism is operative in the very form of the question 'what is this love we have for the invert, boy or girl?', which presumes and believes in 'love' without deciding whether the 'boy or girl?' is at stake. I'd like to analyse how fetishism shapes the formal construction of a scene that both consolidates the romance – it is the couple's first sex scene – and transfers vision, knowledge, desire and narration to Lana. Brandon has returned to Falls City to woo Lana (fleeing a court date in Lincoln that would officially register his identity as female and felon, and might cause his incarceration), and she joins him on the riverbank outside the plant where she works. As Brandon adjusts Lana's naked torso beneath him, she murmurs, 'I feel like I'm in a trance.' The line addresses on one level the prurient question of how the sexual partner of a transgendered or passing woman can avoid noticing the absence of the penis. But it works on a phantasmatic level as well. We watch a remarkable, lingering overhead closeup of Lana's face as she receives oral stimulation (in qualifying the film for an R rating, the censors objected to the shot's duration); her expression and the musical accompaniment rise in intensity and climax with a cut to a low-angle point-of-view shot of moving lights that resolve into streetlights seen from a car. A match cut to Lana's open mouth in the next shot shows her partying in a car with Brandon and her girlfriends Candace (Alicia Goranson) and Kate (Alison Folland) at her side. The slow-motion shot relays her sexual euphoria with Brandon into an image of pleasure felt in her female friends' company.

The next scene in Lana's bright yellow, teenager's bedroom strengthens this connection, as she narrates the sexual encounter to the girls. In response to their prodding, Lana sinks back between them where they lie on the bed passing a bong and covers her eyes: 'I can't talk about it, it is too intense!' The girls prompt her to continue and the camera cuts from a tight overhead shot of all three girls on the bed to an overhead closeup of just Lana that is strikingly reminiscent of the orgasm shot we have seen just a few moments before. Within what is now a subjective flashback to the sex scene, Brandon penetrates and pleasures her, and a shot from Lana's optical point of view reveals the hint of a cleavage in Brandon's chest. Lana doesn't verbalize this moment when the film cuts back to the closeup of her face on the pillow, but next a series of shots in flashback show her touching Brandon's jeans at the crotch, then tracing his jawline, and looking into his eyes. 'Well, did you do it?' her friends demand, the question seeming inadequately to grasp the pleasure that we have been able to see on her face, both in the protracted shot during the oral sex scene and in the shots in which she now recalls it. 'What do you think?', she answers with satisfaction.

Why is this a satisfactory answer? Lana's flashback is offered to us visually, so we know 'more' than her friends. If we credit her with now 'knowing' about Brandon's gender performance, we might understand why she leaves the question's presumptive 'yes' answer unspoken (it all depends what is meant by 'it'). But because the flashback transpires during screen time in which she is clearly narrating to her friends, I believe that its mise-en-scene is available to her diegetic inter-locutors as well. In other words, both her pleasure (which we see in the act and in its later recollection in the company of the other girls at home in her bed) and her undecided question – 'what do you think?' (or even 'boy or girl?') – are conveyed to us as *if* we were among the girls.[4] We are left to decide whether we think she did it and what we think 'it' is, whether and what we think she knows, and whether we think the knowing worth thinking about. Though the narration seems to disavow a genital 'fact' at this juncture, this is not presented as a costly disavowal, as tragic misrecognition; instead Lana's desire is renewed as she becomes the film's narrator. Thus, on a formal level, the film authorizes the investment of the girl auditors who are our stand-ins (stand-ins who at this moment are lying down – in bed talking about 'boys', a classic topos of girls' culture). Brandon's portrayal as 'one of the girls' partying in the car presents him not as 'castrated' but as a crucial link in a discursive circuit of pleasure and belief.

It is when we recall the implied presence of the 'boys', John Lotter (Peter Sarsgaard) and Tom Nissen (Brendan Sexton III), whom we have so frequently seen partying with the girls, that castration could be said to re-enter the fetishistic equation. Brandon's murderers are not long offscreen. The film's firm location in the 'feminized' realm of melodrama, romance and tears actually allows male inadequacy, impotence, rage and panic to be presented vividly and almost sympathetically.[5] 'Boys don't cry' might be seen as a shaming performative mantra for Brandon – throughout his persecution he strives to 'take it like a man' (the film's original title). But his murderers also try to 'defend' themselves and define their masculinity through negative attributes (boys don't, for example, want to see how they depend on, resemble and fail to communicate with girls) and finally explode into violence. The scary, volatile intimacy with John and Tom that characterizes Lana's and then Brandon's lives also includes the viewer, a chilling reminder that it is also a 'we' who fear and despise the invert.

The box-office and critical success of *Boys* surprised almost everyone involved. But remember: *girls cry*, at least according to market wisdom. It seems to me that in the midst of a notable recalibration of popular entertainment to take into account the knowing genre tastes of adolescent and teenage girls and young women (from *Titanic* [James Cameron, 1997] to *Scream* [Wes Craven, 1996] and its sequels), *Boys'* success makes sense. Still, the film's crossover qualifications have been seen as trivializing the gender crossing that Brandon performed and died for, as well as issues of racism and violence against women at stake in the case. Apparently the emphasis on a central love story left no room even to include a character representing Phillip Devine, another, African–American, victim of John and Tom's murderous rage that night. Indeed, the film is striking for its omission of *any* people of colour in Nebraska. Even from within my emphasis on girls' perspectives, the murder of Candace (a composite character based in part on the third murder victim Lisa Lambert) – an even more obvious stand-in for the sympathetic female viewer than Lana – could be seen as curiously unmourned. She is gunned down in front of her baby, who then disappears from the last scene; the fate of neither is mentioned in the 'where are they now' titles that precede the end credits, titles that carefully elide the film's fictional world and the events upon which it was based. We *are* informed that Lana herself had a baby girl a few years after leaving Falls City and returned home to raise her.[6] Candace's brutal and gratuitous murder and the shrinking of Lana's horizons exist on a continuum of everyday violence against women. These are themes that popular women's genres address; *Boys* rightly recognizes that Brandon Teena's story raised them too.

Rather than dwelling on the commercial constraints or mimetic responsibilities that dog independent films' attempts to tell queer stories, think of what a cultural sea change in imaginings of gender and sexuality we are experiencing if these attempts now resonate with popular forms and audiences. I am not surprised that girls and women in particular are receptive to radical permutations of romance such as *Boys*. Djuna Barnes tells us that it has always been the girl in the boy, the prince in the girl that galvanized our desire; perhaps the 'queerness' of romance need no longer be disavowed. *Boys* female performers themselves worked on some of the most progressive popular youth films and television shows: Swank was featured in the film version of *Buffy the Vampire Slayer* (Fran Rubel Kazui, 1992), Goranson grew up on the long-running ABC sitcom *Roseanne*, and Folland starred in Alex Sichel's *All Over Me* (1997), a lesbian independent feature depicting a somewhat more empowered element of female youth culture than that of *Boys*' dead-end teens. And Chloë Sevigny 'flipped' to play the butch opposite *Dawson's Creek*'s Michelle Williams in the made-for-HBO lesbian compilation film *If These Walls Could Talk 2* (2000); the segment was authored by *All Over Me* writer Sylvia Sichel. Do youth audiences recognize the discontinuities as well as the continuum running from the WB Network to *Boys Don't Cry*? Do girl viewers today 'get' feminism, or grasp what I think is a cultural shift in the status of gay men, lesbians and transgendered people? Do they see beyond makeup and fashion, so aggressively marketed to them in popular culture, to the refiguring of desire and agency also being provoked there by subcultures, activism and independent media? What do you think?

Notes

1   Djuna Barnes, *Nightwood* (New York: New Directions, 1937), pp. 136–7.

2   Christian Metz, *The Imaginary Signifier: Psychoanalysis and the Cinema*, trans. Celia Britton *et al.* (Bloomington, IN: Indiana University Press, 1982); Laura Mulvey, 'Visual pleasure and narrative cinema', *Screen*, vol. 16, no. 3 (1975), pp. 6–18.

3   Interviewed in Susan Muska and Greta Olafsdóttir's 1998 documentary, *The Brandon Teena Story*, Lana Tisdel says that she told Brandon not to show her: 'I'll tell them what they want to hear, what we believe.' The language in *Boys* merely substitutes 'what we know is true' for 'what we believe'.

4   Indeed, this undecidability between visual and verbal information, present and past, perception and fantasy, is what is crucial in the bedroom scene. When Lana removes her hands from her eyes she tells her friends: 'then we took off our clothes and went swimming.' Instead we see Lana climb on top of Brandon in a flashback shot, whispering 'Don't be scared'. As for the swimming story, Kate responds, 'Yeah, right'.

5   In the film's melodramatic topography, the 'public' sphere is represented only by nightmarish law enforcement agents and nightclubs, its many outdoors locations are adjunct spaces to a desolate domesticity.

6   Lana Tisdel's story has been, and will be, told in other ways. Although she signed a release early in Peirce's project, and another when the film was taking more definite shape, after being shown the finished film she filed a lawsuit. In the interim she had become involved in a competing production based on Brandon's story and was represented by its Los Angeles lawyer. The suit objected to her being depicted in *Boys Don't Cry* as 'unfazed by the discovery' that Brandon, whom 'she thought was a man' was 'a female transvestite and/or transsexual who was later murdered'.

The film's rendition of her relationship with Brandon as a 'modern-day, gender-bending Romeo and Juliet' was inaccurate, the suit claimed: 'In sum, the said motion picture falsely depicts plaintiff as a lesbian' as well as someone who, it rather symptomatically goes on to reiterate, was 'unbothered by the discovery' that Brandon was 'a female transvestite and/or transsexual who was later murdered'. A Los Angeles judge refused to halt the film's opening, reasoning that Lana Tisdel's story was public information, and the case was later settled out of court. Conversations with Associate Producer Bradford Simpson, quoting from the court papers, 3 and 4 January 2001.

15 The transgender gaze in *Boys Don't Cry*

Judith Halberstam

In her stylish adaptation of the true-life story of Brandon Teena, director Kimberly Peirce very self-consciously constructs what can only be called a 'transgender gaze'. *Boys Don't Cry* (1999) establishes the legitimacy and durability of Brandon's gender not simply by telling the tragic tale of his murder but by forcing spectators to adopt, if only for a short time, Brandon's transgender gaze.[1] The transgender gaze in this film reveals the ideological content of the male and female gazes and it temporarily disarms the compulsory heterosexuality of the romance genre. Brandon's gaze obviously dies with him in the film's brutal conclusion but Peirce, perhaps prematurely, abandons the transgender gaze in the final intimate encounter, between Lana (Chloë Sevigny) and Brandon (Hilary Swank). Peirce's inability to sustain a transgender gaze opens up a set of questions about the inevitability and dominance of both the male/female and the hetero/homo binary in narrative cinema.

One remarkable scene, about halfway through the film, clearly foregrounds the power of the transgender gaze and makes it most visible precisely when and where it is most threatened. In a scary and nerve-racking sequence of events, Brandon finds himself cornered at Lana's house. John (Peter Sarsgaard) and Tom (Brendan Sexton III) have forced Candace (Alicia Goranson) to tell them that Brandon has been charged by the police with writing bad cheques and that he has been imprisoned as a woman. John and Tom now hunt Brandon, like hounds after a fox, and then begin a long and excruciating interrogation of Brandon's gender identity. Lana at first protects Brandon, saying that she will examine him and determine whether he is a man or a woman. Lana and Brandon enter Lana's bedroom, where Lana refuses to look as Brandon unbuckles his trousers telling him: 'Don't . . . I know you're a guy.' As they sit on the bed together, the camera now follows Lana's gaze out into the night sky, a utopian vision of an elsewhere to which she and Brandon long to escape. The camera cuts back abruptly to 'reality' and a still two-shot of Brandon in profile with Lana behind. As they discuss their next move, the camera slowly draws back, and in a seamless transition places them in the living room in front of the posse of bullies. This quiet interlude in Lana's bedroom establishes the female gaze, Lana's gaze, as a willingness to see what is not there (a condition of all fantasy) but also as a refusal to privilege the literal over the figurative (Brandon's genitalia over Brandon's gender presentation). The female gaze, in this scene, makes possible an alternative vision of time, space and embodiment. Time slows down while the couple linger in the sanctuary of Lana's private world, her bedroom; the bedroom itself becomes an otherworldly space framed by the big night sky and containing the perverse vision of a girl and her queer boy lover. The body of Brandon is preserved as male, for now, by Lana's refusal to dismantle its fragile power with the scrutinizing gaze of science and 'truth'. That Lana's room transforms seamlessly into the living room at the end of this scene, alerts the viewer to the possibility that an alternative vision will undermine the chilling enforcement of normativity that follows.

Back in the living room – the primary domestic space of the family – events take an abrupt turn towards the tragic. Brandon is now shoved into the bathroom, a hyperreal space of sexual difference, and is violently stripped by John and Tom, and then restrained by John while Tom roughly examines his crotch. The brutality of their action here is clearly identified as a violent mode of looking, and the film identifies the male gaze with that form of knowledge which resides in the literal. The brutality of the male gaze, however, is more than just a castrating force: John and Tom not only want to see the site of Brandon's castration, more importantly they need Lana to see it. Lana kneels in front of Brandon, confirming the scene's resemblance to a crucifixion tableau, and refuses to raise her eyes, declining once more to look at Brandon's unveiling.

However, at the point when Lana's 'family' and 'friends' assert their hetero-normative will most forcefully upon Brandon's resistant body, Brandon rescues himself briefly by regaining the alternative vision which he and Lana shared moments earlier in her bedroom. A slow-motion sequence interrupts the fast and furious quasi-medical scrutiny of Brandon's body, and shots from Brandon's point of view reveal him to be in the grips of an 'out of body' experience. Light shines on him from above, and his anguished face peers out at the crowd of onlookers who have gathered in the bathroom doorway. The crowd now includes a fully clothed Brandon, a double, who impassively returns the gaze of the tortured Brandon. In this shot/reverse-shot sequence between the castrated and the transgender Brandon, the transgender gaze is constituted as a look divided within itself, a point of view that comes from (at least) two places at the once: one clothed and one naked. The clothed Brandon is the Brandon rescued by Lana's refusal to look; the Brandon who survives his own rape and murder; the Brandon to whom the audience is now sutured, a figure who combines temporarily the activity of looking with the passivity of the spectacle. The naked Brandon is the Brandon who will suffer, endure, but finally expire.

Kaja Silverman has called attention to cinematic suture as 'the process whereby the inadequacy of the subject's position is exposed in order to facilitate new insertions into a cultural discourse which promises to make good that lack'.[2] In *Boys*, the inadequacy of the subject's position has been presented as a precondition of the narrative, so this scene of the split transgender subject, which would ordinarily expose 'the inadequacy of the subject's position', actually works to highlight the *sufficiency* of the transgender subject. Thus, if the shot/reverse-shot usually both secures and destabilizes the spectator's sense of self, this shot/reverse-shot involving the two Brandons now serves both to destabilize the spectator's sense of gender stability and also to confirm Brandon's manhood at the very moment that he has been exposed as female/castrated.

Not only does *Boys* create a transgender subject position which is fortified by the traditional operations of the gaze and conventional modes of gendering, it also makes the transgender subject dependent upon the recognition of a woman. In other words, Brandon can be Brandon because Lana is willing to see him as he sees himself (clothed, male, vulnerable, lacking, strong, passionate), and to avert her gaze when his manhood is in question. With Brandon occupying the position in the romance which is usually allotted to the male hero and the male gaze, the dynamics of looking and gendered being are permanently altered. If usually it is the female body that registers lack, insufficiency and powerlessness, in *Boys* it is Brandon who represents the general condition of incompleteness, crisis and lack, and it is Lana who represents the fantasy of wholeness, knowledge and pleasure. Lana can be naked without trauma while Brandon cannot and she can access physical pleasure in a way that he cannot; but he is depicted as mobile and self-confident in a way that she is not. Exclusion and privilege cannot be assigned neatly to the couple on the basis of gender hierarchies or class hierarchies: power is instead shared between the two subjects, and she agrees to misrecognize him as male while he sees through her social alienation and unhappiness to recognize her as beautiful, desirable and special.

By deploying the transgender gaze and joining it to an empowered female gaze in *Boys*, Peirce, for most of the film, keeps the viewer trained upon the seriousness of Brandon's masculinity, the authenticity of his presentation as opposed to its elements of masquerade. But abruptly, towards the end of the film, Peirce suddenly and catastrophically divests her character of his transgender gaze and converts it to a lesbian and therefore female gaze. In a strange scene, which follows the brutal rape of Brandon by John and Tom, Lana comes to Brandon as he lies sleeping in a shed outside Candace's house. In many ways the encounter that follows seems to extend the violence enacted upon Brandon's body by John and Tom, since Brandon now interacts with Lana *as if he were a woman*. Lana, contrary to her previous commitment to his masculinity, seems to see him as female, calling him 'pretty' and asking him what he was like as a girl. Brandon confesses to Lana that he has been untruthful about many things in his past and his confession sets up the expectation that he will now appear before Lana as his 'true' self. 'Truth' here becomes sutured to nakedness, as Lana tentatively disrobes Brandon saying that she may not 'know how to do this'. 'This' seems to refer to having sex with Brandon as a woman. They both agree that his whole journey to manhood has been pretty weird and then they move to make love. While earlier Peirce created quite graphic depictions of sex between Brandon and Lana, now the action is hidden by a Hollywood-style dissolve as if to suggest that the couple are now making love as opposed to having sex.

The scene raises a number of logical and practical questions about the representation of the relationship between Brandon and Lana. First, why would Brandon want to have sex within hours of a rape? Second, how does the film pull back from its previous commitment to his masculinity here by allowing his femaleness to become legible and significant to Lana's desire? Third, in what ways does this scene play against the earlier more 'plastic' sex scenes in which Brandon used a dildo and wouldn't allow Lana to touch him? And, fourth, how does this scene unravel the complexities of the transgender gaze as they have been assembled in earlier scenes between Brandon and Lana?

When asked about this in an interview, Peirce reverts to a very tired humanist narrative to explain this extraordinary scene, saying that after the rape, Brandon could be *neither* Brandon Teena *nor* Teena Brandon, and thus becomes truly 'himself' and 'receives love' for the first time as a human being.[3] Peirce claims that Lana herself told her about this encounter and therefore it was true to life. In the context of the film, however, which has made no such commitment to authenticity, the scene ties Brandon's humanity to a particular form of naked embodiment that eventually requires him to be a woman.

Ultimately in *Boys*, the double vision of the transgender subject gives way to the universal vision of humanism; the transgender man and his lover become lesbians and the murder seems instead to be the outcome of vicious homophobic rage. Given the failure of nerve that leads Peirce to conclude her film with a humanist scene where love conquers all, it is no surprise that she also sacrificed the racial complexity of the narrative by erasing the story of the other victim who died alongside Brandon Teena and Lisa Lambert. Phillip DeVine, a disabled African–American man has received scant coverage in media accounts of the case, despite the connections of at least one of the murderers to a white supremacist group.[4] Now, in the feature film, the death of DeVine has been rendered completely irrelevant to the narrative. Peirce claimed that this subplot would have complicated her film and made it too cumbersome – but race is a narrative trajectory that is absolutely central to the meaning of the Brandon Teena murder. DeVine was dating Lana's sister Leslie, and had a fight with her on the night he appeared at Lisa's house in Humboldt county. His death was neither accidental nor an afterthought; his connection to Leslie could be read as a similarly outrageous threat to the supremacy and privilege of white manhood that the murderers rose to defend. By removing DeVine from the narrative and by not even mentioning him in the original dedication of the film ('To Brandon Teena and Lisa Lambert'),[5] the filmmaker sacrifices the hard facts of racial hatred and transphobia to a streamlined humanist romance. Peirce, in other words, reduces the complexity of the murderous act just as she sacrifices the complexity of Brandon's identity.

The murders, in the end, are shown to be the result of a kind of homosexual panic. Brandon is offered up as an 'everyman' hero who makes a claim on the audience's sympathies first by pulling off a credible masculinity, but then by seeming to step out of his carefully maintained manhood to appear before judge and jury in the naked flesh as female. By reneging on its earlier commitment to the transgender gaze and ignoring altogether the possibility of exposing the whiteness of the male gaze, *Boys* falls far short of the alternative vision that was articulated so powerfully and shared so beautifully by Brandon and Lana in Lana's bedroom.

Notes

1   Patricia White has argued that the gaze in *Boys* in Lana's all along. I think in the first two thirds of the film the gaze is shared between Lana and Brandon, but I agree with White that the film's ending transfers the gaze from Brandon to Lana with some unpredictable consequences. See Patricia White, 'Girls still cry', *Screen*, vol. 42, no. 2 (2001), pp. 122–8. See Chapter 14 in this volume.

2   Kaja Silverman, 'Suture', in *The Subject of Semiotics* (New York: Oxford University Press, 1983), p. 236.

3   Interview with Terry Gross on Fresh Air, PBS Radio, 15 March 2000.

4   See Aphrodite Jones, *All S/he Wanted* (New York: Pocket Books, 1996), p. 154.

5   In the review copy of the film I saw, *Boys* was dedicated 'To Brandon Teena and Lisa Lambert'. This dedication seems to have been removed later on, possibly because it so obviously pointed up the erasure of Phillip DeVine.

16 The class character of *Boys Don't Cry*

Lisa Henderson

What might be the value of reading *Boys Don't Cry* (Kimberly Peirce, 1999) as a social class narrative? More to the point, how might we interpret the film as a story of transgender becoming and punishment in a representational field whose class idioms are conspicuously coherent? I pose this question to interrogate popular discourses of transgender experience, the meanings of class belonging and difference in the commercial media and, finally, the reciprocal mediations of transgender embodiment and working-class life.

Such themes are amplified in *Boys* by the film's roots in social reality, naturalizing or at least stabilizing its account of cultural locale and persona. Here, though, I want to emphasize the 'based on' rather than the 'true story', to signify the layered continuities between text and life from which *Boys* emerges as the most recent and probably the best known version of Brandon Teena's death and its preceding days.

Brandon Teena – the person – has been buffeted by various interlocutors and representations as alternately a young transman, a genetic girl, a tomboy, a teenage woman, a butch lesbian who passed as male in the absence of an affirming lesbian community, and as a universal subject who courageously sought to become his 'true self'. These are not just possibilities, however, but claims, and each carries different political weight. For me, Brandon was a young, female-bodied person who identified and passed as a man, and whose physical style and attraction to heterosexual girls and women were expressions and confirmations of his gender identity.[1] Whether and how Brandon might have further materialized his masculinity through hormone treatments or surgery had he the resources – and had he lived – is not clear.

In current parlance, Brandon was transgender, though to my knowledge that is not a term he used to describe himself. In threatening contexts (for example in the sheriff's recordings of investigative interviews following his rape, parts of which were adapted into the script of *Boys* and had been used earlier in the documentary film *The Brandon Teena Story* [Susan Muska and Gréta Olafsdóttir, 1998]), Brandon described himself in more clinical terms as having a 'sexual identity crisis'. It is uncertain, however, exactly what that meant to him or whether he might have used other phrases on other occasions.

In *Boys*, the terms of Brandon's gender identification are mixed. Brandon (Hilary Swank) regards himself as a boy, though sometimes even his self-descriptions shift for strategic reasons. Others see him as a boy, too – until they stop doing so, at which point he is at the mercy of their chaotic and hostile attributions. He finally becomes a transitional body made violently accountable to a gender binarism which permits no alternative embodiment or subjectivity, demanding instead that both one's body and claims about one's self conform to (born) male masculinity or (born) female femininity, and to heterosexuality as their normative counterpart. Brandon as character is not quite exposed and killed for being a dyke (though he is sometimes identified as one, which I shall discuss further below), but as a freak, a gender liar whose nerve in reporting his rape provokes the homicidal rage and fear of his attackers, men whose masculine excess and perilous homosocial bond Brandon had earlier sought to be included in.

Boys has unnerved me since its very first screening. Like many viewers, I have always known what to expect: Brandon's murder and the abjection, intimidation and violence that preceded it. But while most of the violence comes from those fictional others in the social world of the film, gender malevolence, I would argue, also comes from the film's plot, particularly the romantic recuperation of Brandon as Teena in a late (and short-lived) rendering of his and Lana's love affair as a lesbian relationship. This is particularly visible in the surprising, even perverse love scene that follows Brandon's rape. 'Were you a girly girl, like me?', Lana (Chloë Sevigny) asks Brandon, as he props himself up on one elbow and she gently removes his shirt and the Ace bandage strapping down his breasts. 'I don't know what to do', Lana continues. It is her first declaration of sexual inexperience (despite earlier love scenes), and thus becomes a self-conscious reference to the specifically lesbian sex Lana has never had but is about to, with Brandon as a girl. Maddeningly, the scene affirms what Brandon's rapists had imposed (while reclaiming him later as their 'little buddy') – that Brandon is female. While other moments of sex-gender uncertainty or even duplicity are contained by the plot (when, for example, in order to explain biographical inconsistencies and his illegally assumed identities, an incarcerated Brandon tells Lana he is a hermaphrodite), it is disturbing to watch Brandon be humanistically recovered by the script into a love that not-so-humanistically refuses the masculine gender he has struggled to become and for which, indeed, he is finally killed.

As Judith Halberstam has suggested, however, the conventional romantic style of the scene may work for those audiences who would prefer to receive *Boys* in its universalizing, promotional terms – as a tragic love story between two people (Lana, and especially Brandon) who sought personal truth, a gesture familiar or even necessary among commercial protagonists.[2] To be fair, first-time feature director Kimberly Peirce and her colleagues had a complicated artistic task in bringing history and licence to Brandon's volatile biography. But perhaps especially in fiction films based on true stories, licence is the cursed blessing that provokes ideological questions (and culturally telling answers) about events excluded and the terms and conditions of those retained. The most pointed exclusion in *Boys* is Phillip DeVine, the young, African-American man who had been dating Lisa Lambert (renamed Candace in the film) who was killed alongside Lisa and Brandon by John Lotter and Tom Nissen in Humboldt, Nebraska in 1993 (an exclusion Peirce troublingly referred to in a National Public Radio interview as a subplot she just had no room for). But also troubling for me, alongside the putatively 'lesbian' scene, is the extravagant coherence of the film's class-cultural overlay. In *Boys*, working-class life does not cause transphobic murder, but it does over-determine it in ways worth understanding more deeply.[3]

My reading of *Boys* through the lens of class representation is not born of a univocal search for so-called positive images, but I do recoil at what appears to me to be a new instalment in a long history of popular images of working-class pathology. Whatever may have been the layered circumstances of citizens in Falls City, Nebraska, in *Boys Don't Cry* everyone is trapped: by limited options in a limited place; by duplicity; by histories of violence and a lack of autonomy; by single motherhood; by numbing and underpaid work ('You don't have to be sober to weigh spinach', Lana tells Brandon); by drinking too much and thinking too little; by rosy, unrealistic images of the future; by a destructive impulsiveness and, in John's (Peter Sarsgaard) and Tom's (Brendan Sexton III) case, a murderous rage born of its own history of psychic, torture and incarceration. 'Cutting', Tom explains (displaying the self-inflicted knife wounds on his calf), 'snaps me back, lets me get a grip.'

None of these conditions is intrinsically the stuff of working-class life, and each might be as readily understood as a stereotype of some other social form, including youthful immaturity and self-destruction or a small-town, regional culture which imposes conformities at every turn. But dramatized together, such conditions become the very scaffolding of working-class sensibility in *Boys*, a gothic, elemental portrait of a dead-end community whose citizens are rarely able to act on their own behalf and which ends indeed in deadly events.[4]

My response to this image is not (I hope) liberal recuperation, an insistence upon a more noble portrait of thoughtful and hard-working people, among whom are a few crazy bad apples who wreak havoc and commit murder. The conditions which define life in *Boys* do exist and have provoked recognition for many viewers and critics, who (like me) might be more offended still by a 'condescending glamorizing' of working-class subversiveness amid the deprivations and cruelties of poverty, or by working-class images further burdened with the expectation of stoic grace.[5] But the underexplored gothic image, like its flipside narrative of class transcendence that so consoles both middle-class guilt and conservative social policy, erases the human complexity of how and why people act as they do – good or bad – in conditions of privation, exclusion and rage. In *Boys*, when Brandon shows a photograph of Lana to his cousin Lonny and asks 'isn't she pretty?', Lonny responds 'yeah, if you like trash'. It is a moment in which the film makes explicit what it has suggested from the first few frames – a bleak landscape populated by 'white trash' (whose racialization may partly explain why there was no room for DeVine as 'subplot'). As the story unfolds, events known from the historical record become outcomes predicted by class pathology, for an audience of cultural consumers perhaps too primed for such a judgement and too attracted by its gritty and exotic brand of realism.

But that is not the whole story. Within this universe of feeling and reaction structured by lack and tinted blue by country lyrics and a protective and threaten-ing night-time light, characters imbricate gender and class through their longings for love, acceptance and a better life. For Candace (Alicia Goranson) and Lana, Brandon's charm and attentiveness outweigh his ineptitude in such hypermasculine rituals as bar fights and bumper skiing. He is a different kind of man – radiant, beautiful, clear-skinned and clean, the promise of masculinity beside Tom and John, who stand instead as its scarred and mottled failures. They are condemned to prison and poverty while Brandon and Lana aspire to adventure and romantic escape, however unlikely their plan of paid karaoke. Brandon's gender passing, moreover, is anchored in a self-promoting tall tale of class status, with a father in oil and a sister in Hollywood – an erasure of his hustling and criminal evasions made plausible by his angular and unhardened, indeed his boyishly feminine, good looks. Even as Lana's mother (Jeanette Arnette) calls him over to hold and inspect his face more closely (while Brandon and the audience hold their breath), the judgement is splendour, not duplicity, though that judgement will not save him when his passing is discovered and his shame and vulnerability redoubled by gender and class exposure. Received by others as a young man, Brandon's 'pussy' mascu-linity embodies hope for romance and social mobility, and his careful observation of others' gender style becomes reflexively thoughtful, in contrast to John's brutal reactivity and Tom's copycat impotence. Exposed as a sex-gender trickster, however, those same qualities make him fair game for the violent re-enactment of normative gender difference and hierarchy.[6]

My interest in the articulations of class and gender in *Boys* and my anxiety about the film's supersaturated typifications of working-class fate speak to a re-entry into cultural studies of class belonging and representation. As Sally Munt has charted so clearly, cultural studies began with a leftist commitment to working-class inclusion and liberation, a commitment later challenged for its inattention to other axes of social difference and power.[7] But in the last fifteen years or so, class cultures have been pushed to the rearground even as class difference has continued to operate and to make itself felt. Thus, as a cultural studies of class renews itself, it does so conscious not only of the historical fixities of class position and the persistence of exploitation and struggle, but also of the complex trajectories of class location and identity that can occur within the life of even one person. 'We tend now', writes Cora Kaplan, 'to think of class consciousness past and present more polymorphously and perversely: its desires, its object choices, and its antagonisms are neither so straightforward nor so singular as they once seemed.'[8] Here, Kaplan articulates the form of class analysis to which my comments on *Boys* respond, an analysis that not only connects class to (trans)gender and sexuality but also expresses the complexity and recursiveness of the category and its variants. Class cultures are produced, not least by popular representations, and complexly so, in contexts where class life is sometimes central, sometimes not, structured and structuring in critical but incomplete ways. Pressed to identify the primary representational and political terms of *Boys*, I would call the film a transgender story. Pressing further to the layered relations of any such social category takes me to the film's class character.

Thanks to Jackie Stacey and Regna Kunzel for their helpful comments.

Notes

1 The question of where Brandon's sexed body begins and ends is difficult. My description comes largely from Jay Prosser, *Second Skins: the Body Narratives of Transsexuality* (New York: Columbia, 1998), p. 175, though to call Brandon 'female-bodied' sets aside the ways in which his masculinity is indeed felt in and written on his body. Prosser, however, locates material embodiment more centrally in chemical and surgical transsexuality. His discussion of Venus Xtravaganza (pp. 45–50), a pre-operative transsexual woman featured in *Paris is Burning* (Jennie Livingston, 1990), also addresses relations between the 'corporeal materiality' of Venus's sexed and raced body and the 'social materialism' of her class position (p. 50).

2 Judith Halberstam, 'The Brandon Teena archives', public lecture at the John Sims Center for the Arts, San Francisco, 10 February 2001.

3 It is difficult to use the phrase 'working class' to describe the characters in *Boys* without affirming the film's class caricature. But some of the characters are portrayed working in blue-collar jobs (while others are apparently unemployed, though the narrative does not quite confirm that one way or the other), and for this and other reasons, the term is apt. To withhold it, moreover, as a challenge to the film's image of class pathology, would inadvertently endorse the distinction between 'deserving' and 'undeserving' working-class or poor people – a distinction I want to up-end in a more critical analysis of class representation.

4 For example, when the sheriff in *Boys* suggests to Lana and her mother that everyone will be better off if Brandon just leaves town following his 'alleged' rape by John and Tom, Lana quickly responds that everyone would be better off in fact if the sheriff were to lock up John and Tom. It is a wise retort, which expresses what characters and the audience know but what Lana and others are powerless to resist: that John and Tom are violently out of control.

5 The phrase 'condescending glamorizing' comes from Sally Munt, 'Introduction', in Sally Munt (ed.), *Cultural Studies and the Working Class: Subject to Change* (London and New York: Cassell, 2000), p. 12. In North America it is significant that with a few religious exceptions, poverty is most noble in the eyes of those who are not (or are

no longer) poor. With the pain and corrosion of poverty set aside, a poor background can make for noble material indeed if a person moves into (or becomes eligible for) a position of considerable status and authority, for example in cabinet and Supreme Court confirmation hearings. In truth, I think there is human nobility in surviving poverty, and millions of people routinely do so in the USA alone, without ever becoming cabinet ministers or Supreme Court justices. But when popular discourses are not condemning poverty as a personal rather than social failure, they tend to redeem it with attributions of noble modesty. Such an equation says little about poverty or inequality, I would argue, though much about the representational authority of privilege.

6   Brandon is also exposed for car theft and bad cheques, but he is punished for gender, not cheque fraud. The criminal proceedings do lead to his exposure, however, and justify the accusation that he brought his fate on himself as a 'liar'. But here, too, the lie that counts is the judged disparity between his 'female' body and masculine gender identification.

7   Munt, *Cultural Studies and the Working Class*.

8   Cora Kaplan, 'Millennial class'. Introduction to a special issue, 'Re-reading class', *PMLA Journal*, vol. 115, no. 1 (2000), p. 13.

17   Boyz do cry: screening history's white lies

Jennifer Devere Brody

For Western Modernity – which one can date from the peculiar coincidence of Enlightenment thought and the ambitious pursuit of trade in and enslavement of Africans and African Americans – the scopic is the preeminent cultural matrix of power.[1]

In the special *Screen* debate on the film *Boys Don't Cry* (Kimberly Peirce, 1999), Michele Aaron's essay 'Pass/fail'[2] focuses on how the film hails spectators to view its queer, open-ended narrative, and Julianne Pidduck's reading[3] looks at the 'distortions of allegiances' in such interpellations. This essay investigates that which spectators cannot possibly interpret: the unseen black man at the original event upon which the film is based, Phillip DeVine. This paper, like Pidduck's, reads extra-diegetically in order to question the aesthetic pleasures offered by this fictive version of a factual case. Whereas Pidduck suggests that aesthetics cannot wholly replace ethics, I shall argue that they are inseparable. For me, the inextricability of ethics and aesthetics is demonstrated in the way in which the production of a pure white queer subjectivity in this film is achieved through the excision of black humanity. In this reading of Kimberly Peirce's first feature, *Boys Don't Cry* (1999), I am interested in thinking about the 'negative' space of the film; indeed, about material so absent it never even appeared on the cutting-room floor. My evidence for this argument comes from reading the documents of Brandon Teena/Teena Brandon's life-story, studying the rhetoric used in interviews with the director, and finally, looking broadly at the white lies screened in film history.

Reporter Aphrodite Jones's written account of the Brandon Teena tale, *All That She Wanted*, was the first packaged version of Brandon's story for popular consumption.[4] The epigraph Jones selected for the project is: 'We fix our eyes not on what is seen but what is unseen. For what is seen is temporary but what is unseen is eternal' (2 Corinthians 4:17). This biblical reference recalls James Baldwin's riff in his book about the Atlanta child murders, *The Evidence of Things Not Seen*, which suggests that, 'What we do not remember holds the key to who we are.'[5] It was Jones's account that introduced me not only to Brandon Teena, her killers, and her bevy of girlfriends, but also to an apparent interloper: a young black man named Phillip DeVine.

Boys Don't Cry is emblematic of the way in which the radical erasure of blackness makes queer stories queerer. This erasure is all the more problematic because it suggests that visual media in particular follow the trajectory of western modernity that is itself a screen which seeks too often either to efface or exploit difference. Visuality has increasingly become the way in which we know the history of the world (we need only think of the televising of the destruction of the World Trade Centre on 11 September 2001). Focusing on how history is screened in conjunction with history's screenings suggests that such historical translations themselves hide from view other aspects of historical narratives. This chapter focuses on this disjunction between memory and history by posing the following question: what is it about the historical erasure of blackness that appears to make some queer texts queerer? In short, I examine how the white forms of queerness are achieved in the film *Boys Don't Cry*.

The reportage about Teena Brandon/Brandon Teena presents a case of rural violence and early death, and a powerful example of the struggle with normativity. The less acclaimed documentary by Susan Muska and Gréta Olafsdóttir, *The Brandon Teena Story* (1998), is in my view both more ethical and perhaps even more experimental in its telling than is its successor, *Boys Don't Cry*. Contrary to the critic who referred to the film's 'macabre sensationalism and dutiful prosaics',[6] I found the documentary surprisingly compelling, at least in its initial moments. Indeed, *Boys Don't Cry* echoes many aspects of the documentary: the establishing shots of Falls City, the use of superfast photography, and the predominantly country music soundtrack. However, the major difference (besides the *de rigueur* use of talking heads) is the documentary's inclusion of DeVine. It begins with the sound of three shots fired. Then, three snapshots follow – of Brandon, Lisa and Phillip respectively.

The trilogy of sound and images is repeated throughout the film, almost as a *leitmotif*. Unlike *Boys Don't Cry*, *The Brandon Teena Story* documentary begins and ends with the memory of all three victims. There is an attempt to fill in the gaps in DeVine's story. Similarly, the book based on Brandon includes several pictures of DeVine, not to mention a chapter devoted to his life story. But in *Boys Don't Cry* there are only two victims, not three. In this respect, the documentary attends to the role of race as well as class, gender and sexuality. It mentions that there were a few black families in town but no gays. This reading of 'minority' positions is reversed in *Boys Don't Cry*, where there is the mention of gays but no blacks or other people of colour.

Boys Don't Cry reminds us of the violence of removal (and I use this word explicitly because it refers to the Plains Indians of Nebraska mentioned in both the book and the documentary but not the film). As James Snead has argued: 'Omission and exclusion are perhaps the most widespread tactics of racial stereotyping but also the most difficult to prove because their manifestation is precisely absence itself.'[7] Moreover, he suggests that 'since framing, editing, and cutting out are indeed the exigencies of filmic and aesthetic practice, it was possible to hide the ideologically motivated distortions under the mask of artistic economy or exigency'.[8]

Although Snead cites these practices in relation to films of the 1930s and 1940s, his argument applies equally well to the processes of exclusion in *Boys Don't Cry*: the total excision of the black body of Phillip DeVine. The troubling presence (what is a straight black boy doing in a queer story anyway?) of the disabled DeVine (his mother took the drug DES which caused him to need to wear a prosthesis) is relegated to a predetermined absence: what Sharon Holland names 'the space of the dead'.[9]

Here I agree with Pidduck's conclusion that we must be wary of revelling too much in the pleasures of a text for which 'the notion of life and death as "haunting" the frame of entertainment' instead insists upon a limit to our pleasure.[10] Thus, I place *Boys Don't Cry* in the emerging tradition identified by Amy Villerejo and others as 'the new queer cinema'.[11] This new genre/movement proffers a 'post-Stonewall repertoire of images which are mainly white, highly commodifiable to mainstream audiences and anchored in rights-based discourses of political activism'.[12] The overbearing whiteness of this cinema, of which *Boys Don't Cry* is a prime example, relies upon the erasure of blackness. Nothing is included in the film to mark DeVine's death. He is not represented in the printed white letters on an otherwise blank black screen at the end of the film which commemorate the others' lives. DeVine's story is absented from the film: his life and his devastating and tragic death do not merit attention. Where Peirce had an opportunity, if not an obligation, to record the real confluence of racism, classism, misogyny, transgender discrimination and homophobia, she chose instead to ignore the racist issues at stake in this story.

In her reading of the film, Pidduck includes a snippet of dialogue between Brandon and Lana. The two discuss Brandon's decision to participate in the violent 'redneck' ritual that results in his being 'tied to the back of a truck and [being] dragged like a dog'. This conversation screens a reference to an event, utterly current at the time of the film, in which a black man, James Byrd, was dragged to his death in Jasper, Texas, in what many consider to be a lynching. In this sense, Peirce participates, however unwittingly, in a larger pattern of leaving race out of the picture so that other identity categories appear stable and queerness is represented in a way that makes it synonymous with whiteness.

In the film's journey to becoming a classic 'boy' meets girl, 'Romeo and Juliet' story (the latter reference comes directly from director Peirce herself), it actively forgets other complicating, seemingly extraneous material. In interviews, Peirce cites dramas such as *Oedipus Rex* and *Romeo and Juliet* as well as the film *Titanic*, as sources for her production. More specifically, she credits Aristotle's ideas about 'organic unity [which] throws out anything that's not necessary because if it's not necessary you're detracting from the whole' as a major influence on her aesthetic practice.[13] When asked about the facts of the case, she explained that she had jettisoned a thesis about Pauline Cushman, an African-American woman who passed as a white man during the Civil War, in favour of making a film about Teena Brandon. Referring to the decisions involved in making the film, Peirce explains that:

> The story is completely fact based (streamlined slightly for the sake of telling but not altered or Disneyfied). I never really look at them as 'the facts' of the case, because for most people, there were very few facts and for me there were five-and-a-half years of facts. If you think about what the facts were for me, they were the whole interview [of Brandon] with the sheriff to talk about John Lotter, they were Lotter's entire life, they were Brandon's entire life, they were Lana's entire life. When you say stray from the facts, here's the movie [Peirce draws a diagram of a small square on a piece of notebook paper] and then here's what happened [Peirce draws an enormous rectangle around the small square]. So it's interesting when people say, 'What did you change?' Well, you can't look at it that way. Here I was, trying to find the underlying emotional truth and from that, [points to the rectangle] I told one story that attracted me, the tragic events which were motivated by his passing as a boy. Then, what I had to do was yank-yank-yank-yank. Basically, I had to focus on what I call privileged events.[14]

In this lengthy interview, Peirce takes pains to explain her labour in reviving Brandon's story so that, 'Suddenly, it's alive.' Peirce's account of the process, her adherence to classical aesthetics, makes her choice to leave DeVine out of the story at first seem benign – his death just detracted from the main thrust of the story; it was, literally in Peirce's graphic rendering on paper, extraneous, unnecessary, eccentric. On a second reading, Peirce's rhetoric, in word, gesture and deed, makes it seem as if at least two black bodies had to die in order for Teena Brandon/Brandon Teena to live in art.

The narrative Peirce relays parallels a larger narrative about the origins of queer history. As Scott Bravermann discusses in his book, *Queer Fictions of the Past: History, Culture and Difference*, the quintessential origin story of queer figures roots the queer past in Ancient Greece. In his chapter 'It's Greek to whom?', he 'seeks to problematize the racialized history of white queers that positions them differently from black gays and lesbians'.[15] Bravermann's reading of this invented tradition of a classical past gives us a critical genealogy that we can use to rethink the genesis of Peirce's film. This account of the film's 'birth' contrasts with court documents about the deaths, which it names as executions, bringing up the issue of *res gestae*. '*Res Gestae* means that even if the object of the felony is technically over, if the later events occur in such close proximity to the original felony, then it's all part of one transaction.'[16] As the court transcript records:

> Even if we've got felony murder of Teena Brandon, what about Lisa Lambert and Phillip DeVine? These are executions. They are assassinations. And they tell a lot about the intent of the people when they walked in the door. These aren't just wild shots that happened to hit someone . . . these are calculated executions. . . . Consider Phillip DeVine. If you can, imagine the terror of Phillip DeVine sitting in that room, this young amputee, sitting in the other room listening to two people die and knowing – he had to know he was . . . he was next.[17]

What the court transcript reminds us of here is the alignment between crimes of race, class, sexuality and gender.

Given the time Peirce spent attending the trial and visiting the crime scene, her decision not to include DeVine in *Boys* is disturbing. She explains the import of travelling to Falls City with gender activist and writer Kate Bornstein as follows:

> To me it was important to see the blood on the floor, the holes in the wall, to be sitting there at the epicentre of the pain. . . . As a director, it was important for me to sit there and to see . . . 'How long did it take to get from the road to the farmhouse? What does it feel like to go over those wooden steps?' . . . Then you can ask yourself all those dramatic questions: 'Well, who was shot first?' 'Why didn't Brandon go out the window?' and 'What's this place like in the dark?'[18]

Obviously from this well-documented testimony, Peirce was not ignorant of DeVine's presence at the scene of the crime. So why did she choose to reposition him from his marginal place in the other room to the space of the dead? Perhaps one can only speculate about the motivations behind this decision. But the effects are familiar ones in the history of racist representations: the erasure of DeVine from the narrative places the white female bodies as the only true victims of crime: and the film's inability to show DeVine as violated rather than violator perpetuates the myth of the black man as always already a perpetrator of crime. Perhaps it was seen as impossible to read an image of a straight middle-class black male with a white girlfriend as an image of 'innocent' tragedy, particularly in the outlaw story that is Brandon's.

The Global Transgendering Site compiled by Susan Stryker has a link called 'Remembering Our Dead' which begins with George Santayana's line: 'Those who cannot remember the past are doomed to repeat it.'[19] In translating a version of the past into a cinematic narrative, it is as important to analyse how we forget as it is to discuss what we remember. Peirce's film concludes with a white light, fading to a white screen, a slow pan over a dead body and the voiceover of Brandon reading his last love letter to Lana as she drives away down the highway. The choice to idealize and romanticize the main 'couple' in the film is a traditional move. Instead of showing the connections between and among race, class, gender and sexuality by stressing actual alliances with othered others, Peirce chooses to play to target audiences' assumed prejudices and market patterns of identification by making otherwise odious characters palatable through proximity to the normative. Ironically, perhaps, the rebellious gender outlaw Brandon is romanticized in contrast to the middle-class, normative (except for race and able-bodiedness) college student, Phillip.

If nations are tied to hagiography, what can we say about a queer nation whose mediated martyrs are overwhelmingly white (think of Rock Hudson, Matthew Shepard, Brandon Teena)? What of Arthur Warren Junior and the numerous faceless, nameless others who also have died violent deaths but without ceremony? In whose national sociopolitical historical memory will these forgotten dead be housed? Are we indeed living out a fantasy in which our 'historical memory of slavery tends toward amnesia'?[20] As Judith Halberstam notes:

> Radical interventions come from careful consideration of racial and class constructions of sexual identities . . . from consideration of the politics of mobility outlined by the potent prefix 'trans' . . . Butches and FTM's alike need to think carefully about the kinds of men or masculine beings that we become and lay claim to. . . . Alternative masculinities ultimately will fail to change existing gender hierarchies to the extent to which they fail to be feminist, anti-racist and queer.[21]

Boys Don't Cry made Hollywood history but it failed to produce an ethical history, owing much of its success to a film history in which white lies have continued to illuminate black screens.

Notes

1 Lindon Barrett, *Seeing Double: Blackness and Value* (Cambridge: Cambridge University Press, 1997), p. 218.

2 Michele Aaron, 'Pass/fail', *Screen*, vol. 42, no. 1 (2001), pp. 92–6. See Chapter 12 in this volume.

3 Julianne Pidduck, 'Risk and queer spectatorship', *Screen*, vol. 42, no. 2 (2001), pp. 97–102. See Chapter 13 in this volume.

4 Aphrodite Jones, *All She Wanted* (New York: Pocket Books, 1996).

5 James Baldwin, *The Evidence of Things Not Seen* (New York: Henry Holt, 1987). One might compare the differences in these cases in useful ways. For example, numerous black children, mostly young boys, were murdered in the case and a 'gay' black male was accused of and tried for the crime.

6   Danny Leigh, 'Boy wonder'. *Sight and Sound* (March 2000), p. 18.

7   James Snead, *White Screens/Black Images:Hollywood from the Dark Side* (New York: Routledge, 1994), p. 16.

8   Ibid., p. 7.

9   Sharon Holland, *Raising the Dead: Readings of Death and (Black) Subjectivity in American Culture* (Durham, NC: Duke University Press, 2000), p. 4.

10 Pidduck, 'Risk and queer spectatorship', p. 102.

11 Amy Villerejo, 'Forbidden love: pulp as lesbian history', in Ellis Hanson (ed.), *Out Takes: Essays on Queer Theory and Film* (Durham, NC: Duke University Press, 1999), p. 331.

12 Cynthia Amsden, 'On screen preview: *Boys Don't Cry* opens Feb. 18 at the Princess II', *SEE Magazine* (online version) 2000.

13 Kimberly Peirce quoted in Gretchen Lee, 'Passing attraction', *Curve*, vol. 10, no. 1 (2000), p. 16.

14 Ibid.

15 Scott Bravermann, *Fictions of the Queer Past: History, Culture and Difference* (Cambridge: Cambridge University Press, 1997), p. 48.

16 Amsden, 'On screen preview'.

17 From the closing statement of the trial: http://www.foxsearchlight.com/boysdon'tcry/trial2.html.

18 Ibid.

19 *Remembering Our Dead*: http://www.glbhistory.org.html.

20 Eric Foner, 'How the desire for profit led to the invention of race', *London Review of Books*, 4 February 1999, p. 4.

21 Judith Halberstam, *Female Masculinity* (Durham, NC: Duke University Press, 1998), p. 173.

Index

Pages containing relevant illustrations are indicated in *italic* type.

2001: A Space Odyssey (Clarke) 60–1
2001: A Space Odyssey (Kubrick) 10, 55–66, 76–7; narcissism 58–9, 63–5; paranoia 57–8, 65–6

Aaron, Michele 7, 259–64, 265–6, 269, 289
abjection 88–90, 92–4, 100, 231
adaptations, film 183–5, 191, *192*, *193*, 195, 199–200, 202
Adorno, Theodor 65, 232
aesthetics 289, 292
AIDS activism 1, 3, 8, 168, 209
Aimee and Jaguar (Fischer) 148
Alarcón, Norma 31–2
Albertian perspective 214–15, 218, 228
Alien Resurrection (Jeunet) 10, 80–101; abjection 88–9, 92–4; cellular mutations 82–4, 86; homoeroticism 95–100
allegiances 265, 269–70
Almodóvar, Pedro 10, 57, 67–8; *see also Law of Desire* (Almodóvar)
alternative cinema 24–6, 30
anachronism 227
androgyny 95, 237, 249, 252, 265
angels 155, 157, 159
'Angry Young Men' 44–5
Arendt, Hannah 149
art cinema 4, 22, 24
art history 13, 208–12; *see also Caravaggio* (Jarman)
Asian gay men 166–7, 172–6
auteurity 183–4; *see also* authorship

authorship 41–51; female 243; Gay Authorship 42; gay writers 45–7; and identity 50–1; *see also* auteurity
autobiographical film 168; *see also* autoethnography; self-portraits
autoethnography 167–9; *see also Chinese Characters* (Fung); *My Mother's Place* (Fung)
availability of queer cinema 4–5

Baldwin, James 289–90
Bananarama 244
Barnes, Djuna 272, 276
Barrett, Lindon 289
Barthes, Roland 41, 50, 225, 266
Basic Instinct (Vergoeven) 6
Battaglia, Debbora 80, 90
Bauman, Zygmunt 156
Beheading of John the Baptist (Caravaggio) 213
Beloved: a Novel (Morrison) 162n30
Benglis, Lynda *240*
Benítez-Rojo, Antonio 177
Benjamin, Walter 219, 225, 228; history 31, 162n31, 210, 213; *Trauerspiel* 216, 230
Benning, Sadie 169
Benshoff, Harry 7
Beristain, Gabriel 215
Bersani, Leo 209, 218
Bhabha, Homi 150, 153–4, 163, 167, 171, 175
biographies 46, 48, 209–12, 223; *see also* autobiographical film; documentaries

bi-sexed figures 237, 249, 251–2, 254; *see also* She-men

bitter-sweet 47–8

blackness, erasure of 290–1, 293; *see also* race

Black Widow (Rafelson) 34–6

bodies: *Boys Don't Cry* 261, 269; *Caravaggio* 218–20, 230; 'female-bodied' 283, 287n1; She-men 236–9, 242–4, 248–9; *see also* body horror films; corpses; queer male bodies

body horror films 80–1, 88–90, 92, 100–1; *see also* horror films

Borden, Lizzie 26–7

bottoms 166, 174–5

Bound (Wachowski and Wachowski) 5, 11, 106–22; chromatic design 115–16, 119–21; editing techniques 113–14, 117–18; opening sequence 106–7, 114–15

Bowie, David 247–8

Boy Bitten By a Lizard (Caravaggio) 211

Boys Don't Cry (Peirce) 13–14, 259–95; class 283–7; crossdressing 259–63; girl viewers 273–6; race 289–95; road movies 265–9; transgender gaze 278–82

Boys Keep Swinging (Bowie) 247

Braidotti, Rosi 82–3

Brandon, Teena *see* Teena, Brandon

Brandon Teena Story, The (Muska and Olafsdóttir) 13, 266, 271n10, 276n3, 290

Brassard, Marie 184, 190, 192, *193*, 196

Bravermann, Scott 292

Brief Encounter (Lean) 7, 42–51; bitter-sweet 47–8; essentialism and social constructionism 49–51; gay writers 45–7

British film culture 43–4

Brooks, Xan 262–3

butch and femme 110, 112, 118, 121, 254; *see also* Medusan femmes; phallic femmes

Butler, Judith 93–4, 166–7, 200–1

Byrd, James 291

camp 50, 67–8, 76, 227–8

Canada 176–7, 204; Québec 184–7, 191, 196–9, 206n30

capitalism 126, 140, 143

captivity narratives 133, 139

Caravaggio (Jarman) 209–235; anachronism 227; desire 221–3, 229–30; Medusa 231–2; Michelangelo da Caravaggio 209–15; space 218–19; tableaux vivants 215–17

Caravaggio, Michelangelo da 208–11; self-portraits 211–13; studio space 213–15; *see also Caravaggio* (Jarman)

Caribbean 176–7

Certeau, Michel de 212

Chaiken, Irene 5

Chasseguet-Smirgel, Janine 61

Chinese Characters (Fung) 165–6, 172–6, 246, *247*, 248

chromatic design 115–16, 119–21, 196

Civil Rights Movement 14n2, 134

Cixous, Hélène 231, 242

Clarke, Arthur 60–1

class 267–8, 283, 285–7, 293–4

Clay, Catrine 148; *see also Love Story* (Clay)

Clift, Montgomery 190

cloning 80–6; and abjection 89–90; and homosexuality 96, 98; in science fiction films 87–8

closets 106–8, 115, 190

Clouzot, Henri-Georges 229

Cocteau, Jean 72, 74–5

collaboration 147, 149

colonialism 12, 150, 163–5, 168–9, 171, 175–7; *see also* decolonization; imperialism

comedies, crossdressing 259–60, 263

coming out 98

coming-to-terms-with-the-past (*Vergangenheitsbewältigung*) 154–5, 159

Communards 256n18

Constable, Catherine 90–3, 95, 101

contact zones 176

Copjec, Joan 210

corpses 185, 201, 229–30

Coward, Noël 42, 44–6

Creed, Barbara 88–90

crossdressing 236–7, 239, 252–3, 259–63, 266; *see also* transvestism

Cry and Be Free (Marilyn) 251, 252

crystal-images 183, 190, 192, 204

cultural exchange 126, 132, 139–40, 142, 144

cyborgs 10, 98

Czerniakow, Adam 156

Daniels, Don 58, 60
Dargis, Manohla 267
David, Jacques-Louis 228
David with the Head of Goliath
   (Caravaggio) 213, 217
Davis, Douglas 245
Dead or Alive 249, *250*, 251
Death of Marat (David) 228
decolonization 30, 169; *see also* colonialism
Deleuze, Gilles 183, 190, 204, 229
deniability of homosexuality 112
Derrida, Jacques 167, 225, 231
Desert Hearts (Deitch) 25–6
Design For Living (Coward) 45–6
desire(s) 4, 9; *Alien Resurrection* 95, 98; *Boys
   Don't Cry* 272–3; *Caravaggio* 210, 213,
   221–3, 226, 229–30; *Johanna D'Arc of
   Mongolia* 138; *Law of Desire* 72–4, 76–7
Desperately Seeking Susan (Seidelman) 35–6
Des Pres, Terence 149
Devere Brody, Jennifer 289–95
DeVine, Phillip 275, 281, 285–6, 289–94
Dickinson, Peter 12, 183–207; *La Face
   Cachée de la Lune* 202–4; *Le Confessionnal*
   184–90; *Le Polygraphe* 190–5; *Nô* 195–9;
   Possible Worlds 199–202
Dijck, José van 87
disidentification 164, 172, 175
Divine 247, *248*, 249, 252
Doane, Mary Ann 88, 241, 252
documentaries: autoethnography 168,
   171–2, 176; *The Brandon Teena Story* 13,
   266, 271n10, 276n3, 290; *Love Story*
   148–51, 154
drag 164, 237, 240, 247–8, 256n19; *see also*
   crossdressing; transvestism
Dunye, Cheryl 12
Durgnat, Raymond 43–5
Dutoit, Ulysse 209, 218
Dyer, Richard 7, 17n26, 47–8, 143, 173,
   236

editing techniques 113–14, 117–18, 220–1
Edward II (Jarman) 6
empire 164–5, 176–7; *see also* colonialism;
   imperialism
Erhart, Julia 11, 146–62; *Love Story* 148;
   resistance 149–50;
   Vergangenheitsbewältigung (coming-to-
   terms-with-the-past) 154–5, 159

essentialism 42, 49–51, 260
ethics 289, 294
ethnic differences 135; *see also* race
ethnocentric conceit 173
ethnographic film conventions 132, 141–2,
   167
ethnography 166–8; *see also Chinese Characters*
   (Fung); *My Mother's Place* (Fung)
Evidence of Things Not Seen, The (Baldwin)
   289
excessive sameness 81, 89, 92, 98, 100–1
exhibitionism 237, 244
Extremities (Young) 32

Fanon, Frantz 12
Felman, Shoshana 158
female desire 272–3
female gaze 279–80
female sexuality 236, 238–43, 252–4
femininity 139–41, 150, 236, 240–1, 269
feminism 9, 13, 31–4; and authorship 50;
   and female sexuality 239–40; and film
   spectatorship 273; and girls 276; and
   Holocaust film 147, 149; and monsters
   80–1; and paranoia 57; post- 241; *see also*
   women; women's cinema
femme and butch 110, 112, 118, 121, 254;
   see also Medusan femmes; phallic femmes
fetishism 150, 154, 273
fetishized spectacles 141
film adaptations 183–5, 191, *192*, *193*, 195,
   199–200, 202
fingers 109–11, 114, 116
Finley, Karen 254
Fischer, Erica 148
Five Last Days (Adlon) 160n7
Flames of Passion (Kwietniowski) 7, 17n24,
   42
flashbacks 117
Ford, John 133; *see also Searchers, The* (Ford)
foreknowledge 155–6
Foucault, Michel 205n16, 212, 218, 220
Freud, Sigmund 57, 61–2, 65–7; *see also*
   psychoanalysis
Fried, Michael 211–12
Friedlaender, Walter 215
Frith, Simon 244
Fung, Richard 12, 163–8, 246, *247*;
   see also Chinese Characters (Fung);
   My Mother's Place (Fung)

Fung, Rita 169–71
Fusco, Coco 21–2

Garrity, Henry A. 183, 190
gay male bodies 205n5; *see also* queer male
    bodies
gay male culture 173, 176
gay male pornography 166–7, 172–5
'gay sensibility' 49
gay writers 45–7; *see also* authorship
gaze, transgender 278–82
gender 200–1, 259–62, 269, 284, 286,
    288n6, 293–4; *see also* transgender
generic conventionality 10–11, 92;
    see also genres, conflation of
genetic engineering 80–5, 87–9, 100
genres, conflation of: lesbian love stories
    and history films 154; thrillers and
    romances 112, 115–16, 120–2;
    travelogues and ethnographic films 127;
    Westerns and travelogues 133
Germany 11, 146, 156; *see also November
    Moon* (von Grote)
Getino, Octavio 24–5, 30
Gilliatt, Penelope 58
Girard, René 221, 226–7
girls 273–6
Goldstein, Richard 243–4
Gottlieb, Roger 149–50
Great Expectations (Lean) 44–5
Greyson, John *246, 249*
Griffin, Sean 7
Grisham, Therese 125, 132
Grosz, Elizabeth 80
Grote, Alexandra von 146; *see also November
    Moon* (von Grote)
guerrilla cinema 24, 30–1

HAL 57–60, 62–6, 76–7
Halberstam, Judith 278–82, 284, 294
Hall, Sir Peter 41, 46
Hall, Stuart 169
Hallam, Paul 50
Hanson, Ellis 4, 10, 55–79; *Bound* 107–8;
    desire in *Law of Desire* 72–4, 76–7;
    disembodied voices in *Law of Desire*
    69–71; narcissism in *2001: A Space
    Odyssey* 58–9, 63–5; paranoia in *2001: A
    Space Odyssey* 57–8, 65–6
Haraway, Donna 58, 87

Hartman, Geoffrey 217
Hayles, Catherine 99
Henderson, Lisa 283–8
Hennegan, Alison 48
heteronormativity 7, 10, 12, 187, 195, 198,
    279
heterosexuality 47, 95–6, 152–3, 100, 278
Heung, Marina 35
Hibbard, Howard 226
Hilberg, Raul 149
Hine, Daryl 231–2
history 31, 154; *Boys Don't Cry* 290, 294;
    Caravaggio 13, 209–10, 213, 218, 227,
    230; *November Moon* 147, 162n31; queer
    292
Hitchcock, Alfred 186; *see also I Confess*
    (Hitchcock); *Rope* (Hitchcock)
Holland, Sharon 291
Hollywood production code 112–13
Holocaust film 146; *see also November Moon*
    (von Grote)
home movies 170–1
homoeroticism 10, 95–100
homosexuality: cinematic representations of
    112–13; and closets 106–8; and
    government 232n11; male homosexual
    structure of feeling 47; and narcissism
    58–9; and paranoia 57; and political
    correctness 148; as social construction
    49, 51; *see also* gay male culture;
    homoeroticism; lesbianism; lesbians;
    queer male bodies
homosociality 262, 284
hooks, bell 50, 143
horror films 56, 62; body 80–1, 88–90, 92,
    100–1
humanism 281
Human Voice, The (Cocteau) 72, 74–5
hybridity 12, 164–6, 169–70, 177

I Confess (Hitchcock) 186–7, 189–90
identity 50–1, 91, 94, 97, 110–11; gender
    259–61; and hybridity 164–5, 169, 177;
    and mirrors 212; national 12–13, 136,
    185, 187; politics 15n5, 168, 209; racial
    126
imperialism 126, 128, 132, 137; *see also*
    colonialism
independent film and video 5, 30
indeterminacy 4, 10, 106

Interior Scroll (Schneemann) 241, *242*
international film festivals 3
interracial and inter-ethnic romances 154–5
Irigaray, Luce 242–3
I've Heard the Mermaids Singing (Rozema)
    32–4

Jagged Edge, The (Marquand) 32
Jameson, Fredric 166
Jarman, Derek 3, 6, 13, 209; *see also*
    Caravaggio (Jarman)
Jeunet, Jean-Pierre 81; *see also Alien*
    Resurrection
Johanna d'Arc of Mongolia (Ottinger) 11,
    125–44; racialized spectacle 126–7, 130,
    132–3, 137–44; and *The Searchers* 133–8
Johnston, Claire 29
Jones, Aphrodite 289–90

Kael, Pauline 58, 68
Kalin, Tom 4
Kaplan, Cora 286–7
Kember, Sarah 87
Kipling Trilogy: Perils of Pedagogy (Greyson)
    246, 248, *249*
Kiss of the Spider Woman (Babenco) 25–6
knowledge of Nazi genocide 155–7
Kosofsky Sedgwick, Eve 107–8, 164
Krauss, Rosalind 245
Kristeva, Julia 62, 88–9
Kubrick, Stanley 10, 55–6, 58; *see also*
    2001: A Space Odyssey (Kubrick)
Kuhn, Annette 260
Kwietniowski, Richard 7, 42

La Face Cachée de la Lune (Lepage) 202–4
Lambert, Lisa 275, 281, 285, 293
Landy, Marcia 154
Lane, Jim 168
Lanzmann, Claude 155, 158
Last of England, The (Jarman) 228, 230
Latour, Bruno 165
Laura (Preminger) 122n7
Lauretis, Teresa de 9, 21–40; alternative
    cinema 24–6, 30; guerrilla cinema 30–1;
    She Must Be Seeing Things 36–9; *Working*
    Girls 26–9
Law of Desire (Almodóvar) 10, 57, 66–77,
    237; desire 72–4, 76–7; disembodied
    voices in 69–71; reviews of 68

Lean, David 7, 42, 44–5
Le Confessionnal (Lepage) 12, 184–90, 194,
    203
Lefebvre, Martin 185
Lehman, Peter 236
Lejeune, C.A. 44
Le Mystère Picasso / The Picasso Mystery
    (Clouzot) 229
Lennox, Annie *253*, 254
Lepage, Robert 12, 183; *see also La Face*
    Cachée de la Lune; *Le Confessionnal*; *Le*
    Polygraphe; *Nô*; *Possible Worlds*; *Seven*
    Streams of the River Ota, The
Le Polygraphe (Lepage) 190–5
lesbian and gay movements 2
lesbianism: *Boys Don't Cry* 281, 284; and
    desire 95, 98, 138; *She Must Be Seeing*
    Things 38; theme of 32–4, 36; visibility of
    147, 154; *see also Bound* (Wachowski and
    Wachowski)
lesbians 15n15, 146, 254
Lewis, Lisa 243
Lindee, Susan 87
lining up 164, 170–1
Lionnet, Françoise 167, 170
Loiselle, André 185
Longfellow, Brenda 11, 125, 127, 138
Lorde, Audre 29
Love Story (Clay) 148–51, 154–5
Lowe, Lisa 175
Lundin, Michael 99
L Word, The (Chaiken) 5
Lyotard, Jean-François 216
lyricists, gay 47

McGann, Jerome 232
McLaughlin, Sheila 4, 30, 36–7; *see also*
    She Must Be Seeing Things (McLaughlin)
Madonna 253
mainstream cinema 5–6, 13, 25–8
male gaze 279, 282
male homosexual structure of feeling 47
male sexuality 236
Manvell, Roger 43–4
Marilyn 251, 252
Martyrdom of St Matthew, The
    (Caravaggio) 220
masculinity 268, 284, 286, 294
masquerades 11, 152, 236–7, 241, 248,
    252–4, 280

Mayne, Judith 23
Medhurst, Andy 7, 41–52; bitter-sweet
  47–8; essentialism and social
  constructionism 49–51; gay writers 45–7
Medusa 231–2, 242
Medusan femmes 239, 241–3, 248, 254;
  see also butch and femme; phallic femmes
melodrama 154
men: gay male culture 173, 176; gay male
  pornography 166–7, 172–5; 'gay
  sensibility' 49; gay writers 45–7; male
  homosexual structure of feeling 47; male
  sexuality 236; masculinity 268, 284, 286,
  294; musicians 243–4; *see also* queer male
  bodies; She-men
Merck, Mandy 9
Midwest, American 267
Mighton, John 200, 202
Miller, D.A. 106, 112, 114
Miller, Nancy K. 50
mimicry 11, 150, 153–4, 163–4, 172, 175
mirrors 212, 214, 245
Mitchell, W.J.T. 229
modernism, political 209–10, 226, 228
modernity 165, 232
Modleski, Tania 31
Monroe, Mike *250*, 251–2
monsters 80–1, 83; *see also* cloning
Morency, André 197
Morrison, Toni 162n30
mothers 62–4, 66, 87–9, 103n37; *My
  Mother's Place* 169–71; Nazi 148, 151
multiculturalism 125–6; *see also* cultural
  exchange
Mulvey, Laura 141, 241
Muñoz, José 12, 163–80; *Chinese Characters*
  165–6, 172–6; *My Mother's Place* 163,
  165–6, 169–72, 176
Munt, Sally 286
music videos 13, 243–5, 247–52
My Mother's Place (Fung) 163, 165–6,
  169–72, 176

Nancy, Jean-Luc 227
narcissism 245, 252; *2001: A Space Odyssey*
  58–9, 63–5, 69; *Alien Resurrection* 96, 98;
  La Face Cachée de la Lune 203
narrative(s) 24, 29; *see also* genres,
  conflation of; romantic narratives
national identity 12–13, 136, 185, 187

nationalism 196, 199, 204
native informants 166
Nazi period 11, 156; *see also November Moon*
  (von Grote)
Neale, Steve 268
Negri, Antonio 226
Nelkin, Dorothy 87
new queer cinema 2–8, 265, 268, 270, 291
New Queer Cinema (Aaron) 7
Newton, Esther 237, 239
Nichols, Bill 166
Nietzsche, Friedrich 231
Night Porter, The (Cavani) 154
Nô (Lepage) 195–9
Nora, Pierre 230–1
nostalgia, imperialist 137
not-lining-up 164, 170–1
November Moon (von Grote) 146–59; and
  Love Story 148; resistance 149–50;
  Vergangenheitsbewältigung (coming-to-
  terms-with-the-past) 154–5, 159

orientalism 128–31, 144, 175, 177,
  179nn27, 28
other(s) 21–2, 25–6, 32, 127, 166, 176
Ottinger, Ulrike 11; *see also Johanna d'Arc of
  Mongolia* (Ottinger)
Out on Tuesday/Out 6
Owings, Alison 149

paintings 208–9, 211–12, 214, 223; *see also*
  tableaux vivants
panopticon 205n16
paranoia 56–8, 65–6, 69–71, 76–7
passing 98, 259–60, 286
patriarchy 138
Peck, Ronald L. 50
Peirce, Kimberly 265–6, 281, 291–3;
  see also Boys Don't Cry (Peirce)
penises 71, 236, 238–9, *240*, 247–9,
  252–3; *see also* phalluses
performance art 239, 245, 254
performativity 166–7, 260
perverse sexual desires 4, 9, 55
Pet Shop Boys 47–8
phallic femmes 239–40, 248, 254; *see also*
  femme and butch; Medusan femmes
phalluses 61, 69, 236–8, *240*, 243, 247,
  254; *see also* penises
photographs 266

Pidduck, Julianne 265–71, 289, 291
Pink Flamingos (Waters) 237
politics 1, 3, 5, 8, 15n5, 147, 168; and
    modernism 209–10, 226, 228
popular culture 6–7, 16n20, 275–6
pornography 166–7, 172–5, 246, *247*, 254
Possible Worlds (Lepage) 199–202
Possible Worlds (Mighton) 200, 202
post-feminism 241
postmodernism 50
poststructuralism 9
poverty 287n5; *see also* working class
power 175–6, 236–9, 241, 244
Practice of Love, The (de Lauretis) 9
Pratt, Mary Louise 167–8, 176
Preminger, Otto 122n7
Profane Love (Caravaggio) 223, *224*,
    225–6, 228
psychoanalysis 4, 9–10, 49, 57–9, 91–2,
    202, 273; *see also* Freud, Sigmund

Québec 184–7, 191, 196–9, 206n30
queens 91–2, 163, 177, 237
queer, signification of term 1, 55, 164, 270
queer cinema, new 2–8, 265, 268, 270, 291
Queer Cinema, The Film Reader (Benshoff and
    Griffin) 7
queer history 292
queering culture 6–7
queer male bodies 184, 205n5; *La Face
    Cachée de la Lune* 203, *204*; *Le
    Confessionnal 188–9*; *Le Polygraphe* 191,
    193, *194*, 195; *Nô* 197, 199; *Possible
    Worlds* 200, *201*, 202
queer nation 294
queerness 164–5, 170, 260–2, 276, 290–1
queer theory 3, 9–10, 12–13, 66
'queer turn' 2
queer voices 56–8, 77; *see also* voices,
    disembodied

race 11–12, 50, 85, 128, 154–6; *Boys Don't
    Cry* 275, 281, 285–6, 289–94; and gay
    male pornography 172–5; *The Searchers*
    133–7; *see also* ethnography; orientalism;
    racialized spectacles
racialized spectacles: *Johanna d'Arc of
    Mongolia* 126–7, 130, 132–3, 137–44;
    The Searchers 134–6
Rafelson, Bob 34

rape scenes 268–9
resistance 148–50, 209, 226
Rich, Ruby 2–3, 6–7, 12, 138, 155
Riggs, Marlon 169
risk 269–70
road movies 265–9
Rocky Horror Picture Show, The (Sharman)
    237, *238*
romantic narratives: *Bound* 111–12, 115–16,
    120–2; *Boys Don't Cry* 272, 276, 278,
    284, 294; *November Moon* 154
Rope (Hitchcock) 106, 112–14, 121–2
Rosaldo, Renato 136–7
Rosenthal, Abigail 149
Rozema, Patricia 33
Ryder, Winona 96; *see also Alien Resurrection*
    (Jeunet)

Said, Edward 128, 130, 150, 175
St Jerome Writing (Caravaggio) 228
sameness 80–1, 89, 92, 98, 100–1
Save You All My Kisses (Dead or Alive)
    249, *250*, 251
scalping 134–5
Scarlett-Davis, John 245–6
Schneemann, Carolee 241, *242*
Schragenheim, Felice 148
Schreber, Daniel Paul 55–7, 61, 63, 66–7,
    69, 71, 77
Screen 8–9, 14
Screw, A (Swans) 252
Searchers, The (Ford) 133–8, 140, 143
Second World War 156; *see also November
    Moon* (von Grote)
self-portraits 168, 211–13, 217, 230, *240*;
    see also autoethnography
Seven Streams of the River Ota, The (Lepage)
    186, 195–6, 199
Sevigny, Chloë 262, 263n6, 276
sexuality 236, 239, 241–4, 254–5, 269,
    293–4; *see also* homosexuality
Shadey (Saville) 237
Shaviro, Steven 195
Shelley, Percy Bysshe 231–2
She-men 13, 236–56; in art and music
    videos 243–52; power of 237–8, 244;
    and vagina envy 241; women's
    counterpart to 252–4
She Must Be Seeing Things (McLaughlin) 4, 9,
    15n15, 30, 36–9

Shoah (Lanzmann) 155, 158
Shohat, Ella 164
Sidnell, Michael 191
Silverman, Kaja 279–80
Sinfield, Alan 46
Slotkin, Richard 269
Smelik, Anneke 268–9
Smith, Paul Julian 67
Snead, James 290–1
social constructionism 49, 51
Solanas, Fernando 24–5, 30
space 218–19, 279
space–time collapses 183, 200
'special thrill' 43, 48
spectacles 141, 260; *see also* racialized
  spectacles
spectatorship 195–6, 259–63, 265,
  269–70, 273
Spivak, Gayatri 49
Springer, Claudia 91, 98, 100
Stacey, Jackie 1–18, 80–105; abjection in
  Alien Resurrection 88–9, 92–4; cellular
  mutations in *Alien Resurrection* 82–4, 86;
  homoeroticism in *Alien Resurrection*
  95–100; new queer cinema 2–8; *Screen*
  8–9, 14
Stella, Frank 213–15
Straayer, Chris 5, 13, 173, 236–56; art and
  music videos 243–52; Medusan femmes
  242–3; phallic femmes 239–40; power
  of She-men 237–8; women's counterpart
  to She-men 252–4; *see also* music videos
Street, Sarah 1–18; new queer cinema
  2–8; *Screen* 8–9, 14
studios 213–15, 220
subcultural authorship 48; *see also*
  authorship
suicide 73, 77, 156, 185, *189*, 191
supersyncretism 177
survivors 158
suture, cinematic 279
Swank, Hilary 260, 266, 276; *see also Boys
  Don't Cry* (Peirce)
Swans 252
Swoon (Kalin) 4, 11
symptoms 72–3

tableaux vivants 209–10, 214–17, 219–20,
  223, 225, 228–9, 231–2
Taxi Driver 252

technology 10, 55–6; genetic engineering
  80–5, 87–9, 100; HAL 57–60, 62–6;
  and homoeroticism 99–100; and *Law
  of Desire* 67, 69, 72–3, 76; *see also*
  cloning
Teena, Brandon 283, 289, 292–3; *The
  Brandon Teena Story* 13, 266, 271n10,
  276n3, 290; *see also Boys Don't Cry*
  (Peirce)
Telotte, J.P. 87–8
teratomas 83
theatre 184, 195; *see also* film adaptations
Thérien, Gilles 185
third cinema 24–5
thriller narratives 111–12, 116, 120–1
Tillman, Lynne 222
time 183, 200, 279
Tisdel, Lana 276nn3, 6, 281; *see also
  Boys Don't Cry* (Peirce)
Tobing Rony, Fatima 142
Tomlin, Lily 254
transgender 13–14, 259–60, 272, 278–83,
  287, 293
transsexuals 71, 74–5, 237, 249, 287n1
'trans' theory 13
transvestism 236–7, 241, 249, 252, *253*,
  259–60; *see also* crossdressing
Trauerspiel 216, 230
travelogues 127–8, 133
triangular desire 221–3; *see also* desire(s)
Trinidad 163, 176–7
Trip Through the Wardrobes of the Mind, A
  (Scarlett-Davis) 245–6, 248, 252
Turner, Tina 237, 243
Tweedie, James 13, 208–35; anachronism in
  Caravaggio 227; desire 221–3, 229–30;
  Medusa 231–2; Michelangelo da
  Caravaggio 209–15; space in *Caravaggio*
  218–19; tableaux vivants 215–17

United Kingdom 6, 16n20; British film
  culture 43–4; Thatcherite governance
  13, 31, 209, 227

vagina envy 241
Vergangenheitsbewältigung (coming-to-terms-
  with-the-past) 154–5, 159
Vergoeven, Paul 6
Vernet, Marc 223
Veronica 4 Rose (Chait) 16n20

Victorious Cupid (Caravaggio) 208, 223, *224*, 225–6, 228
videos 168, *246*; *Chinese Characters* 165–6, 172–6, *247*, 248; music 13, 243–5, 247–52
Villerejo, Amy 291
violence: *Bound* 112, 116, 120–1, 122n10; *Boys Don't Cry* 267–9, 271n10, 275, 279, 289–91, 293; *Law of Desire* 76, 79n33; scalping 134–5
visibility 11, 147, 154, 166, 290; *see also* racialized spectacle
visual pleasure/labour, cinematic 161n18
voices 57–8, 67, 69–76, 158, 269

Wachowski, Andy 5; *see also Bound* (Wachowski and Wachowski)
Wachowski, Larry 5; *see also Bound* (Wachowski and Wachowski)
Walk Like a Man 247, *248*, 252
Wallace, Lee 11, 106–22; chromatic design in *Bound* 115–16, 119–21; editing techniques in *Bound* 113–14, 117–18; opening sequence of *Bound* 106–7, 114–15
Waller, Marguerite 154
Weaver, Sigourney 95–6; *see also Alien Resurrection* (Jeunet)
Weeks, Jeffrey 49
West, Mae 248, 256n19
Westerns 128, 130, 139, 141, 269; *The Searchers* 133–8, 140, 143
Whissel, Kristen 11, 125–45; racialized spectacle in *Johanna d'Arc of Mongolia*

126–7, 130, 132–3, 137–44; *The Searchers* 133–8
White, Patricia 272–7
White Rose, The (Zanke) 160n7
whites 12, 128, 134–6, 143, 172–4, 289–94; *see also* race
Willemen, Paul 25
Williamson, Judith 237
witnessing 158
Wittig, Monique 201
women: in *2001: A Space Odyssey* 59; counterpart to She-men 252–4; female gaze 279–80; femininity 139–41, 150, 236, 240–1, 269; girls 273–6; in Holocaust film 146–9; and love triangles 234n42; musicians 243; and sexuality 236, 239, 241–4; and violence 269; *see also* feminism; lesbianism; lesbians; mothers; She-men; women's cinema
women's cinema 9, 21–39; and guerrilla cinema 30–1; history of term 22–3; *She Must Be Seeing Things* 36–9; *Working Girls* 26–9
Woods, Gregory 41, 48
working class 267–8, 283, 285–7
Working Girls (Borden) 26–9
Working Space (Stella) 213–15
writers, gay 45–7; *see also* authorship
Wust, Lilly 148, 150–1

Yentl (Streisand) 260, 262

Žižek, Slavoj 72
Zupančič, Alenka 185